Y0-BRV-592

LIBEL

RIGHTS, RISKS, RESPONSIBILITIES

Robert H. Phelps
and
E. Douglas Hamilton

REVISED EDITION

DOVER PUBLICATIONS, INC.
NEW YORK

International Standard Book Number: 0–486–23595–5
Library of Congress Catalog Card Number: 77–086709

Manufactured in the United States of America
Dover Publications, Inc.
180 Varick Street
New York, N.Y. 10014

Contents

Preface to the Dover Edition   vii

Introduction   ix

1   LIBEL IS NOT A DIRTY WORD   1

2   A WORKING GUIDE   6

3   WAS IT PUBLISHED?   13

4   IS ANYONE IDENTIFIED?   16

5   IS CRIME OR DISHONOR CHARGED?   33

6   IS RIDICULE OF MISFORTUNE PRESENT?   50

7   IS THERE A REFLECTION ON RACE, NATIONALITY OR
PATRIOTISM?   63

8   IS THERE INJURY TO ANYONE IN HIS OCCUPATION?   71

9   THE ABSOLUTE DEFENSES   100

10   TRUTH—THE GLORIOUS DEFENSE   106

11   PRIVILEGE OF REPORTING—THE BREAD-AND-BUTTER
DEFENSE   126

12   THE NEW YORK TIMES RULE—THE EXPANDING
DEFENSE   170

13   FAIR COMMENT—DEFENSE FOR OPINIONS   195

14   CONSENT—THE BACKSTOP DEFENSE   224

15   REPLY—THE SELF-DEFENSE   233

16   MALICE AND DAMAGES   248

17   DEFENSES AFTER PUBLICATION   281

18   HOW TO APPLY THE RULES   301

19   IN THE EDITOR'S HAND   314

20   RADIO AND TELEVISION   342

21   DETECTIVE WORK   357

22   CRIMINAL LIBEL   370

23   ONE LAST WORD   378

EPILOGUE: PRIVACY   380

Index of Cases   403

Subject Index   413

Preface to the Dover Edition

In the 12 years since the first edition of *Libel: Rights, Risks, Responsibilities* was published, judges have handed down many rulings. Fortunately for those interested in writing, publishing and broadcasting, the courts continue to reduce the legal barriers to freedom of expression. In fact, it is accurate to say that never before have Americans had so much freedom to discuss public events without fear of retribution in the courts. The Watergate scandal of the Nixon administration demonstrated the value of such liberty.

This new edition follows the same format as the old, offering an easy-to-understand approach to libel and a method of handling specific problems. Important new cases are, of course, included, and the text has been altered to conform to these rulings.

In addition, a chapter on privacy has been included at the end of the book. Privacy is a subject still in its formative stages. While some guidelines can be laid down, there are areas so fuzzy that the only sound advice is to rely on journalistic practice that has worked in the past.

Whether the problem is libel or privacy, journalists should remember the words of Justice Oliver Wendell Holmes: "The life of the law has not been logic, it has been experience."

R.H.P.
E.D.H.

Introduction

This book represents a sharp departure from previous discussions of libel. It was written with three objectives in mind. The first was to cut through the fuzzy thinking about libel. Fallacies and misconceptions have needlessly blocked the public, newsmen, lawyers and, at times, even the courts from a sound understanding of the law. The need for clear thinking is great since the libel laws represent a restriction on freedom of the press as well as a bulwark in defense of an individual's right to his good name.

The second objective was to give those who deal with controversial opinions—the press, for the most part, but the public in general, too—guidelines to how much they can say with safety. The methodology presented is simple. It tells how to recognize libel and how to publish it without losing your life savings. But the law is complex and the reader who demands absolute certainty will not find it here. As Oliver Wendell Holmes said at the Boston University School of Law in 1897, "The language of judicial decision is mainly the language of logic. And the logical method and form flatter the longing for certainty and for repose which is in every human mind. But certainty generally is illusion, and repose is not the destiny of man."

What the reader will find here is reasonable security without sacrificing his role as a participant in the democratic process of discussing controversial issues.

The third objective was to set forth the vast changes made in the law by recent court decisions. This book does not ignore the old landmark cases, since they are necessary to an understanding of the law. But principles can best be understood in a contemporary context. For that reason most of the cases discussed here are recent, and the reader does not need to be in his second childhood to recognize many of the personalities who parade through the pages.

If the authors have succeeded in their objectives, they have fulfilled the hope of Theodore M. Bernstein, assistant managing editor of *The New York Times*, who first proposed that this book be written and who offered suggestions for its execution.

Thanks are also extended to Richard E. Cheney, vice-president of Hill and Knowlton, the public relations firm; Kenneth Millar, the novelist; Bob G. Slosser, copy editor of *The New York Times;* and John D. Kousi and Donald G. McCabe of the New York bar for reading the manuscript and making valuable suggestions.

Our appreciation also goes to the librarians of the Columbia Law School Library and to Paul Greenfeder and James Sayler of *The New York Times* library and to Joel D. Katims and Robert Schwartz, law students, for aiding with the research. Of great help, too, were the hundreds of lawyers who took time to answer queries. Would that all of their cases could have been used. But even those cases that were not used helped, by guiding the authors, to make the book more meaningful.

Special thanks are reserved for Elizabeth K. Phelps, who gave unselfishly of her time and energy in every phase of the work, from the drudgery of the secretarial tasks through the research, writing and editing, and who suggested dozens of titles, including the one finally selected.

ROBERT H. PHELPS
E. DOUGLAS HAMILTON

Chapter 1

LIBEL IS NOT A DIRTY WORD

ONE OF THE AFFLICTIONS OF THE AMERICAN PRESS—AND IT HAS many—is that reporters and editors know so little about libel. Speak but the word and fear stabs at the cub reporter, the grizzled copy editor and the hard-boiled city editor alike. The rash ones may drop a few glib phrases about libel per se, libel pro quod, qualified privilege and malice, but, faced with the hard questions of how to compose a specific article and whether to print it, they soon grow silent.

This fear is unnecessary. While libel is one of the most complex subjects of jurisprudence, writers and editors who master the art of applying the principles discussed in these pages will soon move confidently, even in sticky situations. They will learn how to tell their story and at the same time stop many an outraged citizen who thinks he has been defamed from rushing off to his lawyer. They will discover how, by changing a word here or striking out a word there, to shape the article so that the outraged citizen who does see his lawyer will realize he had better not go to court. And they will develop work habits that take advantage of the leeway in the libel laws to win cases that do wind up in litigation.

The responsible journalist will reject at once any suggestion that either through trickery or other stratagem he evade the libel laws although they are without doubt the foremost restriction on freedom of the press in the United States. He knows that without the restrictions of the laws of defamation the individual would stand helpless before the onslaught of any liar with access to a printing press or a broadcasting station. Lies could cost a man his job, deprive him of his friends, ruin his life. If Western civilization treasures anything, it is the inviolability of the individual. He needs the libel laws to protect his reputation.

The responsible journalist will also reject the temptation to walk such a safe path in protecting the individual that he forgets his main goal: supplying the people with the facts, comments and opinions they need if they are going to fulfill their role in a democracy of helping formulate decisions. These facts, comments and opinions often involve libelous charges about the individuals concerned.

In the old days the authorities reasoned that lies served no public good and therefore those who published false statements of fact about individuals could not be protected from damages. This reasoning made no distinction between calculated falsehood and honest misunderstanding. It did not take into account the fact that truth is often recognized only after it has been defended. Nor did the authoritarians realize that truth is usually not the monopoly of any side but rests somewhere between various points of view. Here, too, falsehoods help shape the final conclusions. Judge Learned Hand put it this way:

> The First Amendment . . . presupposes that right conclusions are more likely to be gathered out of a multitude of tongues than through any kind of authoritative selection. To many this is, and always will be, folly; but we have staked upon it our all. [United States v. Associated Press, 52 F. Supp. 362]

Once this philosophy is accepted, it follows that communications media can help a democratic society act intelligently only if they carry a wide variety of reports—true, untrue and half true—about those in public life. The leeway in the libel laws was designed for just this purpose.

Libel, then, is not a dirty word. It becomes one only when the press sticks its nose into purely private affairs or resorts to the outright lie. Most of the time, great brilliance is not required to distinguish between socially useful libel and scandal mongering. But there are times when the demand of the public for information and the right of the individual to his private reputation conflict. The ideal society will balance these sometimes-conflicting interests by giving maximum protection to discussions of public problems, while calling for strict accounting of accusations about purely private affairs and punishing the outright liar. Sometimes distinctions will be difficult to draw, as when a police chief is accused, at a poker party at his club, of stealing chips. Are the people who depend on the police chief to combat crime entitled to know that he's not above a little pilfering himself? Or is such an incident part of his purely private life that the public has no right to invade? Perhaps some day the courts will have to determine such a case. Until then, all that newsmen can do is guess, with the aid of good counsel, what the courts would probably find and then decide whether publishing the accusation would be ethical and, if it is, whether the risk should be taken.

This is not such a hazardous procedure as it sounds. The courts have taken great strides in the last half century to improve the democratic structure for finding truth. In no field of law is this more true than in the laws of defamation. The right of a newsman to print or air news has never been so great as it is now. Yet editors, writers and broadcasters have only a vague understanding of their widening freedom to speak up on controversial issues.

Fear and Confusion

There are several reasons for this lag between the winning of crucial battles for freedom of the press and actual occupation of the new ground. One is the fear produced by costly libel judgments. Related to this is the fact that the libel law is beclouded by so many legal ifs, ands and buts. The legislators, the courts and the writers of lawbooks have done little to clear up the muddle. Each of the fifty states and the District of Columbia has its own statutes and precedents on the subject. Thus it is not libelous in New York, New Hampshire and Maine to call a white man a Negro, but it is in Georgia and other states in the South.

Adding to the confusion are the constantly changing interpretations of defamation, so that what is libelous at one time may not be years later. To write that a man joined the Mormon church and went to Utah would not be libelous today, but it was in the late 1800s, when Mormons were held in ill esteem (Witcher v. Jones, 17 N.Y. Supp. 491). Similarly, it was not libelous in the 1930s to write that a man was a Communist, but now public feeling is at such a point that it is defamatory to call a man a Red or even a pro-Communist (Grant v. Reader's Digest Assn., Inc., 151 F. 2d 733).

Compounding the problem is the fact that newsmen are held accountable for merely quoting libelous remarks, as well as for making any on their own. The law is clear that talebearers are as guilty as talemakers—with certain exceptions.

On top of all these problems is the difficulty that the newsman faces when he gets into court. Everything seems the reverse of the usual legal procedure. Instead of being presumed innocent, the defendant (in this case, the writer or editor) is, in a sense, presumed guilty. All the complainant has to do is show that the story was published and insist that it was false and that it damaged him. The newsman has to prove his innocence. The explanation for this unhappy state of affairs is, it must be admitted, sound. For the publisher of a libel is standing in the shoes of a prosecutor since he is accusing someone of bad conduct, while the person named in the publication is—as he should be—presumed innocent of the accusation. The traditional Anglo-Saxon principles of justice still apply.

The Danger and the Solution

When one considers all these complexities, it is no wonder that those responsible for communicating ideas quake when the word "libel" is mentioned. Like many fears, it stems from a lack of knowledge. Being unsure, editors and writers operate on a by-guess-and-by-golly basis—on some occasions taking unnecessary risks and on others tossing out vital news that could safely be published. If he is lucky, the newsman escapes libel suits. Should he trip up, the paper or broadcasting station may find itself paying stiff damages. In other cases, the news medium may be caught in litigation more expensive to defend than it would be to settle. Yet the wise publisher knows that he should not settle because the word soon would get around that the paper is a soft touch and he would be deluged with suits. Regardless of the situation, both the newsman and the publisher may lose more than a libel suit. They may lose their courage to handle libelous stories. Their fears may brush off on other publishers and newsmen, with a debilitating effect on news coverage.

Those who doubt that reporters, editors and broadcasters often take the simple way of avoiding libel suits—by just throwing the suspect material away—need only make a cursory examination of the press, both printed and electronic. The timidity displayed in covering local news, where most of the danger of libel occurs, compared with the thunder about Cuba, Red China and the Soviet Union is ample proof that what critics call Afghanistanism is rampant. While social and economic factors contribute to this timidity, the reporters' and editors' lack of a working knowledge of libel is an important cause. If the press is going to meet its obligations, it has to learn the maximum information it can supply before running undue risk. To stop one step short is abdication of duty; to go many steps beyond is to devolve into scandal mongering.

Chapter 2

A WORKING GUIDE

BEFORE THE NEWSMAN CAN MARK THE OUTER PERIMETER OF HIS freedom to communicate harmful reports about an individual, he must learn what libel is. Not any old definition will do. It has to be one that will help the newsman transfer principles into practice under pressure of a deadline. In spite of many attempts, no one has ever come up with an entirely satisfactory definition. Some are inaccurate; others are accurate but not comprehensive; still others are both accurate and comprehensive but too complex to be of much help to the working newsman.

The New York Penal Law definition, which prior to its repeal in 1966 was similar to the statutes of other states, read as follows:

> A malicious publication, by writing, printing, picture, effigy, sign or otherwise than by mere speech, which exposes any living person, or the memory of any person deceased, to hatred, contempt, ridicule or obloquy, or which causes, or tends to cause any person to be shunned or avoided, or which has a tendency to injure any person, corporation or association of persons, in his or their business or occupation, is a libel.

This may have been a fine definition as far as the Penal Law was concerned, but it raises more questions than it answers for the newsman.

Civil and Criminal Libel

Note that this definition speaks not only of living persons but also of "the memory of any person deceased." The outstanding difference between civil libel and criminal libel is that civil libel is a tort—an offense of one individual against another. The injured party sues in the civil courts. His lawyer argues the case, and if he wins, damages are awarded. Criminal libel is an offense against the state, a breach of the peace. The public prosecutor brings the charge. If he wins, the defendant is fined or thrown in jail. A civil suit cannot be brought for libeling the dead, but a criminal charge can be based on nasty remarks about those who have gone to their reward, as well as about the living. The theory is that the government has the right to punish a man if, for example, he calls George Washington a rogue and a liar, thereby provoking the public to riot. Criminal libel of the dead does not have much practical importance for most writers and editors, partly because people don't usually throw bricks at those who defame the dead—even the Father of Our Country—and partly because district attorneys do not like to tangle with communications media over someone who is no longer around.

How Slander Differs

The New York definition is also useful in that it makes clear that libel must be expressed in writing, printing, pictures, effigies or other visible forms. The only other form of defamation is slander, which is expressed orally.

The differences between slander and libel are purely historical. Originally no distinction was made in England between spoken and written defamation. Since few people could write, the question seldom arose. The injured party could turn to two kinds of courts for justice, to the church courts, where defamation was punished as a sin, or to the local manorial courts, where damages in money were designed to maintain the peace of the community and prevent dueling and blood feuds. As kings consolidated their hold on the entire country, their common-law courts started to take over jurisdiction. At first the king's courts were not interested in defamation, but with the introduction of movable type in the mid-fifteenth century the press was viewed as a threat to authority, and the state soon took over all cases of defamation.

Printing also created another problem, the question of a more permanent form of defamation than the spoken word. It did not take the courts long to conclude that written defamation was a greater evil than slander, and libel as a separate offense was born. The doctrine of civil libel, as distinct from slander, was promulgated in 1670. The case involved a barrister named King who contended that he had been "damnified in his good name and profession" by Sir Edward Lake. The complaint charged that Lake had described a petition that King had drawn up for Parliament as "stuffed with illegal assertions, ineptitudes and imperfections and clogged with gross ignorances, absurdities and solecisms." That sounds tame these days, but King demanded £5,000 in damages. In upholding an award of £150, the court said:

> There is no material variance betwixt the declaration and the special verdict; and although such general words spoken once, without writing or publishing them, would not be actionable; yet here they being writ and published, which contains more malice, than if they had but been once spoken, they are actionable. And the court being all of that opinion, judgment was given pro quer nisi causa, &c. [King v. Lake, Hardres 470]

Since *King v. Lake,* libel has always been regarded as a greater evil than slander. In addition to its permanence, libel is considered the result of a studied attempt to defame while slander is often the product of a flash of anger. Everyone knows that there are things he would say on the spur of the moment that he would not put down in writing about the neighbor who lets his dog relieve himself on his lawn. The law recognizes this distinction by letting a person get away with more when he speaks than when he writes. If you call the girl next door a "bleached blonde bastard" during an argument, you will probably get away with it, at least as far as the courts are concerned. A Brooklyn man used that bit of alliteration to elevate the tone of back-fence name calling. The court held it not slanderous. (Notarmuzzi v. Shevack, 108 N.Y.S. 2d 172). But there is no doubt that those same words printed on a handbill and circulated in the neighborhood would have been libelous.

The historical distinction between libel and slander has become somewhat absurd with the introduction of modern inventions. Radio and television deal with the spoken word, yet they can reach much larger audiences than a newspaper and often

the impact is greater. Most courts have decided that if a broadcaster is using a script, the defamation is libel; if he is speaking
extemporaneously, it is slander. However, it would be dangerous
for a station to lay down a policy of giving performers wider
latitude when ad-libbing than when reading scripts. Programs
in which outsiders—or even station personnel who tend to go off
the deep end—appear should be taped for monitoring. Even if the
tape is played back almost immediately there is some time for
the alert producer to prevent defamatory matter from being
broadcast.

Spoken Libel

The man who thinks he can get away with libel by transmitting
the defamatory material orally to a reporter who publishes it
is playing with fire. The law leaves no doubt that an oral statement made to a reporter for the purpose of publication is libel,
not slander. Thus the news source who holds a press conference,
who grants an interview, who answers telephone queries is as responsible for any libels he utters as is the newsman who prints
them. Even if the printed account differs somewhat from the
spoken words, the speaker is liable as long as the substance of
the libel is accurately reported. Nor can the speaker escape
responsibility by insisting that he did not ask the reporter to print
the remarks; that fact, the law says, can't be inferred (Roberts v.
Breckon, 31 App. Div. (N.Y.)431).

Libel Can Be True

A careful reading of the laws and court decisions clears away
a misconception common not only among newsmen but also
among lawyers and judges—that to say a story is libelous means
that the person named in it can recover damages. That is not
true. To say a story is libelous merely means that the person has
been defamed. He will recover damages only if there is no defense in the libel law for publishing the article. A lawyer charged
in print with ambulance chasing has been defamed, but he can
collect damages only if his accuser can show no legal defense for

the publication. Libel is not a defenseless publication; it is a publication requiring a defense.

Pursuit of the same thought will dissolve another widespread misconception—that to be libelous a statement must be false. That too, is erroneous, even though some statutes define libel as "false defamation." What they mean is that a statement is actionable, that is, it contains a sound basis for the award of damages, only if it is false. Truth does not enter the case when the court is determining whether the words are defamatory. It is just as libelous to write that a lawyer is an ambulance chaser, if he really does find clients by following up accident reports in the newspapers, than if he slavishly adheres to the bar association's code of ethics. In the early part of the case the court assumes that the libel is false. Later the defendant has the opportunity to prove that he had a right to publish the libel either by proving the statement true or by invoking some other legal defense.

The Basic Approach

This distinction between libel and its defenses lays the basis for sound work habits. Writers, editors and broadcasters must train themselves to be constantly on the lookout for suspect material. When it pops up, the newsman should ask himself a simple question: Is the material defamatory?

If the answer is no, the material can be used with little risk.

If the answer is yes, then a second question must be asked: Is there a legal defense for publishing it? If such a defense exists, the newsman is home free. If he finds no defense, then the article is actionable—that is, it can be the basis for a successful libel suit.

Take a simple case. The legislative correspondent calls and says that he has a good story. He has discovered that Dr. Beanbag, who works out of plush offices on Park Avenue, is a quack. Following the recommended procedure, the editor asks himself if this is libelous. There is no question about it. Of course it is libelous to call a doctor a quack, because the charge injures him in his profession. So he immediately asks the second question: Is there a legal defense for publishing it? The reporter supplies the answer. The state medical board has investigated Dr. Beanbag, has found out he is a fraud and is taking away his license. Since a public agency is reporting that Dr. Beanbag is a quack, the editor has a legal defense for publishing the charge if his account is balanced and substantially accurate. On the other hand, if the reporter had skulked around and found a dozen patients who were angry because their astronomical doctor bills reflected Beanbag's luxurious offices, that would not be a legal defense for calling him a quack. He might be one, but the paper would face the possibility of a large loss in damages if it printed a charge on so flimsy a basis. Under the circumstances, since the "quack" charge against Dr. Beanbag would have to be deleted, the correspondent is left with only a story that a dozen people are angry over the high cost of medicine. That is scarcely news these days, so it would probably never be written.

Nonlibelous Falsehood

But say that instead of the legislative correspondent, it is the police reporter calling with the story. "The DA," he mutters in that low, confidential tone that police reporters develop, "has finally caught up with Dr. Beanbag. Another patient has died in his office—the third in two weeks." The editor again follows his routine. First question: Is this libelous? This time the answer is no. It is no reflection on Beanbag that so many of his patients are doddering old ladies who go to him too late to get much help.

Since there is little risk in running a nonlibelous story, the editor decides to use a paragraph or two noting that a third patient has died in Dr. Beanbag's office. He cautions the reporter to check his facts again, but the next day when the editor walks into the newsroom, Beanbag is on the phone, screaming in protest. "That woman died in my brother's office over on Sixth Avenue," he yells. Before hanging up, he warns that he is going to sue.

Can he? You bet he can. You can not keep him out of the courts. A better question is whether Beanbag can collect. That is a different story. Beanbag must show not only that the reporter made an intentional mistake, but also that his practice was damaged. He can collect only an amount equal to the loss directly attributable to the false story. He would have to put on the stand patients who switched to another doctor because they were afraid old Beanbag might kill them. He would have to prove the loss of every dollar he asked in damages. Chances are that Beanbag would not want to parade witnesses before the public who would tell how their opinion of him had dropped after reading the story. Even if he were angry enough to do so, he could not wind up with very much in damages. He might collect $30 by proving that a little old lady from Greenwich Village canceled two appointments before overcoming her fear and going back to him.

In fact, few cases have been found in the records of the award of a major sum for publishing nonlibelous falsehoods. The responsible editor will strive to eliminate them, but he will be motivated by his devotion to truth, not any fear of damages.

The problem of libel now comes into focus. The newsman must be able to recognize libel when he sees it, and he must be able to invoke the defenses the law allows for publishing it. From this perspective, a helpful definition of libel is the following: A publication is libelous of any person if it identifies him to any reader and its natural effect is to make readers generally think worse of the person identified.

Note that there are three requirements: There must be publication; there must be identification; and there must be a harmful effect. If any one is missing, there is no libel.

In the following pages each of these requirements is discussed in detail. Then the defenses available to the press are explained. The constant aim is to show the newsman how he can communicate the maximum amount of information in the public interest with the least possible risk.

Chapter 3

WAS IT PUBLISHED?

THE FIRST REQUIREMENT OF A LIBELOUS PUBLICATION IS THAT IT BE communicated to a third party.

You can sit alone in your room before your fireplace and type out all sorts of lies about anyone you please. But if you throw every sheet into the fire, no one will think worse of the reputations of the people you have been lying about. It is prescisely the same as the situation with respect to obscene literature. You can compose as many dirty ditties as you wish, but if no one sees or hears them, you are not liable for what you have written. The law does not pay off on thoughts and it is just as well; the courts would be trying nothing but libel and obscenity suits.

The case of poor Flora Shepard illustrates the necessity for publication. Back before World War I this comely New York widow opened her mail one day and read to her dismay the following anonymous letter:

Mrs. Shepard:

I am very much impressed with your looks, appearance, etc., and have been for a long time. I am writing this to know if you would meet me at some place where we could talk with each other and make some arrangements where we could get out and have a nice time. I am a married man that you know well, live in Brocton, and highly respectable and no one would think that I would go out for a good time, but I would like to with you. If you will write me and address the letter to C. A. Bennett Dunkirk, N. Y. Box 71 before next Tuesday as I will be there at noon that day and will get it. I will tell you who I am or will call and see you or write so that we can meet each other for a good time. I am strictly in earnest about this in every way, and anything you may write me will be strictly *confidential* and expect you to treat this the same.

Now you will say what is there in it for me. Well if you go out with me it will be a good time, pleasant treatment the best I know how, and $5.00 in money and a good true friend in every way one that will never say a word about this in any way. Kindly ans. this so that we may be able to get together and talk things over and have a good time. I will not sign this but will come and see you or write you all of it after I hear from you.

Flora's indignation rose as she read the letter, either because of the erotic suggestion implicit in the letter or the $5 offer, which even in those days was a paltry sum to offer a respectable widow for a compromising date. Her indignation soon became a tidal wave that would subside only by the recovery of a substantial sum of money. So, she went to the post office and showed the letter to the officials, and with the aid of friends, discovered that the man who had propositioned her was Louis G. Lamphier. She promptly sued him for libel.

The court commended her good citizenship in going to the postal authorities with the letter and expressed no little regret that it was forced to the conclusion that it had to turn Flora away empty handed. Lamphier had not published the letter to a third party, so there was no cause for an action for libel (Shepard v. Lamphier, 84 Misc. (N.Y.)498). Flora's reputation had not been damaged one iota in the eyes of any third party while the letter remained in her hands. It was not until she herself laid the letter before the postal authorities that it was actually "published" according to the law—that is, communicated to a third person. The late Calvert Magruder, the distinguished United States Circuit Court of Appeals Judge and professor of law, observed, in commenting on a similar case, that the court apparently took the position that "there is no harm in asking"— as long as you do not tell anyone else about it ("Mental Disturbance in Torts," 49 *Harvard Law Review* 1055, May, 1936).

Attempts That Failed

Some ingenious attempts have been made to show publication of a libel. In Providence, Rhode Island, Emma Lonardo protested that she had been libeled because her aunt and a funeral director had omitted her name from the list of survivors in an obituary notice of her mother's death and that they had prevented her from attending the wake, from riding in one of the lead cars of the funeral cortege, from sitting with the family in a front pew at the church and from standing near the coffin at the interment. The Rhode Island Supreme Court decided on December 21, 1964, that such actions were not "publication" by printing, writing, signs or pictures, as demanded by the state's law (Lonardo v. Quaranta, 205 A. 2d 837).

In Illinois, a suit was filed on behalf of an infant against his father for being stigmatized a bastard for having been born out of wedlock. One of the charges was libel. The Appellate Court of Illinois held, in dismissing the case, that there was no proof of communication of the libel to a third party (Zepeda v. Zepeda, 41 Ill. App. 2d 240).

No Middle Ground

For the journalist, the question of publication requires a flat yes or no. There is no middle ground. The twice-a-week Uvalde (Texas) *Leader-News* offered an argument in defending a libel suit in 1964 that few newspapers would want their advertisers to hear: that there was no proof that anyone had read the article, although 3,900 copies of the edition had been distributed. The Texas Court of Civil Appeals gave the paper more credit than it had asked:

> We hold that a libel committed by a newspaper publication is accomplished when the publication goes into circulation. It is not necessary to prove that the article was read as that can be presumed. [Hornby v. Hunter, 385 S.W. 2d 473]

Once the story is in print and the paper is distributed or the words are broadcast, there is no escaping the fact that any libel in it was published. The results may sometimes be disastrous, but libel suits are an occupational hazard of the newsman. Above all, he wants to be published.

Chapter 4

IS ANYONE IDENTIFIED?

THE WRITER WHO THROWS RESPONSIBILITY TO THE WINDS CAN DASH off scurrilous remarks as fast as he can operate his typewriter. He can get them printed and broadcast over the entire nation. But he can't be successfully sued for libel unless he points an accusing finger at a particular person. The law requires that the defamed person be identified. If no one is identified, there can be no libel because no one's reputation has been injured. This does not mean that all readers must be able to identify the person referred to, or readers generally, or even the average reader. It is sufficient if only a single reader is able to identify the person bringing the suit.

The use of a name identifies the defamed to all readers, whether they know him or not. But a newsman cannot escape liability by just leaving the name out, despite widespread belief to the contrary. A person can be identified by nickname, pen name or circumstances. A reference to Mark Twain would immediately identify Samuel L. Clemens. A radio broadcaster once sued the New York *Herald Tribune* on the basis of a story that referred to him only as the Mystery Chef—the name he used on his show. That was sufficient for the court. Initials will also identify a person.

Mere circumstances are sometimes sufficient. In April, 1958, a Cholly Knickerbocker column syndicated by the Hearst corporation carried the following item regarding the Palm Beach, Florida, jet set:

> Palm Beach is buzzing with the story that one of the resort's richest men caught his blonde wife in a compromising spot the other day with a former FBI agent. Cameras, screams of anguish and the whole nawsty bit . . .

Frederick H. Hope, a Palm Beach attorney and former FBI agent, sued, contending that the item identified him and Mrs. Gregg Sherwood Dodge, wife of Horace Dodge. Hope testified that he, as a comparatively new member of the County Solicitor's office, had received extensive publicity as an ex-FBI agent. While there were other former FBI agents in Palm Beach, he said that he was known primarily as an ex-agent and that he was the only one who traveled in the resort's high-society circles. The United States Court of Appeals for the Second Circuit upheld a $58,500 verdict (Hope v. Hearst Consolidated Publications, Inc., 294 F. 2d 681).

In another case an article reported the death of a young man and his declarations to his attending physician that he had been poisoned by a young woman with whom he had been keeping company. This identified her to some of his acquaintances, although she was not named (Nunnally v. Tribune Association, 111 App. Div. (N.Y.)485).

In a Pennsylvania case, an article described one of the occupants necking in a parked car at a west-side lakefront ball park at four in the morning as a "buxom brunette of Latin vintage employed by the state to attend to the needs of the indigent." Elsewhere she was described as a "raven-haired and owl-eyed, home-wrecking social worker." These words were sufficient to identify her (Commonwealth of Pennsylvania v. Donaducy, 176 Pa. Super. 27).

If the editor decides that his defenses are weak and that he had better delete names and other identifying material because libel is present, he must remain alert to make sure that follow-up articles do not provide the identification. An example will show the danger. A newspaper runs a story charging that the Mafia is muscling in on the city's restaurant and motel business. The paper is not afraid of being sued by the Mafia chieftains and it names them. But it says that the front for them and the real brains behind the operation is a lawyer. Since it lacks sufficient evidence admissible in court to prove its case, the newspaper decides it dare not name the lawyer. This is safe practice. But if in a subsequent and otherwise harmless article it names a specific lawyer as the attorney who handles all the business affairs of the Mafia chieftains, the newspaper has identified the lawyer as the brains behind the mob. The courts sometimes say that the articles can be read together to prove identification.

In another aspect of the same problem, a Texas newspaper published a brief article saying that a Negro woman had been robbed and beaten on a certain street corner. No name was given. Two days later the paper printed a more detailed account, this time naming the victim. It did not give her color, but she was white. She sued, asserting that when the two articles were read together, the conclusion was inescapable that they referred to the same person. The court agreed that she had been identified (Express Publishing Co. v. Orsborn, 151 S.W. 574).

Mistaken Identity

When libelous matter is present, great care must be taken to make sure innocent parties are not hit. The newsman's intent is of no consequence; the test is not at whom he aimed but who has been hit. Some of the most clearly unnecessary cases of libel result from mistaken identity.

The classic examples are the Annie Oakley cases. Annie toured the country with the Buffalo Bill Show and was an expert in the use of firearms. Some years after her fame had reached its pinnacle, a woman was brought into court in Chicago and charged with drunken and disorderly conduct. She identified herself as the famous Annie Oakley but spelled her name Oklay. Although she wasn't Annie Oakley, press associations, without checking, sent the story out identifying her as the sharpshooter. The real Annie Oakley, who had been leading a respectable life as Annie Butler, filed many suits around the country and collected on some (Post Publishing Co. v. Butler, 137 F. 723).

The Annie Oakley cases do not mean that if the police pick up a man who identifies himself as a famous personality the reporter must leave that fact out of the story. The writer can put that fact in his article and even hold the reader in suspense, as the Long Island *Daily Press* did in this story:

> Five, ten minutes go by and in comes this blonde kid with that clean-cut look. Nobody minds that he's dressed like a businessman because he is a regular there, and is really about as square as a 10-ball. He plays the skins—a drummer—and he has let it get around

that he, Mickey Sheen, has been with the big-timers, Stan Kenton, Buddy Scott. You know.

He sits down next to the motorcycle character.

Five minutes more go by. The door opens and into the gloom walks a middle-aged man wearing a what-am-I-doing-in-a-place-like-this look. He edges over to the bar, motions to the bartenders, and croaks:

"I'm looking for Jonesy."

Nobody looks up when drummer-boy Sheen says, "I'm Jonesy." That's his affair. Nobody, that is, except Mr. Motorcycle Jacket. He stays glued to the bar as Sheen and the middle-aged fellow walk to a booth in the back, but his head is like on a swivel. He watches.

There is a short conversation in the booth, then Sheen gets up and heads for the coat-rack. As he does, the middle-aged man takes out a handkerchief and coughs, discreetly, but loud enough to cut through the bar-talk.

BANG!

Mr. Turtle-neck is out of his seat and before you can say make mine extra dry he is pinning Sheen's arms behind him and hustling him back to the booth. Sheen's lower jaw is approaching the floor.

"Yes," says the middle-aged fellow, pointing to Sheen, "that's the one."

.   .   .   .

Turtle-neck reaches into Sheen's jacket and lifts out an envelope. Inside is $500, in marked bills.

All three go back to the Rockaway Beach stationhouse and Sheen is booked on an extortion charge. Only the name isn't Mickey Sheen. It's John Watson. He's 19 years old and lives at 1815 Marine Parkway, Brooklyn.

And Turtle-neck gets out of his costume. He turns out to be Detective Sgt. Vincent Chisari, commander of the Rockaway Beach Squad.

The real Mickey Sheen, an entertainer, then went to his lawyer and complained that the article made people think that he had been arrested for extortion. The judge disagreed, insisting that the story, when read in its entirety, made it "very, very clear" that someone else had been using Sheen's name (Schein-blum v. Long Island Daily Press, 239 N.Y.S. 2d 435). The fogginess over whether "Mr. Motorcycle Jacket" and "Mr. Turtle-neck" were the same person did not, of course, enter into the case.

It should be standard operating procedure in any newsroom to insist on full details of identification—addresses, ages and occupations—when strong legal defenses for publication exist. Every effort should also be made to check on the original information with those named, especially when prominent persons are involved. Such a check—ordered but not made by the city desk of the New York *Herald Tribune*—could have avoided a damage award. The story ran on Oct. 23, 1926:

> Garrison, N.Y., Oct. 22—William Kehoe, formerly Assistant Corporation Counsel for New York City, who was convicted in milk scandal, has purchased from Bertram Delancey Drake a twelve-room house and estate here. Mr. Kehoe examined the property about five weeks ago and the deal was completed through John P. Donohue & Son, local real estate dealer. The price was not disclosed.

If the reporter had followed instructions and had checked, he would have found out that the William Kehoe who had purchased the house was not the one convicted in the milk scandal but a man with the same name. (Kehoe v. New York Tribune, Inc., 229 App. Div.(N.Y.)220). Admittedly, the fact that both had been lawyers in the Corporation Counsel's office increased the chance of error, but such factors are why reporters should be careful and diligent. Not all newspapers are so fortunate as the *Tribune* was in the Kehoe case. After two verdicts—one for 6¢ and one for $10,000—were overturned, the case was settled for about $2,500.

The lesson for the reporter is that he must not assume, as the police and other agencies sometimes do, that similarity of names means similarity of identification. He must check and recheck.

Innocent-Construction Rule

In Illinois sloppy reporters are the beneficiaries of what is known as the innocent-construction rule. This means that if an article is ambiguous and one of the meanings is innocent, the court must declare it nonactionable as a matter of law. A case involving two articles in the Chicago *Tribune* in March, 1952, illustrates the latitude the rule gives the press. The first article read:

Five women, one identified as a former girl friend of Tony Accardo, Capone gangster, were seized by vice squad police last night in a raid on a lavishly furnished nine-room apartment at 4417 Ellis Avenue.

Detectives Jack Woessner, Edward Puhr and Patrick Rafferty said they made the raid after an unnamed policeman paid a $100 fee to one of the women to obtain evidence of prostitution in the apartment. Two men seized as they were entering the apartment were questioned and released. Dolores Reising, 57, alias Eve Spiro and Eve John, who, police said, was known years ago as Accardo's woman friend, was held as the suspected keeper of the apartment.

The next day the *Tribune* carried the following item:

Five women arrested by Detectives Jack Woessner and Edward Puhr of Hyde Park station in a vice raid at 4417 Ellis Ave. Saturday night will appear in Women's Court Wednesday.

Dorothy Clark, 57, who gave 4417 Ellis Av. as her address, was charged with being keeper of a disorderly house and selling liquor without a license. Police said she also is known as Dolores Reising, Eve Spiro, and Eve John, and was known years ago as a girl friend of Tony Accardo, Capone gangster.

Dorothy Clark, the owner of the building, occupied one of the apartments. Living in the apartment below the one raided was a twenty-seven-year-old practicing psychologist. Her maiden name had been Eve Spiro and her name at the time of the raid was Eve John, although she had been divorced. Mrs. John sued the *Tribune*, contending she had been libeled.

The Illinois Supreme Court held that she had no case since the articles referred to the landlady, not to a tenant of the building. In support of this finding it said that it was clear that "Eve John" and "Eve Spiro" were aliases, which the law has traditionally defined to mean assumed, not true, names. Invoking the innocent-construction rule, it said that the articles were non-actionable (John v. Tribune, 28 Ill. App. 2d 300; 24 Ill. 2d 437).

The rule is a valuable protection to newspapers that innocently make a mistake, as the *Tribune* did in the above case, but newsmen who harm an individual through carelessness and then escape damages by falling back on the innocent-construction rule merit no praise. They would be in a more defensible position if they exerted maximum care in reporting the facts rather than banking on strained court interpretations of the law.

Illinois seems to be the only state that still adheres to the innocent-construction rule. This rule used to be applied rather generally.

Group Identification

In the majority of libelous situations identification must be so precise that the reader knows without question who is being defamed. The reporter will not hesitate to name names or describe the circumstances that point to an individual, because the reporter has a strong legal defense for publishing the libel. If his defenses are in doubt, then the reporter must consider fuzzing his identification. The situation often arises in exposés and other exclusive articles. Investigatory reporters and crusading newspapers dig up information that casts light on a particularly bad situation but which is not protected by any of the traditional defenses to libel suits. Ideally, the culprits should be named, but the newsman might run into grave difficulties in defending himself. In such cases the stories need not be thrown away. The situation can be exposed, but precise identification of the wrongdoers must be avoided. If no one is identified, no one can sue successfully.

The key to taking advantage of this approach is understanding group identification. No one is libeled if a charge is made against a group to which the wrongdoer belongs—provided the group is large enough. No one could collect damages because a television commentator proclaimed that "all men are liars." Nor could any attorney win a suit if the charge was that "all lawyers are thieves." The group is still too large. No one has been identified.

This rule seems unfair when minority groups are castigated. Jews, Negroes and Puerto Ricans suffer en masse when bigots attack them. But the doctrine gives the writer wide freedom to expose fraud and corruption. The *Saturday Evening Post* carried an article about the District of Columbia cabbies titled "Never Give a Passenger a Break." Among other things, the article said:

> Only the natives who make a life study of the zone system know exactly how much is legal. It's easy to tell whether you've got one of those or some poor trusting visitor. For instance, when they point to the Capitol and ask if it's the White House, that automatically

doubles the fare. Any guy unpatriotic enough not to know his Capitol should be penalized.

Thomas W. Fowler and Charles B. Howery brought suit. There was no problem so far as Mr. Fowler was concerned because he was not a taxi driver at all. He was the owner and operator of a fleet of taxicabs and he was sent home without the award of even cab fare. Mr. Howery was in a different position. He said he was the driver of a Columbia taxicab, and he sued in behalf of himself and fifty-nine other taxicab drivers. Although the article was illustrated by a photograph of a Columbia cab, Mr. Howery was also told that he had no cause of action, and he also had to go home without any money. The court said in dismissing the complaint:

> . . . in case of a defamatory publication directed against a class, without in any way identifying any specific individual, no individual member of the group has any redress. The reason for this rule is that ordinarily a defamatory statement relating to a group as a whole, does not necessarily apply to every single member. A minority not intended to be castigated has no legal cause for complaint. The only exception involves cases in which the phraseology of a defamatory publication directed at a small group is such as to apply to every member of the class without exception. [Fowler v. Curtis Publishing Co., 78 F. Supp. 303]

Time magazine took advantage of this rule of law in the following item from its edition of June 4, 1956:

> . . . top Western officials of the International Brotherhood of Teamsters were conspiring with Seattle gamblers to 1) control Portland's law enforcement agencies, 2) organize all the city's rackets, from pinball machines to prostitution. . . .
>
> Among other accusations, the *Oregonian* reported that the plotters had threatened Portland Mayor Fred Peterson with political reprisals by the Teamsters if he did not get rid of his police chief.
>
> Mayor Peterson confirmed the charge. The Oregon Teamsters' representative, Clyde Crosby—whom the *Oregonian* revealed as an ex-convict—admitted that he had tried to get the mayor to fire Police Chief Jim Purcell, but only, he said, because the chief was in cahoots with racketeer Elkins. . . .

In tossing out Crosby's libel complaint, the United States Court of Appeals for the Seventh Circuit said:

On the face of the article under attack, it is not discernible how the ordinary reader (we have read the article many times) would have any reason to believe that plaintiff had any part in the corrupt activities attributed to others. He was referred to as an Oregon representative of the Teamsters' Union. To assert, as plaintiff does, that in that capacity he was included among "The top Western officials of the International Brotherhood of Teamsters," against whom charges were made in the first paragraph, is little more than a figment of the imagination. [Crosby v. Time, Inc., 254 F. 2d 927]

How small does a group have to be before the newsman must begin to worry about making all-embracing charges? The cautious editor will begin to take more care when the number falls below one hundred.

True magazine lost a libel suit because of a 1958 article that implied that Oklahoma's 1956 national championship football team had been hopped up with drugs. While the article referred only to "Oklahoma players being sprayed in the nostrils with an atomizer," the Supreme Court of the state said that it had libeled every one of the more than sixty players on the squad. Dennit Morris, a fullback, who was not mentioned in the article, offered evidence to the court that the substance had not been sprayed in the nostrils, but in the mouth, and was only "spirits of peppermint" to relieve dryness. Undoubtedly he got more relief from the $75,000 he collected in damages from *True* (Fawcett Publications v. Morris, 377 P. 2d 42). Twelve companion cases were settled out of court for substantial sums.

When the group numbers less than one hundred, the writer can reduce and often eliminate risk by saying "certain," "many" "most" or "some" instead of indicating that all are involved.

Another Oklahoma Supreme Court decision shows how effective this device can be. O. O. Owens, a candidate for the state legislature, ran ads in the Tulsa *World* in 1926 calling for an investigation of the state Supreme Court and accusing "certain members" of the court of making "the legal machinery of the state a tool for use in private controversies, in depriving or attempting to deprive citizens of their property and in looting or attempting to loot business enterprises." One of the nine Supreme Court justices, J. W. Clark, sued for libel. When the case reached the Supreme Court on appeal, all the justices disqualified themselves and Gov. William H. Murray appointed nine special jurists to hear the case. The special court ruled that the advertisement had not identified Justice Clark (Owens v. Clark, 154 Okla. 108).

How about saying "all but one"? Does that get the writer off the hook? Eddie Cantor, the comedian, wrote a letter to the editor of *Radio Guide* in which he said of the New York City radio editors: "There is but one person writing on radio in New York City who has the necessary background, dignity and honesty of purpose."

There were twelve radio editors in New York City at that time. Prior to publication of the letter, Cantor had publicly referred to one of them as a fine radio editor and the plaintiff was not the man. So the New York Court of Appeals concluded that there was sufficient evidence to make out a case (Gross v. Cantor, 270 N.Y. 93). If Cantor had not identified the one fine editor beforehand, would he have won his case? That is an unknown factor, but the wisest advice would seem to be to stick to the "many," "most" and "some" in the smaller groups.

Even then the writer cannot be absolutely safe because it is difficult to draw a clear line between identification of the individual and the group. The book *U.S.A. Confidential* by Jack Lait and Lee Mortimer illustrates the problem. It said this in discussing Stanley Marcus, president of the Neiman-Marcus Company, the stylish Dallas store:

He may not know that some Neiman models are call girls—the top babes in town. The guy who escorts one feels in the same league with the playboys who took out Ziegfeld's glorified. Price, a hundred bucks a night.

The salesgirls are good, too—pretty, and often much cheaper—twenty bucks on the average. They're more fun, too, not as snooty as the models. We got this confidential, from a Dallas wolf.

Neiman-Marcus also contributes to the improvement of the local breed when it imports New York models to make a flash at style shows. These girls are the cream of the crop. Oil millionaires toss around thousand-dollar bills for a chance to take them out.

Neiman's was a women's specialty shop until the old biddies who patronized it decided their husbands should get class, too. So Neiman's put in a men's store. Well, you should see what happened. You wonder how all the faggots got to the wild and wooly. You thought those with talent ended up in New York and Hollywood and the plodders got government jobs in Washington. Then you learn the nucleus of the Dallas fairy colony is composed of many Neiman dress and millinery designers, imported from New York and Paris, who sent for their boy friends when the men's store expanded. Now most of the sales staff are fairies, too.

Even though the book said "some" Neiman models were call girls, the court ruled that the language included all nine. Fifteen of the twenty-five salesmen sued on the basis that "most" of the staff had been defamed. The court held that since previous rulings regarding members of groups of this size had been conflicting, it would permit the suits. As for the salesgirls, 385 was just too many, the court said, and threw out the case of the 30 who were suing (Neiman-Marcus v. Lait, 13 F.R.D. 311). As a result of a legal snarl, the case was settled without going to trial. None of the plaintiffs received any compensation, but their attorney fees were paid.

Obviously, when subjects of particular emotional impact are concerned, like beautiful women and football heroes, more risk is taken than with politicians, labor leaders or racketeers. In such cases the writer should cloud the identification even more.

The Either-Or Technique

Another technique available to the skilled writer in cases where he is not sure of his legal defense for publication of libel is to place the target of his writing in an either-or situation, one possibility being libelous, the other nonlibelous. The book *Red Channels*, purportedly designed to combat Communist influence in the radio and television industry, did this adroitly. It emphasized that it was going to "indicate the extent to which many prominent actors and artists have been inveigled to lend their names, according to these public records, to organizations espousing Communist causes." Then, in a number of places it made clear that not all the performers listed were actual Communists, fellow travelers or part of a "transmission belt." It also mentioned "innocents," "well-intentioned liberals," persons who "advance Communist objectives with complete unconsciousness," "genuine liberals," "actors and artists who have been inveigled to lend their names•. . . whether they actually believe in, sympathize with, or even recognize the cause advanced." In a section listing the names of 151 performers, the book made no attempt to categorize each person, but it did list factual information on membership in left-wing groups and attendance at certain rallies. When Joe Julian, an actor, sued, New York's highest court rejected his case, asserting that "the alleged libelous material upon a fair reading and evaluation has not been shown to have been published of and concerning the plaintiff." It pointed out that there was exculpatory material and warnings against misjudging those listed (Julian v. American Business Consultants, 2 N.Y. 2d 1).

Needless to say, the use of such a device calls for the utmost responsibility on the part of the writer to prevent unnecessary damage to the innocent. It can, however, be used effectively in crusades when reporters are unable, because of a lack of investigatory authority, to ferret out facts needed to prove the truth of their charges or when the actions of individuals raise sufficient suspicions that the fair-minded newsman believes an exposé is in order.

Extrinsic Facts

Related to the question of identification is one of the most difficult kinds of defamation for an editor to detect. It is called libel by extrinsic facts. The reason it is hard to spot is that the editor cannot tell by merely reading the material whether it is libelous. Everything in the article seems innocent on its face.

What makes the article defamatory is that there are additional facts that throw a false and injurious light on the person named in the story. These extrinsic facts usually are not known to the editor. Thus, he has no way of seeing the harmful way he is portraying the person in the news to those who do know these other facts.

This type of defamation often occurs in the most innocent type of story and almost always because of a failure to make a thorough check. Almost every newspaper carries birth announcements every issue. On November 3, 1956, The Clay Center (Kansas) *Dispatch* carried the following item:

Stork-O-Grams. Ellen Marie is the name Mr. and Mrs. Phillip Karrigan of Clay Center gave to their daughter, who was born Thursday, Nov. 1, at the Clay County Hospital. The little girl weighed nine pounds, three ounces.

The Karrigans have two other children, Gary 7 and Timothy, 3. Grandparents are Mr. and Mrs. E. H. Carpenter of Lovell, Wyo. Great grandparents are Mrs. Ida Davis of Clay Center and Mrs. Kate Carpenter of Omaha, Nebraska.

Philip Karrigan sued, but not because the paper misspelled his first name. He said that the item, innocent on its face, was scandalous because he was a bachelor and because it made many readers think that he was married to "one Betty Ellen Carpenter, a woman of ill repute and who has given birth to four children out of wedlock." The Kansas Supreme Court ruled that Karrigan had stated a cause of action, even though the newspaper contended that it had obtained the facts for the story from the hospital, which, in turn, had been told by the patient that she was Karrigan's wife (Karrigan v. Valentine, 184 Kan. 783). The Clay Center *Dispatch* was fortunate. As the result of legal maneuvering the case was ultimately dismissed without payment of damages.

Large newspapers are particularly susceptible to errors of this type because so many of their news subjects are strangers. *The New York Times* once ran an item about the birth of a baby. The mother was a married teacher and there was nothing in the announcement that suggested anything unusual or improper. The paper did not know that the teacher's husband was an Army officer who was, and had been for a long time, stationed in the Philippines. He had not visited, lived with or even seen his wife for five years. The teacher sued, asserting that "my friends who knew of our long separation, upon reading the article, believed that I was the mother of a child by a man other than my husband."

One of the best-known cases of extrinsic fact is based on an article about Fatty Arbuckle, a comedian in the days of silent films, that appeared in the old New York *Evening Graphic* (sometimes known as the Pornographic). He had earned the reputation of being a philanderer and the article was headlined: "Arbuckle to Marry? Maybe; Maybe Not." It went on to say that "maybe Roscoe (Fatty) Arbuckle is going to marry Doris Keane and maybe he is not." Accompanying the article was a photograph of a young lady and under it the caption:

> Doris Keane is, according to rumor, Fatty Arbuckle's latest lady love. Doris is pretty and "Fatty" is cross, or was, when some of those prying newspapermen attempted to interview him about the reported match. "Fatty" dislikes the publicity.

The trouble was that there were two movie actresses, one named Doris Keane and the other named Doris Deane. The former was the wife of Basil Sydney, an actor, and the latter was the girl friend of Fatty. The newspaper confused the two because of the similarity of names.

Though false, there was nothing libelous about saying an attractive movie actress was the girl friend of Fatty Arbuckle, even though Fatty was not the most presentable male in existence. Once the extrinsic fact was known that Doris Keane was married, the story—innocent on its face—became defamatory because even married movie actresses are considered to be defamed when a paper alleges that they are running around with other men (Sydney v. MacFadden Newspaper Publishing Corp., 242 N.Y. 208).

Mistakes such as these can often be avoided if careful procedures are followed. Birth, death, marriage and engagement announcements should not be blindly accepted over the telephone or through the mail but should be treated as tips to be checked out with the sources like any other story. Caution must be taken to identify persons in pictures, as discussed on page 322.

These cautionary warnings should not be interpreted to mean that a newsman must be frozen by the fear that somehow libel may be present in every story he writes. Libel by extrinsic fact is not the most dangerous or costly kind. Often a mistake will turn out to be a nonlibelous falsehood.

A shopping news magazine in Albuquerque, New Mexico, carried the following item in its February, 1961, edition:

> Marge Hoeck (Marge White of KOB-TV) off on a six month jaunt . . . true story: persuaded to take a charm course by employees as standard procedure . . . is knitting little things as she and her husband expect an addition to an already half-grown family.

Marge Hoeck sued, protesting that she was neither married

nor pregnant, although she had been married twice previously and was the mother of two grown sons. The New Mexico Supreme Court ruled that the article was not libelous and rejected claims for damages (Hoeck v. Tiedebohl, 74 N.M. 146).

In another case, the New York *Herald Tribune* published a picture of a man and woman at a costume ball. Although they were both single, the caption described them as man and wife. Since she was attractive, the man did not complain, but the woman indignantly claimed that this constituted a charge that she was living in sin with the man with whom she was photographed and that her friends knew that she was single and might doubt her chastity. The *Tribune*'s reply was that the layout might well charge that she and the man were living together, but under the holy bonds of matrimony, and it asked, in effect, what's wrong with that? The charge was held nonlibelous.

In other words, the advice is not don't print, but be careful.

Fictitious Names

Fictitious names can get a writer into trouble, but there is no reason why they cannot be used if they are selected properly. The trouble arises when the name happens to coincide with that of a real individual. The classic case resulted from an article, printed in the Manchester (England) Sunday *Chronicle* in July, 1906, about an imaginary gentleman named Artemus Jones, who, on one side of his life, was a blameless churchwarden at Peckham, and, on the other side of his life, indulged in wild orgies at Dieppe, France.

The article was headlined "Motor Mad Dieppe" and included the following passage:

> Upon the terrace marches the world, attracted by the motor races —a world immensely pleased with itself, and minded to draw a wealth of inspiration—and, incidentally, of golden cocktails—from any scheme to speed the passing hour. . . . "Whist! There is Artemus Jones with a woman who is not his wife, who must be, you know— the other thing!" whispers a fair neighbour of mine excitedly into her bosom friend's ear. Really, is it not surprising how certain of our fellow-countrymen behave when they come abroad? Who would suppose, by his goings on, that he was a churchwarden at Peckham?

No one, indeed, would assume that Jones in the atmosphere of London would take on so austere a job as the duties of a churchwarden. Here, in the atmosphere of Dieppe, on the French side of the channel, he is the life and soul of a gay little band that haunts the Casino and turns night into day, besides betraying a most unholy delight in the society of female butterflies.

In England a lawyer named Artemus Jones went to court and said that his fellow members of the bar had been snickering and poking fun at him and he wanted some money to assuage his wounded feelings. The *Chronicle* protested its innocence and even ran a disclaimer insisting that its imaginary Artemus Jones was not the barrister; but the jury, after deliberating only fifteen minutes, awarded £1,750 in damages (E. Hulton & Co. v. Jones, 2 K.B. 444).

The key to the selection of fictitious names for news stories and columns is to make sure that they are products of the imagination. If the article is supposed to be humorous, manufactured names like Dr. Computer would be fine for a scientist, Ben Dover for a physical education teacher, Pip Squeak for a midget and Last National Bank for a bank. It is true that the Manchester Sunday *Chronicle* thought that the name Artemus was so unusual that the reader would instantly realize the character was imaginary. But, since Artemus Ward, the American humorist, had been popular in England before the turn of the century, it was not beyond comprehension that some youngster had been named for him. Even then the *Chronicle* would have been on safe ground if it had combined Artemus with a plainly fictitious last name. By using the ubiquitous Jones it increased the odds of selecting the name of a real person.

If the article is not humorous and the writer wants to use a more realistic name, a good procedure is to manufacture it from the names of his coworkers or his immediate family. The "Ann" from Terry Ann Harrison could be combined with the "Evans" from Winifred Evans to produce the name "Ann Evans." Then the telephone directory ought to be checked to avoid unnecessary duplication of names. While there is still a chance that a girl by the name of Ann Evans will pop up and claim she has been defamed, the writer can offer convincing evidence that his character was purely fictional. He can produce the two girls in court, explain how he had thought up the name and how he had checked the phone book to avoid mistaken identity. The plaintiff might have a theoretical case, but she would not get very far with her claim.

The timid writer can always fall back on John Doe and Richard Roe, but these names are too dead for those who care about the effect they are trying to create.

Chapter 5

IS CRIME OR DISHONOR CHARGED?

THE ARTICLE IS PUBLISHED AND THE INDIVIDUAL IDENTIFIED. STILL there is no libel unless the natural effect of the writing is to make readers generally think worse of the person.

Who are readers generally? Some have high standards and some low. Most people would think worse of a man described as a bookie. But a considerable segment of the community might think so highly of him that they would want his name and telephone number. The test is not the opinion of those readers whose standards are abnormally high nor those whose standards are abnormally low, nor the majority. You could not take a Gallup Poll to determine if something were libelous. Defamation is not determined by counting noses or brains. The test is whether the matter is calculated to induce an evil opinion of the person in the minds of a considerable segment of the average right-thinking people, the fair and reasonable people, of the community.

This is admittedly an uncertain yardstick. Among other things, what it means in practice is that the standards of a particular segment of the community cannot be picked out to judge libel. An Irish priest found that out back in 1869. He had sued on account of an allegation that he was an informer against a certain class of Irish criminals. He argued that this exposed him to odium among criminals and those who sympathized with criminals. "That," said the court, "is quite true, but we cannot be called on to adopt that standard. The very circumstances which will make a person be regarded with disfavour by the criminal classes will raise his character in the estimation of right-thinking men. We can only regard the estimation in which a man is held by society generally" (Mawe v. Piggott, 4 Irish Rep. C. L. 54).

By the same token, if an article says that Dr. Tonic recommends whiskey for medicinal purposes, he is not libeled even though people in the community with extraordinarily strict standards might deplore the use of liquor in any form.

Judge or Jury

Who decides whether the words are libelous? Generally the rule is that if the words are capable of only one meaning the judge presiding at the trial makes the ruling. This is what happens in almost all cases. If the judge announces that the publication is not libelous, the trial ends and everyone goes home. The jury never receives the case. On the other hand, if the judge decides that the article is libelous, the fun is just beginning. The defendant is required to prove his defenses, and the case in all probability will wind up with the jury.

In some cases, however, the judge tosses the question of whether the article is libelous to the jury. This procedure generally occurs when the words are capable of two meanings—one libelous, the other nonlibelous.

A 1925 slander case shows why a judge is sometimes forced to require the jury to make the decision. The incident occurred aboard the steamer *Orizaba,* which plied between the United States, Cuba and Spain. The second-class steward, a man named Boget, had tried to make love to a Spanish widow, a Mrs. Rovira, and resented the fact that she had been doing some work in the chief steward's office. One evening, as the ship was sailing from Havana for Spain, Mr. Boget, Mrs. Rovira and some others sat down to dinner. It was hot and Mrs. Rovira wanted a cool drink. She turned to Mr. Boget and asked, "Will you please ask for some ice water?"

Torn by jealousy and unable to forget the chief steward, Mr. Boget replied, "Why don't you go to your friend's room and ask him for ice water?"

"I have no friends," the Spanish lady said demurely. "I just am nice to everybody, and I have no friends."

The second-class steward could not accept her reply. "Go ahead," he prodded, "you are worse than a cocotte."

With this, Mrs. Rovira slapped his face and fainted.

At the trial an interpreter testified that the French word

"cocotte" meant a woman who leads a fast life and who gives herself for money, and implies to some men the idea of prostitution. In other associations, however, it can mean a poached egg.

It was for the jury to decide, the court ruled, whether Mrs. Rovira's dining companions had understood the jealous steward to mean that she was a prostitute or a poached egg (Rovira v. Boget, 240 N.Y. 314). No jury ever decided; the case was never retried.

Per Se and Pro Quod

Judges are fond of calling such cases libel pro quod to differentiate them from libel per se, or matter that is defamatory on its face. Other examples of libel pro quod are those in which extrinsic facts are needed to make the article defamatory and nonlibelous false matter, which becomes actionable only if the plaintiff can prove malice and special damages.

At this point even some students of the law tend to throw up their hands in despair. The introduction of such complexities is not required. The Latin term "pro quod" is used to avoid thinking the problem through. The only real question is whether the article is defamatory or not. If libel is present, chances of damages are great; if it is not, the risk is small. Therefore, the term "pro quod" will not be used in this system of dealing with libel. Instead, every situation will be described precisely to enable the newsman to make a reasonable determination whether a judge or jury will find the material defamatory. In this way the newsman can get a good idea of how much risk he is taking.

Now comes the temptation. Why not separate troublesome words and phrases into two groups, one labeled "libelous" and the other "nonlibelous"? The lure of the lists is irresistible to those who refuse to think. In theory, all the writer or editor has to do when he is worried is thumb through the lists. If the word or phrase is under "libel," out it goes; if it is under "nonlibel," in it stays. In this way even if the subject in the news complains that the charge against him is false he can not successfully sue for libel.

Words, however, cannot be forced into one group or the other. The situation in which they are used is crucial in determining whether they are libelous. The phrase "Hitler-like" has been held nonlibelous when applied to a lawyer in his private practice, but libelous regarding him as a public prosecutor. Geography also plays a vital part, as rulings on calling a white man a Negro show. Besides, words have a way of jumping from one category to another, as "Mormon" has, when social, political and economic conditions change.

The major objection to lists is that they tend to reduce the amount of information communicated to the reader. The newsman develops a habit of deleting words or phrases from stories if they are on the "libelous" list. Such information can be the most vital in the story.

Three Kinds of Harm

Despite the uncertainty in some areas of libel, the writer, editor and broadcaster need not despair. Guidelines are available that clearly mark most of the risks. In general a libel can harm an individual in three respects: first, in personal reputation and good name; second, in his right to enjoy social contacts; and third, in his profession, business or calling. The libel can touch an individual in all three respects, but need harm him in only one.

For example, the article might say that Joe Blowhard, a lawyer, was divorced in New York in 1965. That would not injure him in his profession because the very best lawyer might find it hard to live with one woman for more than a few years. But such a statement would affect his personal reputation and good name since in New York the only ground for divorce in 1965 was adultery.

To write that Joe was suffering from smallpox would also be libelous. That would not affect him in his profession, since lawyers are, like all of us, susceptible to diseases; nor would it affect his personal reputation and good name. But Joe would be defamed because he would undoubtedly get kicked out of his car pool and his girl friend would look for someone else to take her on a skiing weekend to Vermont. The libel would deprive Joe of his social contacts.

The article might say that Joe was a wretchedly poor lawyer.

That would not affect his personal good name, for a poor lawyer might be a person of the highest integrity, good morals and reputation. Nor would he lose any friends, except, perhaps, those seeking free legal advice. But the article would damage him in his profession and therefore would be libelous.

Crime and Dishonor

The most common libel cuts across all three of these aspects of a person's life. It is an accusation of crime, fraud, dishonesty, immorality or dishonorable conduct. The charge can be made directly or indirectly. There can be a flat statement that Gorkol Glutz held up Tillie the Teller and escaped with $5,000 of the bank's money. Or it can be attributed—with the police, or the district attorney or some other authority, accusing Gorkol of the holdup or saying he had been arrested for it. Either way there is libel.

To say that a person is guilty of a crime is much more severe than to say that he has been accused or is suspected of a crime. Therefore the defense faces more difficulty with flat statements of guilt than with accusations or suspicions.

The crime can be charged by name, by narrating the facts or by describing the punishment. If the article should say that Seaman Snorkel assaulted Lieutenant Martinet, it would impute the specific crime of assault. The article would also accuse him of a crime if it said that Snorkel suddenly smacked Martinet on the nose without provocation, because the facts would meet the definition of assault under the penal law. The article would also impute crime if it said that Snorkel spent his vacation at Sing Sing instead of Florida, because it would be clear that he had gone to prison for a crime and not for his health.

As long as the reporter is shielded from a libel suit by a solid legal defense he is free to use the exact legal terminology in describing the criminal charge. If, however, he uses the legal term for a crime and lacks a defense, he is in serious trouble.

Under the headline "Church Labels Shooting as Murderous," the Savannah (Georgia) *Evening Press* ran an item on a protest against a policeman's shooting of a boy believed to have been stealing a truck or something from it. The article began:

The Bethlehem Baptist Church today condemned as "unwarranted" and "murderous" the shooting of 13-year-old Claud Sutton Thursday. In a letter addressed to Mayor Mingledorff, church officials wrote:

"We feel that it is one of the most disgraceful things a law enforcement officer could do in the light of circumstances given. We do not condone crime and believe that all criminals should be punished, including Patrolman J. R. Harley, for his unjustifiable shooting of this boy, but we do feel that law violators should be treated as human beings, and not as beasts to be shot down unmercifully."

A Georgia appellate court, in ruling on the case in 1959, said:

Certainly the facts as set out in the published letter and also in the plaintiff's petition do not show that the plaintiff was guilty of the offense of murder as defined by statute. But the ordinary signification of the word "murderous" as defined in Webster's New International Dictionary, is "characterized by, or causing, murder or bloodshed; having the purpose or quality of murder; bloody; sanguinary; blood-thirsty, fell, savage, cruel." "Criminal," likewise, means not solely one convicted of a crime in a court of law, but "involving, or of the nature of, a crime; relating to crime or its punishment; guilty of crime or serious offense." The article thus affirmately charged the plaintiff with guilt of the crime of making an attack upon another which was unwarranted and likely to produce death.

The *News* won the case, however, because it could rely on the defense of truth, which, as we shall see later, is the best defense of all. The court found that Patrolman Harley had no legal right to shoot the boy because he did not do so in self-defense and, as a Georgia police officer, he was not justified in firing in trying to make an arrest when the offense was only a misdemeanor (Savannah News-Press v. Harley, 100 Ga. App. 387).

It is also libelous to cast grave suspicion on an individual with hints. Such a case involved the following from the Boston *Record American:*

The Veterans Hospital here suspected that 39-year-old George M. Perry of North Truro, whose death is being probed by federal and state authorities, was suffering from chronic arsenic poisoning, the *Record American* learned Wednesday.

State Police said the bodies of Perry and his brother, Arthur, who is buried near him, would probably be exhumed from St. Peter's Cemetery in Provincetown.

George Perry died in the VA hospital in Jamaica Plain last June 9, 48 hours after his 10th admission there since Dec. 29, 1959.

His brother, who lived in Connecticut and spent two days here during George's funeral, died approximately a month later.

About two months later, in September, George's mother-in-law, 74-year-old Mrs. Mary F. Mott, who had come to live with her daughter, died, too. Her remains were cremated.

.   .   .   .

An autopsy, performed with the permission of his [Perry's] wife, Mary, disclosed that 500 times the usual amount of arsenic was in his hair and abnormally high quantities of the same lethal substance were in his brain and liver.

Perry, according to police, was his wife's second husband.

When Mrs. Perry sued, the court decided that a jury could readily find that the deaths had resulted from a crime and "the only question is whether the article could be read to indicate the plaintiff as a suspect." It explained why it thought readers could conclude that Mrs. Perry "was engaged in highly sinister conduct":

> This is not a case where it was asserted simply that the plaintiff's husband met his death by acts of persons unknown. The identity of a possible suspect was made more specific by the suggestion that the brother had met with the same fate following his visit "here" from Connecticut. It was much further localized by the mention of the death, "too," of plaintiff's mother two months after she had "come to live with her daughter." The reference to the fact that this mother's "remains were cremated" could be found to imply that the fact was regrettable under the circumstances. Indeed, in this total context the otherwise irrelevant observation that the plaintiff had had a previous husband might even be regarded as having significance. [Perry v. The Hearst Corporation, 334 F. 2d 800]

Mrs. Perry received $25,000. The story would have been less of a risk if it had given Mrs. Perry's views on the deaths and provided details indicating some undetermined person might have been responsible or that foul play might not have been involved.

Crime can be charged in an even milder way. An article asserted that a police officer was riding free on passes issued by a taxicab company and that if he would go before a grand jury and waive immunity the district attorney would be glad to have him repeat his denials. No crime was directly charged, but the plaintiff was held up to public condemnation by suggesting that he was the subject of some impending accusation or suspicion of some crime. The jury awarded $15,000 in damages (Dooley v. Press Publishing Co., 170 App. Div. (N.Y.)492).

A Way Out—No Crime

While such restrictions may seem suffocating to the crime reporter, the United States Supreme Court long ago provided authority for publishing details of many incidents that might otherwise go unrecorded. Its decision made it possible for a careful newspaper or broadcasting station to report police news without fear. The article on which the decision was made ran in the Washington *Post* on April 3, 1909:

> John Armstrong Chaloner (Chanler), brother of Lewis Stuyvesant Chanler, of New York, and former husband of Amelie Rives, the authoress, now Princess Troubetsky, is recuperating at Shadeland, the country home of Maj. Thomas L. Emry, near Weldon, N. C., where he had gone to recuperate following a nervous breakdown as a result of the tragedy at his home, Merry Mills, near Cobham, on March 15, when he shot and killed John Gillard, while the latter was abusing his wife, who had taken refuge at Merry Mills, Chaloner's home. Following the shooting, Chaloner suffered a nervous breakdown, and was ordered by his physician to take a long rest. He decided to visit his old friend, Maj. Emry, who with Chaloner, was instrumental in founding Roanoke Rapids, a manufacturing town 5 miles from Weldon. Chaloner arrived at Weldon after traveling all night and was immediately hurried to Shadeland, where he received medical attention and temporary relief.

Chaloner sued, contending that the *Post* had accused him of murder. The truth was, Chaloner told the court, that he had been trying to protect Gillard's wife from her husband when a pistol accidentally exploded, killing Gillard. The trial judge agreed with Chaloner that the article was libelous because it did accuse him of homicide. The judge told the jury that "the only question really, for you to consider, is how much damages the plaintiff should be allowed." The jury decided on $10,000 and the verdict was upheld by the Court of Appeals. In overturning the decision, the Supreme Court held that this case should not have gone to the jury because the article "does not set forth the commission of a crime in unambiguous words." It went on:

> We are unable to conclude that, as matter of law, addition of the words, "while the latter was abusing his wife, who had taken refuge at Merry Mills, Chaloner's home" would convert such a statement into a definite charge of murder. On the contrary they might at least suggest to reasonable minds that the homicide was without malice. [Washington Post Co. v. Chaloner, 250 U.S. 290]

What the court was saying was that it is not libelous to accuse a man of something that he has a legal right to do. Killing is not always a crime, hence it is not always libelous to attribute that act to someone. Needless to say, such writing demands the writer's highest skills if he is going to stay out of trouble. When doubt exists, a check with a good libel lawyer before publication is advisable.

The value of the rule is that it allows a newsman to disclose information to the public about actions of individuals that, while not criminal, are often unpopular. Thus no libel is involved in mistakenly writing that a witness invoked the Fifth Amendment forty-seven times in refusing to testify at a Senate rackets committee hearing. The Fifth Amendment to the Constitution gives every American the right to protect himself against self-incrimination by refusing to testify against himself. Use of the right may be unpopular; some may insist that it proves the witness' guilt. But since a person has a legal right to invoke the Constitution, the writer who reports that a witness did is not libeling him, even if the article is erroneous.

Nor is it libelous to say that a person who was sued for a just debt pleaded the statute of limitations and got off scot-free. Many people may consider such conduct contemptible, but the statute of limitations is designed to outlaw stale claims so that judicial machinery will not get bogged down. Thus society should not react against the person who uses this right, nor can the reporter who mistakenly writes that a debtor pleaded the statute be successfully sued for libel (Bennett v. Williamson 4 Sandf. 60).

The courts have also held not libelous reports that a person attempted to escape the performance of an agreement by pleading the statute of frauds. This law provides that certain agreements must be in writing to be binding and, while the public generally might not approve the conduct of a man who ran out on an oral deal, he has a legal right to do this.

When Anna Rosenberg was up for confirmation as Assistant Secretary of Defense, she was opposed by a man from New York who hired an attorney by the name of Richardson to represent him before the Senate committeee. The New York *Herald Tribune* published an article about the case and pointed out that Richardson formerly represented a man by the name of Williams who was a notorious rabble-rouser. Richardson sought an indictment, but the court held that it was not libelous to say that he had once represented such a man (*People* ex rel. *Richardson v. Reid,* unreported). A lawyer has a legal right, some would say duty, to represent such a man in legal matters.

A word of caution, however. Dependence on this rule in periods of excessively strong passion is dangerous. A court has found libelous a statement that a man was a profiteer in wartime, even though he had a legal right, in the absence of special legislation, to charge anything he wanted to for his product (Lunn v. Littauer, 187 App. Div. (N.Y.)808). Such a statement is no more than an assertion that a person did what he had a legal right to do. But in wartime, emotions are aroused and it would be extremely unpopular and therefore defamatory to accuse someone of profiteering, although in peacetime it would not be, unless crime were involved.

Sex and Women

A large percentage of libel suits are based on stories imputing crime in one form or another. A substantial percentage of the remainder are based on stories relating to unchastity or other breaches of the currently sanctioned moral code. The overwhelming majority of such suits are the result of some error in reporting, and not because the writers and editors did not understand that libel was involved.

A typical example is a listing in the April 21, 1961, edition of the Spokane (Washington) *Chronicle,* under "Brief City News," of the divorce of Hazel M. Pitts from Philip Pitts. Actually Philip

Pitts had been divorced in February, 1960, and had remarried seven months later. The listing was a misreading by the reporter of a court action brought by Pitts to seek custody of the youngest child by his first marriage. This case is an example of libel by extrinsic fact, since the reader would have to know that Pitts was living with another woman before the listing would be defamatory. Pitts said that several friends called him and his wife and made sarcastic remarks about their being bigamists. One family in the neighborhood would not allow their children to play with the Pitts children. Even Pitts' coworkers gossiped about the matter. As a result, even though the *Chronicle* had published a correction, the Supreme Court of Washington held that the listing was libel per se (Pitts v. Spokane Chronicle Co., 63 Wash. 2d 763). A judgment of $2,000 plus interest was paid.

There is no substitute for care in reporting.

One of the few fixed rules is that an imputation of unchastity to a woman is always libelous. The rule is so very harshly applied that it can be regarded as settled law everywhere that it is libelous not only to impute unchastity but also to print anything indicating that a woman's chastity has been brought into question.

Back at the turn of the century, the New York *Recorder* published an article that included this passage: a "dashing blonde, twenty years old, and is said to have been a concert-hall singer and dancer at Coney Island." Is it wrong to call a girl a "dashing blonde"? Certainly not. "Twenty years old"? Many women would like to be twenty. But how about Coney Island? Was that such a bad place at the turn of the century? The girl said it was, that "a concert hall at Coney Island is a place of evil repute and a resort for disorderly and disreputable persons of both sexes; that the female singers and dancers therein are generally depraved and abandoned, or are so regarded and understood to be, and as such are shunned and avoided by orderly and respectable people." The court said she was right and ruled that the description of her as a former concert-hall singer and dancer at Coney Island had held her up "to the public gaze not only as unchaste but as belonging to one of the lowest classes of the great army of fallen women" (Gates v. New York Recorder Co., 155 N.Y. 228).

What about saying that a woman has been raped? Does this

libel her? It does not attribute any moral delinquency; she is but the innocent victim of the crime of another. The motion picture *Rasputin, the Mad Monk*, which dealt with the murder of the lecherous man who had exerted an evil control over the Czar and his family before World War I, included a scene in which a "Princess Natasha" was either seduced or raped. When a Russian princess living in Paris sued in England, Metro-Goldwyn-Mayer, which made and distributed the film, argued that the film portrayed a seduction, not a rape, and that therefore it had not defamed her. But the British court that heard the case decided that it did not make any difference, from the standpoint of defamation, if rape or seduction were depicted. If she were seduced, one judge pointed out, she would be pictured as immoral; if she were raped, she would be shunned and avoided (Youssoupoff v. Metro-Goldwyn-Mayer Pictures, Ltd., 50 Times Law Reports 581, 99 A.L.R. 864). That one verdict netted the princess, who had fled Communism, £25,000 or $125,000 at the rate of exchange in 1934. Her suits in other countries were settled for $250,000. Those were large amounts, especially with the world in the grip of an economic depression.

Police reports of rapes should be double-checked, especially if names or other identifying circumstances are included in an article.

Society's views on what is right and wrong about sexual behavior have changed a great deal in the last fifty years and are still changing. Eventually, moral standards may relax so that sexual relations are much freer. Medical science is hastening the way toward change by developing drugs that control conception. But for now, at least, the prohibition on accusations of unchastity in women is still inflexible.

The writer should be wary of the use of quotation marks that convey, by innuendo, an improper relationship.

In the early 1900s Mrs. Edith M. Irving found herself in the plight of being unacceptable to her father-in-law. Matters went from bad to worse, and the father-in-law lost no opportunity to cast suspicion on her past and break up the marriage. A good chance arose when somehow he received a bill from her doctor. He sat down and wrote the doctor the following note:

In regard to your bill for this woman, which you ask me to forward to the proper person, I'm afraid I can't help you much. There is a fellow who used to be a "friend" of the woman about three years ago, and perhaps I can find out something from him.

The daughter-in-law struck back with a libel suit. In upholding her cause of action, the court noted that the "suspicious quotation marks" in the letter when considered in conjunction with the word "fellow" might communicate the idea that the daughter-in-law had had a paramour (Irving v. Irving, 121 App. Div.(N.Y.) 258).

A modern case finds that the courts still hold the same opinion. The New York *Post* carried an article with the headline "Slain Exec Faced Liens of 2 Million" and the following paragraphs:

> As police delved into his tangled business affairs, several women described as "associated" with Brenhouse were questioned at Hastings Police Headquarters.
> Among those questioned were Mrs. W. B. Wildstein who, with her husband, shared the second half of the two family house in which Brenhouse lived.

Mrs. Wildstein sued for libel. The *Post* argued that it had merely been quoting the police when it used the word "associated." The court rejected the argument and made clear that the *Post* could have avoided trouble merely by removing the quotation marks. It said:

> The use of quotation marks around the word "associated" might be found by a jury to indicate that an inverted meaning was intended by the writer and so understood by the average reader of that newspaper in the community, and not its normal or customary meaning. . . . There was no need to impart such emphasis or imply such connotation if the purpose was merely to indicate that the police had used the word "associated" in describing these women. The fact, if it be so, that the writer was only quoting the word used by the police would not immunize defendant from liability if it be held that it constituted a libel; one who repeats a libel must respond in damages, even if he indicates that he is quoting another. [Wildstein v. New York Post Corporation, 243 N.Y.S. 2d 386]

When a woman's chastity is questioned, however gently, courts are chivalrous. They take a less protective view of comments about female beauty. A Mississippi case is indicative. Mrs. Florence Temple Edens, a twenty-two-year-old Natchez woman, had neglected her teeth for a long time and they began to give her trouble. In June, 1956, she went to Dr. Emile W. Salvo, Jr., who advised her to have all her upper teeth—there were only eight left—removed and false teeth made. When Mrs. Edens said that she did not have the money to make a down payment on the work, Dr. Salvo said that he would take an impression and make the denture and when she returned with the money he would extract the teeth. This seemed to be satisfactory to Mrs. Edens, so Dr. Salvo made the impression. Mrs. Edens left his office but did not return until spring of the next year. Dr. Salvo took out her eight upper teeth and immediately put in the denture that he had made. Proud of his work, he asked Mrs. Edens to look in the mirror and see how nice she looked. Mrs. Edens was not so delighted. She pointed out to the doctor that blood was oozing through a crack in the front of the denture. But she wore it home. According to her story, she couldn't eat and she suffered all night.

Her husband took the plate back and said he was told the charge was $20. Mr. Edens said he would pay the bill when he received his wages in a few days. Without waiting for payday to roll around, Dr. Salvo sat down and wrote the following note:

Dear Mrs. Edens:

I sincerely regret that you are without your denture, and your teeth. Had I suspected that you and your husband would have been satisfied with paupers' care I should have offered that to you. Had I also known that you and your husband had no aversion to your running around toothless and thereby loosing permanently your, until now, somewhat pleasant facial contours, I should never have suggested immediate denture service for you.

Your husband should not be blamed for his serious mistake but pitied for his understandable ignorance relative to dental care. (The seriousness of his mistake will only be fully realized at a later date.)

Since my generous offer of services (for such a negligible fee) has been so rudely declined I shall be moved nevertheless to overlook at this moment your rightful and legal indebtedness to me for denture-services as rendered to date. I shall mark it up as a profitable experience.

However, a statement of my fee for examination, diagnosis, medication, local anesthesia and extraction of your teeth is enclosed herewith. Under the circumstances I shall appreciate prompt settlement so that we both can forget the whole matter.

Most Sincerely yours,

E. W. Salvo, DDS

encl. Statement fee: $30.00

cc. Credit Assoc. Natchez Dental Society

When Mrs. Edens read the letter, she responded by getting angry and crying. But it was Dr. Salvo who sued first. He asked a justice of the peace to award him his fee, upping the amount first to $50 and later to $100. Nearly two months after he was awarded $100, Mrs. Edens sued for libel. It was not that the fee had jumped so high. It was that third sentence in the letter, indicating that she was no longer a beauty, that had kept gnawing at her. A jury agreed that she deserved damages and awarded her $2,500, but the Mississippi Supreme Court said No. Such words may embarrass and are tactless, the court said, but they are not libelous (Salvo v. Edens, 237 Miss. 734).

Sex and Men

In writing about sexual behavior of men, more leeway is permitted, as an article in the December, 1960, issue of the magazine *Motion Picture* demonstrates. It was titled "Janet Leigh's Own Story—I was a Child Bride at 14!" Included in the goo were the following paragraphs:

> For the small tawny-haired blonde and the lean, dark boy their world was coming to an end that desperate summer. They put their arms around each other in the dark and held tight, afraid.

.   .   .   .

> That summer in Merced, a small town south of San Francisco with only one motion picture theatre, Jeanette Morrison—the girl who was to become Janet Leigh—was 14 [actually she was 15]. The dark boy we'll call "John" was 18.
>
> "Never make fun of young love," Janet Leigh says today.
>
> "Never laugh at it."
>
> "I might have become a tramp," says Janet Leigh.

.   .   .   .

> "You know what I mean. Or I might have become a frigid woman, afraid of men."

A salesman, John Kenneth Carlisle, who said he had been the "lean, dark boy," sued Fawcett Publications, Janet Leigh and a magazine distributor for libel and invasion of privacy. He asked $2 million in damages, asserting that the article describing the courtship and marriage had accused him of being a "tramp, a vagabond and a depraved and predatory male, who conspired to, and did in fact, abduct and exploit a young maiden of the age of fourteen years, and who was capable of causing and did in fact attempt to cause said maiden to become a frigid woman afraid of men." The court agreed that Carlisle had been sufficiently identified, although his real name had not been used, but dismissed the case on the basis that he had not been defamed:

> The description of the plaintiff as a "dark boy" refers obviously to his complexion or hair color, and his personal appearance is described rather attractively than otherwise; the allegation that he went through a marriage ceremony while he and the girl were minors does not expose the plaintiff to "hatred, contempt, ridicule or obloquy" or cause him to be "shunned or avoided" or have "a tendency to injure him in his occupation" . . . in view of the current mores of the people of this state. The allegations that they put their arms around each other in the dark, that the plaintiff kissed her and that she knew for the first time what a kiss was, that they held hands and kissed at the moving picture show can scarcely be held to be libelous in the surrounding circumstances. The statement that a young man has kissed a willing and pretty girl is not generally considered degrading. "All the world loves a lover." [Carlisle v. Fawcett Publications, 20 Cal. Rptr. 405]

Any charge that a man or wife failed to fulfill marital obligations is defamatory. On June 22, 1951, Florence E. Browne executed her last will and testament, which contained the following paragraph:

> I am mindful of the fact that I have made no provision for John H. Browne, my husband. I do so intentionally because of the fact that during my lifetime he abandoned me, made no provision for my support, treated me with complete indifference and did not display any affection or regard for me.

Actually, Florence was divorced by her husband in 1917 because of adultery and he remarried seven years later. New

York's highest court held that the will was defamatory in validating a $5,000 award, although it did not pass on the legality of a libel suit against an estate (Brown v. DuFrey, 1 N.Y. 2d 190).

In Michigan, a husband ran an ad in the paper asserting that his wife had deserted him in his illness. The state Supreme Court said that the notice was libelous because "if this charge be true, Mrs. Smith was guilty of the basest ingratitude, and of conduct deserving the contempt of all right-minded people" (Smith v. Smith, 73 Mich. 445).

The United States Court of Appeals for the District of Columbia has held that a mere assertion of marital discord is libelous (Thackrey v. Patterson, 157 F. 2d 614), but this ruling does not bar reports of isolated disagreement.

Chapter 6

IS RIDICULE OR MISFORTUNE
PRESENT?

Laughter

WHEN THE NEWSMAN EMERGES FROM THE REALM OF THE SEVERE types of charges such as crime and sexual misbehavior, he enters the more debatable land where people's standards differ. This uncertainty is especially true of articles that ridicule someone. The newspaper, magazine or broadcasting station sometimes has to take a calculated risk. It cannot be determined with complete certainty in advance what a court will rule as libelous. There have been instances where a judge was upheld by a three-to-two vote by one appellate court and later reversed by a four-to-three vote in a higher one.

The principle that controls ridicule is simple to state; the difficulty of applying it is what makes infallible predictions of libel cases more difficult. Mere ridicule is not libelous. Ridicule that injures reputation—that has a tendency to deprive a man of normal social relations—is libelous. A publication that generates a laugh at the victim's expense and makes him the subject of a joke or his conduct the occasion for amusement is not libelous. It must be more than a jest, more than a mere shaft of humor; it must carry some kind of sting that harms a person's reputation.

Bealey Cohen awoke one morning to read to his great dismay in the obituary columns of *The New York Times* the following: "Died—Brooklyn: Cohen—Bealey, 133 St. Marks Avenue, May 6."

Bealey knew he was alive but decided to demonstrate it to *The New York Times*. So he sued. The *Times* had been victimized by some of Bealey's friends, who were playing a joke. Was this libelous? No, the court said, and explained in a 1912 decision:

The item states that an event has come to pass which is looked for in the history of every man, is regarded as beyond his control, and, therefore, does not permit the inference that the man has done any act or suffered any act which he could not have done or which he need not have suffered. . . . Such publication may be unpleasant; it may annoy or irk the subject thereof; it may subject him to joke or jest or to banter from those who knew him or knew of him, even to the extent of affecting his feelings; but this in itself is not enough. [Cohen v. New York Times, 153 App. Div.(N.Y.)242]

Some forty years later a similar joke was played on John Cardiff of Brooklyn. He sued the Brooklyn *Eagle*, which had published the announcement, on the basis that it not only falsely said he had died, but also said that he was lying "in state at 566-4th Avenue," which was his saloon. Still the court held that there was no libel. "At its worst, the publication might cause some amusement to the plaintiff's friends," the court held. "But it is difficult to see where his reputation would be impaired in the slightest degree and the law of defamation is concerned only with injuries thereto" (Cardiff v. Brooklyn Eagle, Inc., 190 Misc. (N.Y.)730).

A saloonkeeper is one thing, a clergyman quite another. Both may have sensitive natures, but the man of cloth is by far more dangerous to poke fun at, as the New York *Herald Tribune* found out after running this article on December 11, 1920:

CHAUFFEUR HITS PASTOR, THEN WISHES HE HADN'T

REV. H. M. HANCOCK, OF HUNTINGTON, FORGOT
TO TURN OTHER CHEEK; WALLOPS FOE INSTEAD

The Rev. H. M. Hancock's automobile and one owned by the Long Island Lighting Company crashed together yesterday at Main and Green Streets, Huntington. The Lighting Company's car was overturned and the clergyman hastened to it to assist the driver, George Carbone.

Carbone crawled from the wreckage as Mr. Hancock approached, and as soon as the clergyman got within reach punched him in the face.

A gasp of horror went up from the witnesses of the accident and its sequel, and its echo came from the lips of Carbone, the husky chauffeur, as an ecclesiastical fist smote him in the midriff.

Between astonishment and lack of breath Carbone's appreciation

of the succeeding events was somewhat dulled, but the onlookers
said that the pastor of Huntington Methodist Episcopal Church gave
as nifty an exhibition as though he were a professional bag-puncher
instead of a pulpit pounder.

Carbone got in one more blow during the entire encounter. It
reached the clergyman's jaw, but did not disconcert him in the
least, seeming rather to increase his agility and the vigor of his
punches.

The chauffeur is said to have been close to taking the count when
Dr. Samuel Cook pushed through the crowd and separated the
fighters.

Witnesses said that Mr. Hancock had done his utmost to avoid
the collision and he was asked if he wanted to make a charge
against Carbone. Mr. Hancock's good eye roved over the panting,
staggering figure of his opponent and said he guessed he wouldn't.

"Why should I?" he asked. "I guess I gave back as much as I
received."

The article did not charge that the minister had assaulted
Carbone. It said merely that he had acted in self-defense, but
the court concluded that the frivolous tone in which the episode
was described damaged Mr. Hancock's reputation (Hancock v.
New York Tribune, Inc., 198 App. Div.(N.Y.)917).

The article would not have been libelous of a newspaperman, a
doctor or a lawyer, but courts are sensitive to the reputations of
clergymen. They have also been more than gallant regarding
women, as the ruling on the following article on August 4, 1894,
showed:

ROW, NELL! PULL, MAME!
TWO GIRLS ROW A RACE FOR A BEAU WITH A
HANDSOME FACE
PROSPECT PARK LAKE TURNED INTO A CUPID'S COURSE WITH
A FRINGE OF FEMININITY

"Hurry up, Nellie! Oh, do hurry!"

Shrill shrieks from fair feminine friends enthusiastically encouraged each earnest, anxious aspirant as she shook shining drops
daintily from the blades of her oars and pulled for dear life.

"Move up, Mame! Look out! She's crawling away from you!"

Mamie bent to her work like a little man, and sent the scull shooting through the shimmering stream as she strove frantically to over-
take her opponent.

"Hurry up, Nellie! Hurry, hurry! Oh!"

The occasion was the great Prospect Park quarter mile junior singles for the Cupid cup. Miss Nellie McFadden (a prize for Aladdin) and sweet Mamie Barton (you'd sure lose your heart on) had both set their caps for young Frederick Bohn, so, with a friend and relation they went to the Park to give demonstration ('twas just before dark), by rowing a race, an aquatic love chase of their love for this perfectly proper Don Juan.

Nellie insisted that the article in the *Morning Journal* was not only pure fabrication but was also libel because it described her as competing in an unladylike way for a husband. The court agreed (McFadden v. Morning Journal Assn., 28 App.Div.(N.Y.) 508). Nellie collected $3,000.

Columns of personal items should be closely watched because writers may go too far in poking fun. Here is an example of one from the "Milling Around" column by Sonny Oleson in the Westbrook (Maine) *American* on June 26, 1957, that the court held went too far:

> George Powers, Coating Department, is a fellow who believes in looking ahead. He's also a classic example of typical Yankee thrift. Take his idea on caskets now—George says, "Why spend a lot of money for a casket when, for $15 or $20 you can build one, yourself. After all, your family can always use the money you've saved in that one item, alone."
>
> Suiting the action to the word, George is now busily sawing and hammering away on his own tailored-to-fit coffin. And, as a sort of package deal, he's making plans to dig the space for it next.
>
> From all outward appearances, this thrifty, if slightly ghoulish gent can take his time on his project, because . . .
>
> He turned (approximately) 35 on his last birthday.

The workers in the Coating Department of the S. D. Warren Co. paper plant roared with laughter and kidded Powers about the item, but he saw nothing funny about it and sued. The newspaper tried to get the case thrown out, but the Supreme Judicial Court of Maine upheld the action. It said:

> The reader is given the impression that the plaintiff is at best an odd or unusual character acting in a manner far removed from the ordinary standards of the day. The man who builds his own coffin and is planning to dig his own grave is described as "thrifty, if

slightly ghoulish gent." The reader may well laugh with the writer at the victim with a laughter mixed with contempt.

The defendant does not escape liability on the ground the article was written in jest, if such was the fact. The joke that goes too far and causes harm, not laughter, is within our common experience. [Powers v. Durgin-Snow Publishing Co., 154 Me. 108]

Eventually the case went to a jury, which awarded Powers $50 in damages against the publishing company and $50 against the writer. Luckily for the press, Maine juries tend to shy from awarding punitive damages.

Tears

Tearjerkers and other articles of misfortune also present a peril. This kind of article differs from most of the ones previously mentioned in an important respect: generally the articles relate to incidents for which the libeled person is not responsible. The libelous classifications previously discussed usually involved some act of commission or omission, such as a crime or a breach of sexual ethics, and, as a result, reflect on personal reputations. The misfortune articles, on the other hand, generally deal with things for which the person could not have been responsible and therefore do not injure his personal reputation. Nevertheless, they are frequently held libelous because the contents have the tendency to cause the person to be shunned and avoided and deprive him of normal social contact even though high-minded people might not agree.

Mental Illness

It is libelous to say of a person that he is insane, an idiot, mentally deranged or the like, or to impute any other form of mental defect. Such an afflicted person is not and cannot be responsible for being an idiot and such a charge does not attack his reputation for good behavior. Nevertheless, a man described as an idiot might find himself shunned and avoided and such a charge would be held libelous. Statements that a person is suffering a nervous breakdown, or a psychological upset, or needs psychiatric treatment or is undergoing psychoanalysis would not be considered libelous by most modern courts since these do not necessarily imply abnormality or a depth of mental illness severe enough to result in the loss of social relationships.

Any suggestion of an abnormal mental state in relation to sex is especially dangerous. The Michigan Supreme Court ruled libelous in 1958 a political advertisment by a judge that said:

> . . . numerous complaints were said to be on file against Kenney in the Benton Harbor police department indicating that he had been frightening women and required institutional treatment for mental illness for the protection of himself and society.

The judge defeated the suit for libel brought against him because he showed a good legal defense for publishing the charge, but the court noted that "it is generally held that a publication imputing impairment of mental faculties" is libelous (Kenney v. Hatfield, 35 Mich. 498).

Any indication that mental illness interferes with a person's ability to make a living adds to the danger. One of the landmark cases of libel through a charge of mental illness involved a man who had been a teller at the Manufacturers' National Bank of Troy, New York, for eighteen years. The article ran in the Troy *Times* of September 15, 1882, and said:

> Several weeks ago, it was rumored that Amasa Moore, the teller of the bank, had tendered his resignation. Rumors at once began to circulate. A reporter inquired of Cashier Wellington if it was true that the teller had resigned, and received in reply the answer that Mr. Moore was on his vacation. More than this the cashier would not say. A rumor was circulated that Mr. Moore was suffering from overwork, and that his mental condition was not entirely good. Next came reports that Cashier Wellington was financially involved, and that the bank was in trouble. A *Times* reporter at once sought an interview with President Weed of the bank, and found him and directors Morrison, Cowee, Bradwell and others in consultation. They said that the bank was entirely sound, with a clear surplus of $100,000; that there had been a little trouble in its affairs occasioned by the mental derangement of Teller Moore, and that the latter's statements, when he was probably not responsible for what he said, had caused some bad rumors.

The court upheld the teller's libel suit, saying:

While the statement was calculated to excite sympathy, and even respect for the plaintiff, it nevertheless was calculated also to injure him in his character and employment as a teller. On common understanding, mental derangement has usually a much more serious significance than mere physical disease. There can be no doubt that the imputation of insanity against a man employed in a position of trust and confidence such as that of a bank teller, whether the insanity is temporary or not, although accompanied by the explanation that it was induced by overwork, is calculated to injure and prejudice him in that employment, and especially where the statement is added that in consequence of his conduct in that condition the bank had been involved in trouble. [Moore v. Francis, 121 N.Y. 199]

Attitudes toward mental illness have changed a great deal in the last century, but false statements about a person's mental condition when related to his occupation are still perilous. Thus, statements that a person possesses an intelligence quotient below the normal range of 90 to 110, or descriptions of subpar intellect, such as "moron," "idiot" or "imbecile," would automatically be libelous.

Disease

To say of a person that he is suffering from a loathsome and contagious disease, such as leprosy, smallpox or the plague, is also defamatory. The courts have ruled not libelous, however, statements that a person is suffering from consumption or diphtheria or other milder forms of contagious disease, because these are not considered, by that fictitious group known as the general public, to be loathsome. The tense in the article is important: if the present tense is used, there is danger, because the implication is that the person should be shunned and avoided; if the past tense is used and the story makes it clear that the disease has been cured, there is almost no risk.

For a time there was a question about infantile paralysis, but since this disease has been practically eliminated in the United States, it does not create any problem insofar as libel is concerned.

Any indication that a person is suffering or has suffered from a disease involving a violation of the moral code, such as syphilis or drunkenness, is dangerous. Here the tense is not important, since the sting of the charge is not so much in being afflicted with the disease as violating the moral code (Williams v. Holdredge 22 Barb. (N.Y.)396).

Poverty and Wealth

Almost everyone would agree that poverty is a misfortune. Is it libelous to say so? There are decisions on both sides. In one, the article said:

> That the battle for existence is not won by brains alone is illustrated in the sad plight of Professor Alfred Nolan Martin, at Richmond Park, Staten Island. A man of extraordinary attainments in classical learning and once a professor in Oxford University, he is now in sad straits because his education hampers him in earning a living. He is living with his young wife and two small children in a house which has not a single door or window inclosed. He is too poor to finish his dwelling and too proud to ask aid. His neighbors say he is starving. In his life—he is now over fifty—Professor Martin has been, besides an Oxford professor, a sanitary engineer, a lecturer, a social agitator, a school teacher and author. Seven years ago while with the Staten Island Health Department he married Miss Cooper of Stapleton, a graduate of the New York University Law School. Then he lost his place.

In ruling the item libelous the court said that as an abstract generality it is true that mere poverty ought not to expose any citizen to ridicule, but insisted that this article made the old professor look like an educated moron (Martin v. Press Publishing Co., 93 App. Div.(N.Y.)531).

This account by the Brooklyn *Spectator* of an accident also was held libelous:

> Unless financial aid is forthcoming immediately the body of a four-year-old boy who was run over Tuesday will be buried in Potter's Field, burial ground of the homeless, friendless and penniless who die or are killed in New York City. The parents of this youngster are in dire financial straits and at this writing have no alternative but to let their son go to his final rest in a pauper's grave. [Katapodis v. Brooklyn Spectator, 287 N.Y. 17]

But the New York *Daily Mirror* won a case in the depression of the 1930s based on an article concerning a suicide of a woman. It said that "she had two little boys, herself and her husband to take care of and their only income was from Tom Birmingham's W.P.A. job." The husband sued, asserting that the article indicated that his job on a Federal make-work project was not sufficient to support his wife and children and that he was responsible for her suicide. In rejecting the claim the court noted that many people held WPA jobs and that this was not a charge of extreme poverty (Birmingham v. Daily Mirror, 175 Misc. (N.Y.)372).

A useful distinction to keep in mind is whether the articles tend to place blame on the individual or society for his plight. If the onus is on the individual, libel may be present.

Incredible as it may seem in this materialistic world, it can also be libelous to impute extreme wealth or an excessive eagerness to acquire wealth to someone. In 1904 the New York *Star* ran a story that said:

> A sensation was created recently by the announcement made by Mrs. Woolworth that her life had been made unhappy because her husband neglected everything, herself included, in his absorbing pursuit of millions. She declared that he sacrificed everything to his one passion. Mrs. Woolworth and her husband are now separated, which she ascribes as due to the incompatibility of the artistic and money-making temperaments.

The court commented:

> One of the meanest of all vices is the mere love of money, and when a man is accused of being affected by that vice so far as to lose sight of the duty he owes to his wife or to his family, he is made at once contemptible. [Woolworth v. Star, 97 App. Div.(N.Y.) 525]

Friends and Relatives

Another category of misfortune stories is those that point out an individual's relationship to someone who has an unsavory character. Is it libelous of a person with a pure heart to report that he has a sister who is a gang moll or a brother who is a spy for Communist China? Could the pure-in-heart collect if the newsman had no legal defense for writing such stories? This kind of writing poses an ethical question, too, since it could imply guilt by association if not handled with care. But it is also risky from the standpoint of libel. Two cases of almost parallel situations illustrate what seems to be a contradiction in the courts.

Whittaker Chambers, the man who helped send Alger Hiss to the penitentiary in a trial involving a Communist spy apparatus, wrote a book titled *Witness.* In it the following appeared: "Some years later I was to see the Commissar of War himself, Joseph Pogany, the brother of Willi Pogany, long a scene designer in the Metropolitan Opera House."

When Willi sued, a New York Court rejected his case on the basis that there was no libel because a man cannot be held responsible for his brother's actions. According to this decision, it would not be libelous of a man to say that a close relative is a Communist (Pogany v. Chambers, 206 Misc.(N.Y.)933).

Five years later the Federal District Court for the District of Columbia ruled exactly the opposite. This case involved a broadcast by Fulton Lewis, Jr., over about 500 radio stations. In it the commentator criticized Mrs. Pearl A. Wanamaker, the Superintendent of Public Instruction of the state of Washington, for, among other things, her handling of a case concerning a teacher who had invoked the Fifth Amendment's protection against self-incrimination when questioned about Communism by the House Committee on Un-American Activities. Lewis also said that Mrs. Wanamaker had a brother who had been in the Department of State and who, renouncing his citizenship, had fled behind the Iron Curtain. The court held that the broadcast was libelous (Wanamaker v. Lewis, 173 F. Supp. 126).

How far, then, can a writer go in showing a person's relationship to someone of disreputable character? If the article carries the implication that the subject of it shares in or is sympathetic with the disreputable activities of his friend or relative, then the article is dangerous. This is apparently what made the Lewis broadcast libelous. The false piece of information about the brother's defection to Communism was not an aside; it was coupled with the commentator's criticism of Mrs. Wanamaker on other anti-Communist grounds. The two seemed to go together. In the Chambers book, however, the relationship between the Commissar for War and the Metropolitan Opera's set designer was more in the way of a parenthetical observation.

This distinction is also supported in a Chicago case. On May 8, 1949, the Chicago *Herald-American* ran the first of a series on the notorious outlaw John Dillinger. The article carried the headline "How Dillinger Curse Pursued Pals to Grave" and included the following:

> (Some people are drawn to the vultures of crime like flies into a web. The lure is tawdry and mean and gaudy with false glamor. It's a fatal attraction.
>
> Greed or distorted vanity led many to serve John Dillinger in that brutal killer's epic career of outlawry. This series, inspired by the recent squalid death of Dillinger gang moll Patricia Cherrington, shows that the bandit chief's influence was wholly evil and that none escaped the Dillinger curse.)
>
> .   .   .   .
>
> Probably the most innocent of all the victims was Prosecutor Robert Estill of Lake County, Ind.
>
> Estill felt so expansive when they brought Dillinger to Crown Point for a too-brief sojourn in the county jail that he posed for pictures with an arm about John in an apparently brazen show of friendship and admiration.
>
> It was literally a fatal mistake. Following Dillinger's epic crashout with a wood-carved gun, Estill lived long enough to be laughed out of office. Then, a broken man, he died.

Illustrating the story was a picture showing Dillinger standing next to Estill. The caption explained:

> Victim of the Dillinger curse was Robert Estill, Lake County Indiana, prosecuting attorney, who foolishly struck a friendly pose with the noted outlaw. The killer's subsequent toy-gun escape from a Hoosier jail spelled the end of Estill's career. He was virtually laughed out of office and public life.

Far from being dead, Estill was not only alive but still practicing law, and he lost no time in filing suit. The *Herald-American* argued that a false report of a man's death is not libelous. That is ordinarily true, agreed the United States Court of Appeals for the Seventh Circuit, but in this case it was libelous because the story purported to relate the circumstances under which he died "a broken man" (Estill v. Hearst Publishing Company, Inc., 186 F. 2d 1017).

Note that while the article referred to Estill as "probably the most innocent of all the victims," it also contained indications that those who were drawn to Dillinger were motivated by "greed or distorted vanity" and that Estill knew what he was doing when he threw his arm around the outlaw in "an apparently brazen show of friendship."

The either-or technique (discussed on page 26) can be helpful when the writer is faced with the need to show the association of persons he is writing about with disreputable individuals or situations. The technique will certainly reduce the risk because one of the possible interpretations of the article is nonlibelous.

Association is often used in exposés of racketeering, crime, vice, racism and political extremism. It is valuable, but the writer should plumb his conscience deeply to make certain he is justified in drawing the relationship. He does not want to forget his responsibility to the innocent and the fact that he is flirting with danger.

The risk is illustrated by the case of the unfortunate George E. Garrison. The New York *Sun* published a story asserting that his wife had deserted him and disappeared from Newark with a man named Archer who was under indictment for forgery. In Denver she had second thoughts, the article said, and wrote back and asked for forgiveness. Mr. Garrison, being a good man, forgave his wife, the *Sun* reported, and sent her money to return home. But, the *Sun* added, she soon disappeared a second time and was last heard from living in sin with Archer on the West Coast. This was a readable story that must have echoed daydreams of many a middle-aged man and woman. There was only one trouble with it. The *Sun* had mistaken the Garrisons for another couple with a similar name.

Mr. Garrison sued the *Sun*. The court, however, dismissed his first cause of action, for libel, pointing out that the article merely said that he was an innocent victim of his wife's unfaithfulness. However, it did uphold the second cause of the suit—that because of the false publication his wife had become so mentally disordered and distressed that she was unable to perform her duties. So Garrison was able to show special damages because of the nonlibelous falsehood. He had lost a housekeeper and could recover the amount that he had to pay out to get another (Garrison v. Sun, 74 Misc.(N.Y.)622).

Comparison to Animals

Related to the misfortune cases are articles that compare a person to an animal. The law holds libelous any comparison of a person to an animal whose habits are disgusting and revolting, but not to those animals people are fond of.

The New York *American* learned of this after it ran an article titled "How Science Proves Its Theory of Evolution." Near the top of the page appeared a photograph of a man in a wrestling pose, with the caption: "Stanislaus Zbyszko, the wrestler, not fundamentally different from the gorilla in physique." Nearby was a picture of what the court described as a hideous-looking gorilla. This was held libelous (Zbyszko v. New York American, 228 App. Div. (N.Y.)277).

The courts have also ruled libelous comparison of a person to a snake, because of the common—although erroneous—belief that a snake is sneaky and slinks up on its quarry.

Some years ago a newspaper intended to describe an actress "in all her perky vivaciousness." A typographical error made it come out "in all her porky vivaciousness." Was it libelous? Readers striving valiantly to hold down their weight would say Yes; those from rural areas with a fondness for pink pigs might say No. We shall never know, because the actress did not sue.

Chapter 7

IS THERE A REFLECTION ON RACE, NATIONALITY OR PATRIOTISM?

Race

Despite adoption of three constitutional amendments designed to wipe out the political and legal inferiority of minority races, courts in the South still hold libelous any statement that a man is a Negro, or a mulatto. The reasoning is that whites generally view the black race as inferior. The Negro campaign in the mid-twentieth century for civil rights will eventually lead to social equality as well. When that status is reached, there will no longer be any basis to award libel damages as the result of mistakes about race. Even now, northern courts deny damages based on such errors. But southern courts have stuck to the traditional rule.

On March 11, 1954, the Anderson (South Carolina) *Daily Mail* printed an item under the headline "Negro News" and a picture of a Negro soldier that the son of Maudie Bowen had been transferred to a government hospital. Mrs. Bowen sued on the basis that she was white. In upholding her claim, the South Carolina Supreme Court refused in a 1957 decision to alter the long-established rule and explained:

> The earlier cases were decided at a time when slavery existed, and since then great changes have taken place in the legal and political status of the colored race. However, there is still to be considered the social distinction existing between the races, since libel may be based upon social status. . . .
>
> Although to publish in a newspaper of a white woman that she is a Negro imputes no mental, moral or physical fault for which she may justly be held accountable to public opinion, yet in view of the social habits and customs deep-rooted in this state, such pub-

lication is calculated to affect her standing in society and to injure her in the estimation of her friends and acquaintances. [Bowen v. Independent Publishing Co., 230 S.C. 509]

The danger increases if a woman and a man are involved in the story. The Natchez (Mississippi) *Times* lost a $5,000 verdict because a reporter described a young married white woman as a Negro woman traveling in the company of two Negro men at 3:50 o'clock in the morning (Natchez Times Publishing Co. v. Dunigan, 221 Miss. 320). Most of these cases could be avoided if editorial policy did not require identification of persons in the news by race unless that fact was really pertinent.

Sight alone can often determine race, but on occasion even the eyes can lead to mistakes. A 1946 Virginia slander case involved a soda-fountain attendant's refusal to serve a glass of Coca-Cola to a white customer he mistook for a Negro. The attendant consented to sell him a Pepsi-Cola in a paper cup and charged an extra penny. The customer was also supposed to go outside to drink it. A few minutes later another white customer entered the store and asked for a Coke, which was served him in a glass. The first customer protested, and the attendant replied, "We don't serve Negroes Coca-Colas and we don't let them drink out of glasses." The first customer then pulled on a lock of his hair and asked if it looked like a Negro's. The attendant said, "Yes, I have seen whiter Negroes than you are." The argument shows how silly the whole question of race is, since the customer did have what the court termed a "brunette" complexion and the attendant had such bad eyesight that he had been rejected by the Navy (Cook v. Patterson Drug Co., 185 Va. 516).

The Negro's inequality before the law in the South is also shown by the fact that the word "nigger" has not been considered legally opprobrious when applied to a Negro there. As recently as 1938 a court rejected a libel suit based on use of that word, asserting that "nigger" is frequently employed by both whites and blacks in a friendly way and is not normally insulting (Franklin v. World Publishing Co., 183 Okla. 507). Its use in the North would undoubtedly be more dangerous. While the North has a long way to go before it gives justice to the Negro, the courts have held that the use of the term "Negro" is not defamatory. An article that referred to Isiah "Chink" Mitchell as a Negro was ruled not libelous in Illinois (Mitchell v. Tribune Co., 343 Ill. App. 446).

The Negro civil-rights movement has created court questions regarding libelous words. In the old, subservient days, "Uncle Tom" was considered a friendly description. Nowadays Negro leaders generally look down on those of their race who knuckle under to whites. But a 1965 decision by the Ohio Supreme Court invalidated a $32,000 judgment against the Cleveland *Call & Post* for reporting that former Gov. Michael V. DiSalle had called Mrs. Bertha B. Moore, an Akron Negro leader, an "Uncle Tom." (Moore v. The P. W. Publishing Co., 3 O. S. 2d 183). An all-white jury had upheld her claim on the basis that "Uncle Tom" implied that she had betrayed her people in the civil-rights struggle. Until there have been more decisions on the question, the newsman should make doubly sure of his defenses before using the term "Uncle Tom." If he has no legal right to say so, he should fall back on such definitely nonlibelous adjectives as "moderate," "conservative," "old-line" or "cooperative" to describe nonaggressive Negroes.

The extremists also cause concern. While no court cases have arisen, it would not seem to be libelous to identify Negroes as belonging to groups that are countenanced by the law, such as the Black Muslims or Black Nationalists. But linking Negroes with organizations dedicated to violence to achieve their ends, such as the Five Percenters, who vow to kill whites, would be defamatory. So would a description of a Negro as a Mau Mau, since the antiwhite terrorist group in Kenya operated outside the law.

The libel problem insofar as white attitudes are concerned generally revolves around the character of opposition to integration. Everyone has a right to resist change, as long as the opposition takes legal form. But freedom does not mean license to resist with violence. The question of dedication to violence should mark the distinction between libel and nonlibel. On this basis, it would be libelous to accuse a person of belonging to the Ku Klux Klan, but not the Citizens Council. The word "racist" would be in doubt, since to some it would mean an advocate of violent resistance. "White supremacist" would certainly not be libelous because a person can be such an advocate without resorting to violence. "Nigger lover" would not be libelous since the defense could easily argue that segregationists as well as integrationists insist that they have great affection for Negroes. The problem with all these words is that the interpretation would often be left to the jury, and in the South (and some parts of the North) the jurors might well decide that such allegations as membership in the Klan are not accusations but praise.

While integrationists are anathema to many in the South, a court has held not libelous the statements that a white person was a member of the National Association for the Advancement of Colored People, participated in a sit-in demonstration and was a protégé of a moderate southern publisher. The case involved Billie Clyde Barton, a journalism student at the University of Mississippi and managing editor of the student newspaper. The Governor, Ross Barnett, and other staunch segregationists circulated statements that Barton belonged to the NAACP, that he was a "left-winger," that he took part in an Atlanta sit-in and that he was a protégé of Ralph McGill, the publisher of the Atlanta *Constitution,* who has sought to wake up the South to the desirability of opening new opportunities for the Negroes. Barton said that the statements were false, that they embarrassed and humiliated him and damaged him in his projected profession. After they appeared, he was defeated as a candidate for editor of the student paper. A Federal court rejected his claims for damages, making it clear that the statements were not libelous (Barton v. Barnett, 226 F. Supp. 375).

The description "poor white trash" is marginal and therefore would probably go to the jury for determination. In some communities the outcome would undoubtedly be a victory for the plaintiff.

In the North, as noted earlier, it has been ruled libelous to say that a union leader is anti-Negro. But times have not changed enough, at least not yet, to make it defamatory to say that a person believes white Anglo-Saxon Protestants to be superior. A case along these lines was dismissed in the New York Appellate Division. The New York *Post* ran an article quoting a woman who obtained contestants for television quiz shows. One of the statements attributed to her said that the ideal couple for a daytime show would be from Indiana, white and Protestant, age twenty-six and twenty-four and have two children. The woman sued, saying that the article indicated that she was prejudiced in favor of members of the Caucasian race and

Protestant faith. But the court held that the statements were not libelous, but merely suggested that "perhaps because of nationwide audience identification, candidates having the stated characteristics are generally more acceptable" (Lawson v. New York Post Corp., 10 A.D. 2d(N.Y.)832).

Nationality

In Chapter 4 the point was made that no one can collect damages because of defamatory remarks about a group. This rule includes remarks about national and ethnic groups. Anyone so inclined can use such scurrilous terms as "Wops," "Spics," "Chinks" and "Polacks." There is no danger of damage because there is no identification of any individual. Even if a specific person is identified, libel is not present. The rule is that words referring to nationality, even though insulting or opprobrious, are not actionable unless specific injury can be proved.

A New York court has ruled not libelous a statement that a person is a refugee and not an American citizen. But again, the bigot must beware, because if the portrayal is such that it invites scorn and ridicule, it might well be considered defamatory. Such was the holding regarding an article comparing a "refugee and an alien" with a "two-fisted American airman." The article went on to say:

> Does deSeversky's unsuccessful career as the promoter of an aircraft manufacturing company—which recently lost millions of dollars and had to be reorganized—make him an expert and an American wrong? [DeSeversky v. P. & S. Publishing, Inc., 36 N.Y.S. 2d 271]

Such statements are also dangerous when they cast doubt on the individual's loyalty to the United States, especially in wartime.

Patriotism

The writer reporting on an individual's political beliefs runs into a libel problem when devotion to country and its ideals is questioned. Unorthodox political beliefs sometimes win acceptance. When they do, the general public no longer doubts the patriotism of those who espouse the once-hated policies. In 1915 an Illinois court held libelous a statement that a man was a Socialist (Ogren v. Rockford Star Printing Co., 288 Ill. 405). In those days Socialists were looked on as bomb throwers. Today Socialists are viewed as out of tune with the times, but certainly not dangerous. In view of the change, a statement about Socialist affiliation would not be defamatory.

When Americans and Russians were allies, a report that a man was a Communist was held nonlibelous (Garriga v. Richfield, 20 N.Y.S. 2d 544). Now the law is settled, at least for a time, that charges of Communist affiliation are libelous. Libel is present regardless of whether the statement is a flat one that a person is a Communist or merely says that he is pro-Red or a fellow traveler. The leading case involved an article in Reader's Digest titled "I Object to My Union in Politics," in which the following passage appeared: "And another thing. In my state the Political Action Committee has hired as its legislative agent one Sidney S. Grant, who but recently was a legislative representative for the Massachusetts Communist Party."

Insisting that the article was false, Grant sued. Taking up the question of whether there is a difference between saying that a man is a Communist and saying that he is an agent for the party or sympathizes with its objectives and methods, Judge Learned Hand wrote in 1946:

> Any difference is one of degree only: those who would take it ill of a lawyer that he was a member of the Party, might no doubt take it less so if he were only what is called a "fellow-traveler"; but, since the basis for the reproach ordinarily lies in some supposed threat to our institutions, those who fear that threat are not likely to believe that it is limited to party members. Indeed, it is not uncommon for them to feel less concern at avowed propaganda than at what they regard as the insidious spread of the dreaded doctrines by those who only dally and coquette with them, and have not the courage openly to proclaim themselves. [Grant v. Reader's Digest Assn., Inc., 151, F. 2d 733]

Westbrook Pegler wrote an article that appeared March 15, 1945, in which he noted similarities between a man named Novick, the head of the Electronic Corporation, and Abraham N. Spanel, president of International Latex Corporation. The article first described the activities of Novick, who purchased time on the radio to interpret the news. It stated that his press agent was a "prominent and aggressive Communist," that his news "interpreter" was a convicted thief and that Novick was associated with Communists in a projected corporation. The second part of the article dealt with Spanel, whose company espoused political beliefs in two- and three-column advertisements in newspapers around the country. Novick and Spanel were compared as natives of Russia, successful manufacturers of war products and disseminators of political propaganda. The strongest Pegler remark about Spanel was the following:

> Another of Mr. Spanel's rhapsodies was a reprint of a column by a member of the Roosevelt newspaper following in Washington, which described Wallace [former Vice-President Henry A. Wallace] as a champion and symbol of the "aspirations of the common man and the underdog." This was a poetic construction well expressing the attitude of some demagogues of the extreme left who regard the American citizen as a soulless lump to be fed, quartered, ordered and disciplined even as a dog.
>
> A native of Russia and an admirer of the Soviet system might be pardoned in the error.

By a two-to-one vote the United States Court of Appeals for the Seventh Circuit ruled the article might be found libelous of Spanel because the ordinary reader could conclude that there was little difference between him and Novick (Spanel v. Pegler, 160 F. 2d 619). If Pegler had written just about Spanel or had made a sharper distinction between Spanel and Novick, he would not have committed libel.

The use of the term "un-American" is fairly safe, as long as the article is not loaded with overtones strongly suggesting Communism. The context is vital. The New Jersey Supreme Court found nonlibelous a letter to the editor that included these words:

> Mr. Charles Mosler is definitely influenced in his thinking by a foreign philosophy alien to the American way.
>
> .   .   .   .
>
> I would further suggest that the real Democrats in town divest themselves of this type of writer, whose un-American tactics upon other citizens have no place in the true American manner of conducting a campaign.

The court noted that "un-American" in political debate was frequently used as a "rhetorical effusion to any social, economic or governmental program espoused by an adversary." As for the "foreign philosophy alien to the American way," the court said that that also did not necessarily mean Communism (Mosler v. Whelan, 28 N.J. 397).

A New York court handed down a similar ruling in a case in which an industrialist was accused by a union of having "a stubborn, unreasonable, un-American attitude" (McAuliffe v. Local Union No. 3, etc., 29 N.Y.S. 2d 963).

Even the word "subversive" when used in a general sense has been held not libelous. A court upheld an article saying that the plaintiff had been named in an American Legion resolution as a "person fostering subversive activities" (Dilling v. Illinois Publishing and Printing Co., 340 Ill. App. 303).

To be safe from libel the word must have such a general meaning that it does not indicate a definite adherence to a specific philosophy which, like Communism, stands for the violent overthrow of the Government and the undermining of democratic institutions.

On the other end of the political spectrum, similar admonitions apply. General terms such as "far right" and "ultra old guard" create no problem whatsoever. The Detroit *News* carried this paragraph on its editorial page:

> Every time John D. Dingell, Democratic incumbent, gets re-elected we keep hoping he will live up to his potential for better service. Maybe, if re-elected, he will this time. In any event we cannot endorse his opponent, Robert J. Robbins, a Republican who represents the thinking of the ultra old guard group which complains that President Eisenhower has made socialism respectable.

The Michigan Supreme Court lost little time in dismissing Robbins' libel suit (Robbins v. The Evening News Assn., 373 Mich. 589).

Chapter 8

IS THERE INJURY TO ANYONE
IN HIS OCCUPATION?

Unfitness and Failure

SO FAR THE LIBELS WE HAVE LOOKED AT HAVE BEEN PERSONAL, reflecting on an individual's private reputation or his right to enjoy social contacts. Now we turn to the most dangerous of all libels insofar as the possibility of large damages are concerned. These are known as business or occupational libels. They can harm an individual, in respect to his office, his profession, his trade or his business; they can injure a corporation, or they can damage unincorporated groups, such as partnerships.

Simply stated, the doctrine is that the law will protect a man from any false attack that tends to impair his means of livelihood or discredit him in his profession, business or occupation. It is not necessary that the words actually prejudice or injure the man in his occupation. It is sufficient that they have a tendency to or are calculated to harm him.

There are some general rules for spotting this kind of defamation.

It is defamatory to charge a professional man with acts constituting a breach of professional ethics. In a 1956 slander case, Walter F. O'Malley, president of the old Brooklyn Dodgers, was found to have defamed a physician by saying he had performed an unnecessary operation and must have thought he was operating on the patient's bankroll (Shenkman v. O'Malley, 2 A.D. 2d(N.Y.)567).

Charging a person with general unfitness or inefficiency in his occupation or business or office is defamatory. A court ruled that an architect had been libeled by an article that a new school building of which he was the designer was in a dangerous condi-

tion and that the architect, although he had been notified, had
ignored the notification, and that the condition did not speak
very well for those who designed and built the school (Vosbury
v. Utica Daily Press, 183 App.Div.(N.Y.)769).

Any charge of bankruptcy, insolvency or financial embarrassment, past, present or future is libelous. In one case it was found
defamatory to publish of an officer of a corporation that "his
extravagances startled people and finally got the company into
trouble" (Daily v. Engineering & Mining Journal, 94 App.Div.
(N.Y.)314).

Accusations of fraud or dishonesty in one's occupation, profession or office have been held libelous. With respect to these
libels the newsman must remember that suspicion or accusation is
as sufficient as an outright charge of guilt. A story reporting that
a firm of butchers had knowingly sold goats' meat for lamb was
declared libelous. A caption carried the admonition: "Leg of
Lamb in Brooklyn May Be Goat. The Price is Very Low and
Gives Big Profit" (Kornblum v. Commercial Advertiser Assn.,
183 App.Div.(N.Y.)615).

The protection against libelous statements is not limited to
the professional man, although the principle is often stated in
terms that sound that way. The businessman and the tradesman—
even newspaper editors and publishers—enjoy the same protection.

In May, 1962, Frank Anthony must have been proud when he
mailed from the post office at Stow, Massachusetts, the four-page
letter-size Vol. 1, No. 12, of *New Frontier.* The lead story bore
the headline "Fraidom of the Press," and Anthony had so much
confidence that readers would support his far-right editorial
policy that he had decided to start charging $2 for a year's
subscription instead of giving the publication away. In nearby
Bolton, however, two couples were shocked by the "Fraidom"
article—one passage, for example, explained John F. Kennedy's
election by saying "A young Socialist Billionaire has had his rum-
running father buy him the Presidency of the richest country of all
time." The four, William Barss, an artist, his wife and their
friends, Mr. and Mrs. Mowry Baden, decided to act. On June 20,
1962, they sent the following letter to various businesses in
Worcester and Middlesex Counties:

Sir:

We have noticed your ad in Mr. Frank Anthony's circular *Frontier.* Perhaps, in the pressure of business, you have not had time to examine the editorial content of *Frontier,* or to question whether the editor's motive is to enlighten or merely to irritate his readers. Nothing is more irritating than a presentation of the news (item or editorial) compiled without proper regard for the facts. Do you believe that irritating advertising is the best way to keep customers and contact new ones? We believe that Mr. Anthony's readers are perceptive enough to discern his lack of objectivity. A lasting relationship between an advertiser and his customer is based on truth, not distortion. We suggest that you seriously consider whether you wish your name to be associated with a publication of this type.

Anthony sued for $500,000, equivalent to 250,000 yearly subscriptions to his sheet. The Badens went off to India on a Fulbright scholarship and the case against them was never pressed. The Barsses succeeded in getting the Superior Court to dismiss the action, but the Massachusetts Supreme Judicial Court reinstated the case. The court agreed that the statement that the news was compiled without proper regard for the facts was nondefamatory. "It is common knowledge that many newspapers of today are published with an eye mainly to speed and are frequently fraught with error," the court said. But the court added that the implication that *Frontier* had been based on distortion might very well be held libelous and sent the case back to the lower court for trial (Anthony v. Barss, 346 Mass. 401). The Barsses, however, had the last laugh. When the case was called for trial on November 9, 1964, Anthony appeared in court but decided not to push the action. As a result, an entry was made "Judgment for neither party" and attachments that had been placed on the Barsses' property were lifted. Nevertheless, the case does underline the fact that publishers, even shoestring operators peddling trash, are protected from defamation.

Low-paid office workers are shielded too. The Supreme Court of North Carolina held that a woman who received only $600 over eleven years had been libeled by indications that she had failed to make payments to Farm Bureau clubwomen and that office records were lost. The court said the statements tended to

impeach her in her occupation (Bell v. Simmons, 247 N.C. 488).
She received a token payment in settling the case.

The libel laws are a second shield for policemen. Frederick
P. Upton, a slight, quiet businessman of sixty-five, went shopping
for groceries at a Safeway store on Baltimore Avenue in College
Park, Maryland, one day. He found a parking place and, like a
good citizen, started to put pennies in the meter. But no matter
how many he put in, the arrow would not move past twelve minutes. Sure enough, when he took his groceries back to the car,
there was a ticket. Not wanting to pay $2 for an offense he did not
commit, he drove to the town traffic office to explain, but was
told that he would have to take it up with the policeman who
gave him the ticket. His usually mild temper rising, Upton returned to the Safeway store to see another car pull out with a
ticket on it. He looked around for a while for the policeman but
couldn't find him. Still hoping for understanding, he put a bag,
with the ticket attached, over the defective meter. On it was a
message saying the meter was "N.G." Then he went home. For a
short time everything seemed to be straightened out, because he
heard nothing about the ticket. But one day the city sent him a
letter demanding $2 for the parking violation. That did it.
Upton pulled out some writing paper and wrote a blistering
letter to the Mayor (with copies to several important citizens).
Among other things Upton wrote:

> As nearly as I can determine, your tin-horn cop sits in nearby
> concealment sipping beer until he sees a car parked over 12 min. at
> a defective meter (and who can buy a week's supply of groceries
> in 12 min?), then sneaks over, places a ticket on the car and then
> hustles back to his beer. I can smell skunk perfume a long way, and
> this definitely smells like a racket, whether to raise money for the
> police, or to divert trade to shopping center across Baltimore Blvd.
> In either case, the situation stinks.

The Maryland Court of Appeals, the highest tribunal in the
state, said this letter was libelous because it had accused Policeman David R. Thompson of conduct that would "make him unfit
to discharge, faithfully and correctly, his duties as a policeman"
(Thompson v. Upton, 218 Md. 433). While the jury was out,
Thompson commented dryly, "Well, we will find out what a
policeman's reputation is worth." The jury returned with a verdict

of $1, plus costs. If Upton had not been such a mild little guy, and if members of the jury perhaps had not shared his irritation over defective parking meters at one time or another, the verdict might well have been substantial.

To constitute business defamation, words must refer to the individual's occupation. The Tennessee Supreme Court ruled nonslanderous the following words spoken to a newspaperman, following an auto accident: "You are drunk. Are you going to pay for my automobile? If you are not, I am going to call the police. You are drunk, and you were driving that car under the influence."

The court noted that the words were spoken of the plaintiff as a driver, not as a newsman, and added: "We are unable to conceive of any surrounding circumstances that might be brought out by innuendo that could connect words with the plaintiff's calling, without enlarging the meaning of the words spoken" (Smith v. Fielden, 205 Tenn. 313).

Such statements would be libelous of a clergyman no matter what the occasion. In practice, the charge must be weighed in relation to the occupation to determine whether it is defamatory. It would not be libelous to say that a ditchdigger was illiterate, but it would be of a college professor; it would not be libelous to say that a Peace Corps worker deserted his post when the Communists attacked his town in Vietnam, but it would be of a soldier. A real-estate firm would be libeled by a statement that houses it had rented were condemned and fourteen persons were homeless. Such charges were held nonlibelous regarding a painter-repairman who was one of the owners of a condemned house. The Ohio Court of Appeals said the charge did not reflect on the painter in his occupation (Rudolph v. E. W. Scripps Co., 83 Ohio L. Abs. 538).

Just because an expert's opinion is misstated does not mean he has been libeled. The distortion may annoy him, but he will have to turn to a law other than libel for relief. The critic Ralph Thompson sued G. P. Putnam's Sons for quoting him out of context regarding the book *Memoirs of a Woman of Pleasure,* widely known as *Fanny Hill.* A Note in the book says that Thompson paid both the author and book "grudging respect." The Note also quotes Thompson as saying that the book is "more nearly immortal than anything" Dr. Johnson, Edward Gibbon, William

Wordsworth "and the other great men of the time wrote." Thompson protested that his true opinion, as expressed in his writings, was that *Fanny Hill* was "tediously and bewilderingly pornographic" and "humorless indecency unadorned." The Court said Thompson's right of privacy might have been violated, but he had not been libeled. It explained:

> There is, however, no allegation, as such, that the "Memoirs" are not a work of literary merit. Nor is there an allegation that the public generally considers the book to be one without literary merit. Plaintiff cannot be damaged, by being falsely charged with having expressed the opinion that the book possesses literary merit, unless the reading public considers that opinion erroneous. The mere fact that plaintiff's personal opinion may be that the work is without literary merit is of no consequence. The reading public may disagree with plaintiff's personal view, in which event his reputation would not be adversely affected by the false attribution to him of a favorable opinion as to the literary merit of the book. [Thompson v. G. P. Putnam's Sons, 243 N.Y.S. 2d 652]

In view of the large sale of *Fanny Hill*, Thompson could hardly prove that the reading public generally rejected the book.

The Single Mistake

There is a well-defined exception to these rules that is easy to state but not so easy to apply. Libel is not committed in charging a professional or business man with making a single mistake, or acting unskillfully or unsuccessfully in a particular or single instance. Even the most skillful may make a mistake, since infallibility is not a human trait.

For example, a court has ruled not libelous an article that said a dentist removed a root in an unskillful and negligent way so that three other teeth were exposed, a cavity was created in the roof of the patient's mouth and a disease of the gums and jaw set in. This, the court said, did not necessarily imply incapacity or unfitness, just unskillfulness on a single occasion (Twiggar v. Ossining Printing and Publishing, 161 App. Div. (N.Y.)718).

The decision was no libel in the case of a statement that an artist had fallen down badly and done a bad job with a particular painting (Battersby v. Collier, 34 App.Div.(N.Y.) 347).

But caution is required in applying this rule because a statement can be made relating a particular instance that may be of such character that it imputes general incompetence. If it does, it is libelous. For example, to say that a lawyer's conduct of a particular trial was grotesque would be libelous though it related to a single instance because it would indicate a general lack of skill and fitness. The distinction is a fine one. Undoubtedly some judges would have held the article on the dentist libelous on the basis that it charged incompetence.

In addition, a statement although relating to only one instance would be libelous if it charged something improper. Libel would be committed, for example, in saying that a lawyer had disclosed confidential communications, because, though it related to a particular case, the charge would amount to a gross violation of professional ethics.

On February 20, 1961, *Sports Illustrated* carried an article, titled "Hail, Hail the Gang's All Here," about the "bizarre cast of characters" surrounding the then heavyweight boxing champion, Floyd Patterson. Julius November, a lawyer, sued, arguing that the the article accused him of deliberately giving erroneous legal advice to Cus D'Amato, Patterson's manager, whose license had been revoked, so November would replace D'Amato. One of the paragraphs in the article read:

> D'Amato also got into difficulty when he failed to answer a subpoena issued by State Attorney General Louis Lefkowitz. D'Amato says that November, who serves as attorney for both D'Amato and Patterson, told him to ignore it, that the hearing had been postponed. D'Amato did as he was instructed, but he was arrested, hauled into court, fined $250 and given a suspended sentence of 30 days in the workhouse. The case is now on appeal, but D'Amato was to see Lefkowitz Tuesday and there were reports "something might happen" to him.

New York's highest court commented:

> If that were the whole of it there would probably be no defamation since, as we will assume, the rule still holds that language charging a professional man with ignorance or mistake on a single occasion only and not accusing him of general ignorance or lack of skill cannot be considered defamatory on its face and so is not actionable

unless special damages are pleaded. . . . But there is a great deal
more in addition to that quoted paragraph and a reading of the
whole of it may well have left a sophisticated and sports-conscious
reader of the magazine with the impression that plaintiff had indulged in highly unprofessional conduct. . . .

In cynical but sprightly style writer Boyle painted for his readers
a word picture of shabby intrigue among a group of named persons including plaintiff, elbowing each other for preferred positions
in the champion's entourage. The writer at least intimated that their
several ambitions were not unrelated to the huge financial return
from championship boxing matches. If every paragraph had to be
read separately and off by itself plaintiff would fare pretty well. But
such utterances are not so closely parsed by their readers or by the
courts and their meaning depends not on isolated or detached statements but on the whole apparent scope and intent. . . .

Nowhere in the article is there a charge in so many words that
plaintiff's motives were selfish and sinister when he got his client
D'Amato into difficulties by telling him to ignore the subpoena.
But suggestion lurks in such statements as this: "With D'Amato
somewhat out of the Patterson picture November has filled the
vacuum" and this: "November does all he can to keep Patterson
content with his services."

No single sentence or declaration of alleged fact is directly and
boldly defamatory but a jury should decide whether a libelous
intendment "would naturally be given to it by the reading public
acquainted with the parties and the subject-matter." [November v.
Time, Inc., 13 N.Y. 2d 175]

The case was sent back to the lower court for trial, but Time,
Inc., made an out-of-court settlement that included cash and a
letter saying that it had not intended to harm November.

Is It Legal?

There is another limitation on the rule that it is libelous to
impute lack of capacity to a professional or business man: the
business or profession must be a lawful one. A newspaper article
charging that an individual was the world's greatest failure as
a bookie would be libelous because to charge that a person is a
bookie is to charge him with a crime. But the statement would

not be libelous because it charged failure in the individual's chosen calling. So, if the paper could prove that the man was, in fact, a bookie, it would not have to take on the second charge and prove he was a failure as well.

Related to this limitation is a third. The person referred to must be engaged in the particular business lawfully. There is no libel in calling a man a shyster if he has not been admitted to the bar. A person not licensed as a physician could not recover on an article impugning his medical ability or conduct.

The New York *Herald Tribune* once carried a story describing the arrest of Dr. Hadley V. Carter as the "second electric healer raided in a quack war." Dr. Carter was operating the Central Health Institute. The premises were owned by a dealer in antiques and prehistoric things who, as a sideline, organized the Central Health Institute of New York, Inc., and installed Carter as the doctor in charge. Carter would give a patient a blood test and announce without further examination that the patient had pelvic trouble, a slightly acid condition, a condition of the kidneys, hemorrhoids or something else. Carter also had a machine by which he would depolarize the patient and make him or her neutral—whatever he meant by that. Apparently Carter did not know that it was illegal to practice medicine through a corporation. He glibly admitted at the trial that he was operating through the corporation. The judge declared a recess, called him up and suggested that it was in his interest to discontinue the action immediately and get out of court as fast as he could before the court decided to send the whole record to the District Attorney. That ended the case.

The restriction on charges concerning bankruptcy, insolvency or financial embarrassment does not mean that reports of all financial difficulties involve undue risk. To charge mere nonpayment of a debt or the entry of a judgment is not libelous. A businessman—or anyone—can deliberately refuse to pay a debt or suffer the entry of a judgment that he intends to appeal. A typical decision in such cases was the ruling by the Oregon Supreme Court that a credit report listing a logger as a delinquent debtor was not libelous (Hudson v. Pioneer Service Co., 218 Ore. 561).

Sharp Practices

Cases of fraud or dishonesty in following one's business, profession or occupation go beyond mere illegal activities such as cheating customers or violating the pure-food laws. A New York court found libelous a headline that "Shuberts Gouge $1,000 from Klein Brothers." The article said that the Kleins had been forced to pay $1,000 for a release from a Shubert production contract before they could continue in business. This was termed libelous because it accused the Shuberts of "mean and hard dealing" (Shubert et al. v. Variety, Inc, 128 Misc.(N.Y.)428).

Along the same lines was the article that said a businessman had forced his partner into retirement and seized the profits of the latter's brains and capital. There was no imputation that the plaintiff's conduct had been in any way illegal, but the article was held libelous because those who read it might avoid having business transactions with the plaintiff (Klaw v. New York Press Co., 137 App.Div.(N.Y.)686).

On the other hand, no defamation was found in a publication that a bicycle dealer was cutting prices and thereby injuring the defendant's business and the bicycle trade. Cutting prices is not only normally legal, it is generally considered beneficial by the public (Willis v. Eclipse Manufacturing Co., 81 App.Div.(N.Y.) 591).

The Business Corporation

A business corporation is an artificial entity, created by law, existing separate and apart from the individuals who are its stockholders, directors, manager, employees and customers. Despite what the advertisers say, it has no personality, no dignity that can be assailed, no feelings that can be touched. Since it cannot suffer physical pain, worry or distress, it cannot lie awake nights brooding about a defamatory article. For these reasons courts were at first inclined to think that a corporation could not recover general damages for a libelous publication but were limited in their recovery to specific items of loss that had to be proved.

But as the economic system turned more and more to the corporate structure the courts were forced to recognize that this type of business did have a reputation that could be seriously affected by defamatory statements. The law soon took cognizance of this fact and gave the corporations the same right to collect general damages for libel that individual businessmen enjoyed. Nevertheless, because of the artificial character of corporations, libel suits involving them are much fewer and more limited in scope than those that affect individuals. A man of good reputation possesses attributes of personal honor and dignity, but a corporation cannot be libeled in this regard. It cannot commit crimes of personal violence, such as murder, assault, robbery and rape. Therefore, if a labor union wants to accuse the management of such crimes, it need have no fear of libel. A corporation cannot be defamed by statements that it is guilty of a crime it is physically unable to commit.

A corporation can commit some crimes, however, such as violating the antitrust laws. It would be libelous to accuse a company of restraint of trade or ignoring the Food and Drug Law or circumventing Securities and Exchange Commission regulations.

A corporation may also sue on a publication affecting its management or credit in a pecuniary manner. The New York Court of Appeals said that the thesis "that a corporation has the right to maintain an action of libel when the publication assails its management, or credit, and inflicts injury upon its business, or property, is a proposition which is true upon principle and which has the support of authorty" (Reporters' Association of America v. The Sun, 186 N.Y. 437).

The guidelines for libel of a corporation in regard to its business practices and credit are the same as those already given for individual businessmen. Statements that a corporation is bankrupt or insolvent or that it is embarrassed financially are libelous. But there is no libel in writing that a corporation had not paid certain debts or that it had made a mistake on a single occasion.

Nor does the rule mean that a writer is taking an undue risk in discussing merger possibilities. After the long New York newspaper strike of 1962–63 the American Newspaper Guild published an article to the effect that Hearst and Scripps-Howard had agreed to divide the newspaper markets and that there would be a merger of the New York *Journal-American* and the New York *World-Telegram and The Sun*. Hearst sued, but the United States Court of Appeals for the District of Columbia decided that this was not a charge that reflected injuriously on its credit even though a merger would have meant a reduction in the number of newspapers published (Hearst Consolidated Publications, Inc., v. American Newspaper Guild, 294 F. 2d 239).

A Single Loss

Some years ago the New York *Herald Tribune* printed, as the result of erroneous information, a statement indicating that the play *Molly-O* had been taken from the boards and closed. When the Model Producing Company sued, the court held that the statement was not libelous. A statement that a play produced by the plaintiff had folded did not indicate that the company was about to go out of business, the court held. This variation on the rule concerning accusations of a single mistake permits papers, magazines, financial tip sheets and broadcasting stations to carry reports that a company will close down a plant, will stop production of a particular product or has lost money over a limited period of time. There was no libel, for example, in printing rumors, in the early 1960s, that the Chrysler Corporation was about to stop making DeSoto automobiles, because there were no intimations that Chrysler's other lines—Plymouth, Dodge, Chrysler and Imperial—would be abandoned too.

Cheating Customers

Any indication that a company is cheating its customers is considered a reflection on its management, and the writer should make sure he has a legal right to publish the material. In Hazleton, Pennsylvania, Cosgrove Studio and Camera Shop, Inc., offered a free roll of film for every roll brought into its establishment for developing and printing. The next day Cosgrove's competitor Carl R. Pane inserted the following advertisement in a newspaper:

USE COMMON SENSE ******
YOU GET NOTHING FOR NOTHING!
WE WILL NOT!

1. Inflate the prices of your developing to give you a new roll free!
2. Print the blurred negatives to inflate the price of your snapshots!
3. Hurry up the developing of your valuable snapshots and ruin them!
4. Use inferior chemicals and paper on your valuable snapshots!

Although the ad named no other company, the Pennsylvania Supreme Court held on June 28, 1962, that the circumstances made it clear that it was referring to Cosgrove. As far as the question of defamation is concerned, the court said:

> In the instant case, the advertisement clearly imputes, to the person to whom it refers, characteristics and conduct which are incompatible with the proper and lawful exercise of a business. Certainly, to charge one engaged in such a business with ruining snapshots, using inferior materials and printing blurred negatives in order to inflate the cost to the public would "lower him in the estimation of the community [and] . . . deter third persons from associating or dealing with him." [Cosgrove Studio and Camera Shop, Inc., v. Pane, 408 Pa. 314]

Cosgrove was a rare plaintiff. He refused to follow up his victory by pressing a demand for damages.

Cheating customers is certainly libelous. How about cheating competitors? The courts have held that charges of such tactics are defamatory because they are likely to affect the credit and management of the business. The Union Associated Press, a now defunct press association, was accused by the Cincinnati *Commercial Gazette* of getting news by tapping the telegraph wires of the Associated Press. That, said the court, was libelous (Union Associated Press v. Heath, 49 App. Div.(N.Y.)247).

Fraud

There is also danger in charging a corporation with engaging in a fraud. During World War I the New York *Sun* printed an article with this headline:

WRECK WORKS A SEA CHANGE
"CARGO OF GRAIN" TRANSMUTED INTO COPPER
AND LEAD ON A SCANDINAVIAN LINER
Craft Went Ashore Near Cape Race on July 15

The article went on to describe how a Norwegian steamer, which had sailed from New York carrying a vast quantity of grain, had been wrecked near Cape Race and was found to be heavily ladened with copper and lead. These metals were contraband of war, and Norway was a neutral nation. Hence this was ostensibly a charge of fraudulent and illegal misrepresentation. The company had represented that the ship was carrying a cargo of general merchandise, when actually, the paper said, it was carrying war materials and the company was taking advantage of the neutrality of the flag it was flying to transport contraband of war. The court held that this was libelous (Den Norske Ameriekalinje Actiesselskabet v. Sun. 226 N.Y. 1).

Crime in Business

With criminal elements attempting to move into legitimate businesses, the writer is faced more and more with the problem of stories dealing with this subject. These are risky situations, but they should be reported and can be if the writer makes sure of his defenses. If a corporation was formed by a criminal, but he is no longer with the company, there is no problem. The courts have held that such statements are not actionable as long as there is nothing in the article reflecting on the integrity, solvency or business methods of the corporation (New York Bureau of Information v. Ridgway Thayer Co., 193 N.Y. 666).

If the article says that thugs, gangsters, members of the Mafia or Cosa Nostra or ex-convicts are in key positions in a company, it would undoubtedly be held libelous since the corporation would be injured. In such cases the newsman must make sure that he has written his story to take advantage of the defenses the law allows for publishing defamatory material.

There is another aspect of the libel law and its relationship to professions and business that opens up an opportunity for the journalist to write many stories that would otherwise be barred.

This is the rule that no libel was committed in writing that there was wrongdoing on the premises of an establishment open to the general public. A number of examples show how valuable this rule can be.

The "Harrisburg Windmill" column in the Pittsburgh *Courier* of September 15, 1956, included this item:

> Philosophous, our pet fire-eating dragon, who goes where angels fear to tread, gave us a delayed report of the annual orgy held in Williams Grove Park.
>
> This display of animalism, publicized, quite intentionally and erroneously, as a picnic, produced the usual mawkish fights, automobile accidents, stabbings and drunkenness.
>
> This is one affair promoted by Negroes which is a disgrace to Central Pennsylvania. The crowds will grow smaller each year until these "business" men find it too unprofitable to promote.

The operator of the amusement park sued, protesting that he had been libeled. The Pennsylvania Superior Court disagreed, asserting that it would take "ingenuity and a stretch of the imagination" to find that the article had accused the operator of the park of contributing to, causing or permitting the orgies (Richwine v. Pittsburgh Courier, 186 Pa. Super. 644).

On April 3, 1957, the Florence (South Carolina) *Morning News* ran a story about misconduct of patrons at the Airport Drive-In, just east of the city. Mike Costas, proprietor of the drive-in, promptly went to the editor and protested. He insisted that he operated a reputable business and that he did not allow any conduct at his establishment that would be detrimental to the morals of the youth of the area. He warned the paper not to print any more untrue articles about his business. More than two years later, on August 18, 1959, the Florence *Morning News* carried another article about the drive-in. Over the headline "Youths Fined for Fighting," the story told about a hearing in magistrate's court the previous day, and it included these two paragraphs:

> This was the second fight within a week at the drive-in. On August 10, Jimmy Harper, 17, and Laverne Powell, 18, of Florence, were charged with disorderly conduct.
>
> Harper and Powell, along with two other Florence youths, have been charged with the armed robbery of a gas station in Moncks Corner Friday night.

Mr. Costas sued, complaining that the article not only was wrong, but also harmed his business so much that money—Florence *Morning News* money—was needed to repair the damage. The South Carolina Supreme Court sent him back to his drive-in to dish out hamburgers. Its reasoning provides some clues for the writer who wants to report the news and stay out of trouble:

> We have examined the alleged libelous article set forth in the complaint herein and it contains no statement from which it could be reasonably implied that the respondent had any connection with the arrest made at his place of business, nor does it impute to him or any of his employees any wrongdoing or condonation of wrongful conduct. Certainly, the words complained of do not charge the respondent with any crime, nor with the operation of a disorderly place of business. The allegations of the complaint fall far short of implying or alleging that the published article charged the respondent with any misconduct, by reason of the fact that there had been two fights at his place of business. . . . We know of no precedent, and none has been cited to us, which makes the publication of the fact that a fight took place between parties at the place of business of a merchant libelous per se as to him. [Costas v. Florence Printing Co., 237 S.C. 655]

A New York case concerned a movie titled *The Country Girl,* starring Grace Kelly. As a part of the story, one of the principal characters said he could go to Stillman's Gym in New York and get a punch-drunk fighter. Lou Stillman insisted that the sequence reflected on his establishment, although Damon Runyon once said that a membership at Stillman's was an "open sesame to low society in any part of the world." Stillman asserted that he never catered to punch-drunk fighters. The court gave the decision to Paramount. The movie dialogue did not refer to Stillman himself but to his gymnasium, it said, and to collect he had to prove special damages (Stillman v. Paramount, 2 A.D. 2d. (N.Y.)18).

Hy Gardner once wrote a column in the New York *Herald Tribune* in which he discussed the possibility of a patient's bleeding to death in a hospital while personnel wrangled over the qualifications of the person for aid. He described how he had carried a girl with a badly cut leg into the hospital and the difficulty she had getting assistance. Alfred Richman, doing business as Manhattan General Hospital, sued. But the court said that he had not been named and that the article was, if anything, a libel on the hospital and not on Richman (Richman v. New York Herald Tribune, 7 Misc. 2d(N.Y.)563).

Thus it seems safe to say that amusement parks, hotels, restaurants, saloons, gymnasiums and hospitals are public places where the proprietor has no control over the patrons, and nasty references to such places do not necessarily charge the proprietor with any wrongdoing. The key is to name the place or the patrons and not the proprietors. The writer can safely call a night spot a "den of iniquity" or a "sinkhole" because he is libeling a thing and not those who run it.

When the article deals with a place that is not generally open to the public, trouble can arise. A motion picture titled *The Inside of the White Slave Traffic* carried scenes showing a factory and building bearing the name "Merle" and signs indicating that the establishment made infants' and children's headwear. Mr. Merle said that this meant that he had encouraged the solicitation of his women employees for the white-slave trade. The court agreed on the basis that the owner of the factory is presumed to have control over what goes on inside it (Merle v. Sociological Research Film Corp., 166 App. Div. (N.Y.) 376).

Products

How about criticism of manufactured articles? The leading case involved the Marlin Fire Arms Company and a magazine known as *Recreation*. Marlin had been advertising in the magazine, but stopped doing so in 1899 when the rates were increased. After that, letters to the editor appeared in the magazine criticizing Marlin rifles. The Marlin Company charged that the letters had been fabricated by the magazine to blackmail it to resume advertising. Here are excerpts from one letter:

> I have owned and used a great many Winchester and Marlin rifles of all models. . . . I have come to the conclusion that the Marlin is not to be compared with the Winchester as regards ease, rapidity or certainty of action, beauty of outline, finish and all that goes to make up a first class weapon. I consider the first model Winchester a more reliable weapon than the latest Marlin. Some

will ask, Why? And I answer: Because they handle the cartridges perfectly, and as rapidly as the lever can be worked by the operator, under any circumstances; while the Marlin might fail to handle the cartridges if handled with one half the rapidity of the Winchester. . . . The Marlin has a faulty extractor and ejector. . . .

In dismissing the complaint, the court pointed out that the character and conduct of the manufacturing company had not been maligned. The letters did not charge that Marlin was guilty of any deceit in selling the rifle or want of skill in manufacturing the gun. Every statement related solely to the quality of the rifle and its merits relative to others. Thus the Marlin Company lost its case (Marlin Fire Arms v. Shields, 171 N.Y. 384). If Marlin had been able to prove that its rifle was a good one and to show specific loss, as, for example, that orders were canceled as a direct result of the letters, it could have recovered the exact amount of that loss. Such a case is one of libel of a product— another example of nonlibelous falsehood.

On March 29, 1958, the *Saturday Evening Post* ran an article titled "Don't Fall for the Mail Frauds." Among other things, the article said:

> The hottest gimmick in the mail-fraud field today is the alleged weight-reducing pill. Recent emphasis by medical authorities on the harmful effect of overweight has made avoirdupois a national obsession. The underlying causes of overweight are often obscure: boredom, nervousness, unrequited love are only a few. But the cure—eating less—calls for something most fat people don't have when it comes to food: will power.
>
> That's where the gimmicks come in. Certain drugs, medical authorities agree, have the effect of deadening the appetite. Doctors often prescribe them to help obese patients stick to a diet, but they frequently have harmful side effects and generally are available only on prescription. Yet so common is the desire to get something for nothing—in this case slimness without diet—that some schemes promising this impossibility have taken in over a million dollars a year. Forty-five such schemes, not all quite so profitable, have been barred from the mails during the past two years.
>
> About a year ago, the Wonder Drug Corporation, in a flood of full-page newspaper advertisements, heralded an allegedly new reducing discovery called Regimen, which required "no giving up the kinds of food you like to eat." In the box of green, pink and yellow pills you got for three dollars, however, were instructions warning

you to avoid heavy gravies, oils, thick soup, rice, spaghetti, jam, jelly, noodles, nuts, ice cream, potatoes, cake, candy, chocolate, cereal, crackers, cream, custard, bread, butter, pastry, pudding, sugar and salt.

Last June, after an investigation by postal inspectors, officials of the Wonder Drug Corporation voluntarily signed an "affidavit of discontinuance," agreeing to stop soliciting orders through the mail—after taking in $200,000 in six months, according to inspectors' estimates. Nevertheless, Regimen is still obtainable over the counter in some retail stores, where postal authorities have no jurisdiction. However, the Federal Trade Commission, which has responsibility concerning deceptive advertising when the mails are not used, has Regimen under investigation.

In a four-to-three decision the New York Court of Appeals held that there was nothing in the article that reflected on Drug Research Corporation, the manufacturer of the pills. The majority opinion said:

> The rule is that, if a product has been attacked, the manufacturer may recover in a cause of action for libel, provided he proves malice and special damages as well as the falsity of the criticism. . . .
>
> Giving the pleading its most favorable construction, namely, that it states a libel on the product, it nonetheless must be dismissed for failure to allege special damages. A libel of the plaintiff's product is not necessarily a libel of the plaintiff. [Drug Research Corp. v. Curtis Publishing Co., 7 N.Y. 2d 435]

Drug Research decided that it would be difficult to establish specific loss of sales and dropped the suit.

Similarly, in an earlier case, where *Collier's* attacked "Dr. Williams' Pink Pills for Pale People" as worthless medicine, the court held that this was an attack on the medicine and not a charge that the plaintiff was guilty of fraud (Hanson v. Collier, 51 Misc.(N.Y.)496). This rule does not give the writer or broadcaster license to say anything he wants about a product. If the charge is so sweeping that it indicates that the manufacturer is guilty of fraud or deceit, it is libelous and no proof of special damages will be necessary. The lesson for the writer is that if he wants to expose fraudulent practices or products, he should emphasize the places and products and not charge the individual or the person with fraudulent conduct. He can name names as long as he takes great care to keep the charge pointed at the product and not at the manufacturer.

Nonprofit Corporations

Foundations, charitable associations, religious groups and other nonprofit corporations can also sue for libel. For some time they did not have such a right because the courts held that they had no credit or business reputation since they could not engage in business. Then along came the New York Society for the Suppression of Vice. This corporation was organized by special act of the New York legislature to enforce laws for the suppression of obscene literature. It was long associated with Anthony Comstock and John S. Sumner. Its sponsors regarded it as devoted to "charitable and benevolent or high public-spirited purposes." Others looked on it as a group of busybodies and meddlers. In the middle 1920s the New York *Evening Graphic* published an article with this headline:

DOOM REFORMERS
SUMNER SOCIETY FIFTY-FIFTY SPLIT
OF VICE FINES EXPOSED

The article disclosed that the society had enjoyed the rich privilege of splitting fifty-fifty all fines collected as a result of its action. The story said that the society would have to fight for its existence before the state legislature because of the indignation expressed by the lawmakers when they were told about the split. More exposures were pledged, including details on "how a good storekeeper was importuned to commit a crime."

Outraged, the society sued. The *Graphic* argued that the society, as a benevolent corporation, could not sue for libel. The Society replied that the story was calculated to reduce voluntary contributions to it and therefore hampered it in its lawful purpose. Brushing aside earlier rulings in the field, the New York Court of Appeals held:

> Corporations engaged in charitable, social welfare, benevolent and religious work, have the right to acquire and hold property which may produce a profit or income. Indeed the statute under which

plaintiff was organized expressly grants that power to it. Many such corporations own and control very valuable properties, and in their management such corporations establish a reputation, rights and interests similar to the reputation, rights and interests acquired by individuals and corporations engaged in business for profit. To decide that such corporations have no reputation acquired in the management of their affairs and property which can be injured or destroyed by a malicious libel, unless special damage is proved, would constitute a reflection upon the administration of justice. Benevolent, religious and other like corporations have interests connected with property and its management which should have the same protection and rights in courts in case of injury as corporations engaged in business for profit. [New York Society for the Suppression of Vice v. MacFadden Publications, Inc., 260 N.Y. 167]

This is now the law in almost all jurisdictions.

Unincorporated Groups

Unincorporated groups also had to fight an uphill battle for the right to sue for libel. More than a century ago the New York *Sun* ran an article charging that some members of a volunteer fire company had stolen the author's hat. The company was an unincorporated social group that had fun racing to fires, chopping down doors and otherwise destroying property. Occasionally the members put out a fire. When the article appeared, some of them sued. The case presented an issue of whether an unincorporated group could sue for libel. No, said the court, such a group could not, and added:

I know of no case in which it has been held that a body of men having no pecuniary interest in their associated character, either as members of a company, or directors of a corporation, or trustees of any society, or any particular class, trade or association, may unite in an action for libel against such a body, class, trade or association, much less where the libel only charges the offense to have been committed by some of them. [Giraud v. Beach, 3 E.D. Smith (N.Y.) 337]

As a group there was no ground on which the plaintiffs could recover. The court pointed out that all the individuals making up

the hose company had not been libeled and as a body no business
injury had been sustained by them.

In 1907 the law insofar as it applied to partnerships was clari-
fied. The insurance firm of Tobin & Tobin was accused of following the methods of an unauthorized broker of fake policies
who had been sent to jail. Members of the firm sued and the
court held that this attack on the partnership affected the business reputation of each of the members. It also pointed out that
the article had a tendency to injure the business of the partnership by charging that the persons connected with it were not
honest and that the firm itself was dishonest. In short, the court
came to the conclusion that whatever injures the business reputation of a firm injures each partner and therefore each can maintain an action to recover damages because of the business libel
(Tobin v. Best Co., 120 App. Div.(N.Y.)387).

Labor Unions

On July 3, 1939, the Westchester Newspapers carried an article
by McClure Newspapers Syndicate about the International
Brotherhood of Electrical Workers that said:

> Our report that union officials are feathering their nests from initia-
> tion fees and dues payments is also challenged. The point is made
> that Local Union 3 voted to allow members of out of town locals to
> work here during the World's Fair boom without paying a cent to
> the New York local.
>
> It is argued, therefore, that the North Carolina youngster with
> only amateur experience, who, we stated, got a very profitable elec-
> trician's job, needn't have "paid a price" for the privilege. A recheck
> discloses that he did pay a price—and a stiff one. It was, however,
> paid privately to an official of Local 3 and probably never appeared
> in the union's books. Evidently the rank-and-file members of Local 3
> are not aware of the practices indulged in by some of their associates.
>
> The plain fact is that this union and others took advantage of the
> setup to charge more than the traffic would have borne on any nor-
> mal job.

If normal practice had been followed, every one of the approximately 17,000 members of the local would have had to sue because the union was unincorporated and thus without a legal

entity separate from its membership. The union sued through its president under a statute that permitted this as a matter of procedure. The court pointed out that the article had not been directed at the personal reputations of the individual members and said:

> The article charges wrongdoing by officers of this association in performance of the work of the association. It does not reflect upon, or tend to injure the reputation of the individual members but it does tend to discredit the work in which they have a common interest. The injury is thus a common injury and the members have a common interest in the consequent damages. . . .
>
> The courts have no less a duty in this case than in a suit brought by a corporation or an individual, to protect good name, reputation and credit from slanderous or libelous attacks. . . .
>
> Labor unions play a large and important role in modern life. . . . We know that they are rarely incorporated. We should not require them to assume the form of corporations in order to be recognized as possessing reputations which the law will protect. The courts which recognize a labor union's existence and its traditional form of organization, will not refuse to redress a wrong done to it in its group or unified character. [Kirkman v. Westchester Newspapers, Inc., 287 N.Y. 373]

This is the authority for the individual members of a labor union to sue on a libel that adversely affects their common business reputation in the union.

When it comes down to actuality, however, it is the officers who are the nominal plaintiffs suing in behalf of the members. In almost every case the words that must be watched in articles about unions are those that deal with the leaders. Mere accusations that a unionist is an agitator or antibusiness or out to rule or ruin can safely be carried. So can the charge that an organization is a "company union" (National Variety Artists v. Mosconi, 169 Misc. (N.Y.) 982).

But defenseless charges of crime are dangerous and can slip by an editor if he is nodding. References to rackets and racketeering have been held libelous, the court saying that since the era of prohibition the word "racket" has meant the engaging in an occupation to make money illegitimately and implying continuity of behavior (Bradley v. Conners 169 Misc.(N.Y.)442).

But this rule does not mean that belligerent moves by unionists cannot be reported. On February 25, 1951, the Chicago *Herald American* carried the following article:

BEHNCKE TELLS HOW GROUP JAMMED
WAY INTO SICKROOM
By Meyer Zolotareff

David L. Behncke, a legendary figure in America's aviation history and the man who raised the standards of living for thousands of pilots through the world, today bemoaned what he termed an insult by 17 employees of the union he heads.

From a sickbed in his six-room bungalow at 6459 S. Albany Ave., the national president of the AFL Air Line Pilots Association and first president of the International Federation of Air Line Pilots Associations, denounced their charges of dictatorial treatment and refusal to bargain with union employees for wage increases.

LOWEST BLOW

Behncke, a leading advocate of air safety and one of the great fighters for better working conditions, frankly admitted:

"I think it is the lowest blow ever struck to any representative of workers in the labor world. It really hurts. I've never been against the establishment of agreements with employes of our union."

Behncke was in New York directing hearings of his union before a presidential fact-finding board, involving a dispute with American Airlines about curtailment of flying hours for 800 pilots, when, he said, the charges were made in his hotel room there Feb. 15 by Maurice H. Schy, an association lawyer and head of 17 disgruntled staff employes.

GESTAPO ACTION

Branding the entrance of Schy's group into his room, where he was ill, as a Gestapo Action Behncke said:

"At the time they made their unannounced military-manner entrance, I knew nothing about the troubles of our staff employes or that some were dissatisfied.

"When Schy threw a contract on the bed and asked me to sign it, I told him this was too abrupt and I was in no position to sign any contracts. He threatened to set up picket lines in front of the hotel.

"It is a lie that I am against establishing agreements with employes of the association. In fact, I have long encouraged an agreement for stabilizing their employment, but I will never recognize any shot-gun approach."

When Schy read this slanted story he sued for libel, asserting that it was untrue and that it charged him with using force to accomplish wicked designs. The United States Court of Appeals for the Seventh Circuit said no with the following explanation:

. . . it appears to us that the average person reading the article complained of at bar would conclude that it details a somewhat unusual and ironical situation. The president of the Airline Pilots' Federation, while representing the Pilots' Union in a dispute with American Airlines, an employer of pilots, is himself confronted with a demand for wage increases by the office employees of his own union. He finds under the circumstances, the same tension, antagonism and feeling in representing the employers' side as is usually manifested when he is acting for Air Pilots in controversies with the operators of air lines.

The statement in the publication "I think it was the lowest blow ever struck at any representative of workers in the labor world—it really hurts," when considered in connection with the entire article does not in our opinion indicate or mean that any physical assault was charged to have been committed against Behncke. It seems to be a mere expression of injured feelings. In our opinion it is not libelous per se.

The statement that plaintiff and his co-employees made an "unannounced military-manner entrance," "Gestapo-like" into the sick-room of the president of the union is merely a somewhat rhetorical way of saying that their conduct was dictatorial, and that they used highhanded methods. We find nothing libelous per se in such language. . . ." [Schy v. Hearst Publishing Co., 205 F. 2d 750]

Individual workers who oppose unions often are the target of the waspish tongues of organizers and other union officials. The term "strikebreaker" is probably not libelous if used to castigate a foe of a particular work stoppage. But if facts are added that indicate that this is the regular calling of the individual or that he is violating an antiscab law, the word would probably be defamatory (Farley v. Evening Chronicle Publishing Co., 113 Mo. App. 216).

Sometimes, in the heat of bitter organizing campaigns, unions and employers go far beyond what they should in denouncing each other. Until a Supreme Court decision in 1966, the rule had been that in cases covered by the National Labor Relations Act the defamatory statements were considered part of a labor controversy, to be treated, if particularly heinous, as unfair labor practices. Civil suits for libel were barred on the basis that Federal labor law had preempted jurisdiction in the field.

Then came the case of William C. Linn, an assistant general manager of Pinkerton's National Detective Agency, Inc. During an organizing campaign at Pinkerton's Detroit office, the United Plant Guard Workers of America circulated leaflets that said that Pinkerton Guards in Saginaw, Michigan, had been "deprived of their right to vote in three N.L.R.B. elections," that they had been "robbed of pay increases" and that Pinkerton managers "were lying to us." The leaflets predicted that "no doubt the Saginaw men will file criminal charges" and "somebody may go to jail." Asserting that he was one of the managers referred to, Linn sued for $1,000,000 in damages. The Federal District Court dismissed the complaint, ruling that the N.L.R.B. had jurisdiction, and the Court of Appeals agreed.

The Supreme Court, however, held that either party to a labor dispute could sue for libel in state courts. It noted that the N.L.R.B. had refused to uphold Pinkerton's request that the leaflet be branded an unfair labor practice. For years the board had concluded that such epithets as "scab," "unfair," and "liar" were commonplace in union-management disputes and could be condoned, even if erroneous. The Supreme Court, however, found there was "an overriding state interest" in protecting residents from malicious libels in labor disputes. The court held that the N.L.R.B.'s lack of concern with the personal injury caused by malicious libel, together with its inability to provide redress to the maligned party, vitiated the argument that civil libel suits were barred by the labor law. It said:

> ... the most repulsive speech enjoys immunity provided it falls short of a deliberate or reckless untruth. But it must be emphasized that malicious libel enjoys no constitutional protection in any context. After all, the labor movement has grown up and must assume ordinary responsibilities. The malicious utterance of defamatory statements in any form cannot be condoned, and unions should adopt procedures calculated to prevent such abuses.

However the court set stiff standards for the plaintiffs in such cases. They must show that they were actually injured and they must prove that the defamatory remarks had been made with knowledge of their falsity or reckless disregard of whether they were false. (Linn v. United Plant Guard Workers of America, 383 U.S. 53). As far as the newsman is concerned, these standards for malice permit him to print almost any charges in a labor dispute.

Government

There is one group of legal entities that can be libeled with impunity—governments, Federal, state or local. Governments used to suppress the critical press with criminal prosecution for seditious libel. But the trial of John Peter Zenger in New York in 1735 closed the door to this method of restraint before it ever took hold in the Colonies. Although there were attempts to revive it after the Revolution, including the Alien and Sedition Laws, the suppression of news critical of the Government through criminal prosecution for seditious libel was dead.

Shortly after World War I the question arose as to whether a government could accomplish the same suppression through a civil action. Fortunately for the cause of free speech, that ended in disaster for the plaintiff. The case concerned a long and bitter controversy between Mayor William Hale Thompson of Chicago and the Chicago *Tribune* and the Chicago *News*. Rarely has a man in public office been pilloried as Mayor Thompson was by the two papers, especially the *Tribune*. During the political campaign of 1920 it charged that the city was "broke," that it "owes millions of 1921 funds," that "bankruptcy is just around the corner for the city of Chicago," that its "credit is shot to pieces," that "the city is headed for bankruptcy unless it makes immediate retrenchments," that the city administration, "having busted the city and having reduced it to such insolvency that it is issuing Villa script to pay its bills, is reaching out for the state," that "the city cannot pay its debts—it is bankrupt, the bankers have refused it credit."

Mayor Thompson was, of course, personally libeled, but he did not dare go forth to battle in court against the *Tribune*. However, if he could use the City of Chicago as a plaintiff he might win a large verdict against the newspaper. That might stifle criticism. So the city sued the Tribune Company.

The Illinois Supreme Court told Thompson, in effect, to go back and govern the city and not engage in extracurricular activities, such as libel suits. In dismissing the city's complaint, the court said:

> The fundamental right of freedom of speech is involved in this litigation and not merely the right of liberty of the press. If this action can be maintained against a newspaper it can be maintained against every private citizen who ventures to criticize the ministers who are temporarily conducting the affairs of his government.
>
> . . . assuming that there was a temporary damage to the city and a resultant increase in taxes, it is better that an occasional individual or newspaper that is so perverted in judgment and so misguided in his or its civic duty should go free than that all of the citizens should be put in jeopardy of imprisonment or economic subjugation if they venture to criticize an inefficient or corrupt government. [City of Chicago v. The Tribune Co., 307 Ill. 595]

Thus the law is firmly settled that anyone—in a newspaper, a magazine or tract, on a radio station, a television show or a soapbox—has an unqualified right to criticize his government—even if he lies and knows he lies and does so from base motives.

He can say that the Federal Government has sold out to the Russians, that his state has conspired with racketeers and that his city administration violates the civil rights of its citizens. He can be even more specific. He can with impunity name the agency of government responsible. He can say the Pentagon is a haven for homosexuals, that the police department brutalizes suspects to force confessions, that Congress is guilty of treason. Such talk may be based on nothing more than a guess, on blind acceptance of hearsay—or even less. But everyone, including the newsman, has the freedom to be irresponsible when talking about his government. The newsman's ethics should prevent him from taking advantage of this freedom, but he nonetheless possesses it.

The key to this safeguard of the press is keeping the criticism impersonal, that is, not naming the officials responsible even though every citizen knows who they are. The Alabama Supreme Court ruled that a critical reference to the Montgomery police in an advertisement was a libel on the city commissioner in charge although he was not named, but the United States Supreme Court disagreed, saying in a landmark 1964 decision:

> We hold that such a proposition may not constitutionally be utilized to establish that an otherwise impersonal attack on governmental operations was a libel of an official responsible for those operations [New York Times v. Sullivan, 376 U.S. 254].

Does this mean that impersonal criticism is libel-proof, even though the agency or department of government is small? How about a one-man police force? Until such questions are resolved by further court decision the writer had better not push his luck with unprotected libels of one- or two-man agencies.

As far as libels of individual government officials are concerned, the critic does not have a blank check, although two Supreme Court justices held in 1964 that he ought to. Nevertheless, the defense for such libels is almost impervious (as we will see in Chapter 12). This defense makes any discussion of what is and what is not libelous of officials almost academic.

Chapter 9

THE ABSOLUTE DEFENSES

HAVING DECIDED WHETHER THE ARTICLE IS DEFAMATORY, THE editor turns to his second decision. If there is no libel, he has it easy. He orders the article used and has a moment to relax before turning to the next item. If libel is present, his job is tougher. Then he must make sure that there is a legal defense for using the story.

A defense is a confession that the article may be defamatory and has caused some damage. But it asserts there are facts that will show that there was a complete right to publish the matter or that the damages should be lower than they otherwise would have been. It is true that lawyers frequently assert in the answer to a suit that the article is not libelous or that it is not about the plaintiff and term this a defense. But this is only a defensive maneuver, not a real defense.

In an actual trial the presentation of the defenses are the key to the outcome. As noted in Chapter 1, all the plaintiff must do is show that a libel was published and insist that it identified and damaged him. The publisher is on the receiving end of what looks like a loaded situation; he is presumed wrong. As the trial progresses, however, he moves to a better position. For if his editor and his lawyer have done their work well, the scales will tip completely the other way and court spectators will be saying, "What a scoundrel that plaintiff is; give it to him."

One of the reasons the scales tip is that truth—the whole truth and half-truth—now joins untruth in the trial. In determining whether or not the publication was libelous the judge did not even consider the truth of the article. He assumed it was false and judged the question of whether it was libelous solely on the wording, independent of other considerations.

Complete and Partial

There are two kinds of defenses, complete and partial.

A complete defense is one that wholly defeats recovery. The publisher, in effect, says to the plaintiff, "I admit the article was published; I admit that it identifies you; I also admit that it caused some damage. But I say I had a legal right to publish the article and that you cannot recover one cent."

A partial defense is one that tends to mitigate or reduce damages. In pleading a partial defense a publisher, in effect, says to the plaintiff, "I admit the article was published; I admit that it identifies you; I admit that it might have caused you some damage. I might not have a complete defense, but there are facts that mitigate the damages, so that you aren't entitled to as much money as you would have been if those facts had not existed."

Generally a publisher will plead partial as well as complete defenses. He will plead certain facts as a complete defense, and then to insure against the possibility of not being able to prove all of them, he will replead them all over as a partial defense. Thus he increases his chance of keeping damages down.

There are eight complete defenses in defamation actions against the press. They are:

1. Statute of limitations
2. The privilege of a participant
3. Truth
4. The privilege of reporting
5. The New York Times Rule
6. Fair comment and criticism
7. Consent or authorization
8. Self-defense or right of reply

Some of these defenses are absolute, others are qualified. An absolute defense exists regardless of the motive of the publisher or the purpose of the publication. In other words, it exists regardless of the malice that inspired the libel. A qualified defense is one that is complete only if the publisher harbored no actual malice. The burden of proving actual malice rests on the plaintiff. This is a great advantage that the defense has in libel trials. The publisher, his editors and his reporters need not take on the difficult task of disproving malice. (Methods of avoiding a finding of malice are discussed in Chapter 16.)

Statute of Limitations

The first two defenses are of little importance to the working newsman because they do not depend on the language of the publication. The first of these is the statute of limitations. The law is designed to outlaw stale legal claims by barring suits after a certain period of time. The statute differs for various claims. For libel it is relatively short.

With five exceptions, the statute of limitations on libel is either one or two years in all the jurisdictions in the United States.

In the following jurisdictions the statute is one year: Alabama, Arizona, California, Colorado, District of Columbia, Georgia, Illinois, Kansas, Kentucky, Louisiana, Maryland, Michigan, Mississippi, Nebraska, New Jersey, New York, North Carolina, Ohio, Oklahoma, Oregon, Pennsylvania, Rhode Island, Tennessee, Texas, Utah, Virginia and Wyoming.

In the following states the statute of limitations on libel actions is two years: Alaska, Connecticut, Delaware, Florida, Hawaii, Idaho, Indiana, Iowa, Maine, Minnesota, Missouri, Montana, Nevada, North Dakota, South Carolina, South Dakota, Washington, West Virginia and Wisconsin.

In four states the statute is three years: Arkansas, Massachusetts, New Mexico and Vermont.

In New Hampshire the statute of limitations is six years.

The editor has little need to pay attention to the statute of limitations, but in certain states the circulation department should. In these states an old common-law rule applies. It holds that a libel is published every time that the article is displayed, sold or circulated to a third party. Thus even if the statute of limitations has run, it can be revived by an isolated sale or exhibit of a back number.

Single-Publication Rule

The unfairness of this rule led to adoption of the single-publication rule in many states. For this, the publishing business owes a debt of gratitude to William J. Wolfson, who did not plan things that way. Mr. Wolfson was aggrieved by something that had been published in the Syracuse *Journal* in December, 1935. He had allowed the statute of limitations to run, but one day he and a friend went to the office of the newspaper and said to the clerk, "I should like to see some back copies." The clerk showed them where the back numbers were. Wolfson thumbed through the issues until he came across the article that he said had ruined his reputation. He showed it to his friend and then filed his suit, contending that the newspaper had republished the libel.

The New York Court of Appeals upheld the Appellate Division's decision to throw out the common-law rule and establish a new doctrine: the single-publication rule. Under this rule the statute of limitations starts running from the date of the original publication. Isolated sales or exhibits of the libelous material thereafter do not revive the statute (Wolfson v. Syracuse Newspapers, Inc., 279 N.Y. 716).

In New York the single-publication rule has been extended to books. G. P. Putnam's Sons first printed Curt Riess's *Total Espionage* in November, 1941, and turned out the last copy in December, 1943. About 6,000 copies were sold in 1941 and 6,300 in 1942. Sales dropped after that, and the demand was low enough to be satisfied by books in stock. On July 2, 1946, Armand Gregoire, a lawyer, sued for libel although in the preceding twelve months Putnam's had sold only sixty copies of *Total Espionage*. In extending the doctrine of the Wolfson case, the court said:

> Although it may not be said that the publication and dissemination of books has reached that degree of mass production and widespread distribution now prevalent in fields invaded by newspapers and periodicals, it is our view that the publication of a libelous book, involving styling, printing, binding and those other acts which enable a publisher on a given date to release to the public thousands of copies of a single printing or impression, affords the one libeled a legal basis for only one cause of action which arises when the finished product is released by the publisher for sale in accord with trade practice. [Gregoire v. G. P. Putnam's Sons, 298 N.Y. 119]

What is the date of original publication? It is not the date that the publisher prints in the paper or magazine or book. In the case of magazines the printed date is days and often weeks after it is offered for sale to the public. If this were the effective date, a magazine could cut the time of the statute of limitations by a mere printing technique. Neither is the effective date for the statute of limitations the time when copies are sent to the distributor, for a publisher could accomplish the same purpose of reducing the statute-of-limitations period by a circulation trick. Nor is the statute started by the distribution of a few copies to a small segment of the readership. The rule that is emerging is that "what is really determinative is the earliest date on which the libel was substantially and effectively communicated to a meaningful mass of readers—the public for which the publication was intended" (Osmers v. Parade, 234 F. Supp. 924).

Jurisdictions that adhere to the single publication rule are Alabama, Arizona, Arkansas, California, Colorado, Connecticut, District of Columbia, Florida, Idaho, Illinois, Kansas, Louisiana, Massachusetts, Michigan, Mississippi, Missouri, New Mexico, New York, North Dakota, Oklahoma, Pennsylvania and Texas.

Publishers in states that still follow the common-law rule should take care not to open their back files to anyone wanting a peek unless he can give a satisfactory reason for looking—and signs a waiver.

Privilege of Participant

The other defense for libel that does not depend on the language of the publication is the privilege of a participant in a legislative, judicial or other official proceeding. This defense wholly defeats recovery by the plaintiff regardless of any malice behind the libel. It exists only with respect to statements, made orally or in writing, that are pertinent in such a proceeding. Since this defense is limited to participants, it concerns editors and writers only in a minor way. The privilege they often rely on is the privilege of reporting, which will be discussed in Chapter 11.

The privilege of a participant protects such persons as legislators, judges, lawyers and witnesses from suits based on anything they say, no matter how libelous, how injurious or how malicious it is, as long at it is said in the course of a legislative, judicial or other official proceeding and pertinent to it. The reason for this rule, which seems at first blush to be susceptible to much injustice, is rooted in public policy. This policy holds that it is better that the reputation of an individual occasionally be unjustly assailed than that judges, legislators, witnesses, attorneys and public officials be restrained by fear of libel suits from making pertinent statements in the performance of their duties.

In legislative proceedings, the immunity extends to members of Congress and legislators in most states regardless of whether the comment is pertinent. In lesser legislative groups the absolute privilege is less certain. They are at least protected by a qualified defense—protected as long as there is no proof of malice.

Lawmakers cannot invoke the privilege for remarks made outside official proceedings, as Congressman Adam Clayton Powell, Jr., discovered in a case discussed on page 344.

In judicial proceedings, all legitimate participants are protected —judges, witnesses, litigants, jurors and lawyers.

In regard to other official proceedings, the privilege extends to the President, members of his Cabinet, other executive officers of the Federal Government and heads of departments when they are exercising executive or administrative functions and acting within the scope of their duties. The same protection also exists for Governors, members of their Cabinets and comparable heads of departments. Heads of municipal governments also come within the provisions of the absolute-privilege rule, but subordinate officials in charge of local government departments may be limited to a qualified privilege, that is, freedom only when malice is absent. Yet there are indications that even these local officials may win the absolute right (Sheridan v. Crisona, 14 N.Y. 2d 108).

This privilege is not very often used by newsmen; but if they are called as witnesses in libel suits, they should be cognizant of the fact that they are protected in such testimony no matter how libelous their remarks. Similarly, as defendants in libel suits, newsmen are protected in their answers, affidavits and testimony.

The absolute privilege of a judicial proceeding also offers an interesting possibility for a publisher concerned with a public wrong but fearful of a libel suit if he carries the story. He can file an information—an accusation sworn to before a court—containing the facts he believes to be true and then report what he has done. If he is sued, he can fall back on the absolute privilege of being a participant for that which he has said in the information, and on the privilege of reporting such news for the subsequent publication.

Chapter 10

TRUTH—THE GLORIOUS DEFENSE

TRUTH IS THE GREATEST OF ALL DEFENSES. THERE IS NO FINER HOUR for a newsman than, when hauled before a court on a libel charge, he replies, in effect, to the plaintiff, "Yes, I libeled you, and I'm glad. I would do it all over again, exactly as I did before, because what I said was true and the public ought to know what a scoundrel you are."

That is how Ben Bagdikian, reporter for the Providence *Journal-Bulletin,* must have felt when a Rhode Island jury returned verdicts upholding his designation of Harold Noel Arrowsmith as a Fascist and an anti-Semite. That is how Drew Pearson, the Washington columnist, must have felt when a California jury filed back from its deliberations with a verdict that he had proved his charge that Fred N. Howser, a former State Attorney General, had accepted a bribe. That is how the editors of the *Saturday Evening Post* must have felt when a Pennsylvania jury found that it had told the truth in an article saying that Rocky Marciano almost lost his heavyweight title fight with Jersey Joe Walcott because he had been blinded by capsicum Vaseline smeared on Walcott's gloves by Walcott's manager, Felix Bocchicchio.

Truth was not always a defense in libel litigation. Long after it began to appear as a defense for civil suits, it continued to be ruled out in criminal cases. The reason is easily understood. The purpose of the criminal law is to preserve order. Criminal law is designed to punish the man who commits a wrong against society. If the law does not, the injured individual, or his kinsman, will. If a Hatfield murders a McCoy, Hatfield must be punished or McCoy's kin will reach for their rifles. The original purpose of the criminal libel law was to prevent private vengeance, feuding, dueling and riots. The more truth there is to a libelous charge the more likely the victim will resent his exposure. The person who is most resentful of being called a crook is the crook who is trying to keep it secret. Thus in criminal law the maxim developed "the greater the truth, the greater the libel."

Complete Defense

Now, however, truth is a complete defense everywhere, both in civil suits and in criminal prosecutions. The newsman who can establish it can avoid paying damages in civil action and stay out of jail in criminal cases. Moreover, in civil suits in most states truth is an absolute defense, that is, good even if the publisher spoke the words from malice. In criminal prosecutions in most states and in civil suits in a few states, truth is a qualified defense, good unless the other side shows that actual malice lay behind the libel.

The states where the law says that malice negates the defense of truth in civil cases are Delaware, Florida, Illinois, Maine, Massachusetts, Nebraska, New Hampshire, Pennsylvania, Rhode Island, West Virginia and Wyoming. But the problem is not as serious as it sounds. Even though the law in these states holds that the truth must be spoken for good purposes or justifiable ends, the writer or editor need have no fear if what is printed is true. Nor need they fear criminal prosecution if what they printed is true and there was no personal ill will behind it.

The Wyoming State Tribune and *The Wyoming Eagle* of Cheyenne were sued for carrying Associated Press and United Press dispatches about a disbarment action against a lawyer in 1943. In validating a jury verdict for the newspapers, the Wyoming Supreme Court said:

> The testimony afforded substantial evidence tending to establish that in addition to being true the published articles in question here were published with good intent and for justifiable ends. The general public is entitled to know when an attorney becomes involved in a disbarment proceedings . . . [Spriggs v. Cheyenne Newspapers, 63 Wyo. 416]

The question of malice will be discussed in detail in Chapter 16, but a classic case of a successful criminal-libel prosecution shows the kind of personal ill will necessary to defeat truth as a defense. Mayor James Curley of Boston met Frederick W. Enwright, publisher of the Boston *Telegraph,* on the street one day. The conversation ended in a fist fight. Enwright must have lost, because he retreated to his newspaper office and published a cartoon of Mayor Curley on the editorial page. It showed Curley in prison garb behind bars, with the caption: "Sober Up, Jim." In truth, Curley had served a term in jail (this was before his sentence to the Federal Correction Institution in Danbury in the late 1940s). When he was a young man, he had been prosecuted and convicted for taking a civil-service examination for a pal. He proudly told his audiences that of course he had taken the examination and had gone to jail for a friend.

But when the District Attorney, at Curley's instigation, prosecuted Enwright for criminal libel, the publisher found that he could not fall back on the truth of the charge. For the District Attorney showed that Curley and Enwright had had a fist fight just before the cartoon was published. This was evidence of actual ill will, of malice strong enough to defeat the defense of truth in criminal prosecution. Enwright was convicted on January 31, 1927.

What Is Truth?

In a libel case "truth" means that the substance or gist of the defamatory charge is accurate. If the charge is that a television-repair service defrauds its customers, the reporter cannot prove the accusation by evidence that the picture tubes on TV sets it repairs conk out quickly. The reporter would have to show that the poor repairs result from intentionally deceitful practices.

On the other hand, there can be errors in the story, even serious ones, and the truth be held sufficient. If the article says that a man robbed a bank in Minneapolis when he actually robbed one in St. Paul, truth is still a good defense. The site of the crime is incidental, not relating to the substance or gist of the accusation.

A case that reached the Alaska Supreme Court illustrates the rule. It was brought by Mrs. Elizabeth B. Pitka, a teacher, who complained of a banner headline and read-out lines in the Fairbanks *Daily News-Miner* on October 21, 1957, that said:

NORTH POLE TEACHER FIGHTS BOARD

TERRITORIAL POLICE CALLED
TO EXPEL FIRED SCHOOLMARM

Dispute at Outlying Community Finds Teacher
Defying School Board; She is Arrested
for Disorderly Conduct

The facts were that on October 7, 1957, Mrs. Pitka had written the school board of North Pole, a small community near Fairbanks, notifying it that she wanted to resign, "effective in thirty days from this date." At a meeting the next day the board asked her to leave her position immediately, but she insisted on working out her thirty-day notice. On October 18, she received a letter from the board advising her that it had relieved her of her duties on that day. Three days later she was warned in a letter not to set foot on school property and told that law-enforcement agents would prevent her from doing so. Nevertheless, she entered the school, and Lowell Jenkins, the board president, arrested her for disturbing the peace.

In the libel trial Mrs. Pitka insisted that the headlines had not portrayed the truth. The newspaper asked the judge to instruct the jury that it was invoking the defense of truth and to explain to it the requirements for such a defense. The judge refused, and the jury returned a $25,000 verdict against the paper. On appeal, however, the Alaska Supreme Court ruled that the judge had erred, because the jury might well have concluded that the words in the headline were true. It explained:

> Plaintiff's insistence upon continuing her teaching job after being told she had been relieved of her duties and was no longer permitted to enter upon school property could legitimately be characterized as a "fight" with the school board and an act of defiance of the board's decision. The statement that plaintiff had been arrested for disorderly conduct could be justified by proof that she had been arrested for the specific offense of "disturbing the peace" which, according to the terms of the North Pole ordinance, was included in the definition of "disorderly conduct." The statements "territorial police called to expel fired schoolmarm" was erroneous. The police were not called for that purpose, but instead had been summoned by plaintiff because she thought she needed their protection. But she was actually expelled from the school when arrested by Jenkins who, among other

things, was a North Pole police officer. Thus, the reported purpose for which the territorial police were called could be considered an immaterial variance from the literal truth. It is not necessary to prove the literal truth of the precise statement made. Slight inaccuracies of expression are immaterial provided that the defamatory charge is true in substance.

What is left, then, is the assertion that plaintiff had been "fired" as a schoolteacher. Whether this was true was also a question of fact that ought to have been submitted to the jury for determinaton, rather than being summarily disposed of by the trial judge.

. . . the trial court was mistaken in holding that whether plaintiff had voluntarily resigned or had been fired was not a "close enough question" for jury determination. The word "fired" means "to eject forcibly; to discharge from a position; to expel summarily." The jury might well have concluded that this is precisely what happened to plaintiff, which would mean that the newspaper report of her being fired would have been found to be true. [Fairbanks Publishing Co. v. Pitka, 376 P. 2d 190]

Half-Truth

Another way to state the rule for truth is that the proof must be as broad as the charge. In other words, you must prove the truth of what you have published in all its essential particulars. If you charge a man with perjury, it will not be sufficient for you to show that on the witness stand and under oath he testified to something false. That is no more than false swearing and is not perjury. To meet the legal proof for the crime of perjury you must also show that he willfully and knowingly gave false testimony or that he had reason to know that his testimony was false. Perhaps you would not have to marshal as much evidence as the District Attorney, but you would still have to satisfy the jury with a preponderance of evidence that your opponent had willfully and knowingly given false testimony.

A Utah slander case brings the requirement of proving essential particulars into focus. In the spring of 1949 a telephone operator, Mrs. Thomas, was accused of saying of another phone operator, "Mrs. Crellin was a whore," and later of saying, "Mrs. Crellin worked in a house of prostitution." Mrs. Crellin sued, and Mrs. Thomas offered the defense of truth. Her evidence was that a friend had told her that Mrs. Crellin had "come from a house of prostitution." The jury was not satisfied with this indefinite evidence and returned a verdict for Mrs. Crellin. Only hours later Mrs. Thomas learned that Mrs. Crellin had worked as a dance-hall girl in Ely, Nevada. With this newly discovered evidence, Mrs. Thomas asked for a new trial and the judge agreed. At the second trial Mrs. Crellin admitted that in the early 1920s she had worked for a short time as a "dance-hall girl" or "percentage girl" in Rhiney's in the red-light district in Ely. The evidence was contradictory as to what kind of place Rhiney's was and what the duties were of the girls who worked there. Concerning Rhiney's, a man who had worked in the locality testified as follows:

Q. What was the general reputation for morality?
A. It was a good place. . . .
Q. Do I understand you to say it was a good place for morality, a good reputation?
A. It had a reputation for the place it was, as a good place. . . . It was known as a whorehouse—a good one.

The witness explained that places such as Rhiney's had a bar and a dance floor. Down the street were establishments with little rooms known as "cribs," where the prostitutes plied their trade. He described how the men who went to Rhiney's were treated:

. . . We would go there into the dance hall. There was always a girl to come and ask you to buy her a drink and dance with you. While dancing there was generally a proposition to go to the crib . . . and a fellow most generally did because he was there for that business.

. . . .

Q. Did you always go into the dance hall and take the girl out and down the street to the crib?
A. Yes.
Q. And after completing your interview with her you took her back to the dance hall?
A. Absolutely.

In rebuttal, the plaintiff presented a witness who had lived in Ely for thirty-two years and who had operated dance halls in the red-light district. The dance-hall girls were not supposed to be prostitutes, he said, but were a "better class" of girls, the "best girls they could get," and were not permitted to work the cribs.

Their job, he said, was to dance with patrons and encourage them to buy drinks. The girl would be served colored water and would receive 50 cents of the $1 charged the patron for her drink. The plaintiff insisted that she was a "percentage girl" and not a prostitute.

In instructing the jury, the judge said that if it found that the plaintiff had worked in a house of prostitution "in any capacity" at any time, then the verdict would have to be for the defense. The jury returned a verdict of no cause for action, but the Utah Supreme Court ruled that the charge on truth as a defense had been prejudicial error. The court said:

> The evidence would have permitted a finding that the dance halls were also houses of prostitution, and hence that the plaintiff "had worked in a house of prostitution" but as a "percentage girl" and not as a prostitute. Under such a finding, the utterance "Mrs. Crellin was a whore" would be false.
>
> Admittedly, when truth is pleaded in justification, it is not necessary to prove the literal truth of the precise statement made. Slight inaccuracies of expression are immaterial, providing that the defamatory charge is true in substance. . . . Nevertheless, the language of the utterance just referred to is of such a fixed and certain meaning . . . that it cannot be said that a dance hall girl who does not act as a prostitute comes within that language, even though the dance hall may have been a house of prostitution or that prostitution may have been practiced in connection with it.

The case was remanded to the lower court for a new trial (Crellin v. Thomas, 122 Utah 122). Again the jury found no cause for action.

Accuracy Not Enough

"Truth" does not mean mere accuracy in reporting. Suppose a reporter interviews a Congressman who says that the president of a union is a thief, and this charge is carried in the newspaper. If the union president should sue the newspaper, the reporter cannot satisfy the defense of truth by showing that the quotation was accurate—even if the Congressman admitted he said it. The reporter would have to go further and show that the union president was in fact a thief. The defense of truth is not met by showing that the report was an accurate repetition of a libelous charge.

The difficulties that a newspaper faces as a result of this rule are graphically demonstrated by the troubles that beset the Little Rock (Arkansas) *Gazette*. On February 25, 1959, Hugh Patterson, *Gazette* publisher, was invited to the home of the attorney for Harold F. Dunaway, a pinball-machine kingpin. There he heard a remarkable story involving Bob Troutt, a crime reporter for the rival *Arkansas Democrat*. The gist of the story was that nearly a year before, Troutt had asked for a payoff from Dunaway and Dunaway's partner Cecil Hill to keep him from writing false stories for the *Democrat* on the pinball-machine business. As a result, Dunaway and Hill said, they had paid Troutt $2,000 in cash. All went well for almost a year, they went on, but then Troutt had spoken of additional compensation, suggesting a fee of $5,000. The pinball-machine operators said they had warned Troutt that if certain threatened articles appeared, tape-recorded conversations of the 1958 payoff demand would be released. Soon thereafter the *Democrat* printed an article and the tapes were taken to the sheriff and played for him, the county prosecutor and grand-jury foreman.

To back up the story, Dunaway and Hill played the tapes for the *Gazette* publisher. No written transcripts of the tapes were available, but the next day Patterson stopped by and picked one up. That same day Dunaway and Hill called a press conference and released the charges to the *Democrat* and radio and television stations, as well to the *Gazette*. The *Gazette* put a bannerline on the story on page one and carried the text of the transcript of the tapes, as well as Troutt's denial of the charges. The *Democrat* used the Associated Press account. Troutt then sued the *Gazette*, Dunaway and Hill for $500,000. Troutt insisted that the only conversation he had had with Dunaway and Hill about money was a short time before, nearly a year after the reported blackmail attempt. Dunaway and Hill called him, Troutt said, to ask if the pinball association could get some publicity if it made a donation to the March of Dimes. Eventually about $2,000 was donated. Troutt said that the tapes had been altered to make his conversations about the March of Dimes seem like a demand for a payoff for himself.

The *Gazette's* account had been an accurate reflection of the

Dunaway and Hill transcript of the tapes. But accuracy could not prove that the *Gazette* had told the truth. The careful writing only showed that the newspaper had faithfully repeated the charges originated by Dunaway and Hill. The *Gazette* thus found itself in a position of being forced to prove that Troutt had indeed been guilty of blackmail. As witnesses the paper had to rely on two men, Dunaway and Hill, of doubtful credibility because of their gambling background. Troutt's lawyer capitalized on this weakness by forcing Dunaway into contradictions. In a deposition, read at the trial, Dunaway gave the following testimony regarding Troutt:

> Q. Was he lying about your business?
> A. Definitely.
> Q. Tell us who he lied to and what the nature of his lies were.
>
> . . . .
>
> A. Well, he contended in—in several articles that he wrote in the paper that gambling was being carried on on pinball machines and which in my opinion was a lie.
> Q. And that is the reason you paid him?
> A. That is the reason I paid him, to keep him from telling lies, that is right.
> Q. And that is the only reason?
> A. That is right.

In cross-examination at the trial Dunaway testified:

> Q. Now, what lies had Mr. Troutt reported on you—your business prior to the time you made this contact?
> A. He had reported no particular lies. He had reported no lies at that time. He had mentioned us in his series of private club articles, I think, a couple of times.
> Q. Had mentioned you, Harold Dunaway, and Cecil Hill?
> A. I say, I don't know whether he wrote them or not, but I say we were mentioned in those articles a couple of times during the private club series.
>
> . . . .
>
> Q. What was the real reason that you state to these ladies and gentlemen that you gave this money to Troutt?
> A. The real reason I gave this money to Mr. Troutt was to keep him —we didn't mind at all any publicity at all regarding our business of a truthful nature, and the real reason I gave this money to Mr. Troutt was to keep him from publishing anything untrue.

Q. Well, now, up to this time had he ever published anything untrue about your marble machine—pinball machine business?

A. Not to my knowledge. I will say he—his paper had mentioned it.

Q. Was it untrue?

A. Part of it was, yes sir.

Q. Just exactly then, what had he printed untrue about your business?

A. I am making it very plain, Mr. Howell. I don't know who wrote the article. I don't know if he wrote it or not.

Q. What was it? What especially?

A. The paper made a statement that we owned an interest in a certain club in town and we did not own that interest.

In another part of the cross-examination, Dunaway testified:

Q. And you told us he made threats against you and that was the purpose of your paying him?

A. Yes.

Q. And the only threats he made to you was in the newspaper, is that it?

A. He never made no threats——

Q. The only threats made to you was through one hundred thousand other readers in the newspaper?

A. That's right. That's right.

The *Gazette* introduced the tapes as evidence. Troutt's lawyers expected this and had not been idle. They produced an expert in recording devices who testified that tapes could easily be altered. In his opinion, there were fifty to sixty spots in the tapes indicating that they had been altered in one way or another. Fifteen of these spots made him absolutely certain, he said, that the tapes had been changed. The defense countered with its own expert witness, who testified that in his opinion the tapes had not been altered, although he did agree there was evidence that they had been spliced.

Many of the rulings at the trial hampered the *Gazette*'s defense. The newspaper had hoped to obtain evidence through a key man in the alleged blackmail, Judge Robert W. Laster, a member of the school board. According to Dunaway and Hill, Laster was a go-between. The court refused, however, to let the *Gazette* subpoena Laster's bank accounts, income tax returns and other financial records. The court also decided against playing tapes of Laster's conversations and refused to question a juror about reports that he had discussed the case in public.

Although Troutt's background was not flawless (he had married three times, fathered a child by one of his wives sixteen months after divorcing her and fallen behind in paternity payments), the jury decided not to believe the word of the two professional gamblers. The verdict was $50,000 in compensatory damages and $50,000 in punitive damages—the largest libel award in Arkansas history. Despite a passionate plea by the *Gazette,* the State Supreme Court ruled that there was substantial evidence to support the verdict. It did reduce the over-all award to $50,000 (Dunaway v. Troutt, 232 Ark. 615).

Wire-Service Dispatches

Truth is also not proved by showing that the newspaper or broadcasting station merely used a wire-service dispatch, even though the dispatch was unaltered. On December 24, 1956, the Associated Press sent a story to Texas members that began:

> AUSTIN, Dec. 24 (AP)—Texas Ranger Walter Russell shot and killed a Laredo man late Saturday night after the ranger had been fired on, the Department of Public Safety said here today.
>
> The dead man was Raymundo Davila, about 36, who was killed with a single shot-gun blast on a highway about six miles east of Freer. The DPS said Russell and Manuel Amaya, San Diego, chief of police, had stopped a truck Davila was riding in for investigation.
>
> The DPS said Davila and his two companions, Rodolfo Cruze Mata, 28, and Pedro Martinez, 24, both of Laredo, had marijuana in their possession and were planning to deliver some in San Diego.

The truth was that the dead man was not Raymundo Davila but his brother, Jesus Davila, who also lived in Laredo. Raymundo sued the Corpus Christi *Caller-Times.* The Court of Civil Appeals of Texas held that the newspaper, "however innocent may have been the mistake, is liable for actual damages" (Davila v. Caller-Times Publishing Co., 311 S.W.2d 945).

Note that the liability was only for actual damages. In other words, punitive damages, the kind that can run high, were not an issue. In this case there was an out-of-court settlement for $1,000. This is an indication that newspapers and broadcasting stations should not hesitate to use press dispatches of the Associated Press, United Press International and other recognized agencies. Of course, if the dispatches involve local people, every effort should be made to verify the information. That is not only good journalism—it is also good protection from errors that could lead to libel suits. It is better to attribute the matter picked up from the wire association when ticklish stories are involved, but even if no credit is given, the newspaper or broadcasting station can fall back on its source to reduce damages. On March 2, 1932, the New York *American* carried this short:

> Setting aside a jury's verdict, Supreme Court Justice Dunne yesterday adjudged Mrs. Irene Walsh guilty of marital misconduct. She is the wife of Dr. Joseph Walsh, prominent Brooklyn physician.
>
> They counter-sued for divorce, he naming Dr. Stephen Szalay corespondent while she cited a chambermaid. The jury last November denied divorce to both and the judge suggested a reconciliation. The suggestion was not adopted.

The fact was that a jury had found neither party guilty of adultery, but a judge had set aside the verdict as against the weight of evidence insofar as it applied to Mrs. Walsh and ordered a new trial. The article went one step beyond the judge's decision to say that Mrs. Walsh had been found guilty of marital misconduct. In defense of its story the *American* said, among other things, that it had based the article on the report of a reliable news agency. Referring to this defense, an appellate court said:

> . . . it would be well to call attention to the fact that no punitive damages can be awarded if the jury believes that defendant based its publication on a communication from a reliable news service and published the same in good faith in the ordinary course of business believing it to be true. That defense, however, if established, does not apply to compensatory damages. [Szalay v. New York American, 254 App. Div. (N.Y.) 249]

In Florida, news media are exempt from all damages for carrying libelous press dispatches of established agencies. The rule was formulated by the Florida Supreme Court in 1933 and has been affirmed in subsequent cases. There is one qualification. There must be no reckless, wanton or careless disregard of the rights of the person in the news (Layne v. Tribune Co., 108 Fla. 177).

In addition to responsibility for press dispatches, news media are also liable for any defamation contained in syndicated columns. Liability was made clear in a chain of sixty-eight suits brought by Representative Martin L. Sweeney, an Ohio Democrat, against newspapers that carried a column by Drew Pearson and Robert S. Allen. The accusation was that Congressman Sweeney was opposing the naming of a Cleveland attorney to a judgeship because he was a Jew. Sweeney won some of his cases and lost others (e.g. Sweeney v. Patterson *et al.* 128 F.2d 457).

How to Prove Truth

If truth cannot be shown by mere accuracy of reporting, how can it be proved? One way is by incontrovertible documentary evidence. When Edmond C. Fletcher, an attorney, complained that he had been libeled by a report that he had been disbarred, the Norfolk (Virginia) Newspapers proved its statement with a copy of the court orders of disbarment (Fletcher v. Norfolk Newspapers 239 F. 2d 169). Such legal judgments are always impressive.

Truth can also be proved by affidavits when the defense moves for summary judgment. The magazine *Motor Trend* pubished an article in its April, 1959, issue criticizing a battery rejuvenator known as VX-6. As we have already noted, an accusation that a product is worthless is not libelous of the manufacturer. But *Motor Trend* carried its criticism further and questioned the advertising of the manufacturer, National Dynamics. The advertisement had contained this letter of endorsement:

HOSPITAL ENDORSES VX-6

Batteries which were due for replacement were treated with VX-6. These batteries are now working at high performance levels thanks to VX-6.—Cedars of Lebanon Hospital, Los Angeles, Cal. [Excerpt from Letter]

In commenting on the advertising the magazine said this:

Motor Trend talked with the head of one organization whose endorsement appeared in some of National Dynamics' advertising. He was very surprised to find his company was using the product and much more surprised to find they endorsed it, as they "do not endorse any product." Questioning personnel in his organization brought to light a letter that an employee had written on company stationery stating that he used the product. We understand that legal action has been taken to stop the use of the company name in connection with VX-6.

National Dynamics had based its advertisement on a letter on Cedars of Lebanon stationery from a man named Ernest L. Metz that said:

> The results of the tests made on the cars of members of the maintenance staff has proven successful. The said men are nothing less than enthusiastic over VX-6 and heartily endorse it.
> The tests involved "worn-out" batteries which were due for replacement. These batteries are now working at high performance level, thanks to VX-6.

The company sued for $1.5 million, alleging that *Motor Trend* had falsely accused it of misrepresenting VX-6. To prove the truth of its allegation, *Motor Trend* offered an affidavit of Robert W. Lyons, the assistant administrative director of Cedars of Lebanon Hospital. In the affidavit Lyons stated that the letter had been written by a former employee and was not "an official statement of Cedars of Lebanon Hospital, and that the use of hospital stationery and titles for this purpose was not authorized . . . the use of VX-6 was not authorized for hospital use and was never tested as a product to be used by the hospital." In upholding the truth of the article the court noted that the letter had not even suggested that the hospital, as distinguished from some of its employees, had authorized tests of VX-6 or had endorsed it (National Dynamics v. Peterson Publishing Co., 185 F. Supp. 573).

If affidavits contain material that is questioned, however, they are not sufficient to prove truth, as *Saturday Evening Post* editors found out in a case described at length on page 256.

Another method of proving truth is to cross-examine the plaintiff to show that he really is the kind of person the newsman said he was. Counsel for the Providence Journal Company followed this method in defeating the $750,000 libel suit brought by Harold Noel Arrowsmith, a wealthy Baltimore man who described himself as a researcher into governmental agencies and the international Communist conspiracy. Two of Arrowsmith's chief complaints were that he had been labeled a "sophisticated fascist" and "a shy, reticent anti-Semite."

Cross-examination brought out that Arrowsmith believed that an international Zionist conspiracy brought about World War II, that Franklin D. Roosevelt was a part of the conspiracy, that "there would be obvious need of isolation" of Jews to protect the security of the United States and that he might have said that there was "no more vicious anti-Semite than Jesus Christ."

Interrogation also revealed that Arrowsmith met George Lincoln Rockwell, the American Nazi, in 1958 and entered into an oral understanding that Rockwell would print documents Arrowsmith had collected relating to the "Communist and Zionist conspiracy." The two worked on arrangements for picketing in Washington, Atlanta and Louisville after the United States Marines were sent into Lebanon in July, 1958. One picket sign, "Save Ike from the Kikes," was a "poetic necessity," Arrowsmith said. Asked what the sign meant, he replied, "To save President Eisenhower from the political blackmail of the Zionists and their agents was patriotic." Arrowsmith also admitted that he gave to friends and pasted up on a major avenue in New York City red stickers, printed by Rockwell, reading "Communism is Jewish!" "Zionism is Treason!" and "Don't fight ANOTHER WAR TO SAVE THE JEWS!" Asked if the stickers were pro-Jewish, Arrowsmith responded, "It all depends. It may be pro-Jewish from the point of view of friends of the Jews. I have talked to many, many Jews in my life and some of them say they may need me to save them from themselves."

The jurors were out less than three hours and brought back a verdict for the defense. The jurors did not say whether they believed that the truth had been proved, but there was no question that the cross-examination had skillfully disclosed the actual state of Arrowsmith's feelings.

Arrowsmith filed other suits around the country with little success. As the result of judicial pressure he was given a $1,000 settlement by the New York *Daily News*. In Atlanta he was awarded $1.

The Test of Truth

One of the landmark cases on the question of truth laid down the rule that courts everywhere follow. The defendant was Benny

Friedman, who had been a first-class quarterback at the University of Michigan and later a star for the New York Giants in the early days of professional fooball. He wrote an article for *Collier's* magazine about the perils of the game, naming players who played dirty football. Both college and professional football, Benny wrote, "suffer from the occasional player with a mean streak—the bully of boyhood who knows his physical superiority and takes sadistic pleasure in displaying it." This theme was first illustrated by reference to the conduct of an anonymous college player and then by reference to William P. Fleckenstein by name. The "Fleckenstein Formula," Benny said, was "loser take all—on the chin." Fleckenstein was described as "a specialist at infighting during scrimmages" and as "a rough gent who's discreet enough to slug under cover."

When Fleckenstein sued, Benny filed the following answer in justifying the charges:

> During the said period, 1927–1931, inclusive, while engaged in playing professional football, in violation of the rules of football, fair play and good sportsmanship and to the detriment of the game of professional football, the plaintiff employed and practiced the unlawful tactics of striking opposing players in scrimmages with the closed fist or the heel of the palm or of butting opposing players with the knee or elbow in the groin or stomach or face or jumping or falling on the back of opposing players landing on the knees and employing unlawful use of the hands by gouging and choking, and unlawful use of the feet in tripping and unnecessary roughness in charging, blocking and unnecessarily piling and unnecessarily trampling or treading on opposing players with heavy cleated shoes and otherwise playing "dirty" football; and at the time of the publication of the alleged article the fame and reputation of the plaintiff as a professional football player was bad, the plaintiff being generally in disrepute for slugging and the other illegal tactics above enumerated and for playing unsportsmanlike and "dirty" football.

Fleckenstein made a motion to strike the answer and said, in effect, "What of it? Suppose I did slug and gouge and trample and tread, that doesn't make me a sadistic bully." But the Court of Appeals, New York's highest court, sustained the answer and said in its decision, which has been quoted and requoted:

> A workable test is whether the libel as published would have a different effect on the mind of the reader from that which the

pleaded truth would have produced. "When the truth is so near to the facts as published that fine and shaded distinctions must be drawn and words pressed out of their ordinary usage to sustain a charge of libel, no legal harm has been done." [Fleckenstein v. Friedman, 266 N.Y. 19]

If truth is such a glorious defense, why is it so seldom used in libel cases? The chief reason is that it is generally difficult and sometimes impossible to prove and, what is more, it is occasionally even dangerous to attempt it. Newspapers and broadcasting stations lack the investigatory powers and experience of the police. The reporter generally has no personal knowledge of the facts he is reporting and therefore cannot testify in support of the defense. Such proof as there is must come from persons not connected with the publication. In addition, people who do something wrong do not usually surround themselves with witnesses. The result is that the reporter must necessarily rely on what other people have told him, and these people may be liars or irresponsible or unreliable witnesses. They may even be dead when the case is tried. The difficulty of proving the truth was shown by Drew Pearson's trial on a charge of defaming Fred N. Howser, former Attorney General of California. In a radio broadcast, Pearson accused Howser of accepting a bribe. To sustain this charge Pearson offered evidence to show that Joseph A. Irvine, a bookmaker, had turned over an envelope containing twelve one-hundred-dollar bills to James T. Mulloy, who worked in Howser's campaign headquarters. Other evidence was designed to show that Mulloy had delivered the money to Howser and had told him it came from Irvine. Not being able to count on Irvine, Pearson did not call him as a witness. Howser did, however, and on the stand Irvine denied the transaction *in toto*. Pearson's lawyer, William P. Rogers, later United States Attorney General, had to counteract this testimony in some way, and he did so in skillful cross-examination that intimated that perhaps Irvine had been leniently dealt with on a gambling charge because of his acquaintance with Howser. The jury returned with a complete victory for Pearson. Because libel law is so complicated, juries are often given a list of questions to answer. In the Pearson trial it answered the first three this way:

Question No. 1. Has the defendant established that the statement made by him concerning the plaintiff was true?

Answer: Yes.

Question No. 2. Has the defendant established that the statement was made by him without actual malice?

Answer: Yes.

Question No. 3. Has the plaintiff suffered any damages as the result of the broadcasting of the statement and, if so, in what amount?

Answer: None. [Howser v. Pearson, 95 F. Supp. 936]

Even when the defense can count on a solid witness the going is not always easy. After Rocky Marciano retired in 1956 as the undefeated heavyweight boxing champion, the *Saturday Evening Post* carried a series of six articles under his by-line but actually written by two professional reporters. The fourth article dealt with his winning the championship in 1952 in a bout with Jersey Joe Walcott and carried this headline:

DIRTY WORK AT RINGSIDE

For the first time. Rocky discloses the startling truth about his title fight with Jersey Joe Walcott

In the body of the article, which was written in the first person, Marciano said:

. . . it seemed like everything in the world was done to steal it from me before I even got it.

. . . .

. . . here's the truth, as it was told to me by the policeman who found out. I was blinded by capsicum Vaseline. According to the policeman, Walcott's manager, Felix Bocchicchio, rubbed it on Joe's gloves and on the upper part of his body. From the sixth round through the eighth, every time Walcott jabbed me and his glove came in contact with my eyes, or everytime I clinched with him and got my face against his body, my eyes would smart.

The magazine realized that the charge might bring repercussions, so it went over its ground carefully before publishing it. Marciano said that the information had come from a Philadelphia police officer named Melchiore he had talked with at Grossinger's, the Catskill resort, in 1953. But Melchiore refused to disclose the name of his informer. One of the reporters than tape-recorded an interview with Melchiore, who confirmed that he had information that capsicum Vaseline had been given to Bocchicchio for the fight, but again would not release the name of his source. The editors at the *Post* reviewed this tape. They also took into account the fact that Bocchicchio could not go into court with an unblemished character. He had been convicted of a felony. If it came to a showdown on whom the jury would believe, the *Post* thought its side would win. So it ran the article.

Bocchicchio sued. At the trial, Melchiore, then a county detective, was the star witness for the *Post*. Asked what information he had concerning the cause of Marciano's impairment of vision during the Walcott fight, Melchiore replied, "I had received some information that capsicum Vaseline was used on the gloves of Jersey Joe Walcott. . . . the complete information I had was what was given to Felix Bocchicchio by Blinky Palermo, capsicum Vaseline, and it was put on the gloves of Jersey Joe Walcott."

But even when questioned by the trial judge, Melchiore refused to divulge his source, "because I have—I have other informants . . . and if I reveal the name of one, there is not one of them out there will ever trust me again in other information." Despite repeated efforts by the plaintiff's counsel, the judge permitted the witness to remain silent on his informant. Score one round for the *Post*. Three witnesses testified that a kinescope of the fight showed Bocchicchio rubbing Walcott's gloves and a doctor offered his expert opinion that a foreign substance that could have been capsicum Vaseline had caused Marciano's eyes to burn. Score another round for the *Post*.

There was also the problem of getting the plaintiff's criminal record before the jury. First the defense sought to show that Bocchicchio had been guilty of pandering and of breaking and escaping from prison. But the judge refused, on the basis that Bocchicchio had been pardoned on both counts. Finally it succeeded in introducing merely the fact that he had been convicted of a felony. Another round for the *Post*. Bocchicchio offered a number of witnesses whose testimony was confusing, if not contradictory. A member of the Pennsylvania Athletic Commission testified that it was customary for fighters to rub Vaseline on their faces and bodies, but another witness, who had examined in April, 1961, the gloves used in the September, 1952, fight, said he had found no evidence of Vaseline on them. He said that if there had been Vaseline on them he would have found traces of it even though the capsicum "might change and disappear."

When the jury returned, Marciano won another battle—this one by a decision. The article was found to have been substantially true and no damages were awarded (Bocchicchio v. Curtis Publishing Co., 203 F. Supp 403).

Peter E. Droner was a retired police officer who shot and killed a doll peddler in Times Square. *Look* magazine carried an article entitled "Death of a Hooked Heiress," and in the article there was the following paragraph:

> Bob Friede was placed in the Manhattan House of Detention for Men—"the Tombs"—in a cell on the eighth floor, the "tight" floor reserved for the potentially psychotic, the potentially suicidal and the notorious. Among Friede's floor mates were the men who murdered Malcolm X, a retired policeman who shot and killed a doll peddler in Times Square and Mark Fein, a wealthy young man convicted of killing his bookmaker.

Droner sued and said that he was not potentially psychotic, potentially suicidal or notorious and that only one of the three men who murdered Malcolm X was a floor mate. The publication was held to be substantially true (Droner v. Cowles Communications Inc. and World Journal Tribune, Inc., 34 A.D. 2d (N.Y.) 823).

Chapter 11

PRIVILEGE OF REPORTING—
THE BREAD-AND-BUTTER DEFENSE

TRUTH IS THE MOST THRILLING OF ALL THE DEFENSES FOR LIBEL, but the privilege of reporting is the most commonly used protection of those who write, edit and transmit the news. This privilege grants anyone—not just the press—immunity from libel damages for publication of fair and true reports of legislative, judicial and other official proceedings. Since so much of the news originates in government or legally authorized proceedings this defense is invoked more often than any other. It is also the easiest to prove since such proceedings are usually documented.

The reporter of a proceeding does not have the same protecttion as the participant. A lawyer participating in a trial can libel a person even if he does so from base motives and escape damages. On the other hand, reporters, except in four states, lose their immunity in stories of official proceedings if malice can be proved against them. In New York, California, Georgia, Michigan, Oklahoma, Texas and Wisconsin reporters need not fear damages even if they harbor malice.

The second distinction is that the participant must make sure his remarks are pertinent. If they are not, he loses his privilege. If a district attorney in a vehicular-homicide case, for example, should suddenly accuse the defendant of seducing his secretary, he does so at his peril. But the newsman reporting the proceedings can go right ahead and report anything that goes on during them. He is not burdened with the problem of guessing what is pertinent and what is not. So long as his report is fair and accurate, he is safe.

The privilege of reporting can be used for any article that meets four requirements:

1. The article must deal with a legislative, judicial or other official proceeding.

2. The article, including the headlines, must be a fair and true report.

3. The article must contain no extraneous libelous matter.

4. Outside of New York, California, Georgia, Michigan, Oklahoma, Texas and Wisconsin, the writer can harbor no actual malice.

Legislative Proceedings

Legislative proceedings are the official proceedings of a body created by law and authorized by law to legislate, to enact or repeal statutes for the guidance of the public generally or recommend the repeal or enactment of such laws, or to investigate the desirability of enacting or repealing laws. In other words, the body must have legal status and must be authorized to make, recommend or investigate the subject of legislation.

Clearly then, the proceedings of the United States Senate and the House of Representatives fall within the protection of the privilege of reporting. The same is true of state legislatures, city councils, school boards, town meetings, boards of aldermen and the like. If the worst scalawag in the legislature gets up in the Assembly chamber and calls the most ethical lawyer in the state an ambulance chaser, reporters can write the story without fear of having to prove the truth of the charge.

The privilege is even broader. It applies to the duly constituted committees of these bodies. Congressional committees are in session even after Congress adjourns, and these meetings are protected. So are the hearings they hold on various subjects. If a witness or a member of the committee makes libelous statements at a meeting, they may be reported. Thus, most of Senator Joseph R. McCarthy's libels could be safely reported because they were made during legislative hearings.

The same shield protects the reporting of committees of the state legislatures and all city and local lawmaking bodies. It even applies to reports in this country of proceedings of the English House of Commons, the Israeli Knesset, the French Assembly, the Japanese Diet and the legislative bodies of all countries. If an American businessman is accused in the Supreme Soviet of cheating on a deal, this defense can be used by American news outlets that carry the reports.

The privilege of reporting also protects stories about petitions, complaints and other communications made to the legislative bodies as soon as they are officially received and some action taken on them. Strictly speaking, the privilege does not exist until the legislative body acts, because until then there is no legislative proceeding. In actuality, however, there is little risk in reporting a petition or complaint once it has been filed with the legislative body. In most cases it is referred at once to a committee.

The important thing is that the body be legally created and that its proceedings be official. But suppose that its proceedings turn out to be illegal. Suppose that a governor called a special session of the legislature and that at one of its meetings a member made a defamatory remark that was reported in the press. Suppose that it turned out later that the governor had not followed the constitution in calling the special session and that none of the meetings of the lawmakers was sanctioned in law. Is the press protected in reporting what was said at the session? No court cases have arisen on this point, but there seems little doubt that if the meeting appears on the surface to be legal, that if it has all the trappings of a duly constituted session, then the press is taking little risk in reporting what goes on at it.

This question is more likely to arise in the case of some controversial legislative committee, such as Senator McCarthy's. In the period when he was running rampant there were times when doubt was expressed whether a legal quorum was present at the hearings or whether the committee had the authority to do what it was doing. A cloud was cast over the entire proceedings. If the reporter has any doubts about the legality of such hearings, the safest thing for him to do is to ask the legislator in charge to put on the record a statement giving the legal basis for the proceedings. This should be sufficient to guarantee the privilege of reporting, since the courts do not require that newsmen be constitutional lawyers.

News Conferences

Senator McCarthy's methods created another problem, not so easily solved. He would often hold a closed hearing and then brief reporters on what had taken place. Were these press conferences privileged? The Supreme Court of New Jersey decided they were in a case involving Senator McCarthy's investigation of the Fort Monmouth radar laboratories. On October 22, 1953, McCarthy's Permanent Subcommittee on Investigations held an executive session. Immediately after the meeting the Senator held a press conference. The next day the Newark *Star-Ledger* carried the following story based on that news conference:

EX-MARINE LINKED TO ROSENBERG
MONMOUTH RADAR AIDE WAS SPY'S ROOMMATE
McCarthy Presses For Espionage Trial

Fort Monmouth—An ex-Marine officer, suspended from his job at the Fort Monmouth radar laboratories in 1949 after Military Intelligence found 43 classified documents in his apartment, may have been the direct link between the laboratories and the Rosenberg spy ring, Sen. McCarthy said yesterday.

McCarthy said the man at one time roomed with Julius Rosenberg, the executed atom spy, and has admitted that several other known Communists had keys and free access to his apartment during the time the classified material was there.

The senator added he has conferred unofficially with Justice Department officials and they have decided the man can be brought to trial under the espionage act.

.   .   .   .

The man's apartment was raided by Military Intelligence in 1946, McCarthy said, and 43 classified documents were found.

In December the *Star-Ledger* carried another article, this one based on an open hearing, asserting that McCarthy was moving to have the suspended radar scientist cited for perjury and naming Aaron H. Coleman of Long Branch, New Jersey, as the man in question. Coleman sued for libel. While he based his suit on both stories, the one that was most in question was the first because it had stemmed from a news conference, while the second was based on an open hearing.

At the trial Senator McCarthy testified that the news article of the press conference was a "very accurate report and summation" of what he had said, and he insisted that he had talked to newsmen under authority given him by the subcommittee. Coleman argued that since the McCarthy news conference was not part of the executive session it was not part of the official proceeding and thus not protected by privilege. The jury returned a verdict for the *Star-Ledger*. On Coleman's appeal to the state Supreme Court only Chief Justice Joseph Weintraub agreed with Coleman that the press conference was outside the protection of privilege. In the majority opinion five justices noted that closed sessions of Congressional investigating committees were often necessary "in the interest of the common safety, but this does not exclude the publication of such information as the committee may in its discretion deem fit and proper for the general good." It was up to the jury, the opinion said, to decide if the privilege had been abused (Coleman v. Newark Morning Ledger Co., 29 N.J. 357). Coleman then dropped his case. The court's decision has been widely criticized.

While this case presses the privilege of reporting a legislative proceeding to the outer limits, it would seem to have the support of the second *Restatement of the Law of Torts* (1977) § 611, which extends privilege to "the publication of defamatory matter concerning another in a report of any official action or proceeding. . . ." One comment under § 611 states: "The privilege covered in this Section extends to the report of any official proceeding, or any action taken by any officer or agency of the government of the United States, or of any State or of any of its subdivisions. Since the holding of an official hearing or meeting is in itself an official proceeding, the privilege includes the report of any official hearing or meeting, even though no other action is taken."

The wise reporter covering news conferences of legislators issuing libelous statements should try to force the legislator to concede that he has the authority to speak for his committee. As additional protection, the reporter should also seek out those who are defamed and obtain, if possible, responses. Besides making the story better, the replies may invoke another defense against libel—authorization or consent (which will be discussed in Chapter 14).

Closed Sessions

What if there is no news conference but the reporter noses around and finds out what happened at a closed session of a legislative body? The law is not clear on the subject and the courts have not provided sufficient clarification. In New York the statute on privilege used to apply to reports of "any judicial, legislative or other public and official proceedings." This wording was ambiguous because it could be interpreted three ways. It could mean that the statute applied only to proceedings at which the public was generally present. Or it could mean that the law covered only proceedings at which the public was entitled to be present. Or it could mean that all proceedings with a public interest were protected. Then the legislature deleted the word "public" from the statute. Thus in New York, at least, the law would seem to grant the reporter immunity even if he exposed the contents of a sealed document or the candid discussion of legislators behind closed doors.

However, since the law is still not clear anywhere, the best procedure would be to weigh the reasons for the secrecy against the need of the public for the information and then make the decision. In almost all cases of legislative bodies the answer will probably be to go ahead and use the material because the subject is probably one the public has a right to know about—that is often why the legislators favor secrecy. There are cases, however, that require an opposite decision, such as those involving military secrets.

Informal Sessions

In small towns a legislative body, such as a city council or a school board, often will hold informal conferences before or after the public meetings to decide what to do. The lawmakers feel freer to speak their minds if the voters are not there to check on them. If decisions are actually made at these meetings, there seems little reason why the privilege of reporting could not apply. There is almost no question about it if a reporter is permitted to be present, even if the meeting is informal and the tradition is that he not write about anything controversial that occurs.

On December 27, 1956, the Clifton (New Jersey) City Manager, John L. Fitzgerald, had a couple of drinks at the Board of Health Christmas party, then went to a City Council meeting. After a session in the regular chamber the councilmen moved to a conference room where they could say what they really thought. The Clifton Council had been following this procedure for about twenty years, and that night, as usual, there was a reporter present from the Passaic *Daily News*. No sooner had the conference come to order than City Manager Fitzgerald was pummeled with questions by Councilman Brogan as to why he was not going to promote Patrolmen Charles R. Swede and Raymond DeLuca, who had finished first and second in the civil-service test, to the rank of sergeant. The *News* reported Fitzgerald's reply this way: " 'You want to know why they were skipped?' Fitzgerald said, 'I'll tell you why. Insubordination, that's the reason. I should have fired them.' "

When the item appeared, Fitzgerald's opponents demanded an explanation. Fitzgerald was not too concerned, because he was retiring, and took off for Florida on a vacation. But the sniping continued and to get his foes off his back Fitzgerald finally wrote a letter denying that he had ever said that he "should have fired" two patrolmen. Eventually the City Council voted four to three to censure Fitzgerald and exonerate the two policemen of any wrongdoing. Knowing a good local story, the *News* covered all the developments and each time repeated the quote it had attributed to Fitzgerald concerning the patrolmen. The disgruntled policemen were not satisfied with the official exoneration. They went to court and asked for money from the *News* and from

Fitzgerald. Eventually the complaint against Fitzgerald was dropped. The lower court dismissed the case against the *News* and on appeal the decision was upheld by the New Jersey Supreme Court. Noting, among other things, that the city had kept minutes of the conference and that a councilman had tried to introduce two resolutions, the court said that the mere fact that the press had been admitted for twenty-odd years was "sufficient proof of the public and official nature of the meeting." The defense of privilege thus applied (Swede v. Passaic Daily News, 30 N.J. 320).

Judicial Proceedings

The man who covers the courts is the one who knows the value of the privilege of reporting. Without it he would not have a job, because almost every article he writes is protected from damages only by this defense. Almost every story from the courts involves crime or violations of the moral code or accounts of misfortune and trouble. With the shield of this defense, these events (like the libel cases in this book) can be safely reported, but the task is not easy. The great bulk of legislative proceedings is usually not too technical and takes place on the floor of the body in open session. The road is clear to follow. Except for open court trials, this is not true for judicial proceedings. Much of what goes on in court is so technical that it is difficult for one who is not versed in legal jargon to understand it. Lack of knowledge, disregard of warnings and carelessness lead to mistakes. Here is where the danger lies; here is the source of so many libel suits.

Needless to say, there must be judicial actions to report before the privilege is available. The ones in open court before a judge are obvious. Every trial is a judicial proceeding, of course. So is every decision by a judge, every verdict by a jury, every indictment handed up to a judge by a grand jury, every order signed by a judge, every warrant of arrest signed by a judge, every judgment entered in the office of the clerk of the court. These are the main instances, but the privilege of reporting extends beyond the reports of trials, arguments and decisions. It is in dealing with these other aspects of judicial proceedings that we

enter a realm less easy to understand. The greatest danger
lies in the first few stories about a case. One reason is that the law
does not always protect the reporter until the judicial process
begins, and there is often a mistaken idea about when this happens. Freqently news articles report the commencement of a
civil suit. Such suits can be commenced by the service of a
summons, which generally, though not always, is accompanied
by a complaint. In most states, an attorney can generally prepare
a summons, issue it, cause it to be served and get a lawsuit
started without the aid of the court. In Federal cases, however,
while the attorney prepares the summons and complaint, he must
cause them to be filed before the summons can be properly
issued. The clerk of the court issues it. Is the service of a summons and complaint a judicial proceeding that falls within the
scope of the privilege of reporting? This is an important question because legal moves involving stories of great news value
are frequently started before there has been any judicial action.
If the newsman is not protected until the judge acts, he faces
substantial risks.

Prior to the mid-twenties the courts dealt only indirectly with
this issue. The only hints in judicial opinions had an ominous tone,
but no one could say with confidence what the decision would be
when the issue was squarely presented. Finally in 1927 a court of
last resort made its decision and it was favorable for news
reporters.

The case involved the sensational story of Mrs. Elizabeth S.
Nichols, a wealthy New York widow. She had sued Mrs. Anne
McCoy Campbell, a widely known Christian Science practitioner,
and a man named Canton, whom the court described as "a
prominent inventor of remarkable devices." Mrs. Nichols asserted
that Mrs. Campbell had succeeded in winning a controlling
mental influence over her and then had defrauded her out of
$16,000. The scheme was said to have involved an investment of
$9,000 and a loan of $7,000.

The summons and complaint in that action were duly served
on Mrs. Campbell and were then filed in the county clerk's
office. They then became public records, and all the metropolitan
newspapers published accounts of the complaint, which, of
course, were libelous because they indicated charges of fraud.
The headline in the *Post* on March 30, 1922 read:

HEALER AND INVENTOR FACE SWINDLE CHARGE
Mrs. Elizabeth Nichols Says They Took
$16,000 From Her Through Fraud

A few months later Mrs. Nichols formally withdrew her charges against Mrs. Campbell and abandoned her lawsuit completely. Mrs. Campbell was not satised with that kind of vindication; she wanted money, so she filed libel suits against five newspapers. She had the papers in a fine fix. They could not fall back on the defense of truth because the only possible source of proof was Mrs. Nichols and she had, in effect, disavowed the charges by withdrawing her suit. There were only two possible defenses available for the newspapers. One of them—authorization or consent—we shall deal with in Chapter 14. The other was the privilege of reporting. All the papers asserted this defense and thus raised for the first time in New York State the question of whether the service and filing of a civil suit constituted a judicial proceeding within the privilege of reporting.

In the lower courts the newspapers took a beating, since the courts in almost all jurisdictions had ruled that there had to be an action by a judge before the privilege of reporting applied. In the Appellate Division the *Post* decision was reversed, the court pointing out that when complaints were filed they became public property, subject to inspection by anyone at any time. It followed, the court said, that they were properly available to the public press and subject to the privilege of reporting.

Mrs. Campbell, however, would not give up and took her case to the highest court in New York, the Court of Appeals. In deciding to disregard the "overwhelming weight of authority elsewhere and start with a rule of our own," the court said:

> To publish truly and without malice of one that an action has been brought against him for fraud, seduction, assault, breach of promise, divorce, et cetera, has become so common that the opportunity is seldom passed in silence except when forbearance or obscurity protects the victim. So general has this practice become that the public has learned that accusation is not proof and that such actions are at times brought in malice to result in failure. To say that the newspapers may freely publish the entire proceedings in a case from an ex parte application for an order of arrest or other remedial process under the protection of privilege, but may speak only at their own

risk before the case actually comes before a court or judge in some
form, is to make a distinction to which publishers give little heed. . . .

   Questions of public policy should be considered. In this case it appears that the action against plaintiff was discontinued; that Mrs.
Nichols thus got her alleged false and scurrilous charges before the
public as news and then dropped her case. It is contended that such
acts should not be deemed privileged so as to protect the publisher.
The contention is too far reaching. Scandalous matter may come
before the public in connection with lawsuits. Personal malice may
thus be given a hearing. A complaint withdrawn may not be the
vindication that a decision favorable to the accused would be. But
complaints are withdrawn after applications have been made to the
courts and suits have been dropped before verdicts. Consistency requires us to go forward or to go back. We cannot go back and exclude the publication of daily reports of trials before a final decision
is reached. The present distinction is indefensible. Therefore, we
proceed to a logical conclusion and uphold the claim of privilege on
the ground that the filing of a pleading is a public and official act in
the course of judicial proceedings. [Campbell v. New York Evening
Post, Inc., 245 N.Y. 320]

The rule in New York thereupon became formally established
that no libel suit could be maintained for the publication of a
fair and true report of the commencement and filing of an action
in a civil suit, including the contents of a complaint that has
been served and filed.

   This ruling also protects the newsman in reporting any other
pleading or any other paper in an action that has been actually
served and filed, even though a judge has not taken cognizance
of it. The court emphasized that the complaint in the Campbell
case had been served and filed. Therefore, before writing a story
about a legal paper that has not been subject to judicial action,
the reporter should check to make sure it has been served. If it
has not, he should be wary of it. He should not rely on a lawyer's
promise. With the best of intentions in the world, lawyers will
say they will serve a paper and then change their minds or
change the statements in the paper. Sometimes they are unable to
serve them. The fact that the papers are in the hands of a process
server or the sheriff for service does not help. Actual service is
what counts.

   Must the papers also be filed? In the Campbell case the
Court of Appeals stressed both service and filing. Eventually the

courts will probably hold that mere service is enough, but so far they have not. If a reporter has an article about a suit in which the complaint has been served but not filed, he would be wise to talk to the attorney and ask him to file the paper. Attorneys know the value of good publicity, so they will usually lose no time in complying.

In the Federal court the rule is that the complaint has to be filed before a summons is issued, so the same problem does not arise. But a different one does. There are times when the summons and complaint have been filed but not served. The papers are then public property. Anyone can examine them in the office of the clerk of the Federal court even though they have not been served. Therefore newsmen seem to have the privilege of reporting the contents in states that follow the New York rule.

A 1966 case in the federal court of the Southern District of New York held that service alone in an action in the state courts and filing alone in the federal courts is sufficient to give the privilege of reporting. (Phillips v. Murchison, 252 F. Supp. 513)

The New York rule is still in the minority. California, Georgia, Kentucky, South Carolina, Pennsylvania and Tennessee follow the New York rule by judicial decision and Ohio and Wyoming by statute.

In other states some judicial action must be taken before the action falls within the defense of privilege. The matter need not be disposed of finally; it is enough if some action be taken, no matter how minor. The action does not have to relate to the merits of the case. Nor does it matter whether the action is ex parte, with only one side appearing before the judge, as in an application for an injunction.

Depositions

Depositions taken after a suit is started are privileged in the same way as is evidence in a trial. Even though the judge is not present, the examination of one party by another is under control of the court and witnesses testify under oath. The fact that some of the statements made at such proceedings are not admissible as evidence does not bar their use in news stories. There are many statements made from the witness stand in open court that are

stricken from the record, but they are nevertheless privileged. If
the deposition-taking is closed, newsmen can write reports based
on questioning of those who were at the proceedings, but extreme
care should be taken to make sure a balanced account is published.

Post-Proceeding Libels

The privilege can easily be lost by failure to realize when the
proceeding is over. The Camden (New Jersey) *Evening Courier*
and *Morning Post* carried articles that reported an argument
between the Assistant Prosecutor of Camden County, Anthony
Mitchell, and the Chief of Police of Pennsauken township,
Thomas Thorpe. The prosecution had just closed its case against
a man named Roberts, who was accused of larceny, and the court
had adjourned. Mitchell had just learned that two of Roberts'
accomplices had not been reported to him for indictment by the
grand jury but had been taken before the local recorder on a
disorderly charge and let off with light fines. The *Courier* and
Post reported:

> Assistant Prosecutor Anthony Mitchell today charged that politi-
> cians in Pennsauken township "covered up" criminal cases handled
> by the police. Mitchell named W. Leslie Rogers, Republican leader
> there, as one of those who "give orders" to the police department.

Rogers sued. In rejecting the defense of privilege of reporting,
the New Jersey Supreme Court noted that "obviously these
statements were not made in the course of a judicial proceeding"
(Rogers v. Courier Post Co., 2 N.J. 393). Having lost the point,
the *Courier* and *Post* made an out-of-court settlement with Rogers.

Closed Court Sessions

How about judicial proceedings that are closed to the public?
Here the reporter is not on as sure ground as he is when writing
about closed sessions of legislative proceedings. The standard is
still the same: if there is not an overwhelming public policy in
favor of secrecy, then the proceedings are privileged, even
though closed to the public gaze. But the application of the
standard to specific judicial situations oftimes tips the balance
against privilege, at least in the eyes of responsible newsmen.

In children's court and women's court, for example, there is a strong public policy in favor of secrecy to protect the defendants. The filing of divorce actions and judges' decisions can be reported, but in some jurisdictions the pleadings are often sealed to protect the parties involved as well as others who might be mentioned. In the mid-1950s the highest court of New York State held that the privilege of reporting did not cover papers sealed by a rule of law (Danziger v. Hearst Corp., 304 N.Y. 244). But immediately following the decision, the legislature deleted the qualification "public" from the statute dealing with official proceedings covered by privilege. Since then a strong legal argument exists that the reporter who digs out the dirt in divorce cases—even if they are sealed—is protected. However, there have been no court tests.

Public policy loses some of its weight when obscenity cases are considered. When obscene testimony is anticipated, the public may be excluded to protect witnesses and maintain decorum in the court. But it is questionable whether these arguments apply to reports of what went on.

Grand Jury Hearings

Grand jury proceedings are sensitive, and stories about them should be handled with special care. Indictments, of course, can be safely reported, but not until handed up to the judge. Generally speaking, the rule has been that testimony before a grand jury and the votes of the grand jurors are not privileged. The trend, however, has been to widen the right to include such testimony. That brash experimental New York newspaper of the 1940s, *PM*, carried an article referring to testimony of "ten Queens bookies" concerning "graft and protection money." A New York Appellate Court held that *PM* had the right to plead that the article was a fair and true report of a Grand Jury investigation (Bridgewood v. Newspaper PM, Inc., 276 App. Div. (N.Y.) 858). Nevertheless, the writer is taking a chance, especially if he relies on quotes from Grand Jurors about what went on during deliberations. The writer who puts together an article from such reports should be extremely careful of identification.

Illegal Proceedings

The reporter is also protected in case a judicial proceeding, which has all the earmarks of a legal one, turns out to be illegal. One of the early cases involved a charge by Fannie Stubbs that the Rev. Sedley Lee, the pastor of a small Brooklyn church, had spent some of the church's money on himself. He was summoned before a magistrate to explain, and the Brooklyn *Standard Union's* story of the hearing included these two paragraphs:

> Lawyer Perry didn't confine his comments to the case in hand, that of the pastor's sudden draft on the church's available funds, but told of a recent prayer meeting in a little church, which is situated in Erasmus Street, during which he broadly hinted that the pastor got away with the collection.
>
> The lawyer said the colored flock had gathered for an evening of prayer and praise, and had donated generously when the collection plate had been passed. The plate was placed on the table on the pulpit, he said, when the Rev. Sedley Lee announced to the brethren and sisters assembled, "Let us pray." The money was all there before the pastor knelt at the table and crossed his hands in an attitude of devotion over the plate, but it was gone when the prayer had been concluded, the lawyer said.

Mr. Lee sued. The article was, of course, libelous because it charged crime, or at least bad conduct on the part of the clergyman. The *Standard Union* thus had to find a defense and cited the privilege of reporting a judicial proceeding. Lee, however, said that there had been no judicial proceeding at all because magistrates at that time had no power to issue summonses. If Mr. Lee was right, the *Standard Union* was up against a wall: it would have to prove the truth of its charges. But even more serious was the problem the press in general would face if the case were lost. For newsmen would have to make sure that the courts were acting legally every time they reported any judicial action. Fortunately the court ruled against the pastor. It said:

> The reporter could not be expected to know whether all of the requirements of law had been complied with, or whether everything said in the course of the proceeding was strictly relevant to the subject of the inquiry. He was required, if he made any report at all, to make it full, fair and impartial, but he was not bound, nor was the defendant bound at its peril, to determine doubtful questions of law. The point is that the proceeding was one which the public had the

right to hear and the defendant had the right in the public interest to report. [Lee v. Brooklyn Union Publishing Co., 209 N.Y. 245]

The finding in the Lee case is now settled law in almost all jurisdictions, so that a hearing that has all the external appearances of a judicial proceeding may be safely reported even if it turns out to be defective for some reason.

Other Official Proceedings

Reporters covering stories of other official proceedings can also count on the privilege of informing the public of what is going on, but the proceeding must fulfill two requirements. First, it must have some basis of sanction in law, and second, it must concern the public welfare in some measure. These are not difficult conditions to meet; in fact, reports of almost any meeting open to the general public and dealing with matters concerned with the public welfare are shielded by this privilege.

An Idaho case provides a good illustration. On December 14, 1952, Murray Estes, a Moscow, Idaho, attorney, accosted Richard Shoup, a University of Idaho student, at a campus café known as the Perch and allegedly threatened to shoot him. The police were summoned and Estes was allowed to leave, reportedly still carrying his pistol, while Shoup was taken to the jail for questioning. Felony charges were twice filed against Estes, but both times they were dismissed. Subsequently Estes permitted the dismissal to be set aside and pleaded guilty to a lesser charge of battery and was fined $100. But a number of citizens, including Capt. Thomas C. Thomas, commander of the university naval ROTC unit, were outraged by the extraordinary handling of the affair. A public meeting was called and on May 13, 1953, the *Idahonian* carried a long story about it that included these paragraphs:

> A faction of the Moscow population, numbering some 175 persons, not satisfied with recent actions, which brought an abrupt conclusion of the legal cases involving a Moscow attorney and a University of Idaho student, went on record at a public gathering last night "requesting a grand jury" call to clear away what the group called a "miscarriage of justice."

> . . . .

> Thomas reported certain facts and incidents which have never be-

fore been told publicly and were not a part of any court record . . .

.   .   .   .

After several instances where Shoup had been dissuaded from filing any charges against Estes, a charge was filed soon after Melvin Alsager took office as prosecuting attorney, some four weeks after the incident, Thomas said.

Thomas then made reference to legal maneuvers in which a hearing was set for January 15 at 9 A.M. At 8 A.M. that day, Thomas explained, Alsager notified Judge John K. Borg that he would be ready at 9. Alsager and his witnesses were present at police court, normally the place where such hearings are held. But the judge and Estes, Thomas said, had gone to the county courthouse to hear the case.

"This was a ridiculous situation," said Captain Thomas. A motion for dismissal was made and it was dismissed. "If this had been an honest mistake, it could have been easily rectified by lifting a telephone and telling the prosecutor to bring his witness and come on over."

Judge Borg sued newspapers, including the *Idahonian,* that carried reports of the meeting. But the Federal Court of Appeals for the Ninth Circuit held that the reports were sheltered from libel awards and explained: "There is a general doctrine that what is said at a public meeting, at which any person of the community or communities involved might have attended and heard and seen for himself, is conditionally privileged for publication" (Borg v. Boas, 231 F. 2d 788).

The legal basis for the privilege to report public meetings of this character is the Constitutional right that the people have to assemble in peace and to petition for redress of their grievances. This is a broad enough right to embrace all meetings open to anyone in the community. Political gatherings, civil-rights rallies, protests against the erection of a private business—all are covered.

The law is widening its interpretation of privilege as more and more people become more and more involved in economic, social and political affairs. Nevertheless, a word of caution is necessary because some courts have insisted that not all that takes place at an official proceeding is safeguarded by privilege. The New York *Herald* found that out more than a century ago. A man named Warren Wood had been convicted of first-degree murder and had been sentenced to hang. As he mounted the scaffold on January 20, 1854, he looked around and decided that this was a fitting time for a farewell address. The gist of his speech was that his lawyer, a man named Sanford, had botched the case by failing to use all available witnesses.

The *Herald* published this speech and Sanford sued. The *Herald's* best potential witness, Wood, was no longer around, so any chance to prove the truth of the charge was gone. But the *Herald* did rely on the privilege of reporting, contending that the hanging was a public proceeding and that its story was a fair and true account of what had occurred. The court turned it down. The hanging, it agreed, was an official proceeding sanctioned by law, but the convict's farewell address was not. It explained:

> It is quite usual for the convict to make a statement or speech either by way of confession, or in vindication of himself as the case may be; and it is also customary for the attending clergyman to conduct the devotions in a public and audible manner. But these are simply incidental to the public proceeding, and not a portion of it; whether they take place or are omitted is of no legal consequence. [Sanford v. Bennett, 24 N.Y. 20]

It is doubtful that this ruling could be sustained in any court today. Courts have expanded the concept of an official proceeding. In addition, there were special circumstances in the Sanford case. The court was so aghast at the libel of an attorney that it deleted the offensive passage from its opinion, substituting instead the phrase "he again commented harshly." Newsmen today would not hesitate to publish the quotations of a convict under similar circumstances. The reporter stands in the place of the public at an official proceeding. It is not his function to decide to delete certain matters by making a judicial interpretation that they are not sanctioned by law; it is his job to give an accurate account of all that the reader would have seen if he had attended the event. Nevertheless, in New York at least, the prevailing rule is that last-moment speeches by doomed murderers are not protected by the privilege of reporting.

Private Gatherings

Private gatherings, even if held in public places, are definitely outside this privilege. Gossip columnists who pick up their tawdry items in the plush saloons of New York and Hollywood must look for other kinds of libel-proofing. Newsmen who move in such circles may have fun but they are not reporting a public meeting. The Washington columnist who works the cocktail circuit is in the same untenable situation.

Besides being rooted in law, a proceeding must also affect the rights or welfare of the public if it is going to fall within the ambit of this defense. An event may be of unusual news interest and be sanctioned by an affirmative provision of law and yet not touch the rights of the public generally. The annual meetings of the stockholders of the American Telephone and Telegraph Company are such an example. They are not only sanctioned by law, they are also required. They affect vast numbers of people; so many thousands attend the meetings that armories or convention halls are rented; they excite wide public interest. But they are not concerned with the public generally. They deal only with the interest of the private stockholders. Therefore the proceedings are not privileged. Labor-union meetings dealing with the affairs of the members also do not meet the requirement, although their decisions, such as to continue a strike or go back to work, often affect the welfare of the entire community.

There are signs, however, that the reports of the meetings of stockholders and unions, if held in public, may eventually be guarded by privilege. In five states, California, Idaho, South Carolina, Utah and Texas, this privilege has been extended by statute to all public meetings. In other states the risk of reporting libelous remarks decreases with the size of the meetings, and it can be safely said that the peril is almost negligible in the case of large gatherings.

Even now the proceedings of a few private corporations come within this privilege. These are corporations that by statute perform a legal duty concerning matters that touch on the right of the public generally. Bar associations and medical societies, for example, are authorized to police their professions. When a bar association or medical society acts against a practitioner for some unethical or improper conduct, reports of the proceedings are protected.

The newsman is not taking an undue risk if he reports a trial before a private tribunal, such as a church board, provided the public has a legitimate interest in the outcome. On November 13, 1927, the St. Louis *Post-Dispatch* ran a long feature article under the headline

THE WAY OF A MINISTER WITH A HOUSEMAID

SHE COULDN'T RESIST HIS EYES, SO DURAND [ILLINOIS] PASTOR IS NOW OUT OF A PULPIT AND IS SUING SIX MEMBERS OF HIS FLOCK FOR SLANDER.

The article told in great detail how the Rev. John A. Logan Warren had been dismissed from the ministry by a Methodist trial board after having been charged by Hazel Lamb, his maid, with seducing her. The Missouri Supreme Court ruled that reports of the trial were privileged, even though the proceedings had been closed to the public. It explained:

Ministers of the gospel are spiritual teachers and leaders of the people. Their influence and the influence of the church which sponsors them is great. It must be obvious, therefore, that proper qualifications and character for such a position are matters of public concern, especially in a country, such as ours, where there is complete religious freedom and the appeal of every church is solely the character of its teachings and the sincerity of its leaders. . . .

This public interest certainly extends to charges affecting these matters publicly made and tried before a tribunal which has jurisdiction, even though the tribunal be that of a church. Upon both reason and authority, we think the rule of qualified privilege should be applied here. The charges were made for the purpose of determining the fitness of plaintiff to continue in the ministry as one of the leaders of his church and its communicants, and not to punish him for a crime against the law of the land. No other tribunal had jurisdiction of this matter, a fact which plaintiff recognized in submitting his case to it.

The court also held that the qualified privilege of publishing an account of the trial was not lost because the article was cast in a feature vein. But it did note that the headline and the characterization in the lead of Mr. Warren as "a sprightly young Methodist minister" who had a "roving eye and a disposition to be friendly," especially to young girls, could hardly be considered objective accounts of an official proceeding (Warren v. Pulitzer Publishing Co., 336 Mo. 184). The case was settled for about $2,500—sufficient to pay the minister's legal fees.

Under this rule, trials before union boards, civic clubs, political parties, professional societies, charitable groups and other private organizations whose policies touch on the public could be safely reported even though libel was present. Naturally the accounts would have to meet the requirements for fair and true reports of official proceedings.

Government Agencies

By far the largest number of protected proceedings involve government agencies. Such quasi-judicial agencies as the Interstate Commerce Commission, the Federal Trade Commission and the Federal Power Commission are covered. So are military courts-martial, state milk boards, local school boards and trials of policemen, to mention only a few. Even the billing of delinquent customers by a local water board has been ruled privileged (Briarcliff Lodge Hotel v. Citizen-Sentinel Publishers, Inc., 260 N.Y. 106).

Executive Actions

Government executives can hold official proceedings and these are also privileged for the reporter. It is impossible to list all actions of officials that are privileged, but a guideline can be laid down. The courts sometime hesitate to regard executive or administrative action as an official proceeding unless it is semi-judicial in nature. If the official holds hearings, has the power to investigate and can take actions on complaints, chances are high that reports of these actions are privileged.

If a state attorney general looks into a city administration and recommends that the mayor be tried on charges of malfeasance in office, that report is privileged. If a mayor fires his police commissioner, his reasons, given orally or in writing, can be published without fear. If a police commissioner demotes certain officers, his report—even if in a press release—is considered an official proceeding and is also privileged.

But the newsman must make sure that what he is reporting is the official act of the executive. If a district attorney issues a report on an investigation into loan sharking by finance companies, the reporter can use all the names and the charges with impunity. But he cannot add to the story the fact that the district attorney, after issuing the report, went around to his club and told the boys over a few drinks that the real reason for giving the business to the Neverpayback Company was that it was operating a car-theft racket. That makes readable copy, but the DA was merely engaged in a frolic of his own. The newsman cannot afford to take the risk.

The privilege of reporting an executive's actions is shown by a libel case successfully defended by the New York *Post* in the 1930s. The Depression was still on and the Civil Works Administration was providing work relief for those who could not find jobs. Cheats found easy pickings, and in due course the acting administrator of the CWA held an investigation, then issued a report that included the name of Ray W. Farrell as a payroll padder. Farrell was not a payroll padder, and he sued the *Post*, which had carried a story on the report. The court threw out the suit, asserting that the actions of public officials should not be hidden under a cloak of bureaucratic secrecy (Farrell v. New York Evening Post, Inc., 167 Misc.(N.Y.)412).

Arrests

The most important official proceeding from the standpoint of avoiding libel damages is the arrest of a person on a charge of a crime. The report of an arrest, although not necessarily indicating guilt, does include a charge of crime and is automatically libelous. If it is not privileged, the newsman's only complete defense usually is truth. That is a heavy burden to shoulder, because those who sue almost always have been cleared of the crime. The newsman must try to do what the police and district attorney, with all their investigatory power and staff, have failed to do. This happens all the time in television shows and in comic strips, but in actuality it is rare.

Arrests are almost always made by policemen, but private citizens may legally be called upon to assist, and, in some circumstances, they have the legal right to make arrests themselves. If the arrest is legally made, it and the charge can be safely reported.

One of the most important things for the newsman to know is when a person is actually arrested. Sometimes the cop clamps his hand on the suspect's shoulder and says, "Come on, I'm taking you in." Is that an arrest? Sometimes a detective knocks on the door and extends an invitation to visit the headquarters for a short quiz. Is that an arrest? Sometimes Federal agents raid gambling establishments and seize a dozen persons. Are those arrests? Sometimes state troopers haul a dozen civil-rights demonstrators to jail. Are those arrests? Sometimes pickets against American foreign policy fall limp on the street and the gendarmes drag them into paddy wagons so that traffic can move. Are those arrests?

This is the same question—when does an official proceeding begin?—popping up again. Actually, an arrest is not officially made until the suspect is booked, that is, his name is entered on the police blotter and a charge is lodged against him. While there is a question in some localities whether the police blotter is an official record, the newsman who relies on it in writing his articles will run into no serious trouble if he is careful. A recent case in Louisiana involved the privilege of reporting entries in a blotter. The article, in the January 2, 1962, edition of the *Morning Advocate* of Baton Rouge, said:

> Opelousas—An eighth person, identified by state police as a member of a narcotics ring, was arrested early Monday morning at Kenney's Lounge in Eunice, Capt. Lonnie Rogers, commander of Troop K in Opelousas, reported.
>
> He identified the man as Floyd Fuselier, 37, of Morrow. Fuselier was charged with possession of narcotics, Rogers said.
>
> The seven others were arrested in a predawn raid Sunday by state and Eunice police. They were: David Warren Jr., 28, Deweyville, Tex.; Lionel Richard, 30, Ville Platte; Lionel Fuselier, 30, Mamou, all charged with possession of narcotics; Nuborn Francois, 33, Eunice, charged with possession of narcotics and contributing to the delinquency of a juvenile. . . .

Actually no narcotics had been found on Francois. He sued, asserting that he had been libeled by the false statement. The *Morning Advocate* produced evidence showing that the logbook of Troop K of the Louisiana State Police carried this entry:

> 12-31-61
> 4: A.M.
> Nubon Francois—W/M—33—Eunice
>   CHARGED
> *Possession of narcotics & contributing*
> *to the delinquency of a juvenile.*
> *Placed in jail. Eunice.*
>   *Lt. Fruge*

The Louisiana Court of Appeals held that this was a privileged report of an official proceeding because it was an accurate account (it disregarded the Advocate's misspelling of Francois' first name) of a record that the state police were required to keep and because it did not assume the guilt of the accused (Francois v. Capital City Press, 166 So. 2d 84).

Until the police actually book a suspect the newsman should use great care in describing what happened. The reporter can say that the police "seized" or "picked up" or "held for questioning" or "rounded up" (or even "nabbed" or "netted" if the editor is so lax that he permits such slang). The circumstances are vital in making the determination. If a person with an unblemished reputation is involved, the story should go no further than to say that he is being questioned by the police in connection with the crime. An innocent person can be questioned by the police, perhaps as a possible witness, so such a report is not libelous.

The names of innocent people are often on police records. Some are listed as witnesses. Some are the victims of criminals. Some are involved in automobile accidents. Some are accused of crimes, but later cleared. When the newsman links a person to police records, he should make clear what the relationship is. An article in the January, 1961, issue of *Official Detective Stories* magazine shows the trouble that arises from the telegraphic shorthand "police records." The article dealt with the exploits of Jack Friday and his apprehension by the police. It contained this passage:

> A search of police records yielded the names of several associates, as well as all Friday's relatives who lived in West Texas. These persons were warned to notify police if they received any communication from Friday and their homes were placed under surveillance.

Ten relatives of Friday in West Texas sued, asserting that the passage accused them of criminal involvement with the fugitive. A Federal judge said that they had a good enough case to go to a jury (Friday v. Official Detective Stories, Inc., 233 F. Supp. 1021). The case cost the magazine $3,000 to settle. A simple rephrasing of the passage or deletion of the first sentence would have prevented the legal trouble without any substantial loss in meaning.

Some individuals want to be arrested, and in their cases there is little risk in jumping the gun on the actual booking. Civil-rights demonstrators and political pickets, for example, consider it a mark of distinction to be seized by the police. Often they are picked up just to halt a demonstration that threatens to wind up as a riot. After being held for a while they are released without any charges having been made against them. These people will love the newsman who writes that they were arrested. Instead of attaching a clipping of the story to libel-suit papers, they will carry it around in their wallets to show to friends.

In most states privilege is limited strictly to the arrest and the charge. It does not cover reports of the investigation leading up to the arrest, the discovery made by the police officer during the investigation or his conclusions as to the guilt or innocence of the arrested party. Needless to say, you will rarely hear a policeman admit that he arrested the wrong person or that the one he did pick up was innocent.

The reporter who goes beyond privilege to add collateral details to his story is running a risk. If the additional material is libelous, its presence may destroy the privilege protecting the rest of the report. That puts him back in the position of trying to out-investigate the DA to prove truth or of settling with the injured party.

However, the situation is not as grim as it sounds. For one thing, a number of legislatures have passed laws extending the privilege to official statements issued by heads of police departments, county prosecutors and coroners. New Jersey adopted such a law, and when it was discovered that most of the statements came from the second instead of the first in command, the privilege was extended to assistants. A similar statute in Georgia extends privilege to reports of an arresting officer. In other states, some judges have also interpreted the law to cover statements issued by prosecutors and the police.

On November 14, 1957, a group of hoodlums held a convention in the little town of Apalachin, just outside of Binghamton, New York. Like other conventions, this one was held to let the delegates eat, drink and consult about their common problems. The state police thought they might be interested, too, so they jotted down the license numbers of the Cadillacs and Continentals that pulled up to the estate of Joseph Barbara and then surrounded it. When the boys saw what was happening, they panicked. Some of them jumped out windows and tried to run through the woods to escape. But a fat hoodlum does not get very far in rugged country, particularly when his stomach is loaded down with good food and expensive whiskey. So fifty-eight were soon overtaken and interrogated by the police. The authorities discovered that one of the distinguished members of the assemblage had a pistol permit issued by the New York Police Department. The embarrassed New York City Police Commissioner immediately revoked the permit, but he felt that more drastic measures were indicated. So he started an investigation of all the other persons who had been at this convention to ascertain whether any others had applied for police permits. To show the public he was really making amends, he handed out a press release naming names. Among the thugs at Apalachin was a man by the name of Frank Valenti of Rochester. There was another Frank Valenti in Brooklyn, a well-to-do contractor who had unsuccessfully applied three times for a gun permit. The police thought that the Brooklyn Valenti was one of their pigeons and started investigating him. The press release carried the name Frank Valenti of Rochester, formerly of Brooklyn. The New York *Herald Tribune, The New York Times,* the *World-Telegram and the Sun* and the *Journal-American* ran stories based on the news release, and the Brooklyn contractor sued. The court sustained the contention that newspapers had a right to report the police investigation, even if the cops were checking on the wrong man (*Valenti v. New York Herald Tribune, Inc., New York Law Journal,* January 28, 1959). Unfortunately facts were at issue, and all four papers contributed to a nominal settlement.

A 1959 ruling by the Kansas Supreme Court is even more sweeping. It concerned a banner-headlined story and follow-up articles in the Wichita *Beacon* about the cracking of a burglarly ring. The article quoted police officers as saying that John Stice, a Wichita judge, was the leader of the gang. It contained specific statements to the police by an informer, who reported on a conversation he said he had overheard between the judge and a member of the gang. The judge was said by a detective to have demanded $1,000 "advance fees" from a robbery. Charges had not even been filed against the judge or any of the fifteen alleged members of the ring, but the police said that state burglarly warrants would be sought. The chief of police apparently assumed the case was all wrapped up, because he issued a statement asserting that the detective would be cited.

Judge Stice, who was never formally accused of any part in the burglary ring (he was later disbarred), sued for $1 million in libel damages. When the case reached the Kansas Supreme Court, the justices could have thrown it out on one basis alone: the *Beacon* had a right to carry libelous charges, even of crime, against Judge Stice because he was a public official (this defense is discussed in Chapter 12). The court did cite this defense, but it went further. It held that the article was also privileged:

> It is well settled in this jurisdiction that newspapers have a qualified privilege to publish as current news all matters involving open violations of the law which justify police interference, and matters in connection with inquiries regarding the commission of crime, even though the publication may reflect on the individuals concerned and tend to bring them into public disgrace. . . . [Stice v. Beacon Newspaper Corp., 185 Kan. 61]

Background Information

Newsmen in other jurisdictions would be foolhardy to go so far as to carry stories implicating nonpolitical figures with crime before any charges have been filed. However, once the charges have been made, the newsman can use details that do not go beyond the charge. He can add background material and information that helps make for a well-rounded account of what really happened. He must make sure, however, that he does not go beyond the official charges when he is referring to the suspect so that he does not accuse him of a more serious crime. Nor should he assume the guilt of the suspect, except in rare instances, as when Jack Ruby, the Dallas nightclub operator, shot Lee Harvey Oswald, President Kennedy's assassin, in front of a nationwide television audience.

There should be no hesitation about carrying background information that puts the crime in proper perspective. For example, the Wenatchee (Washington) *Daily World* carried the following item:

Moses Lake—Donald Swartz, 30, Moses Lake, electrician, was arrested at 2:20 A.M. Saturday by Sgt. Kelly Rogers and Officer Dave

Penn of the Moses Lake police on a drunk and disorderly charge.

Sgt. Kelly says investigation of the incident brought about the signing of a complaint by a 62-year-old Moses Lake woman charging Swartz with third degree assault and attempted robbery. Police say there have been four reports in recent weeks of attempted assault and robbery of elderly women in Moses Lake.

In suing for $50,000 in libel damages, Swartz asserted that the second sentence of the second paragraph implied that he had been responsible for previous attempts at assault and robbery. The trial judge told him no, and the Washington State Supreme Court, in a six-to-three decision, upheld dismissal of the suit, saying that no reasonable person could draw that conclusion. The three dissenters thought that the ordinary reader would make that inference and their reasoning provides a clue to the careful writer who wants to add background information without getting into trouble. They noted that the recollection of the previous attempts at assaults and robbery had been part of the same paragraph as the charge against Swartz. Since a paragraph is generally considered a grammatical unit dealing with a particular point, the dissenting judges concluded that a reasonable person might infer that the person named in the first sentence (Swartz) was responsible for the crimes mentioned in the second sentence. If the second sentence had been set apart in a separate paragraph, they said, they would have agreed that the item had not accused Swartz of the earlier crimes (Swartz v. World Publishing Co., 57 Wash. 2d 213). The moral is clear—keep background material in separate grammatical units.

In adding unprivileged details, attribution is essential, even if in some instances specific officials cannot be quoted. In the Kansas case involving Judge Stice and the burglarly ring, the State Supreme Court justices were impressed by the fact that the articles did not contain flat charges by the newspaper but statements always attributed to authorities through such devices as "police say," "detectives said," "named as," "police investigation has revealed," "implicated by police investigation," "detectives disclosed" and "according to the police evidence." The reporter should always hang his details on a public official and name him whenever possible. While courts in less-enlightened jurisdictions might not rule the stories privileged, such phraseology will provide a partial defense and help keep any damages down.

Illegal Arrests

So far the discussion has dealt with legal arrests. What if the arrest is illegal? That, too, is apparently protected by privilege. The newsman should not be required to determine at his peril whether the arresting officer had the jurisdiction or power to make the arrest.

The newsman must discipline himself according to the rules established by the law and the courts. But he still possesses a great deal of freedom within these boundaries. He need not limit himself to courtroom jargon but can dress the story in humor, pathos or irony. In a case noted on page 145 regarding the threat of a municipal water board to shut off the water at the Briarcliff Lodge, the Yonkers (New York) *Statesman and Daily Argus* began its article: "Water, water everywhere, but never a drop to drink." The court held that the newspaper did not lose its privilege of reporting an official proceeding just because of the jesting manner of the article. The court said, in a passage that judges are fond of quoting:

> Facts do not cease to be facts because they are mixed with the fair and expectant comment of the story teller, who adds to the recital a little touch by his piquant pen [Briarcliff Lodge Hotel v. Citizen-Sentinel Publishers, Inc., 260 N.Y. 106].

The account does not have to be full or complete or verbatim. It may paraphrase, condense or summarize, provided it is substantially accurate and impartial. *Time* magazine reported that David R. George's claim for royalties against the Victor Talking Machine Company had been dismissed as "fraudulent." Although the word "fraudulent" had not been used by the court, *Time's* use of it was upheld in a libel suit because "a reading of the entire opinion establishes beyond question that the claim was so characterized" (George v. Time, Inc., 259 App. Div.(N.Y.)324). The New York *Daily News* quoted a judge in a marital case as saying that a Florida divorce was "improper and invalid." Actually the judge had said, "No decree of divorce has ever been obtained by the defendant against the plaintiff in any court of competent jurisdiction." Despite the misquotation this was held to be a fair and true report (Schachter v. News Syndicate, 270 App. Div. (N.Y.) 378).

It Must Be a Report

There are, however, certain requirements that must be observed to benefit by the privilege of reporting an official proceeding.

The first is that the article or broadcast must be a report, and it must be plain to the reader or viewer that it is a report. It should be clear to the reader or viewer that the reporter is merely the transmission belt for conveying information about what went on in an official proceeding. This is a simple requirement to meet. While no flat rule should be laid down, a useful guide is to make clear in the headline, in the lead and occasionally throughout the body of the article that an official proceeding is being reported.

Obviously the proceeding itself will have to be named high in the story—"in a trial in the district court," "at a hearing of the Senate Finance Committee." The good writer will strive to avoid clumsy repetitions after that. He will use such devices as "the witness asked," "the evidence indicated" and even, perhaps, on occasion, the hackneyed but useful "alleged" or "reported." Long libelous narrations can be introduced with a colon construction, to avoid attributions in every sentence ("the Senator gave the following account of the attempt to 'bribe' him: . . .").

While this requirement seems simple, the reporter sometimes forgets it in his hurry to meet his deadline. The Pittsburgh *Courier* carried these paragraphs in a story headlined "Claims Cops Took $1,225":

> According to Miss Roxie A. Henry . . . she saw Detective Sergeant Irving Lubore take $1,225 from her clothes closet. . . .
>
> "I was standing less than five feet from the detective when he took four fifty dollar bills, two ten dollar bills, a five dollar bill and a $1,000 bill that I had hidden in a fur-trimmed boot in my closet," Miss Henry said.

What the *Courier* failed to state was that Miss Henry's statement had been made orally to a United States Attorney and had been reduced to affidavit form. Affidavits by themselves are not privileged unless they are part of a privileged proceeding, and in this case no charge had been filed against the detective. But even if there had been an official proceeding, the court questioned whether the story would have been privileged, because it never reported that Miss Henry had told her story to prosecutors. It just left the reader guessing as to how the statement was made (Pittsburgh Courier Publishing Co., Inc., v. Lubore, 200 F. 2d 355).

It Must Be Fair and True

The second requirement is that the report must be fair and true. As used here, "fair" means a balanced report and "true" means a substantially accurate report of what happened at an official proceeding.

An article in the Uvalde (Texas) *Leader-News,* mentioned briefly on page 15, said:

> Clarence Large, Deputy Sheriff of Uvalde County, reported that a stolen 1959 Cadillac was discovered on the Jack Griffin ranch, five miles northeast of Sabinal, Saturday, October 5.
>
> The car was stolen in Corpus Christi, according to Large. The lawman reported that he and Texas Ranger Levi Duncan were checking the area when they discovered the automobile. They radioed to their headquarters in Uvalde to see if the car had been stolen and received an answer from the Hondo Sheriff who was monitoring the call. It appeared that the car had been stolen and that a warrant for C. H. "Curly" Hunter of Corpus Christi had been issued in connection with the theft.
>
> Hunter and another man, Al Smith, had previously leased the pasture where the car was found. The seven room house on the lease was well stocked, according to Deputy Large, with food, ammunition, a radio and TV set.

Hunter was under indictment for receiving and concealing stolen property and for burglary, but no warrant had been issued for him in connection with the theft of an automobile. Thus the article was not a fair and true report of the judicial proceedings involving Hunter. His suit for libel was upheld by the Texas Court of Civil Appeals (Hornby v. Hunter, 385 S.W. 2d 473). In an out-of-court settlement he was given $3,000. His counsel felt that the settlement was satisfactory because proof of damages in a jury trial would have been difficult in view of the two felony indictments pending against him. Hunter was later convicted of criminal charges and given a two-year suspended sentence. ·The case shows how important accuracy is, even when the subject of the news has a tarnished reputation.

The requirement that a report be fair and true means, in essence, that the account reflect what went on at the proceeding, with both the accused and the accuser given their say. Even if charges in the proceeding are self-contradictory and obviously false they are protected. An article on the 1957 Apalachin crime convention in the Scranton *Times* illustrates the point. Under the headline "Barbecue Gives Four a Bellyache," it contained these words:

> Four Northeastern Pennsylvania residents are identified as having participated in the beef barbecue New York State Police broke up last Nov. 14 at the palatial Apalachin, N.Y., home of former Pittstonian Joe Barbara.
>
> Prior to the so-called hoodlum meeting, the quartet was little known outside of upper Luzerne County. But for some of them, the meeting spelled nothing but trouble.
>
> Russell Bufalino, for instance, was arrested and held for deportation. Following a lengthy hearing, he was ordered deported. The order is being appealed.
>
> A report issued this month by former New York State Investigations Commissioner Arthur L. Reuter identified the four local delegates to the meeting as:
>
> Russell J. Bufalino, 304 Dorrance St., Kingston, owner of the Penn Drape and Curtain Co., 161 South Main St., Pittston.
>
> Dominick Alaimo, 6 Cherry St., Pittston, co-owner and manager of the Jane Hogan Dress Co., Pittston.
>
> James Anthony Osticco, 156½ Elizabeth St., Pittston, transportation manager for Medico Industries, Inc., Pittston.
>
> Angelo Joseph Sciandra, 108 South Main St., Pittston, a garment manufacturer.
>
> All four, according to the Reuter report, have criminal records.
>
> .   .   .   .
>
> The listing on Sciandra is relatively short. He was identified as having been born in Buffalo and arrested in that city on July 12, 1935 on rape charges. The charges were later reduced to third-degree assault and he received a suspended sentence.
>
> His "reputed associates" were listed as including Jack Benfantie, Modesto LoQuasto, Nick Benfantie and Joe Barbara. After each name was the notation in parenthesis, "(union rackets)."

When Sciandra read this article and the others in the Scranton *Times* series he got so angry he called in a lawyer and asked him to do something about it. The result was a libel suit that complained that the article was unfair on a half-dozen counts, including the headline and the use of such terms as "gangland convention," "hoodlum meeting" and "local delegate." He also pointed out that the Reuter report of the Apalachin meeting had listed his birthday as November 26, 1924. Thus he was only eleven years old at the time the report says he was arrested for rape. Since the *Times* had omitted this fact, which would have raised the question of mistaken identity and vindicated him of the rape accusation in the eyes of most readers, Sciandra charged that the paper had forfeited its privilege of reporting an official proceeding. The trial court rejected all these points but it upheld another. This was the *Times'* omission of the report's sections emphasizing that none of the delegates to the crime convention had been wanted by the police anywhere, that they had committed no crime in meeting and that there was no competent proof that "any were presently living as thieves or criminals." This omission, said the court, abused the privilege of reporting, and it sent the case to the jury, which quickly discovered that it was unable to reach a verdict. The court then decided to resubmit the case to a jury, this time with instructions that it decide only how much damages could be paid. This was too risky for the *Times;* it appealed to the Pennsylvania Supreme Court. The high court upheld the *Times* all the way. It said that the Reuter report, having been released by Governor Averell Harriman of New York, was privileged. It upheld use of such phrases as "gangland convention" and "local delegate" and the headline about the "bellyache." It showed no concern over the omission of the material that would have vindicated Sciandra of rape. The failure to print the date of his birth was inadvertent, the court said, and in any event was immaterial. As for the part of the report asserting that no crime had been committed at the meeting, the court said that *another* article in the series had made that point (Sciandra v. Lynett, 409 Pa. 595).

In the Sciandra case the court leaned over backward to help the press. Judges usually are much stricter in their interpretation of a "fair and true report." An example of a court's leaning in just the opposite direction followed the publication of this article in the New York *Daily News* on August 18, 1948:

> That double-dealing husbands are a dime a dozen in any large city is an accepted cinch. But Robert R. Stevenson, $27,000-a-year treasurer of General Foods Corp., does not fool around on so small a scale, his wife, Grace, charged yesterday in Supreme Court, Manhattan. Bob, said Grace, is a triple-dealer.
>
> By this, Mrs. Stevenson explained in a suit for separation, she

means that the 41-year-old vittles tycoon not only has been double-dealing her with a lady in his employ but also is cheating on the co-respondent.

Mrs. Stevenson, who lives in Scarsdale, left little to be imagined as far as identifying the women is concerned. One, she said, is Mrs. Helen Dobson McCormick, a divorcee with a job in General Food's Birdseye Division. The other, the wife contends, is a close pal of Mrs. McCormick, a cute little trick called "Socks" by her intimates.

First let us take the case of Mrs. McCormick. This gal, charged Mrs. Stevenson, was married to a service man, James McCormick, who spent several years away from home on military duty.

"At first," said the trusting wife, "I was under the impression that my husband and I were taking Helen to dinner and other social functions just to be kind to the wife of a service man."

In due time, however, she asserted, Bob took to staying out all manner of hours and "there were many nights when he did not get home at all." Then Helen's marriage went blooie, Grace said.

TRIPLE PLAY CHARGED

Now, enter Socks and the triple-deal aspect of the fascinating case.

"In addition to his activities with Mrs. McCormick," Grace goes on, "my husband has also been overfriendly with a woman I will identify for the present only as 'Socks.' Socks is a friend of Mrs. McCormick, with whom I believe my husband is obviously two-timing—or, more accurately, three-timing—Mrs. McCormick right under her nose. Apparently my husband sees Socks surreptitiously on nights when he tells Mrs. McCormick that he is coming to my home to give some semblance of living together."

Bob, according to his wife, does not appear to be much interested in his marriage since, she says, he has told her to take steps to terminate the contract and has told her: "You may as well line up a new husband."

Grace asks for a decree of separation, $175 a week for herself and $5,000 for her lawyer, Parnell J. T. Callahan, 37 Wall St.

Mr. Stevenson sued the *News*. Ultimately Grace got a divorce. During pretrial proceedings the court ruled against the paper, asserting that it had lost the shield of privilege because:

> The article said that Stevenson's wife made her charge against him "yesterday"—an assertion that was false. The article made no mention of the fact that the charges were made as part of a motion which had theretofore been withdrawn—an omission that was unfair. In short, the article was neither true nor fair. . . . [Stevenson v. News Syndicate Co., Inc., 302 N.Y. 81]

While it was on solid ground in criticizing the fairness of the *News* article, the court was tougher than usual in its definition of "truth." The customary rule is that the words must be substantially accurate. Errors are usually permitted as long as they do not change the substance of the meaning; and the wrong time element, such as "yesterday," would rarely be considered of so serious a nature. If the effect produced by the story is substantially the same as the effect of the facts, the report is considered true. A jury awarded Mr. Stevenson $25,000.

The *News* made out better in another case, where the ruling followed the usual pattern. In this incident the *News* reported that the police had arrested a man on a charge of burglary. It added the erroneous fact that he had been found under the bed in the burglarized apartment. The court ruled that this added detail did not destroy the defense of privilege of reporting, even though it might have been inaccurate, because it did "not add or detract from the sting of the charge of burglary" (Josephs v. News Syndicate Co., Inc. 5 Misc. 2d(N.Y.)184).

Interpretations of clauses in legal papers and synonymns for legal terms must be closely watched for misunderstandings that lead to trouble. A typical example was an item the Cleveland *Call & Post* published on January 10, 1953, about a divorce action involving Mr. and Mrs. Carroll E. Williams. After noting that Mrs. Williams had petitioned for divorce, the article said:

> Williams, in his cross-petition, made the following accusations against his wife:
> 1. Immediately after their marriage she sought to have unnatural sexual relations with him and harassed and nagged him to allow her to commit these unnatural sexual acts. Because of her continual worrying him to submit to such sex perversion which he always refused, he had to seek living quarters away from her.

Williams had never used the words "sex perversion" in his cross-petition in the divorce action, but did allege that his wife sought to have sexual relations "in an unnatural manner, much to the disgust of the defendant." Mrs. Williams won a $2,500 libel verdict, which the Ohio Court of Appeals upheld. The court said that the term "sex perversion" imports a "more abhorrent concept than do the words 'sexual relations in an unnatural manner'" (Williams v. P. W. Publishing Co., 76 Ohio L. Abs. 404).

The Alaska Supreme Court ruled in 1964 that the use of the term "in cahoots" was an accurate description of a fire chief's report of the relationship between a fireman and some firemen who had been discharged. It also upheld the word "sabotage" as a description of intentional abuse of a fire truck. But it said that a jury should decide if the words "permanently fired" meant what the fire chief said—an indefinite suspension (Fairbanks Publishing Co. v. Francisco, 390 P. 2d 784).

The term "legal technicality" as a description of a lawyer's move for a sanity examination for his client has been upheld by the Arkansas Supreme Court. On March 5, 1959, the Warren *Eagle Democrat* carried this story:

> Through a legal technicality, Judge G. B. Colvin, Jr., Tuesday was forced to send A. C. Duncan, admitted culprit in an attempted rape case here, to the State Hospital for 30 days observation.
>
> Duncan's hearing before Judge Colvin was held Tuesday evening, and Paul K. Roberts, Warren attorney, was appointed as the Negro's lawyer.
>
> When Duncan was asked to make a plea of guilty or not guilty, Attorney Roberts arose and made a motion that he be sent to the State Hospital for observation. Roberts said he thought the Negro might be insane.
>
> Prosecuting Attorney A. James Linder of Hamburg asked Roberts if he really thought that or if he was "grasping for straws." Roberts assured the Court that he felt the Negro might be insane.
>
> Judge Colvin deliberated about the matter for several minutes before granting Roberts' motion, but he told those present that under the law, he was forced to do it. . . .

Roberts sued for libel, asserting that the statement "through a legal technicality" had been designed to leave the impression that he acted improperly and had prevailed through trickery. He argued that a thirty-day observation period is a substantive right of any person accused of a crime and is not a legal technicality. In rejecting the suit, the state Supreme Court said that the public would understand "legal technicality" to mean that the question had been decided on grounds other than the merits of the case. One of the points in the story that convinced the court that the paper had been fair in reporting the proceeding was that it carried Roberts' assurance that he felt that the Negro might have been insane (Roberts v. Love, 231 Ark. 886).

The courts are more lenient than the stern-faced judges sometimes give the impression they are. Even when the reporter takes liberties with quotations, the courts have ruled them to be truthful as long as they did not distort the meaning.

On November 3, 1953, the *Arizona Republic* ran an article on a forum held the previous night by the Phoenix Junior Chamber of Commerce on the local political campaign. The article contained these paragraphs:

> Opposing candidates in the forthcoming city election collided head-on last night over the issue of prostitution and gambling.
>
> Charter Government candidates, seeking to retain the present city administration in office, declared they feared relaxation of present controls on vice within the city if members of the Economy Ticket gained power Nov. 10.
>
> K. S. Brown of the Economy ticket heatedly denied any such danger exists and demanded an apology from Adam Diaz. He failed to get one.
>
> .   .   .   .
>
> Diaz set off the fireworks when he said, "I've heard that Economy Ticket candidates have promised the city will be opened up to prostitutes and gambling if they were elected. If such a thing happens I fear for my children."
>
> Brown, fighting mad, demanded an apology and asserted: "I am for a decent clean city. I would never stand for prostitution or anything of the type if elected."

At the trial uncontradicted testimony showed that Diaz had not mentioned prostitution. What he had said was:

> There are rumors that some of the opposition and their supporters have made promises that if they are elected the town will be opened up. I have four children, including three wonderful daughters, and I certainly hope they will be able to grow up in the clean, wholesome community we now enjoy. I fear for my children and for the children of all other Phoenix residents if there is a return to the type of government we had before 1950.

Members of the Economy Ticket sued for libel and won a judgment of $154,000. The Arizona Supreme Court rescued the newspaper, however, by ruling the article a privileged report of a public proceeding. As for the misquotation, the court held that despite it the article conveyed the true meaning of what listeners thought Diaz meant. The court said that the statement that a city will be "opened up" immediately suggests to the mind of the ordinary person that "prostitution and gambling will exist without restraint," because they are the major vices of urban communities. As evidence of this interpretation the court noted that one of the plaintiffs, Brown, had so construed the Diaz statement because he had immediately replied that he would never "stand for prostitution or anything of the type" if elected (Phoenix Newspapers v. Choisser, 82 Ariz. 271).

The fairness of the article is usually dependent on whether it gives a fair picture of the entire situation. If the article is accurate but gives a distorted picture of the proceeding, privilege is lost. A good example of a true but unfair article was contained in the December 20, 1957, edition of the San Antonio (Texas) *Sunday Express and News* under the headline "Sisters Win Oil Land Suit." It said:

> Ninety-nine-year-old twin sisters, perhaps the oldest twins in the United States, Saturday had won their suit for 13 acres of oil-rich land in Starr County.
> The sisters, Inez Garcia Ruiz, and Aniceta Garcia Barrera, had alleged that the land was fraudulently taken from them by a nephew, Benigno Barrera, and Enrique G. Gonzalez, both of Starr County.
> The women said they signed a deed to the land when Barrera represented it as a document permitting him to erect a corral fence there. The sisters cannot read or write Spanish or English.
> Judge C. K. Quinn in 45th District Court last year returned the sisters the land, which had been in their family since a Spanish grant.
> Saturday it was announced the appeals court had ruled against Barrera and Gonzalez.
> The sisters' address was listed as 2605 Guadalupe Street, San Antonio.

What the story did not say was that the two sisters, while originally accusing both Barrera and Gonzalez, had dropped their charge against the latter. Gonzalez sued for libel. In its defense the *Express* insisted that its article was a fair and true report. Although the charges against Gonzalez had been dismissed, the *Express* pointed out, he had rejoined the suit by signing Barrera's appeal bond. But the Texas Court of Civil Appeals disagreed. It said that the implication of the report was that the District court had sustained the fraud charge against Gonzalez and the statement that the appeals court had ruled against Barrera and Gonzalez reinforced that false impression. It said:

> . . . it is not a defense to show that a statement contained in a publication, if taken alone, is literally true, when other facts are omitted which plainly refute the false impression of the partial statement. [Express Publishing Co. v. Gonzalez, 350 S.W. 2d 589]

Gonzalez was awarded $12,500 in damages.

Many misinterpretations and mistakes in covering official proceedings could be avoided if reporters would follow a simple rule that every cub knows: get the other side of the story. After a number of years on a beat some reporters get lazy. The court reporter and the legislative correspondent know that their stories are shielded by privilege and they learn to stay within its confines. But they forget that they can misinterpret and misunderstand. A simple phone call to the lawyer or party on the other side of the case will often correct inaccuracies and thus make the story substantially true.

The Campbell litigation discussed earlier in this chapter demonstrates how valuable such checking can be. This was the suit by a Christian Science practitioner against New York papers for carrying charges of fraud against her before there had been judicial action. The papers fell back on the privilege of reporting a judicial proceeding, but only one could sustain it. The others ran into trouble. The reason was that Mrs. Campbell had presented a legal answer to the fraud charge against her, but her answer had been misfiled by the court and none of the reporters knew it existed. In the eyes of the law, however, the answer was part of the judicial proceeding and a fair story of the case would have had to include it. *The New York Times'* reporter did not stop with the examination of the complaint against Mrs. Campbell. He telephoned her and asked if she wanted to comment. This was an invitation that she could not resist, and she became very articulate. She denied the allegations and made a substantial statement for publication. This gave the *Times* and the *Sun*, which copied the *Times'* account, the material they would have had if Mrs. Campbell's answer had been in its proper place in the court files. As a result there was a verdict for both papers. The material also provided an additional defense—of her consent to publish the libel—that will be discussed in Chapter 14.

An editor can avoid a lot of heartaches if he insists that reporters seek out the other side of the story, especially at the commencement of legal actions, at ex-parte hearings or at other one-sided proceedings. Such checks often unearth more facts that make for a better story, and they can also provide the balance that keeps the article objective.

While the beginning of a legal proceeding is the period of greatest risk for the reporter, there are times during trials when difficulties arise. One day all of the testimony may be for the prosecution and the next day for the defense. It is permissible at such times for the report to be as one-sided as the proceedings. But care should be taken not to omit anything that would tell in favor of the accused or against anyone else who had been subject to a defamatory charge. Moreover, the newspaper that prints the prosecutor's case extensively on the day it dominates the trial is obligated to print the defense's side fully when it is offered.

Bits of color, like descriptions of the defendant's nervous drumming of his fingers, a witness' anger, the rise in a lawyer's voice, can be used as long as the effect is not to show guilt or impeach the credibility of testimony. Such material can cause trouble, however, as shown by an item in the Plainfield (New Jersey) *Courier-News*. It told how a "skeptical" judge had awarded a fifty-four-year-old carpenter named Walter H. Bock only $500 of the $3,000 he had asked for injuries suffered in a bicycle accident. The article included this description of the trial:

> . . . Judge Chiaravalli proceeded to question the severity of the back injury which Bock claimed prevented him from bending properly. "Show me what you mean," Judge Chiaravalli said. Bock got off the witness stand and squatted twice, each time coming to a standing position slowly.
>
> "Now demonstrate how you bent down before the accident," Judge Chiaravalli said. Bock squatted and came to standing position quickly. He repeated the exercise again at the request of Judge Chiaravalli, but this time Bock's attorney, Robert M. Read of Plainfield objected somewhat strenuously. . . . "I can readily see why you are objecting," Judge Chiaravalli commented.
>
> In paring the petition for a $3,000 judgment to $500 Judge Chiaravalli said the award was made mainly for a chest injury also suffered by Bock in the accident.

Bock's suit for libel protested that the article had attempted to "make a fool out of me." He insisted that he had never squatted and had returned to a standing position at exactly the same speed each time. The New Jersey Superior Court decided that he had enough of a case to be sent to a jury (Bock v. Plainfield Courier-News, 45 N.J. Super. 302). At the trial Judge Chiaravalli testified that the article was an accurate account of the occurrences in his court. The jury upheld the paper in a ten-to-two vote.

The privilege of reporting an official proceeding is invaluable to the crusading newspaper or broadcasting station. Skillful use of material from various governmental reports protected by this privilege can be interwoven with nonlibelous matter from other sources to produce an effective exposé. Wallace Turner of *The New York Times* did this in a series of articles and a book, *Gambler's Money,* which showed that money from the winnings of casinos in Las Vegas was tainting legitimate business enterprises in the country. He used material from the Senate investigation of racketeering, court trials, the Securities and Exchange Commission and the Nevada Gaming Commission. The relation of such well-known public figures as Frank Sinatra, Roy Cohn and Jimmy Hoffa to the gambling czars was discussed and the $5-million Guterma stockmarket swindle detailed.

Exposés must be handled with extreme caution or the privilege will be lost. The writer should be able to point out the places in the official proceeding where he obtained his information, and these citations must support his story. He must be careful to avoid false interpretations, judgments and insertion of indefensible libelous facts.

The New York *Daily News* suffered its greatest loss in a libel suit as the result of a story in its February 26, 1957, editions that began:

TAG 5 PROJECT MGRS. AS RED

By Joseph Martin, Dominck Peluso and Sydney Mirkin
(Eighth of a series of articles)

The headquarters employes of the New York Housing Authority who have already been tabbed as Reds are not the only Communists in the authority—not by a long way.

At least five project managers also have been identified as Communists by witnesses testifying before the staff of Commissioner of

Investigation Charles Tenney. The names of these persons are known to The News, but Tenney has asked that they be withheld. But there are some details available. One manager once was arrested as a participant in a Communist riot. One manager is the wife of a man currently under investigation by federal authorities.

The information on these people is so detailed that it is known that one woman manager fought in the inner councils of the Communist Party to avoid a transfer from one cell to another.

This woman belonged to a neighborhood Red cell and didn't want to be assigned instead to the cell within the Housing Authority. She claimed her neighborhood work was more important. She won—but one result is that she has been unpopular even with her comrades in the authority.

There is strong evidence that Reds and fellow travelers began their determined assault on the Housing Authority years ago—soon after the agency was born.

An interesting record on this subject was built up more than 15 years ago by an official City Council investigation into the activities of the Civil Service Commission and the man who was then its president, Paul J. Kern.

The Council resolution setting up the inquiry directed that the probers look specifically into attempts to set up "an alien espionage system" in the city government.

The investigation, which lasted more than a year, built up an impressive record of left-wing affiliation by Kern and revealed that he ran the Civil Service Commission as a one-man show. And much of his operation was aimed specifically at the New York Housing Authority.

Tenney did not issue a report until nearly eight months later. On November 12, 1957, the *News* ran a story saying that Tenney had reported that 150 Housing Authority aides were under investigation on suspicion of Communist membership or subversive activity. The story said that the Tenney report "supports disclosures in a series in the *News* earlier this year that the city's two-billion dollar taxpayer-supported housing empire had been infiltrated by a solidly entrenched Communist clique."

Kern sued the *News* for libel. At the trial the *News* asserted that the lead portion of the article, dealing with the five project managers tagged as Communists, had been obtained as a result of the paper's own investigation and confirmed by Tenney in an interview. The paper could not rely on the Tenney report as a defense because it had not been issued until eight months after the story appeared. The second portion of the article, dealing with Kern, came from the 1942 investigation, known as the Ellis report, the *News* stated.

The writer will quickly learn the hazards of succumbing to the temptation of leaving the protection of the privilege of reporting an official proceeding if he puts himself in the shoes of Dominick R. Peluso, one of the *News'* reporters, as he was cross-examined. The plaintiff, Kern, a lawyer, conducted the cross-examination himself. Kern first took up the lead:

> Q. Turning to Exhibit 6, the main document underlying the claim of libel as published February 26, 1957, says "Tag 5 Project Mgrs. as Red." What project managers did you have in mind?
> A. If you will consult the Tenney Report, you will see that they had five project managers listed and these are those to which we were referring.
> Q. Then the five project managers you tagged as Red there, were the names known to you at this time?
> A. Yes.

So far so good for the reporter. But Kern asked Peluso to point out the places in the Tenney report where five project managers had been identified as Communists. Peluso did not do so. Then Kern gave Peluso the roster cards of all those who had held the job of project manager at the time the February article was written and asked him to check the names overnight. The next day Peluso was again on the stand:

> Q. Did you find the five people?
> A. I examined more than one hundred or approximately one hundred roster cards last night and I find that they do not refresh my recollection.
> Q. Then we can say that if these are the roster cards, as testified, of the persons occupying the position of project manager or any position which might be included under that general headline, as of February 26, 1957, then there were no five project managers as of that date who were tagged as Red; is that right?
> A. I don't know that, Mr. Kern.
> Q. You don't know that. I make another question out of it. You examined these cards and you did not find the five project managers tagged as Red?
> A. That is not what I said, Mr. Kern.

Q. What did you say?

A. I said those cards do not refresh my recollection. It could be that they may be among them.

Q. Did you find any cards here of a person appointed during the Commissionership of Kern who was terminated in 1957 or early 1958 for Communist activity or for any purpose?

A. I believe I have stated, Mr. Kern, that those cards do not refresh my recollection, so I cannot answer your question.

Q. You are not able to give us the names of the five persons tagged as Red to whom you referred over Kern's picture in the February 26th article that you wrote; is that correct?

A. That is correct, Mr. Kern.

Kern asked Peluso to show him the sections of the Ellis report on which he had based the paragraphs saying that "there is strong evidence that Reds and fellow travelers began their determined assault on the Housing Authority years ago—soon after the agency was born" and "an interesting record on this subject was built up more than 15 years ago" by an investigation into the Kern-led Civil Service Commission. Peluso cited:

1. A letter from the Commissioner of the New York Housing Authority to Kern noting that "numerous people" had expressed suspicion that civil service had been used as "a clever agency for other purposes than employment."

2. A reference in a resolution setting up the investigation to "Mr. Kern and his alleged un-American acts and viewpoints evidenced by attempts to establish 'alien espionage system.'"

3. A letter from Robert Moses as head of the Park Department upbraiding Kern for attempting "to establish a spying system within City Departments" and suggesting that he "send this communication to OGPU in Russia whose American representative you seem to be."

The jury obviously believed that the article had not been a fair report of an official proceeding, because it returned a verdict giving Kern $1,000 in compensatory damages and $200,000 in punitive damages. On appeal the court agreed that the *News* had been reckless, but cut the award to $51,000 (Kern v. News Syndicate Co., 20 A.D. 2d (N.Y.) 528). In a related suit the Chase Manhattan Bank, which had sent a clipping of the article to a railroad, paid Kern $15,000 in an out-of-court settlement.

Chapter 12

THE NEW YORK TIMES RULE—
THE EXPANDING DEFENSE

ON MARCH 29, 1960, *The New York Times* PUBLISHED THE KIND OF advertisement newspaper business departments love. It was a full-page appeal for funds by the Committee to Defend Martin Luther King and the Struggle for Freedom in the South—one of those groups with astonishing titles that spring up constantly to take sides in social and political disputes. For the *Times* the $4,800 it charged for the space represented almost pure gravy because of the low production costs of this type of all-word advertisement. Two years later, as a result of libel suits, that advertisement looked as if it might cost the *Times* $3 million in damages. But on March 9, 1964, despair turned into joy when the United States Supreme Court issued a ruling that not only removed all danger of libel damages as a result of the ad but also erected new safeguards for freedom of expression. The rule extends to all, the individual as well as the journalist, the privilege of uttering or printing in good faith defamatory falsehoods about a public official as long as a few simple rules are met.

Five libel suits were filed on the basis of the advertisement. Governor John Patterson of Alabama asked $1 million in damages, while four officials in Montgomery asked $500,000 each. One of the first cases to be tried was that of L. B. Sullivan, Commissioner of Public Affairs for Montgomery. The advertisement, titled "Heed Their Rising Voices," contained these paragraphs:

As the whole world knows by now, thousands of Southern Negro students are engaged in widespread non-violent demonstrations in positive affirmation of the right to live in human dignity as guaranteed by the U. S. Constitution and the Bill of Rights. In their efforts to uphold these guarantees, they are being met by an unprecedented wave of terror by those who would deny and negate that document which the whole world looks upon as setting the pattern for modern freedom. . . .

> .   .   .   .

In Montgomery, Alabama, after students sang "My Country 'Tis of Thee" on the State Capitol steps, their leaders were expelled from school, and truckloads of police armed with shotguns and tear-gas ringed the Alabama State College Campus. When the entire student body protested to state authorities by refusing to re-register, their dining hall was padlocked in an attempt to starve them into submission.

.   .   .   .

Again and again the Southern violators have answered Dr. King's peaceful protests with intimidation and violence. They have bombed his home, almost killing his wife and child. They have assaulted his person. They have arrested him seven times—for "speeding," "loitering," and similar "offenses." And now they have charged him with "perjury"—a felony under which they would imprison him for ten years. . . .

Although he was not mentioned by name in the advertisement Commissioner Sullivan contended that the word "police," in the paragraph on Montgomery referred to him and everyone knew it did because the public knew that he was in charge of the police. Thus he said he was being accused of "ringing" the campus with his men and of padlocking the dining hall to starve the students into submission. Furthermore, he contended that since arrests are ordinarily made by the police, the "they" in "They have arrested" Dr. King would be read as referring to him. The reader, he said, would also identify him as among the "Southern violators" who committed the other acts mentioned in the same paragraph.

The *Times* could not deny that some of the statements were inaccurate. Although students staged a demonstration on the State Capitol steps, they sang the National Anthem, not "My Country 'Tis of Thee." Nine students were expelled by the State Board of Education, not for leading a demonstration at the Capitol but for demanding service at a lunch counter in the Montgomery County courthouse on another day. Most, but not all, of the student body had protested the expulsion—not by refusing to re-register but by boycotting classes on a single day; virtually all the students had reregistered. The campus dining hall was not padlocked on any occasion, and the only students barred from eating there were the few who had neither signed a preregistration application nor requested temporary meal tickets. Although the police were deployed near the campus in large numbers on three occasions, they did not at any time "ring" the campus and they had not been called to the campus in connection with the demonstration on the State Capitol steps, as the ad implied In addition, Dr. King had been arrested four, not seven, times. There was conflicting evidence whether Dr. King had been assaulted.

At the trial Sullivan made a number of effective points to prove malice. He showed that the *Times* had in its newsroom files, only one floor above the advertising department, clips of previously published articles demonstrating the falsity of the ad, but nobody had checked the ad against the clips. He cited the fact that the *Times* had not published a retraction when he had requested one, but had done so for Governor Patterson. And he said that the newspaper had proved its malice right in court by insisting that, apart from the statement that the dining hall was padlocked, the ad was "substantially correct."

The jury awarded Commissioner Sullivan every dollar he asked, 500,000 of them, a stiff price for the *Times* to pay for the 394 copies of the issue that went to Alabama. The *Times* appealed, but the Alabama Supreme Court upheld the judgment. Then the *Times* went to the United States Supreme Court and won a reversal. In its decision, which for the first time found libelous utterance protected under the First Amendment, the court said:

> The constitutional guarantees require, we think, a Federal rule that prohibits a public official from recovering damages for a defamatory falsehood relating to his official conduct unless he proves that the statement was made with "actual malice"—that is, with knowledge that it was false or with reckless disregard of whether it was false or not. [The New York Times Co. v. Sullivan, 376 U.S. 254]

In other words, the Supreme Court ruled that the Constitution permits anyone—Ku Klux Klansmen and American Nazis, John Birchers and Communists, Old Guard Republicans and liberal Democrats—to make or report libelous statements about a public officer's conduct. For the newspaperman, the magazine writer, the book publisher and the television commentator, the rule offers vast possibilities. The court set only two conditions as necessary to invoke the privilege: the libel must concern the official's public, not his solely private, conduct, and the remarks must not be a knowing lie or reckless disregard of the truth.

No other legal defense is necessary. The newsman can write or broadcast the libels on his own or attribute them to other sources. He need not prove the truth of the charges nor show that they were part of official proceedings or invoke any other defense.

Most important of all, the protection covers false facts as well as opinions, from simple accusations of mistakes in ordering paper clips to fraud, corruption and treason.

There is no question that the rule covers accusations of major crimes as well as less important actions. In a 1921 California case mentioned favorably by the Supreme Court, the Los Angeles *Record* was charged with libel by the city's police chief, C. E. Snively. A *Record* cartoon depicted Chief Snively holding a halo over his head with one hand and extending his other behind him, to take some money from the end of a stick. The California Supreme Court ruled that the cartoon was libelous because it obviously accused him of accepting bribes or being ready to do so. But the court held that the *Record* enjoyed a privilege of publishing such libels (Snively v. Record, 185 Cal. 565).

What the Supreme Court did in the *Times* case was to amplify and extend to the press in the entire country a protection that existed in only sixteen states. Known as the Kansas rule, it had stemmed from the classic exposition of the principle by the Kansas Supreme Court in 1908 in a suit brought by state Attorney General C. C. Coleman against the publisher of the Topeka *State-Journal*. Coleman said that he had been libeled by an article regarding a school-fund transaction. In upholding the *State-Journal*'s privilege of publishing false statements of facts about a public official the Kansas Supreme Court noted that there was a popular demand that the press expose "actual and suspected fraud, graft, greed, malfeasance and corruption in public affairs." It said that its decision should encourage the press to fulfill its duty and noted:

> . . . it is of the utmost consequence that the people should discuss the character and qualifications of candidates for their suffrages. The importance to the state and to society of such discussions is so vast, and the advantages derived are so great, that they more than counterbalance the inconvenience of private persons whose conduct

may be involved, and occasional injury to the reputations of individuals must yield to the public welfare, although at times such injury may be great. The public benefit from publicity is so great, and the chance of injury to private character so small, that such discussion must be privileged. [Coleman v. MacLennan, 78 Kan. 711]

The ultilitarian value of freedom to speak out against public officials without fear of libel damages was shown in a North Carolina case decided before the New York Times rule was laid down. On November 11, 1959, William E. Cobb, the chairman of the North Carolina Republican Executive Committee, issued a statement asserting that two statewide bond issues had been defeated by "fraud" in counting the vote in Madison County in a referendum October 27. He singled out the Marshall Precinct as a special offender. Newspapers throughout the state carried the charge. On May 6, 1960, Cobb repeated his charge of "ballot stuffing" and noted that in the Marshall Precinct 905 votes had been tallied against one issue and only 30 for it.

The three election officials in the Marshall Precinct sued Cobb for libel. One of them was Zeno H. Ponder, a powerful Democratic figure in the area. The jury returned a verdict for the plaintiffs, including $40,000 for Ponder, but the North Carolina Supreme Court ordered a new trial, quoting the Kansas Coleman case with approval (Ponder v. Cobb, 257 N.C. 281). No new trial has been held. The Ponder machine was smashed in 1964 and a solid slate of Republican candidates elected.

Eight months after the Supreme Court issued its decision in *The New York Times* case it applied the same rule to criminal libel. District Attorney Jim Garrison of Orleans Parish, Louisiana, had held a press conference in which he attributed a large backlog of criminal cases to the inefficiency, laziness and excessive vacations of the eight criminal-court judges. By refusing to authorize funds to pay for undercover investigations of vice in New Orleans, Garrison said, the judges had hampered his drive to stamp out crime. In impugning their motive he said, "The judges have now made it eloquently clear where their sympathies lie in regard to aggressive vice investigations by refusing to authorize use of the D.A.'s funds to pay for the cost of closing down the Canal Street clip joints."

Garrison was tried by a judge of another parish and convicted of criminal libel. The Louisiana Supreme Court upheld the verdict. In throwing out the conviction the United States Supreme Court said:

> At the outset, we must decide whether, in view of the differing history and purposes of criminal libel, the New York Times rule also limits state power to impose criminal sanctions for criticism of the official conduct of public officials. We hold that it does. [Garrison v. Louisiana, 379 U.S. 64]

The Garrison decision thus blocks a back-door method of circumventing the New York Times rule. It makes it impossible for public officials to use the power of the state to throw people in jail to stifle criticism that is not only permitted but also encouraged under the civil law.

Momentous as the new rule was, the Supreme Court was not declaring open season on all public figures. It had held that public men were public property, but it had not defined who was a public man and just how much of him was public property. Since then the courts have expanded the rule to embrace most prominent figures, but there are still unanswered questions. A similar situation exists regarding loss of the privilege. The court said that actual malice would destroy the privilege. It defined "actual malice" as knowledge that the libelous statement was false or reckless disregard of whether it was false or not. But these are only guidelines. They have to be applied to specific facts in individual cases. Malice is discussed at length in Chapter 16, but again only the deliberate tread of the courts will mark the way with precision.

Candidates, Too

Some signs of just how far the court's decision extends are clear. Misstatements of facts are certainly permitted about officials of all three branches of government—executive, legislative and judicial—and on all three levels—national, state and local. All elected officials are covered, from the President on down. The court also cited with favor state court rulings involving candidates for public office, and, in view of the underlying rationale of the ruling, there is little doubt that they are covered. In a case decided after *The New York Times* decision, Judge Henry J. Friendly, of the United States Court of Appeals for the Second Circuit, explained the inevitability of such an extension:

> Although the public official is the strongest case for the constitutional compulsion of such a privilege, it is questionable whether in principle the decision can be so limited. A candidate for public office would seem an inevitable candidate for extension; if a newspaper cannot constitutionally be held for defamation when it states without malice, but cannot prove, that an incumbent seeking reelection has accepted a bribe, it seems hard to justify holding it liable for further stating that the bribe was offered by his opponent. [Pauling v. News Syndicate Co., 335 F. 2d 659]

The Supreme Court did not limit its ruling to officials selected by the voters; it used the word "public official." Obviously, then, some appointed officials are covered by the ruling. How far down the line does this privilege go?

In writing the opinion of the court in *The New York Times* case, Justice William J. Brennan, Jr., noted this problem but backed away from designating who would and who would not be covered. "We have no occasion here to determine how far down into the lower ranks of government employees the 'public official' designation would extend for purposes of this rule, or otherwise to specify categories of persons who would or would not be included," he wrote. But he did provide a clue by suggesting that the reader look up the court's ruling in *Barr v. Matteo*. In that 1959 case the court had held that a high Federal official had an absolute privilege to issue a defamatory press release about Federal employees (Barr v. Matteo, 360 U.S. 564). States confer similar immunity on their highest officers, and qualified privilege on lesser officials. The philosophy behind this grant of power is that public officials must be free from the threat of damage suits if they are going to be fearless administrators. Citing this rationale, Justice Brennan found in *The New York Times* case that "analogous considerations support the privilege for the citizen-critic of government." "It is as much his duty to criticize as it is the official's duty to administer," he said.

The Justice's phraseology led to the inference that any appointed official who enjoyed immunity from damages for his criticism would be fair game for others. But in a footnote to an opinion two years later Justice Brennan rejected any suggestion that the court was tying the Times rule to the rule of official privilege. In this 1966 opinion the Justice did, however, throw additional light on who was and who was not a public official within the meaning of the New York Times rule. The case involved a $31,500 verdict against the Laconia, New Hampshire, *Evening Citizen*. Alfred D. Rosenblatt, an unpaid columnist for the paper, had written the following in January, 1960, about a county ski area:

> Been doing a little listening and checking at Belknap Recreation Area and am thunderstruck by what am learning.
> This year, a year without snow till very late, a year with actually few very major changes in procedure; difference in cash income simply fantastic, almost unbelievable.
> On any sort of comparative basis, the Area this year is doing literally hundreds of per cent BETTER than last year.
> When consider that last year was excellent snow year, that season started because of more snow, months earlier last year, one can only ponder the following question:
> What happened to all the money last year? and every other year? What magic has [been] wrought to make such tremendous difference in net cash results?

Frank P. Baer, former supervisor of the Belknap Recreation Area, sued for libel. While he had not been named in the column, he contended that it meant that he had been guilty of peculation. The jury's award was upheld by the New Hampshire Supreme Court. In the opinion overturning the verdict, Justice Brennan emphasized that criticism of government is at the core of the constitutionally protected area of free discussion, and added:

> It is clear, therefore, that the "public official" designation applies at the very least to those among the hierarchy of government employees who have, or appear to the public to have, substantial responsibility for or control over the conduct of governmental affairs.
> . . . Where a position in government has such apparent importance that the public has an independent interest in the qualifications and performance of the person who holds it, beyond the general public interest in the qualifications and performance of all government employees . . . the New York Times . . . standards apply. [Rosenblatt v. Baer 383 U.S. 75]

Thus the importance of the official's role is vital in determining whether the Times rule governs. If this were the sole test, then the lowly unskilled worker somehow caught in the news could easily be libeled. Justice Brennan made clear in a footnote that such a test was not sufficient. He said:

> It is suggested that this test might apply to a night watchman accused of stealing state secrets. But a conclusion that the New York Times malice standards apply could not be reached merely because a statement defamatory of some person in government employ catches the public's interest; that conclusion would virtually disregard society's interest in protecting reputation. The employee's position must be one which would invite public scrutiny and discussion of the person holding it, entirely apart from the scrutiny and discussion occasioned by the particular charges in controversy.

In the Baer decision the Supreme Court pointed out the dilemma a plaintiff faces. Referring to Mr. Baer's insistence that the article referred to him, although it did not name him, the court said:

> His theory was that his role in the management of the Area was so prominent and important that the public regarded him as the man responsible for its operations, chargeable with its failures and to be credited with its successes. Thus, to prove the article referred to him, he showed the importance of his role; the same showing, at the least, raises a substantial argument that he was a "public official."

The plaintiff must make a choice—either he is not important (and therefore not eligible for large damages) or he is important (and therefore subject to the vast limitations on verdicts imposed by the New York Times rule).

Ex-Officials

Rosenblatt v. Baer did make certain one point about the New York Times rule—its protection extends to libels of some former officials, as well as to those still holding their posts. Baer had left his post as supervisor of the ski area, but Justice Brennan said that this had no significance in the case because "management of the area was still a matter of lively public interest." Nevertheless, the opinion emphasized that not all former officials could be covered by the rule. "There may be cases where a person is so far removed from a former position of authority that comment on the manner in which he performed his responsibilities no longer has the interest to justify the New York Times rule," the opinion said.

Federal Officials

From Justice Brennan's opinions it is clear that any Federal official whose appointment must be approved by the Senate is certainly subject to criticism under the New York Times rule. Because each must be confirmed on a separate vote, the argument can certainly be made that the public has "an independent interest" in his qualifications. But the public's interest extends much deeper, to Presidential advisers, sub-Cabinet posts, heads of bureaus and agencies and other positions where Senate confirmation is not required. Certainly all such officials "have, or appear to the public to have, substantial responsibility for or control over the conduct of governmental affairs." Below this level the situation is less certain.

Until the courts clear up this cloudy area the newsman must play each case by ear, judging it on the basis of the importance of the official's responsibilities. If the official has important policy-making functions it would seem to be safe to carry libelous remarks about him without much worry. For those who merely carry out orders and make no policy, the newsman should be more wary of defamatory charges, and look for additional defenses.

State Officials

The Supreme Court has made it plain that state definitions of "public officials" do not determine who falls within the New York Times rule. In *Rosenblatt v. Baer,* the court said that the states had developed definitions of "public official" for local administrative purposes, not to determine the extent of the national constitutional protection. Constitutional limits on free expression cannot vary with state lines, the court said.

Undoubtedly, however, the privilege covers statements about all elected officials and appointed officers, like members of the Governor's Cabinet. As for others, until the courts draw firm boundary lines (if they ever do), the newsman would be wise to follow the same practice as that recommended for Federal employees. If the official is a policy maker, the newsman should feel free to carry libelous material about him; if he is only a spear carrier, another defense must be found. Following this guide, it would be safe to carry honest libelous remarks about members of quasi-judicial state agencies, such as public-utility commissions, investigating commissions, unemployment and disability-compensation review boards and labor-relations boards. The principal officers of such agencies —like the chief counsel—would also seem to be safe targets. But below this level there is a great deal more doubt, and in such cases it would be wise to bank on another defense for publishing libelous matter.

Local Officials

Local officials falling within this rule would include, in addition to all elected officeholders, such major appointees as city manager, school superintendents, chiefs of police and fire departments and the heads of any municipally owned enterprises, like waterworks and power companies.

The Supreme Court has already held that the rule in *The New York Times* case covers chiefs of police and county prosecutors. In a decision March 29, 1965, it reversed $40,000 in libel judgments against Aaron Henry, a Mississippi Negro civil-rights leader. Henry had accused Benford C. Collins, chief of police of Clarksdale, Mississippi, and Thomas H. Pearson, Coahoma County prosecutor, of joining in a "diabolical plot" against him. He made the accusation in connection with his arrest amid charges that he had made unnatural advances to a white hitchhiker he had picked up. A jury awarded Collins $15,000 and Pearson $25,000. In reversing the judgments the Supreme Court quoted from the *Times* decision (Henry v. Collins, 380 U.S. 356).

Police officers in almost every case where the problem has been presented have been held to be public officials within the *Times* doctrine. In this category, the courts have included a deputy chief of detectives (Time, Inc. v. Pape, 401 U.S. 279); a police captain (Thuma v. Hearst Corporation, 340 F. Supp. 867); a police lieutenant (Gilligan v. King, 29 A.D. 2d (N.Y.) 935; and, finally, an ordinary patrolman (Coursey v. Greater Niles Township Publishing Corp., 239 N.E. 2d 837, 40 Ill. 2d 257; Moriarty v. Lippe, 294 A. 2d 326, 162 Con. 371).

The court in the Moriarty case explained:

> The plaintiff here has, or appears to the public to have, substantial responsibility for or control over the conduct of government affairs, at least where law enforcement and police functions are concerned, sufficient to be a public official. Although a comparably low ranking government official, a patrolman's office, if abused, has great potential for social harm and thus invites independent interest in the qualifications and performance of the person who holds the position.

Other minor city officials have been held to fall within the ambit of the *Times* ruling, such as an assistant district attorney (Schneph v. New York Post Corp., 23 A.D. 2d (N.Y.) 822 aff'd. 16 N.Y. 2d 1011); a public school principal (Kapiloff v. Duna, 27 Md. App. 514); and the clerk of the Criminal and Circuit Courts of Raleigh County, W. Va. (Beckley Newspaper Corp. v. Hanks, 389 U.S. 81).

Public Figures

Some who are most persuasive in affecting public policy hold no public office. In two cases in 1967 the Supreme Court extended the New York Times rule to such public figures. One case involved an Associated Press dispatch reporting that former Maj. Gen. Edwin A. Walker had "assumed command" of rioters protesting racial integration at the University of Mississippi on Sept. 30, 1962. The other case involved a *Saturday Evening Post* article accusing Wallace Butts, former Athletic Director of the University of Georgia, of giving away his team's football secrets to the University of Alabama.

In both cases, a majority on the Supreme Court held that private individuals who take part in public affairs could not recover damages as long as standards of the New York Times rule were met. However, the victory was only a theoretical one for the *Post*, because the court held that it had been guilty of actual malice and sustained a $460,000 award for Butts. The *Post's* malice, resulting from failure to make a thorough investigation, is discussed in detail in Chapter 16.

The Supreme Court's inclusion of public figures had been foreshadowed by Judge Friendly of the Court of Appeals in upholding a verdict for the New York *Daily News* in an action brought by Linus Pauling, Nobel prize-winning scientist. An editorial on September 2, 1961, said that Pauling had been lukewarm in protesting to "his friend in the Kremlin" when the Soviet Union announced resumption of nuclear weapons testing. (Pauling v. News Syndicate Co., 335 F. 2d 659.)

General Walker based 15 libel suits on the Associated Press dispatch. He asked a total of $33,250,000 in damages. The case that reached the high court involved a $500,000 verdict awarded him in Texas. The AP dispatch was put together by a rewrite man from material supplied by Van Savell, a 21-year-old correspondent who posed as a student. The dispatch, an eyewitness account under Savell's byline, said in part:

> Oxford, Miss., Oct. 3 (AP)—Utilizing my youth to the fullest extent, I dressed as any college student would and easily milled among the several thousand rioters on the University of Mississippi Campus Sunday night.
>
> This allowed me to follow the crowd—a few students and many outsiders—as they charged federal marshals surrounding the century old Lyceum Building. It also brought me into direct contact with former Army Maj. Gen. Edwin A. Walker . . .
>
> One unidentified man queried Walker as he approached the group. "General, will you lead us to the steps?"
>
> I observed Walker as he loosened his tie and shirt and nodded "Yes" without speaking. He then conferred with a group of about 15 persons who appeared to be the riot leaders.
>
> The crowd took full advantage of the near-by construction work. They broke new bricks into several pieces, took survey sticks and broken soft drink bottles.
>
> Walker assumed command of the crowd, which I estimated at 1,000. . . .

In the key opinion in the case, Chief Justice Warren noted that in modern society "many who do not hold public office at the moment are nevertheless intimately involved in the resolution of important public questions, or by reason of their fame, shape events in areas of concern to society at large." He added in words that every newsman should applaud:

> Viewed in this context then, it is plain that although they are not subject to the restraints of the political process, "public figures," like "public officials," often play an influential role in ordering society. And surely as a class these "public figures" have as ready access as "public officials" to mass media of communication, both to influence policy and to counter criticism of their views and activities. Our citizenry has a legitimate and substantial interest in the conduct of such persons, and freedom of the press to engage in uninhibited debate about their involvement in public issues and events is as crucial as it is in the case of "public officials." [Curtis Publishing Co. v. Butts and Associated Press v. Walker 388 U.S. 130]

The court did not define "public figure," but two classifications were indicated. One involves individuals, like Walker, who "thrust themselves into the vortex" of a public controversy. The other classification embraces those, like Athletic Director Butts, who hold a position that commands wide attention and "important responsibility." The opinions in both cases indicate that another requirement must also be met—the individual must be so prominent that the press would run his side of the story if it were available. Both Walker and Butts were so widely known that all they would have to do to get their views published would be to hold a press conference or issue a statement. Thus while leaders of civil rights groups, the Ku Klux Klan and pacifist organizations would certainly be classified as public figures, there is doubt that individual members would—even though they took part in demonstrations or wrote letters to the editor.

The expanding New York Times rule makes newsmen an easier target for libel, too, as Drew Pearson learned when an Alaska court threw out a suit he had brought against the Fairbanks *News-Miner* for calling him "the garbage man of the fourth estate." (Pearson v. Fairbanks Co., 413 P. 2d 711).

A case in New York also supports a broad interpretation of the New York Times rule. In that case the court threw out a suit by a law partner of the Mayor of Mount Vernon who cited a campaign by a foe of the Mayor charging that their law firm was involved in a conflict of interests. The lawyer insisted that he was not a candidate for public office and thus was outside the political arena, but the court rejected his contention that the New York Times rule did not apply. It found that the lawyer had "made himself as much a part of the local political campaign as did his law partner." However, since the court also based its case on the fact that the defamatory remark had been directed at the law firm and had not named the plaintiff, the decision is limited in its ability to set precedent (Gilberg v. Goffi, 21 A.D. 2d (N.Y.) 517).

Courts in some states where the Kansas rule had been the law before *The New York Times* decision also support a broad interpretation of the defense. Delaware, Pennsylvania and Maine permit libelous misstatements of facts about a person if he is offering himself out for public approval and the matter is one of public concern. In a Pennsylvania case the defense was allowed where the plaintiff was advertising his private school, and in Maine it was allowed where the plaintiff erected a city building.

Businesses, Too?

The Kansas court's landmark Coleman case, cited with so much approval by the Supreme Court, calls for a freedom of expression that goes far beyond the New York Times rule. The Kansas court said:

> . . . it must be borne in mind that the correct rule, whatever it is, must govern in cases other than those involving candidates for office. It must apply to all officers and agents of government—municipal, state and national; to the management of all public institutions— educational, charitable and penal; to the conduct of all corporate enterprises affected with a public interest—transportation, banking, insurance, and to inumerable other subjects involving the public welfare.

One of the greatest possibilities for further breakthroughs in the restrictions on freedom of expression imposed by the law of libel is the Coleman decision's inclusion of "all corporate enterprises affected with a public interest." In a case decided after *The New York Times* decision, the Dallas *Morning News* was charged with libeling H. O. Merren & Co., a British West Indies shipping company. The *News* reported that the British company, through a "legal loophole," had profitably transshipped goods from the United States through the British West Indies to Cuba. The article also commented on what it said was a lack of cooperation by the British company and British Government with the United States embargo on Cuba. A Federal district court confused the issue by holding first that the article was not libelous. If this were so, it would not have had to discuss any defense, but it went ahead anyway and said that the *News* had a right under the New York Times rule to publish the article even if it were absolutely untrue (H. O. Merren & Co. v. A. H. Belo Corp., 228 F. Supp. 515).

A 1955 Connecticut decision, based on the Coleman ruling, held that libelous misstatements of fact in a political campaign about a business were privileged if related in some manner to the public welfare. Joseph N. DePaola, the Democratic candidate for Mayor of Meriden, made a campaign speech broadcast over radio station WMMW in Meriden. In that speech he discussed the loss of industry in the city and said:

> My friends in Meriden, you know the Charles Parker Company— formerly the Bradley and Hubbard Manufacturing Company. This old famous firm is now ninety per cent out of production and is up for sale. How many jobs will disappear? The staggering total of one thousand.

The next day the company, none of whose officers had been involved in the campaign, issued a denial and demanded that WMMW retract. Station WMMW refused, and that night DePaola made another broadcast from the same station in which he said he stood by what he had said in the previous broadcast.

The Parker Company then sued the radio station and DePaola arguing that privilege covering false facts extended only to matters of public interest and that the affairs of a private corporation did not fall within this category. But the Connecticut Supreme Court of Errors rejected that argument and said that the loss of employment, which DePaola had been discussing, was "most certainly" a matter of public interest. It then quoted the Kansas court's words in the Coleman case that the privilege should apply to "all corporate enterprises affected with a public interest" and added: "We accept this as the correct viewpoint." Making the

case a complete rout for the plaintiff, the court noted that under
the Federal Communications Act the broadcasting station had no
power to censor political speeches and thus it was protected from
liability under that law (Charles Parker Co. v. Silver City Crystal
Co., 142 Conn. 605).

Chief Justice Warren's opinion in the Walker and Butts cases
indicates that libels about business activities with a wide public
interest may also be covered by the *Times* doctrine. And the
courts have so held.

Sports Illustrated published an article about the hotel situation
in Augusta, Georgia, during the 1964 Masters Golf Tournament. It
was entitled "AUGUSTA: Where Georgia Retaliates for Sherman's
March." It described the Bon Air Hotel, its tiny bedrooms wide
enough so that by turning sideways a guest could walk between
the bed and the dresser. It went on to tell of halls sloped awk-
wardly toward rooms "numbered in such fascinating sequences as
352, 353 and 362," and of Bon Air maids, who usually respond to
any plea by locking the guest in his room. Bon Air Hotel, Inc.
sued Time, Inc., the owner of *Sports Illustrated*. On the basis of
The New York Times doctrine, Time was successful on a motion
for summary judgment. The Court of Appeals in affirming the
District Court's holding reiterated that the record was "devoid of
any showing that defamatory statements were published by the
defendant Time . . . with knowledge of their falsity or with reckless disregard of whether they were true or false" (Bon Air Hotel,
Inc. v. Time, Inc., 426 F.2d 858).

Sports Figures

At first there was a reluctance on the part of the courts to
extend the public-figure concept to sports figures. Jack Dempsey
sued because of an article in *Sports Illustrated* on January 13,
1964, that suggested that he won the world's heavyweight boxing
championship from Jess Willard in 1919 while wearing gloves
loaded with plaster of paris. The court said that "reaching back
45 years" was not even within the suggested extension of the
Times rule (Dempsey v. Time, Inc., 43 Misc.2d (N.Y.) 754).

Then Orlando Cepeda sued *Look* magazine for criticizing him at a time when he was playing first base for the San Francisco Giants. Cepeda scored in the first few innings in court, but he ultimately lost when the Court of Appeals for the Ninth Circuit held that he was a public figure and was unable to show the type of malice required by the *Times* doctrine (Cepeda v. Cowles Magazine and Broadcasting, Inc., 392 F.2d 417).

The court outlined the scope of public figures:

> "Public figures" are those persons who, though not public officials, are "involved in issues in which the public has a justified and important interest." Such figures are, of course, numerous and include artists, athletes, business people, dilettantes, anyone who is famous or infamous because of who he is or what he has done. Orlando Cepeda, the principal character in the instant suit, was and is a "public figure." His fame as an extraordinary baseball player is recited in our former opinion, cited above.

Since the Cepeda case, almost all prominent athletes who have sued have been held to be public figures. They include a retired professional basketball player turned college basketball coach (Time, Inc. v. Johnston, 448 F.2d 378); a little-known college track coach (Vandenburg v. Newsweek, Inc., 441 F.2d 378); and Alex Webster, a former New York Giants football coach (Webster v. American Broadcasting Companies, *N.Y.L.J.*, October 1, 1976, p. 5).

Other Public Figures

Other public figures include a local real-estate developer (Greenbelt Publishing Association v. Bresler, 398 U.S. 6) and the queen of the Rochester belly dancers who gave a press interview and said, among other things, "Men is my business" (James v. Gannett & Co., Inc., 40 N.Y.2d 415).

In the literary field, a doctor and co-author of a book of which four million copies have been sold has been held to be a public figure (Atkins v. Friedman, 49 A.D. 2d (N.Y.),852); the author of *Papa Hemingway, A Personal Memoir* (Hotchner v. Castillo-Pouche, 404 F. Supp. 1041); and the author of a book entitled *Property Power* on how to resist land developers (Gauitar v. Westinghouse, 396 F. Supp. 1042).

And finally, the Rosenberg children, offspring of convicted spies, have been held to be public figures (Meeropol v. Nizer, 381 F.Supp. 29).

But not all persons who obtain transitory prominence are public figures within the *Times* doctrine. Elmer Gertz was a Chicago lawyer. In 1968 a Chicago policeman named Nuccio shot and killed a youth named Nelson. Nuccio was prosecuted for the homicide and was convicted for murder in the second degree. The Nelson family retained Gertz to represent them in civil litigation against Nuccio.

In March, 1969, *American Opinion,* a monthly outlet for the views of the ultra-conservative John Birch Society, published an article entitled "FRAME-UP: Richard Nuccio and the War on Police." Gertz was portrayed as the architect of the "frame-up." The article said that the police file on Gertz required "a big Irish cop to lift" and labeled Gertz as a "Leninist" and a "Communist-fronter." He was also described as an officer of the National Lawyers Guild which "probably did more than any other outfit to plan the Communist attack on the Chicago police during the 1968 Democratic Convention." Gertz sued.

The Supreme Court held that Gertz was not a public figure within the *Times* doctrine (Gertz v. Robert Welch, Inc., 418 U.S. 323). It defined the test to be applied to determine whether one is a public figure.

> That designation may rest on either of two alternative bases. In some instances, an individual may achieve such pervasive fame or notoriety that he becomes a public figure for all purposes and in all contexts. More commonly, an individual voluntarily injects himself or is drawn into a particular public controversy and thereby becomes a public figure for a limited range of issues. In either case, such persons assume special prominence in the resolution of public questions.

The Supreme Court then held that although Gertz had been active in community and professional affairs and had published several books and articles on legal subjects, he had achieved no general fame or notoriety in the community. In connection with the Nuccio case, he had played no part in the criminal prosecution and·had never discussed either the civil or criminal litigation with the press and had not thrust himself into the vortex of a public issue.

In 1976 the Supreme Court held that Mary Alice Firestone had not become a public figure simply because she had participated in a sensational divorce trial, subscribed to a clipping service, and held several press conferences (Time, Inc. v. Firestone, 424 U.S. 448). She had been awarded $100,000, but the court sent the case back for a new trial because there had been no showing of fault.

Public Interest

George Rosenbloom was the distributor of nudist magazines in the Philadelphia metropolitan area. The Philadelphia Police Department in 1963 initiated a series of enforcement actions under the city's obscenity laws. A police squad under the command of Captain Ferguson determined that certain material was obscene and arrested a number of newsstand operators on charges of selling obscene material. Unfortunately for Rosenbloom, he was delivering some of his nudist magazines when the police were engaged in arresting the newsstand operators and Rosenbloom was picked up for good measure. Three days later, the police with a search warrant raided Rosenbloom's home and barn which was used as a warehouse. He was arrested a second time and Captain Ferguson called the defendant's local radio station, WIP, and informed it of the raid and arrest, and the station broadcast the following item.

CITY CRACKS DOWN ON SMUT MERCHANTS

The Special Investigations Squad raided the home of George Rosenbloom in the 1800 block of Vesta Street this afternoon. Police confiscated 1,000 allegedly obscene books at Rosenbloom's home and arrested him on charges of possession of obscene literature. The Special Investigations Squad also raided a barn in the 20 Hundred block of Welsh Road near Bustleton Avenue and confiscated 3,000 obscene books. Capt. Ferguson says he believes they have hit the supply of a main distributor of obscene material in Philadelphia.

Rosenbloom then brought an action in the Federal District Court against various city and police officials, alleging that his magazines were not obscene and seeking injunctive relief.

The radio station of the defendant described the action as seeking to order the police "to lay off the smut literature racket." The station described Rosenbloom as a "girlie book peddler" who said the description of his literature as smut or filth was hurting his business. In May, 1964, Rosenbloom was acquitted in the state court of the criminal obscenity charges, on the ground that the nudist magazines were not obscene.

Rosenbloom then sued the radio station for libel. The jury found for the plaintiff, and awarded him $25,000 compensatory damages and $725,000 punitive damages. The court reduced the punitive award to $250,000 but did not otherwise disturb the verdict. The defense of reporting was not available because the books in the warehouse were described without qualification as obscene. The only basis on which the defendant could prevail was the New York Times rule. Numerous inferior courts, both federal and state, had held that the real basis for that defense was the public interest of the subject matter, not the status of the plaintiff as a public official or a public figure. The Court of Appeals of the Third Circuit adopted that view and emphasized that the broadcasts involved matters of public interest and the fact that the plaintiff was not a public figure could not be accorded decisive importance. It held that *The New York Times* standard applied and that the plaintiff had not met that standard and could not prevail.

When the case reached the Supreme Court, it was argued about the same time as several other libel cases. The opinions in all the other cases came down within two months, but the justices were badly divided over Rosenbloom and did not hand down an opinion until six months later, on June 7, 1971. The Supreme Court affirmed the opinion of the Court of Appeals, but no majority could agree on a controlling rationale. The eight justices who participated in the case announced their views in five separate opinions, none of which commanded more than three votes. While it appeared that the test of *The New York Times* doctrine no longer depended on a finding that the plaintiff was a public official or a public figure but on the public interest of the subject matter, the split in the court created serious doubts (Rosenbloom v. Metromedia, Inc., 403 U.S. 29).

The Gertz case, discussed briefly on page 188, confirmed these doubts. The Supreme Court was again badly split. It retreated from the Rosenbloom decision and adopted a new standard when a private individual is the plaintiff. The opinion of the court was delivered by Mr. Justice Powell, joined by three other justices; Mr. Justice Blackmun, who had joined Mr. Justice Brennan's plurality opinion in the Rosenbloom case, became the fifth justice because "if my vote were not needed to create a majority, I would adhere to my prior view. A definitive ruling, however, is paramount . . . For these reasons I join the opinion and judgment of the court."

The majority decided that where a private citizen rather than a public official or a public figure was the plaintiff in a matter of public interest, each state could impose its own standard of liability so long as strict or absolute liability was not imposed.

This was revolutionary. Strict liability had always been the test in libel actions. The mere fact of publication regardless of fault had been the basis of liability. Since the Gertz holding in June, 1974, the plaintiff has been required to show some fault on the part of the defendant. An innocent mistake can no longer be the basis of liability. The court went on to hold that so long as strict liability is not imposed, each state may establish its own standard less stringent than *The New York Times* standard where the plaintiff is a private individual (not a public official or a public figure). The court said:

> We hold that, so long as they do not impose liability without fault, the States may define for themselves the appropriate standard of liability for a publisher or broadcaster of defamatory falsehood injurious to a private individual. This approach provides a more equitable boundary between the competing concerns involved here. It recognizes the strength of the legitimate state interest in compensating private individuals for wrongful injury to reputation, yet shields the press and broadcast media from the rigors of strict liability for defamation. At least this conclusion obtains where, as here, the substance of the defamatory statement "makes substantial danger to reputation apparent." This phrase places in perspective the conclusion we announce today. Our inquiry would involve considerations somewhat different from those discussed above if a State purported to condition civil liability on a factual misstatement whose content did not warn a reasonably prudent editor or broadcaster of its defamatory potential. [Gertz v. Robert Welsh, Inc., 418 U.S. 323, 347-8]

Since the Gertz decision, some states have continued to adhere
to the *Times* standard; others have embraced a negligence
standard; and New York has adopted a new standard only
slightly less strigent than the *Times* standard.

Colorado, Indiana and Louisiana have retained *The New York
Times* standard of "known falsity or reckless disregard" where the
plaintiff is a private individual and the matter concerns the public
interest.

Hawaii, Illinois, Kansas, Massachusetts, Maryland, Ohio, Oklahoma, Tennessee and Washington have adopted a negligence
standard.

The New York Court of Appeals, in a 1975 decision, adopted a
gross irresponsibility standard which seems to vary in only a
slight degree from the reckless disregard standard. The court said
(Chapadeau v. Utica Observer-Dispatch, Inc., 38 N.Y. 2d 196, 199):

> We now hold that within the limits imposed by the Supreme
> Court where the content of the article is arguably within the sphere
> of legitimate public concern, which is reasonably related to matters
> warranting public exposition, the party defamed may recover; how-
> ever, to warrant such recovery he must establish, by a preponder-
> ance of the evidence, that the publisher acted in a grossly irrespon-
> sible manner without due consideration for the standards of infor-
> mation gathering and dissemination ordinarily followed by respon-
> sible parties.

The Gertz case was also revolutionary on the question of damages, and that will be covered in Chapter 16.

Private Affairs

The Supreme Court's decisions in both *The New York Times*
and the Garrison cases were limited to a public official's public
conduct. In fact, Justice Arthur J. Goldberg went to pains to point
out in his concurring opinion in the *Times* case that "this is not to
say that the Constitution protects defamatory statements directed
against the private conduct of a public official or private citizen."
While he expressed the opinion that in most cases the line could
easily be drawn between public and private conduct, the court in
its Garrison decision showed that they often overlap:

Of course, any criticism of the manner in which a public official performs his duties will tend to affect his private, as well as his public, reputation. The New York Times rule is not rendered inapplicable merely because an official's private reputation, as well as his public reputation, is harmed. The public official rule protects the paramount public interest in a free flow of information to the people concerning public officials, their servants. To this end, anything which might touch on an official's fitness for office is relevant. Few personal attributes are more germane to fitness for office than dishonesty, malfeasance, or improper motivation, even though these characteristics may also affect the official's private character. As the Kansas Supreme Court said in *Coleman v. MacLennan*, speaking of candidates:

"Manifestly a candidate must surrender to public scrutiny and discussion so much of his private character as affects his fitness for office, and the liberal rule requires no more. But in measuring the extent of a candidate's profert of character it should always be remembered that the people have good authority for believing that grapes do not grow on thorns nor figs on thistles." [Garrison v. State of Louisiana 379 U.S. 64]

In 1971, a unanimous Supreme Court made clear that it was eliminating almost all distinctions it had applied in the *Times* and Garrison cases regarding public versus private activities of political candidates. The case involved a column by Drew Pearson that characterized Alphonse Roy, a candidate for the United States Senate in New Hampshire in 1960, as a "former small-time bootlegger." Roy sued the Concord, N.H., *Monitor*, which carried the column, and the North American Newspaper Alliance, which syndicated it. The jury awarded Roy $20,000—$10,000 from the *Monitor* and $10,000 from NANA. The New Hampshire Supreme Court upheld the award.

In his opinion for the United States Supreme Court overturning the state court, Justice Potter Stewart said:

The principal activity of a candidate in our political system, his "office," so to speak, consists in putting before the voters every conceivable aspect of his public and private life that he thinks may lead the electorate to gain a good impression of him. A candidate who, for example, seeks to further his cause through the prominent display of his wife and children can hardly argue that his qualities as a husband or father remain of "purely private" concern. And the candidate who vaunts his spotless record and sterling integrity cannot convincingly cry "Foul!" when an opponent or an industrious reporter attempts to demonstrate the contrary. Any test adequate to safeguard First Amendment guarantees in this area must go far beyond the customary meaning of the phrase "official conduct."

Given the realities of our political life, it is by no means easy to see what statements about a candidate might be altogether without relevance to his fitness for the office he seeks . . .

We therefore hold as a matter of constitutional law that a charge of criminal conduct, no matter how remote in time or place, can never be irrelevant to an official's or a candidate's fitness for office . . . [Monitor Patriot Co. et al v. Roy, 401 U.S. 265, 274-5, 277]

Nothing is more private than an individual's sexual life, but a mere reminder of the Profumo scandal in Britain is sufficient to show that even here public policy can be affected by what seems to be purely private matters. Few would doubt the right and usefulness of reporting that an official with access to the Pentagon's top-secret documents has been found to be a homosexual. It is also obvious that since this liberal rule gives the press the power to destroy a man, it requires that newsmen exert a degree of responsibility that some have not risen to in the past.

Chapter 13

FAIR COMMENT—DEFENSE FOR OPINIONS

SOME OF THE BEST READING IN THE AMERICAN PRESS COULD NOT BE printed with safety except for a fourth defense—fair comment and criticism. Without this defense editorials would be anemic, commentary spineless, art criticism tepid and letters to the editor platitudinous. Sports reporters, feature writers and columnists would be straitjacketed. Fair comment allows another dimension to the news—libelous opinions to supplement facts. Often the best part of an article is an expression of an opinion—either by the subject in the news or the writer. But opinions, by their very nature, can almost never be proved to be true, so the defense of truth cannot be invoked. If the remarks are uttered outside of an official proceeding, there is no privilege of reporting. If they concern someone not covered by the New York Times rule, that defense is unavailing. But the defense of fair comment offers a certain shield to the writer of libelous opinions.

This is a complete defense. Fair comment wholly defeats a recovery on the part of the plaintiff no matter how defamatory or injurious the expression of opinion may be. But the defense is qualified, that is, lost if there is proof of actual malice. Like some of the other defenses this one is based on the belief that it is better that the reputation of a person should sometimes suffer from defamatory criticism than that the citizen's right to express himself on matters of public interest be too restricted by fears of suits. Lord Ellenborough, in a British case, outlined the basis for the defense:

> Liberty of criticism must be allowed, or we should have neither purity of taste nor of morals. Fair discussion is essentially necessary to the truth of history and the advancement of science. That publication, therefore, I should never consider as a libel which has for its object not to injure the reputation of any individual, but to cor-

rect misrepresentations of fact, to refute sophistical reasoning, to expose a vicious taste in literature or to censure what is hostile to morality. [Tabart v. Tipper, 1 Camp. 350]

The editor will find that the defense of fair comment will be used most often in these types of articles or broadcasts:
1. Editorials and columns
2. Criticism of such cultural pursuits as the drama, music, books and art
3. News items that quote statements or comments of a critical nature
4. Letters to the editor
5. Crusading articles

The third and fourth categories often consist of statements by or about occupants or candidates for public office, but more and more, as public interest in other matters rises, they concern other subjects and persons. Such quotations often do not reflect the editorial position of the publisher or broadcaster. Nevertheless, if the opinion is printed or broadcast, the publisher or broadcasting station must defend it. It need not adopt the position of the author, but it has the responsibility of defending it as his fair comment.

This, of course, is why accurate reporting is important. If the source of the story denies that he said what is attributed to him, the publication is in trouble. This problem often arises in analyses and interpretive articles where the source is generalized. An example that the United States Court of Appeals for the Ninth Circuit believed fell in the latter category appeared in *Look* magazine on May 21, 1963. The article, touched on briefly in Chapter 12, started out this way:

By Jim Cohane
Sports Editor of Look

Orlando Cepeda. The name seems to need a Don in front of it or a cigar band around it. Instead, it wears the sale tag: "First-class first baseman, San Francisco Giants, tradable for top-notch pitcher and other considerations."

Until the trading deadline—midnight, June 15—a National League team may decide it can better itself by giving the Giants all they want for Cepeda. The possibility is scant. Nevertheless, it is astonishing that Cepeda, power hitter and slick fielder on a pennant winner, should be considered expendable. And expendable he has been since the end of last season.

The big fellow, whom they call "Chico" and "The Baby Bull," has for some time been in disfavor with owner Horace Stoneham, Manager Alvin Dark and the club's cue takers. The counts against him:

1) He doesn't produce the crucial hit often enough. 2) He is not a team man. 3) When things go wrong, he blames everybody but Orlando. 4) He does not rebound and take it out on the opposition. 5) He is a hardy holdout every year.

A hot and loud bat can drown out the strains of discord, and Cepeda may slug his way back to grace. Or the active bat might impress Stoneham principally as a boost to Orlando's market value. For Cepeda's doghouse status traces less to unfavorable interpretation of his batting statistics than to his overall performance, which Stoneham and the rest of the Giants' hierarchy deem temperamental, uncooperative and underproductive. . . .

There was much more in the same vein. In rejecting the defense of fair comment and criticism, the court said:

A significant feature of the defendant's writing was that, though the author is said by the defendant to be "a nationally recognized sportswriter and baseball authority," the parts of the article in question of which the plaintiff complains contain practically nothing of this authority's opinion or criticism. What it gives the reader is a report of what, the writer says, Cepeda's employers, the management of the San Francisco Giants, were thinking and saying about him. Some of the thoughts were expressly attributed to that source, and the rest of them would be attributed by a reader to that source, since the writer of the article could not have known them except by learning them, directly or indirectly, from that source. We do not, then, have a situation in which the interested but relatively unsophisticated baseball buffs among Look Magazine's millions of readers were being enlightened by a nationally recognized authority's analysis and opinion of l'affair Cepeda. If the article was a true report, the reader still got only what an eavesdropper with an acute ear and an accurate memory might have learned by listening at the keyhole of the Giants' front office. There are obvious difficulties about fitting this kind of writing into the philosophy upon which the privilege of fair comment is based.

The plaintiff says that the Giants' officials did not entertain the unfavorable opinions which the defendant's writer attributed to them. Since one may not escape liability for defamation by showing that he was merely repeating defamatory language used by another person, a fortiori he may not escape by falsely attributing to others the ideas to which he gives expression. The attribution to others may well make the defamation more serious. If, for example, a sportswriter quoted Joe DiMaggio as having said that Cepeda in the batter's box was a helpless clown, that attributed opinion would carry more weight and be more damaging than a similar opinion of the sportswriter himself. Attribution of the opinion that Cepeda's temperament was unsuited to championship baseball, to the Giants' management, the ones in position to know most about his temperament, would, similarly, add to the weight of the opinion. [Cepeda v. Cowles Magazines and Broadcasting, Inc., 328 F. 2d 869, cert. denied 379 U.S. 844]

As explained in the preceding chapter, Cepeda ultimately lost the case.

Nonlibelous Comment

Not all adverse expressions of opinion are libelous. They may be harsh, but they do not necessarily injure the subject in his occupation or calling. In that event, the judge will usually throw the case out before the defense of fair comment is considered, for again we fall back on the basic rule that nonlibelous statements do not require a defense.

As we have seen, even the courts sometimes get mixed up on this point and make such statements as "fair comment is not libelous at all," and then go on to discuss the defenses for publishing the criticism. But if there was no defamation, the publication does not require any defense because there is no ground for a suit.

Writers and editors should keep this in mind when worried about a particular item. Here is an example from a letter to the editor published by the Belleville (Illinois) *News-Democrat* on August 31, 1959, a few days after a parade:

Dear Sir:

A few nights ago we saw the most disgusting thing in our life. There was this girl, about 14 years old, riding around in the back of a convertible, half-naked, and twirling a hula hoop. If it was a man doing this, he'd have been arrested for indecent exposure, causing a public nuisance, or just plain drunk. Now tell me why this girl was allowed to do such a thing. We were under the impression that the authorities had banned strip teasing. Wouldn't this be under the same heading? The very idea of it, exposing little children to something like this, parading around on the public square, the streets and stores in such an outfit. We would like to hear other people's views on this subject.

Mr. and Mrs.

"Mr. and Mrs." did hear other views on the subject, but only indirectly. It was the Belleville *News-Democrat* that heard directly —from Betty Jane Archibald, the hula-hoop girl and president of the Elvis Presley fan club. She sued for libel.

In an appeal to the Appellate Court of Illinois after her case had been dismissed in the lower court, Betty Jane's lawyer explained how the girl had been damaged:

> From the time in her city that the daily evening newspaper appeared she is branded with a name that has connotations and implications that are far from nice. From within a few hours of a certain publication about her in her city she finds that no boy wants to date her. Her girl friends shun her and avoid being seen talking with her in the school halls or on the campus. Wrong intentioned persons start phoning her wanting answers to odd-ball questions and making suggestive advances. The phone goes night and day until after a week and a half they have to have it disconnected to get rest and peace from anonymous callers at all hours of the night. On the evening of the publication she hears for the first time a name that ticks with her and spreads far and wide to do its havoc and ruin her reputation for being a nice retiring and quiet person. The name that works this wrong is one that everyone knows its popular meaning and that name is: STRIPPER

The court denied her claim on the ground that the letter had not accused her of indecent exposure or lewdness or injured her or her projected profession (Archibald v. Belleville News-Democrat, 54 Ill. App. 2d 38).

Public Officials

How can a writer or editor qualify for this defense? The answer depends on whether the subject of the comment is of public interest and concern. If the subject is a public official or for some other reason falls within the scope of the public-man rule enunciated by the United States Supreme Court, he can be criticized under the fair-comment rule. While the court stressed in *The New York Times* case that it was barring recovery for misstatements of fact, it added in a footnote to its opinion that the rule also covered opinions.

Therefore, if the target of the attack is a public official or anyone else who comes within the ambit of the *Times* decision, only two precautions need be taken. First, the comment must concern the individual's public, not his purely private, affairs; this requirement was discussed in the preceding chapter. Second, the comment must not be made with actual malice—that is, with knowledge that it is untrue—or a reckless disregard for truth (this is discussed in Chapter 16).

Otherwise, the comment can be as harsh, as mean, as unfair, as biased, as misleading, as coarse or as vociferous as the speaker is irresponsible enough to make it. The opinion can be completely wild and unjustified and the facts on which it is based absolutely false. No damages can be awarded.

Others

In all other cases stricter rules apply. Articles concerning these other subjects must meet five tests:

1. They must deal with a subject of public interest.
2. The libelous matter must be an opinion and not a statement of fact.
3. The fact on which the opinions are based must be truly stated.
4. The opinion must be fair.
5. There must be no malice.

Public, Not Private, Affairs

First, the criticism must deal only with subjects that invite public attention or call for public comment. Fortunately, for the writer, many subjects now fall within the New York Times rule—affairs of state, including the functions of Federal, state and local governments; political campaigns; much of the administration of justice, including the acts of judges, district attorneys and perhaps juries.

The stricter rules apply to all other public functions that fall outside the public-figure rule. The writer, therefore, must adhere to the more rigid requirements in dealing with such subjects as:

Public institutions, including hospitals, charities, churches, foundations and those concerned with them, such as superintendents, doctors, nurses, ministers and the like.

Cultural and entertainment pursuits, including books, pictures, art, theaters, concerts, films, sports and other public diversions and their participants—authors, painters, singers, critics and the like.

Economic and social welfare events, such as strikes by labor unions, demonstrations by racial and other civil liberties organizations, picketing by pacifist groups, policies of farm associations, as well as the activities of their opponents. Union and management leaders, pickets and marchers in demonstrations and counterpickets and countermarchers and those who form policies are also covered.

Other appeals to the public, such as advertising and public relations campaigns and their creators, developers and participants.

Newspapers, magazines and journalists are also subject to fair comment since they, too, participate in public discussions. Tom McCarthy, a commentator for radio station WKRC found that out after he sued the Cincinnati *Enquirer* for an editorial and "brightener" about his campaign against fluoridation of the city's water. Both appeared February 26, 1953. The editorial contained these paragraphs that McCarthy considered libelous:

In the last few days we have had a depressing demonstration of how much harm one news broadcaster can do in a community. We refer to the daily efforts of Tom McCarthy of WKRC, to create distrust in our public health authorities by misrepresenting the effects of fluoridation of our water supply, scheduled to begin on Sunday.

By misleading statements, delivered in highly dramatic style, Mr. McCarthy has aroused widespread fears that fluoridation will raise the total death rate, cause more cancer and augment tooth decay. This is by no means the first time Mr. McCarthy has set himself against the community's welfare, thus drawing momentary attention to himself. But it is perhaps the least savory of his adventures.

For those people who form their day-to-day picture of the world from McCarthy's dramatization of the news, we submit the facts regarding water fluoridation.

.   .   .   .

These are the facts, for those who want the facts. The same facts were available to Mr. McCarthy. But for reasons quite his own, he prefers not to limit himself to facts. In this case he has done great harm by causing needless fears and by inciting distrust of fully qualified health officials. We are certain that most persons in Cincinnati will take the word of local and national medical authorities against the word of a broadcaster whose record of reliability we will let speak for itself. The pity is that Mr. McCarthy is permitted by Station WKRC to continue in a pattern of "news reporting" that victimizes the gullible listener.

The "brightener," on the same page, under the headline "The Voice of the Enquirer," said:

When the water dispute is washed away, we wouldn't be surprised to see a Tom McCarthy bottled water appear on the market.

The Court of Appeals of Ohio dismissed McCarthy's suit for $1 million in damages on the basis that the remarks were not libelous because they accused him of doing only what he had a legal right to do and which was not a violation of the moral code. But it also made clear that a radio newscaster can be libeled with impunity if the comment is fair. It said that "it is apparent at once that by the very nature of his employment plaintiff assumes a dual role of private citizen and public figure, so that while not an elected public official, his position is one tantamount to that and his broadcasts tantamount to a production or performance for public exhibition, so that he submits it to fair and reasonable criticism within the class of privileged communications."

As proof of McCarthy's influence on the public, the court noted that his campaign had been successful, for the question of fluoridation was put to a referendum and rejected (McCarthy v. Cincinnati Enquirer, 101 Ohio App. 297).

The Drew Pearson case in Alaska (discussed in Chapter 12) shows that the courts are coming around to the idea that newsmen are public men within the scope of the broad New York Times rule.

While the critic can take pot shots at anyone in public life, he cannot follow him into his private life or pry into his domestic concerns unless they are related to the performance of his public functions. One of the best examples of overstepping the bounds came at the turn of the century.

Oscar Lovell Triggs was a professor at the University of Chicago. He was also an author and a person addicted to making public remarks on various subjects, including drama. In one of these public lectures he criticized Shakespeare and referred to Shakespeare in adverse terms and to himself in complimentary ones. The New York *Sun* was annoyed and ran three editorials of scathing criticism of the professor, including some suggestions on how he might rewrite Shakespeare. Instead of Shakespeare's

> Night's candles are burnt out, and jocund day
> Stands tiptoe on the misty mountaintops

the *Sun* offered this "clear, concise Triggsian" as a substitute: "I hear the milkman."

Such rough criticism was perfectly all right, the court said, because it dealt with Triggs' public pronouncements. But the *Sun* did not stop there. It could not resist the temptation to sneer at the professor for taking a year to think up an appropriate name for his baby. The court concluded that this reference to the professor's private life made the comment indefensible (Triggs v. Sun Printing and Publishing Assn., 179 N.Y. 144).

Opinion, Not Fact

The second requirement is that the article be an expression of opinion and not an assertion of a libelous fact. Suppose a drama critic wrote in a review that the performance by one of the actors was atrocious, the worst he had ever seen. That would be libelous because it imputes to the actor general unfitness in his calling. But this is an expression of opinion and not a statement of fact. The facts would be what the actor did on the stage that resulted in the opinion. Some critics might think that the actor did exceptionally well while others watching the same performance might think his work atrocious. The critics would come to opposite opinions based on the same set of facts. Or suppose that a broadcasting station carried an editorial saying that a union president was totally unfit for the office and ought to be removed. This, too, would be libelous, but it would be an expression of opinion and not a statement of fact. The facts would be what the union leader actually did that led the station to make its charge.

Since statements of this kind would be held libelous by the court, it would be up to the defense to prove its right to utter them. Opinions, being opinions, are not susceptible to factual proof, so the only defense would be fair comment and criticism.

Usually it is easy to distinguish between a fact and an opinion, but there are times when it is not. These occasions usually arise when opinions give the appearance of being stated like facts or facts give the appearance of being stated like opinions. If a television commentator accuses a prominent lawyer of "sheer lunacy," is that an expression of an opinion or of a fact? If the commentator was referring to—or listeners understood him to mean—a mental derangement, then it is a statement of a fact, and a libelous one. On the other hand, if the commentator is only criticizing the lawyer's ideas of barring television cameras from the courtroom, then it is an opinion stated like a fact. It still may be libelous, but it can be protected by the defense of fair comment and criticism if the "sheer lunacy" description were preceded with and followed by a discussion of the ideas the lawyer had expressed. Then there would be no mistaking his intent to offer an opinion.

A case that reached the California Supreme Court provides an excellent example of opinions stated as facts. The article, which appeared in the Stockton *Labor Journal* on September 30, 1938, began this way:

HAPPYHOLME DAIRY VIOLATES
CONTRACT WITH TEAMSTERS

UNIONISTS URGED NOT TO
PATRONIZE BY LOCAL COUNCIL

Action Comes After Three Months' Negotiations
Fail to Bring Peaceful Settlement from Operators

Because it had violated its signed agreement with Teamsters Local 439, hiring non-union drivers, and initiated a destructive labor policy, the Happyholme Dairy, located on the Sacramento Road at Lodi and serving the entire Stockton area, was placed on the official "We Don't Patronize" list of the San Joaquin County Central Labor Council Monday night.

All friends of organized labor are urged not to patronize this dairy. All other milk distributors in Stockton are operating on a union-basis, so there is no excuse for dealing with a non-union firm.

According to officials of the Teamsters Union, the Happyholme Dairy had been working under an agreement with the organization for several months. On July 1, however, while the contract was still in force, the management openly violated its word by hiring non-union milk wagon drivers.

In addition, drivers were made to furnish their own vehicles and were put on a straight commission plan. This move wiped out the minimum wage guarantees established in the agreement with the union, although the status of the drivers as employes of the dairy remained unchanged. The destruction of wage minimums is a threat to gains made by organized labor throughout the district.

The two men who operated the Happyholme Dairy sued. They had been defamed, they said, although all they had done was change their method of distributing milk to their customers. Their three drivers were covered by a one-year contract that guaranteed each $160 a month plus overtime pay. A provision of the agreement was that no employe was permitted to make any written or verbal contract in conflict with it. Before the contract ran out, Happyholme proposed to the drivers that they buy their routes and operate them as "independent contractors." All three drivers were Teamster members, but two immediately agreed to the plan and the third eventually went along with it. With the help of the dairy the three borrowed money and bought their trucks and the accounts receivable for their routes. They would buy Happyholme products at a discount and sell at a profit. Union leaders had tried to talk the men out of going ahead with the plan, and when the drivers persisted, they took their union cards from them. Before the new plan could be put in effect, one of the drivers decided to give up the route, he testified, because of threats by union officials. A dairy ranch hand then took it. After attempts to negotiate a settlement failed, the union placed the dairy on the unfair list and the article appeared.

The jury awarded the two Happyholme Dairy operators $15,000 in compensatory damage and $5,500 in punitive damages. The trial judge reduced the first figure to $7,000, but the state Supreme Court invalidated the verdict. In ruling that the publications met the requirements of fair comment the court conceded that many of the statements of fact involved elements of opinion.

It included in this category the statement that the dairy had hired nonunion milk-wagon drivers, that the drivers had been put on a straight-commission plan and that the minimum-wage guarantees had been "wiped out" although the drivers were still employes. In each of these cases the court found that the supposed facts were actually interpretive opinions that the union had drawn. But the court considered the comments to be fair. Elsewhere in the opinion it emphasized:

> . . . the difficulties in determining when the conditional privilege of capital and labor to express their views on labor controversies has been abused and in segregating the compensable items of damage from the noncompensable are readily apparent. And since such disputes, realistically considered, normally involve considerable differences of opinion and vehement adherence to one side or the other, a necessarily broad area of discussion without civil responsibility in damages must be considered an indispensable concomitant of the controversy. [Emde v. San Joaquin County Central Labor Council, 23 Cal. 2d 146]

Sometimes, editorial writers run into trouble by stating supposed facts as if they were opinions. But such devices as saying, "In my opinion Doctor Glutz is a crook," will not fool the courts. That is an assertion of a libelous fact camouflaged to make it look like privileged opinion.

Facts Truly Stated

The third requirement is that the facts on which the opinion is based be truly stated or referred to. The reason for this prerequisite is to make sure that the reader gets the basis for the opinion so he can judge its value for himself. It is best if the facts are well known or admitted. If they are not admitted, then the writer should make sure that they are not libelous, or, if they are, that he had proof of their accuracy. Here is an editorial from Hodding Carter's *Delta Democrat-Times* of Greenville, Mississippi, that meets the requirements for a factual basis for a defamatory opinion:

A LOW BLOW

It has often been true that men convinced of their fellows' ignorance of the difference between good and evil are themselves unwilling to make that distinction. This is the case in one instance of the United Drys campaign.

Henry Edmonds is not a stupid man, nor is the liquor referendum law passed by the legislature an ambiguous law. On the contrary, the law is quite plain and Mr. Edmonds, one suspects, is quite clever. The United Drys executive director has publicly stated that if the majority of Mississippians vote "Yes" in the August 26 liquor referendum, the state would be entirely wet and it would require an election in each county to make the county dry again. Assistant Atty. Gen. Kendall naturally ruled in reply that a majority affirmative vote "would be mandate to enact legislation permitting each county upon petition of 20 per cent of the qualified electors to vote either for or against the legalization of . . . liquor in that county."

It is all too clear that the United Drys organization, or at least its director, is determined to keep the state dry—even if it has to confuse the issue. Mr. Edmonds knew, of course, that his distortion of fact would receive wide attention as fact itself and that the attorney general's ruling would be lost on the general public. People, given half a chance, will believe what they want to believe. This propaganda trick by the United Drys confirms a growing conviction of ours about pressure groups conducting a "grass roots" campaign. The term "grass roots" expresses the absolute determination to gain an end by whatever means.

The editorial appeared June 16, 1952. Edmonds waited until just before the referendum to file a suit for $200,000, leading the *Delta Democrat* to believe that the purpose was not to collect damages but to propagandize the dry position. The court took judicial notice of the factual statements in the editorial, they being of considerable public interest at the time. Edmonds' position and the Attorney General's had been accurately stated. All Edmonds could complain about were the opinions based on those facts. That argument, said the Mississippi Supreme Court, was not enough (Edmonds v. Delta Democrat Publishing Co., 230 Miss. 583).

One of the common misunderstandings is to assume that facts have been stated when in actuality, only opinions have been expressed. The facts must be facts, and not even the opinion of the best experts in the field can provide the basis on which to make a libelous comment. One of the landmark cases in this regard involved a *Reader's Digest* article titled "Those Million-Dollar Aspirins." The gist of it was that manufacturers, using high-powered advertising, were selling huge quantities of drugs containing aspirin and succinate to victims of arthritis. The article referred to medical opinion in the United States to the effect that the drugs were worthless and even harmful, to the extent that they encouraged arthritics to overdose themselves with aspirin. Then it said, "Hence the only value of these 'wonder drugs' is as simple pain killers. They are no more effective than common aspirin." One of the statements in the article said that the "phoniest, and perhaps most dangerous, of all the claims made for these products is that they are 'safe' and 'nontoxic.'" It told of the difficulties that some of the manufacturers had had with Federal regulatory agencies and how, through delaying tactics, serious penalties could be avoided. It concluded with the rhetorical question "Who wants to pay $15 for 58 cents' worth of aspirin?"

The Dolcin Corporation, one of the manufacturers named in the article, sued for libel. At the trial the judge allowed *Reader's Digest* to introduce evidence that the widespread medical opinion in the United States was that a combination of aspirin and succinate was useless and possibly harmful to victims of arthritis. He also permitted the introduction of proof that the Federal Trade Commission had found Dolcin to be useless or harmful and its advertising misleading and deceptive. But Dolcin was refused permission to offer depositions from five British physicians that such chemical compounds were beneficial to arthritics and sometimes even cured them. The judge's reason was that the question was not whether *Reader's Digest* held the correct opinion, but whether it had facts on which to base the view it had advanced. The jury returned with a verdict for the magazine, but an appellate court ordered a new trial. It ruled that the trial judge had gotten his law mixed up. *Reader's Digest* could not cite opinions— even the widespread belief of medical experts—as facts on which to base fair comment. For the same reason, it said, the Federal Trade Commission findings should have been ruled out. Such evidence might be offered at a new trial for another purpose—to show the magazine's good faith in relying on the experts, but this would tend only to reduce, not eliminate damages (Dolcin Corp. v. Reader's Digest Assn., 7 A.D. 2d (N.Y.) 449). After a jury was picked for a second trial the case was settled out of court on undisclosed terms.

While the facts on which the comment is made should be stated, they need not be set out extensively. A commentator's right to limit his recital of the facts was tested in a case involving a number of New York lawyers. In the middle 1930s the Association of the Bar of the City of New York decided to bring disbarment proceedings against Dixie Davis, who had been a lawyer for the infamous Dutch Schultz and his crime syndicate. Every lawyer has the right to defend a person charged with a crime. But it is unethical to give advice on the commission of a crime and then agree to defend the criminal if arrested. This was the charge against Davis. The bar association retained Irving Ben Cooper, later named a Federal judge, to handle the prosecution. The case was referred to John P. Cohalan, an official referee, for a hearing. At the closed hearings most of the rulings went against Cooper, and eventually Cohalan exonerated Davis. The court, however, turned down Referee Cohalan's report and disbarred Davis.

Then Cooper went to several New York newspapers and briefed them on what had happened at the Davis hearings. Both the *Herald Tribune* and the *World-Telegram* ran editorials denouncing the way Cohalan had handled the hearings, and Cohalan sued them both. In its answer, the *Tribune* set forth in detail some rulings that Cohalan had made. Cohalan's attorney moved to strike the answer on the ground that the editorial comment had not given the details of the rulings they had denounced. The court rejected his plea with these words:

> If plaintiff's position in this respect were correct, no editorial or book review could safely be written unless it contained a minute description of all the facts upon which the comment or criticism contained in the editorial or book review was predicated. It is sufficient that the facts upon which the comment or criticism is based are referred to in the editorial, book review or article. In *Foley v. Press Publishing Co.*, the opinion contains a quotation that language "may be held to be comment if the fact so stated appears to be a deduction or conclusion come to by the speaker from other facts stated or referred to by him." The facts relied upon in the editorials involved in the present action had become matters of public record prior to the publication of the editorials, and as such were accessible to any one who wished to examine the record. They did not have to be specifically enumerated and described in the editorials themselves in orders to confer defeasible immunity upon the defendant. [Cohalan v. New York Tribune, 172 Misc. (N.Y.) 20]

Some courts are much stricter in their requirements, as the Baltimore Sunpapers found out in a case decided by the Court of Appeals of Maryland. After a hearing, Baltimore legislators charged that City Police Commissioner Hepbron was incompetent and guilty of misconduct. They said that he conducted illegal wiretaps and had been friendly with underworld leaders, and they asked the Governor to remove him. Later the Governor held a hearing and decided not to remove Hepbron, despite damaging testimony against him. Among those who testified at both hearings was Edgar G. Kirby, who had been dismissed from the police force on charges of planting false evidence on a raided establishment and of refusing to obey orders, including the taking of a lie-detector test. Kirby's appeal from the dismissal was pending in court when he testified at the hearings. On June 17, 1959, the day after the Governor decided not to oust the police commissioner, the *Morning Sun* ran an editorial headlined "Not Proved," in which it said that the driving force to "get" the commissioner had been a legislator fronting for a Baltimore political leader. The editorial contained this paragraph:

> Every important witness against the Police Commissioner, moreover, was a man with a motive. We name especially the infamous Kirby, former Inspector Forrester, and former Chief Inspector Ford whose retirement was requested and granted some time ago with dazzling haste.

Kirby sued the *Sun*, asserting that the reference to him as "infamous" and the imputation that his motive in testifying against Hepbron was corrupt were untrue statements of fact. The *Sun* insisted that Kirby had been in the news and the public knew that he had been dismissed from the force for planting evidence and balking at a lie-detector test. These facts, said the *Sun,* were sufficient to support its libelous criticism. But the court said no, that the only facts stated in the editorial about Kirby dealt with his testimony at the hearings and that these actions admittedly were not derogatory. It added:

> While not suggesting that we agree, we find enough to have permitted the jury to conclude that the editorial had been written more in anger than in sorrow and that there had been a reckless disregard for Kirby's reputation, in calling him infamous without stating or referring to any fact that reasonably justified the characterization.

Then the court did an unusual thing. It pointed out how the editorial could have been written to meet the test of fair comment. "The point sought to be made could have been made," it went on, "by saying, 'Kirby, who was discharged from the Police Department on a charge of failing to take a lie detector test after he had been charged with faking evidence', or some similar statement of fact."

The editorial cost the Sunpapers $45,000, plus $3,000 in interest (A. S. Abell Co. v. Kirby, 227 Md. 267).

Fairness

The fourth requirement is that the comment must be fair. This restriction does not mean that the criticism need be mild or temperate. It does not mean that it must be the correct opinion or the majority opinion or the opinion of the judge or jury trying the case. It does mean that there must be some basis of fact, however slight, for the comment. If this slight basis exists, the criticism, no matter how absurd or erroneous it may seem to others or how caustic the language, meets the test of fairness, as long as it is the real, honest opinion of the critic.

An article in the Pittsburgh *Courier* of January 5, 1952, denounced Joseph Beauharnais, president of the White Circle League of America, in these vehement words:

> There is a sinister character in Chicago who is more dangerous than the nation's worst gangster. He conducts a vicious and risky business—the promotion of racial hatred, with biased whites as his steady clients. He has never engineered, as far as I know, any outrage like the Valentine Day massacre, but his atrocious activities, if permitted to continue, are sure to cause violent death to hundreds of unsuspecting American citizens who become victims of his bias plots. . . . He defies all law and order in the performance of his defaming work. He is a menace to racial harmony in Chicago. This is the introduction to Joseph Beauharnais . . . Beauharnais, tall, loose-jointed, shifty-eyed, was dressed in a shoddy blue suit with red and white stripes, probably in answer to his "patriotic" tendencies.

The United States Court of Appeals for the Seventh Circuit noted that Beauharnais had been convicted of inciting racial hatred and had been soliciting memberships in his organization during riots at Cicero. Although the *Courier's* criticism was couched in strong language, it did not exceed the limits permitted regarding subjects of public interest, the court held. Such crit-· icism, the court said, could include ridicule, sarcasm and invective (Beauharnais v. Pittsburgh Courier Publishing Co., Inc., 243 F. 2d 705).

Heywood Broun's review of a play that had one performance in 1917 is a good example of how far a critic can go under the fair-comment rule. The play was *The Awakening of Spring*, by Frank Wedekind. It dealt with problems of adolescence, and the chief character was a boy in his teens. This character was played by an actor named Geoffrey Stein. Here is part of Broun's review:

> There seems to be little justification for the belief that the author intended his tragedy as a mere bit of propaganda rather than as a serious work of art, yet it was not serious yesterday, because Geoffrey Stein gave a ludicrously inadequate performance in the important role of Melchior. It was easily the worst performance we have ever seen on any stage. . . .
>
> Supposedly a lad of fourteen, Stein costumed himself in a low-comedy pair of short trousers, which were much too tight, and talked in a deep bass voice. His performance gave the suggestion that Simon Legree was attending a masquerade in the character of Little Boy Blue. At such times he was not growling in deep gutturals, Stein was hopping about the stage somewhat after the manner of Mike Debitsky in the Ballet Loose.

Mr. Stein brought suit. An attempt to get the judge to rule that the review was not libelous because it was limited to a single performance by Stein was rejected. The judge held that the severity of the criticism was equivalent to a charge of general professional incapacity. Therefore, the defendant had to fall back on the defense of fair comment and criticism. Testimony was offered that Stein did wear tight trousers and that although he was cast in the role of an adolescent boy, he talked in a deep bass voice. In charging the jury the judge said:

> Every person has a right to publish fair and candid criticism although the actor may suffer loss from it. Such a loss the law does not consider an injury. This privilege of criticism in the absence of actual malice extends even to ridicule and is without limitation, except that it should be fair and honest. If the article sued on in this

case is found by the jury to be criticism as defined, is confined to fair honest comment upon a matter of public interest, the plaintiff's presentation of a character in a play, and does not attack the moral character or professional integrity of the plaintiff or impute to him unworthy motives, it is not defamatory and the verdict must be for the defendant no matter though it may be severe, hostile, rough, caustic, bitter, sarcastic or satirical in the opinion of the jury. . . . If the jury, after reading the article, think the criticism published by the defendant was such that no fair man could possibly have come to that conclusion about it, then and then only will they find for the plaintiff.

The jury returned with a verdict for Broun. This was a perfect example of fair comment and criticism because as severely as it assailed Stein's performance, there was no word of aspersion of Stein as an individual. His motives were not criticized nor was the propriety of his conduct. This case also illustrates the rule that the opinion does not have to be the majority one. Many of the other critics praised Stein's performance and Stein's attorney tried to introduce this fact as evidence, but the court refused to permit it, saying the opinions of others were of no consequence in the trial. Broun was not required to state the correct opinion; he had a right to give his own.

The case that is so often cited in judicial rulings on fair comment and criticism is a 1901 ruling by the Iowa Supreme Court. The following article, in the Des Moines *Leader*, brought the suit:

Billy Hamilton, of the Odebolt *Chronicle*, gives the Cherry Sisters the following graphic write-up on their late appearance in his town: "Effie is an old jade of 50 summers, Jessie a frisky filly of 40, and Addie, the flower of the family a capering monstrosity of 35. Their long skinny arms, equipped with talons at the extremities, swung mechanically, and anon waved frantically at the suffering audience. The mouths of their rancid features opened like caverns, and sounds like the wailings of damned souls issued therefrom. They pranced around the stage with a motion that suggested a cross between the *danse du ventre* and fox trot—strange creatures with painted faces and hideous mien. Effie is spavined, Addie is stringhalt, and Jessie, the only one who showed her stockings, has legs with calves as classic in their outlines as the curves of a broom handle."

In upholding the paper's right to a fair comment, the court

said that ridicule was often the writer's most effective weapon
(Cherry v. Des Moines Leader, 114 Iowa 298).

In almost all cases the writer would be wise to refrain from
doubting motives. One of the earliest decisions on the subject
would probably no longer apply to the kind of plaintiff who
brought the case—an assistant inspector of the New York City
Board of Health—because of the New York Times rule. But the
principles it enunciates are still good law for those who are not
public officials. The case concerned a letter that Amos F. Eno
wrote Februay 11, 1875, and the New York *Tribune* published.
Eno criticized a type of street pavement that had been highly
recommended by Allan McLane Hamilton, the inspector, in a
report to his superiors. In addition, Eno speculated on the possibility that the report had been written either under the dictation
of the Grahamite Pavement Company or without full inquiry and
added:

> It is understood that the stock of the Grahamite Company has
> been placed where "it will do the most good". . . . When such an
> example is known, those who step aside from the strict line of duty
> to advocate something outside of their proper official sphere, cannot
> feel aggrieved if their action is looked upon with suspicion.

That, said the court, was going too far. It was perfectly defensible to criticize the report, because every citizen has a right to
discuss in public the question of which kind of pavement to use,
just as the report had done. But, the court noted, the reference to
the possibility that Hamilton might be holding some of the company's stock was not an expression of opinion at all but was in
the form of a fact and thus constituted an excuse for an aspersive
attack upon the character and motives of the officers. Hamilton
won $3,000 in damages (Hamilton v. Eno, 81 N. Y. 116).

This case illustrates the rule that criticism must be limited to
the thing discussed and that motives generally cannot be attacked.

However, motives can sometimes be criticized. In some states
imputations of corruption or dishonorable motives can be made if
they are stated not as facts but as an inference that a fair-minded
man might reasonably draw from the facts. The New York *World*
questioned the motives of Capt. Paul Foley, the trial judge advocate in a naval court-martial inquiring into the loss of the airship
Shenandoah in an Ohio storm on September 25, 1925. In a long

editorial the *World* noted that Mrs. Zachary Lansdowne, widow of the dead commander of the *Shenandoah*, had insisted that her husband had protested the timing of the flight and despite the Secretary of the Navy's denials, the record had borne him out. Judge Advocate Foley then went to see Mrs. Lansdowne and suggested that she issue a statement he had prepared in which she withdrew her request to testify at the inquiry. The *World* concluded:

> Capt. Foley, technical aide to Secretary Wilbur, had undertaken to do a little fixing.
>
> That is the Lansdowne story as it is written in the record. What it shows is, first, that the bureaucrats of the Navy Department seeking to make propaganda for dirigibles by taking advantage of state fairs, play politics with the *Shenandoah*. Disaster overtakes them. Then the Secretary of the Navy either tries to hide the facts or shows he does not know them. Then the facts come out. Then the widow of a dead naval officer intends to tell her story much too publicly, and an attempt is made to hush her up.
>
> How much longer, may we ask, does the President of the United States intend to wreck public confidence in the Navy Department by retaining at the department's head a man who first lies or blunders, then makes no apology for the blunder or the lie, and then permits his aides-de-camp to rig testimony for important witnesses?
>
> This whole affair, from the first statement of Mr. Wilbur on Sept. 3 to the present bullyragging tactics of more Navy Department bureaucrats who constitute a court of inquiry and seem to think it is their duty not to get at facts but to catch Mrs. Lansdowne in a quibble, smells to the high heavens. The sooner a Congressional Committee of investigation shakes the truth out of it the better for the Navy.

Captain Foley, who was absolved by the court of inquiry of any wrongdoing in his dealing with Mrs. Lansdowne, sued on the ground that his motives had been attacked. The plaintiff contended that some of the libelous statements in the editorial, such as "a little fixing," "to rig testimony" and "bullyragging tactics" were in the form of fact and thus did not qualify for the defense of fair comment. On that question the court said, quoting previous opinions:

> "Comment may sometimes consist in the statement of a fact, and may be held to be comment if the fact so stated appears to be a de-

duction or conclusion come to by the speaker from other facts stated or referred to by him. . . . If, although stated as a fact, it is preceded or accompanied by such other facts, and it can reasonably be based upon them, the words may be reasonably regarded as comment, and comment only, and if honest and fair, excusable; and whether it is to be regarded as a fact or comment is a question for the jury, to be determined by them upon all the circumstances of the case." . . .

"An inference or comment may take the form of a statement of fact. The question is not whether the words which the defendant used stated a fact or not, but whether reading them in their environment the impression conveyed to the audience was that the defendant was merely making a bald statement . . . or an inference which the speaker thought should be drawn from certain facts which he mentioned or referred to." . . .

Judged by these principles, the . . . defense here pleaded is sufficient. The libel in this case illustrates the sound reasons for the existence of the defense. Captain Foley's conduct is described in the title of the first editorial as "A Smelly Business." It is stated that he had "undertaken to do a little fixing," that he had been guilty of "bullyragging tactics," and that there was "too much whitewash." The editorial sets forth as the facts which prompted the writer so to describe the conduct, the attempt to dissuade Mrs. Lansdowne from giving oral testimony, the advice to her "not to make any statement as to the political aspects of said flight," the circumstances surrounding the preparation of the written statement intended to be read before the naval court by Mrs. Lansdowne, and the falsity of that prepared statement in material respects. The position of the defendant is that such statements as are clearly of fact are actually true; that the publication is an editorial, not a news story, and purports to state opinions as well as facts; that phrases such as "rigging testimony," "fixing," "too much whitewash," and "a smelly business" are fairly to be regarded as expressions of opinion; and that a jury may say that they reasonably characterize Captain Foley's conduct. We cannot say as a matter of law that such expressions are statements of fact, nor can we determine as a matter of law that they are unfair comment upon the facts pleaded as true. A jury must decide these issues.

With respect to the attack on Captain Foley's motives, the court said that the facts may justify such comment. On this point the court said:

We concur in the principle enunciated by these authorities that the publication to be justified must contain no imputations of corruption or dishonorable motive, except insofar as they are an inference which a fair-minded man might reasonably draw from the facts truly stated and represent the honest opinion of the writer. If the imputations are thus inferable and honestly stated, the publication is justified. The mere circumstances that comments are exaggerated will not render them unfair. [Foley v. Press Publishing Co., 226 App. Div. (N.Y.) 535]

But motives can be questioned in any jurisdiction if the occasion being reported is the right kind. There must be a public gathering —not necessarily an official one—and the public itself, or some element in the audience, must express the doubts. Thus when Cassius Clay knocked out Sonny Liston in less than two minutes of the first round in the heavyweight championship fight at Lewiston, Maine, in May, 1965, the sportswriters and columnists went ahead and reported that the fans yelled, "Fake, Fake, Fake" and "Fix, Fix." Those were undoubtedly libelous comments, but they were expressions of opinions at a public sports spectacle and as such could be passed along.

Malice

The final requirement of fair comment and criticism is that the opinion not be inspired by malice. Malice will be discussed in full in Chapter 16, but a good rule of thumb for commentators would be to keep personal ill will out of their comments.

Crusading Articles

As is evident in almost all the cases cited, fair comment is invaluable to the newsman who takes sides. The crusading reporter, the doctrinaire commentator, the editorial writer, the political cartoonist could not get very far without it. Fair comment enables them to make their charges safely, without backing away from them or watering them down. The skilled writer knows how he can expose a rotten situation without undue risk of incurring damage. Here is an example from *Life* magazine's December 7, 1959, issue:

WHAT IS SO RARE AS A RARE FIND?

CALIFORNIA PRODUCES THE LATEST REASONS
FOR VIEWING "OLD MASTERS" SUSPICIOUSLY

The news item from California was a rarity even in that land of overnight fairytale fortunes. Ten paintings, owned by Italian immigrants in Pasadena were said to be Old Masters worth millions of dollars—"the greatest art find of the century!" This was the latest of a long line of "fabulous discoveries" that have burst upon the art world in recent years. The California canvases had long been in the Naples family of Maria and Alfonso Follo. When Maria married a GI she brought them to her new home in Pasadena and tucked them away in a closet and under a bed.

A year ago Alfonso Follo, a TV repairman who had come to live with his sister, dropped in at the neighborhood electrical supply store of Charles and Jay di Renzo and invited them to come up and see the family paintings some time. The di Renzos came, saw and promptly made a deal with the Follos to help sell the art. Their first step: to find an expert to identify the paintings. They telephoned one Amadore Porcella, an Italian who had just authenticated a Raphael in Chicago.

Hurrying out to Pasadena, Porcella took one ecstatic look at the paintings and pronounced them masterpieces. One, he said, was a long-lost painting . . . by the 17th Century Italian master, Caravaggio, and he valued it at more than $1 million. Porcella then called in his friend, Alexander Zlatoff-Mirsky, a Chicago art restorer, for some heavy work. After a few weeks of working with "powerful solvents," Zlatoff-Mirsky declared the paintings almost as good as new and ready for unveiling.

Shortly after the "masterpieces" were made public, ominous doubts began to gather about their authenticity. A Pasadena expert said he had seen the paintings several years ago and found them worthless. A New York scholar said the long-lost Caravaggio was known through authentic copies . . . and bore no resemblance to the Pasadena work. Finally an Italian priest disclosed that the Follos' so-called Caravaggio was in fact a copy of a minor 17th Century painting . . . which hangs in Naples. The California fairy tale was showing signs of being just that.

BUSY TEAM AND ITS THRIVING OUTLET

Discovering a trove of valuable Old Masters would be a once-in-a-lifetime stroke of luck for most mortals. But Porcella and Zlatoff-Mirsky have, as one of their friends observed, a "remarkable talent" for it. Just in the course of the past year they have authenticated more than a dozen "masterpieces."

The pair's instinct for art showed up early. Porcella started out to be a painter in Rome. At the age of 17, he explains, he switched to art criticism. Around 1934 he worked briefly at the Vatican gallery (compiling a guidebook of the art collections). Since then he has written a number of books and "authenticated" innumerable paintings. Zlatoff-Mirsky worked as a painter in Russia until the 1930s when he migrated to Chicago and took up the more remunerative profession of restoring art.

In 1958 the two "experts" met for the first time in New York. Soon after, Porcella went to Chicago and settled down in Zlatoff-Mirsky's studio to inspect the paintings which the Russian was restoring. In a short time they identified "millions of dollars" worth of art, tagged with such top-drawer names as Leonardo da Vinci, Rembrandt and Raphael.

The dual role of source and thriving outlet for most of the team's discoveries is played by the Sheridan Art Galleries, a Chicago auction house which specializes in old and modern "masterpieces." For the past 20 years their highly prized consultant and art restorer has been none other than Zlatoff-Mirsky. Recently the gallery's reputation was slightly tarnished when two buyers proved that the paintings they bought there were fakes. The gallery refunded the complainants' money, later sold one of the paintings for an even higher price.

THE INS AND OUTS OF AUTHENTICATING

Active as they are, Professor Porcella and his colleague Zlatoff-Mirsky have not cornered the art "discoveries" market. Rival authenticators continue to turn up, armed with new-found treasures and long-lost masterpieces. Some of them are reputable authorities. Others are "experts" with elusive or spurious credentials. Whatever their background, many authenticators seem to be in the business at least as much for love of money as love of art.

How much an authenticator makes depends generally on the importance of the painter's name and the authenticator's evaluation of the particular painting. An expert is inclined to charge more for recognizing a Leonardo than a Lastman. Often the price of authenticating a painting far exceeds the amount paid for the work. Porcella received $2,000 for authenticating a work that was bought for half that price. . . .

Professor Erik Larsen received $550 for certifying a painting that originally cost his client $20. . . .

To enhance their prestige and give validity to their judgment, authenticators often publish books or articles reproducing their "discoveries." But their talent for writing is apt to show up best in the flamboyant certificates they compose for their "masterpieces."

The more unscrupulous authenticators have found a bonanza in providing income tax outs. A buyer who pays $1,000 for an old painting may call upon an "expert" to evaluate his purchase. For a comfortable fee, the "expert" values the painting at many times its actual worth. The buyer then donates the painting to a museum or some other institution, thereby getting a sizable write-off on his income tax for his charitable donation.

So far in the U. S. there are no legal penalties for such dealings. The quasi experts are not held responsible for their authentications. The auction houses are not required to back up the authenticity of the works they sell. And with the art market currently enjoying its biggest boom, the flood of dubious "masterpieces," both old and new, is sure to continue.

Life was very careful to stick to the facts so that when Porcella sued for libel he could not claim that any were incorrect. Nevertheless Porcella felt that he was being defamed. He had good reason to feel that way, because *Life* had slanted its article by dropping comments throughout (note how the third paragraph begins: "*Hurrying* out to Pasadena, Porcella took *one ecstatic look* at the paintings and pronounced them masterpieces" [italics ours]) and carefully selecting its facts (note how paragraph six describes Porcella's and Zlatoff-Mirsky's training, thus casting doubt on their claim to being experts). But by the time it came to a charge of outright fraud, *Life* had already mentioned that there were rival authenticators so that although doubt was expressed about Porcella's findings, he was never accused of any wrongdoing. Thus the United States Court of Appeals concluded that Porcella had no right to damages. In rejecting his claim it said:

> Our analysis of the alleged libelous article convinces us that, insofar as the complaint charged it to be false, it is an expression of the publisher's comments and opinions upon the activities of plaintiff as an art expert with a description of the entire setting in which he was active. It might well be characterized as a satirical recital by an author who made no effort to conceal his belief that there were some authenticators of painting less reliable than others. The article, insofar as it offended plaintiff, merely expressed the author's opinion, rather than made a false statement of any fact.

Plaintiff was engaged in a field which he admits (and even boasts) was in the public domain and, as such, he was subject to comment by the public press. . . . [Porcella v. Time, Inc., 300 F. 2d 162]

There are times when commentators can, with a minimum of risks, go beyond the ordinary limits of fair comment. Judges follow the election returns, observers have said, and when passions run high on an issue the courts sometimes stretch the law to fit the popular mood. If the commentator agrees with public opinion he can phrase his criticism of those who oppose it in even harsher language than he ordinarily would—if his conscience lets him.

During World War II Vivian Kellems, a Connecticut woman who manufactured cable grips, waged a campaign against government policies, particularly the income tax. She made speeches against the tax, and in June 1944, she announced that she was not paying her December installment and invited businessmen to follow her example. She also wrote to a Count Zedlitz, a German national who was the Argentine representative of a German metal concern, in violation of the Trading With the Enemy Act. During the same period labor organizations had been smarting under criticism for strikes. Here was a chance for unions to dish it out for a change. On April 14, 1944, and again on October 13, 1944, the *Labor Herald*, a publication of the California Council of the Congress of Industrial Organizations, published articles asserting that Mrs. Kellems was engaging in "treasonable operations." Mrs. Kellems sued for $1,000,000. Just as her political beliefs had been rejected by the public, her suit was dismissed by a Federal District Court. It agreed that the charge against her was libelous. True, the labor paper did not use "treasonable" in the statutory definition, the court said, but "rather in the sense of savoring of, or partaking of or akin to treason and in the nature of disloyalty." Nevertheless, the latter designation was said to carry "an equivalent odium in the public mind." In any event, the court said, the *Labor Herald* was found to be within its rights in making the comment. Some passages from the court's opinion indicate how the wartime patriotism was very much on its mind:

> The evidence discloses plaintiff to be a highly placed woman industrialist enjoying during the war profitable government contracts of a highly confidential nature. She took to the public platform to proclaim her grievances against the government and officers of

the government. Moreover, she undertook in so doing to mold and shape public opinion, all undeniably proper and lawful activities. But when, in time of grave national peril, she directly urged and invited citizens to refrain from paying taxes payable pursuant to duly enacted statutes and necessary in the prosecution of the war, in my opinion, it was within the area of fair comment to characterize her activities as "treasonable." Those, who in public utterances seek to formulate and direct public opinion, have an accompanying responsiblity. Particularly is this so at a time when millions of our young men and women were offering life and limb in national defense.

That the published designation of plaintiff's activities is within the field of fair comment is given further substantiation when it appears that during the period of national peril, plaintiff maintained correspondence with a German enemy, contrary to law and recognized concepts of loyalty in time of war. Plaintiff claims the evidence fails to show that Zedlitz was a Nazi. Whether he was Nazi or just plain German, appears to me to be, under the circumstances, of no moment. . . .

The court observed the plaintiff's demeanor and attitude upon the witness stand. I found her to be evasive, argumentative, arrogant and indeed brazen in her reiteration of her claimed right to do and say as she pleased, without regard to the possible dire consequence to her country and her fellow citizens. True, these considerations are not legally controlling in the resolution of the issue here presented. But at least they go to the weight of the evidence and serve to throw light upon the spirit and intent backgrounding the utterances and activities referred to in the alleged defamatory publications. [Kellems v. California Congress of Industrial Organizations Council, 68 F. Supp. 277]

A more recent example concerns Communism. The book *Red Channels* (discussed briefly on page 27) listed Joe Julian, an actor, as having attended two Communist-front meetings. Julian sued, complaining that while he had innocently attended the two meetings, he was not a Communist dupe, tool, sucker or fellow traveler. New York's highest court affirmed the defense of fair comment without letting it go to a jury on the question of malice and honesty of opinion, as is usual in such cases. But the book was published in 1950, when feelings were running strong against the Communists and there was much public discussion on how to meet the menace (Julian v. American Business Consultants, 2 N.Y. 2d 1).

The moral would seem to be that if a commentator is on the side of the majority on an issue where passions are strong, he can go further in his opinions than he ordinarily could. But if the commentator's opinion runs counter to the public's he should pull in his horns, unless he thinks that the subject is so overriding that he must take the risk.

Chapter 14

CONSENT—THE BACKSTOP DEFENSE

IT IS A BASIC PART OF LAW THAT THE PERSON WHO CONSENTS TO an act that hurts him cannot collect for his suffering. The man who asks a drinking companion to swat him in the stomach will not get far if he prefers charges against his pal for knocking him down. In libel this principle means that the person who is defamed cannot win damages if he has authorized the publication. This defense is firmly established in the law of defamation.

Consent does not have to be direct. The reporter could conceivably show the person in the news the libelous story and ask, "Is it all right if I publish it?" But he would more likely get a punch in the nose than a "yes" for his effort. Unless there are unusual circumstances, the direct approach is not advised. Consent, however, can be won in indirect ways. The simplest is to get comment from the defamed person regarding the charge against him.

One of the early cases supporting this indirect consent was that of Mrs. Anne McCoy Campbell, the Christian Science practitioner. (One of the several cases she filed was discussed in Chapter 11.) She had been accused in a suit of defrauding Mrs. Elizabeth S. Nichols through confidence established in a religious relationship. Mrs. Campbell's answer to the suit had been misfiled at the courthouse, so the reporters did not see it. *The New York Times* reporter, however, called Mrs. Campbell and told her that Mrs. Nichols' charges had been made public and asked if she wanted to comment on them. She did and the *Times* published her denials.

After Mrs. Nichols dropped her case, Mrs. Campbell sued the New York papers for libel. The *Times* took the position that Mrs. Campbell, by commenting on the charges and denying them, had impliedly consented to the publication of Mrs. Nichols' original charges, since the denials without the details of the charges would have been meaningless. The New York *Sun*, which had copied the *Times*' story, took the same position.

When the cases came up for trial, the juries were instructed that if they found that Mrs. Campbell, by giving the interview for publication, had consented to the publication of the original charges against her, they should find for the newspapers. Justice Phoenix Ingraham's charge in the *Sun* case was especially significant because the interview had been given to the *Times* and picked up by the *Sun* without checking. The judge held that the fact that the interview had not been given to a *Sun* reporter made no difference as long as the release had been given to a newspaper for general publication. In his charge Justice Ingraham said to the jury:

> It is for you to determine whether or not from all the evidence before you, the plaintiff in an interview with a reporter of a newspaper gave out for publication the facts which are contained in this article. If after a careful consideration of all the evidence you find that she did give out these facts to a reporter, then your verdict should be for the defendant. And the fact that the reporter with whom the interview was had was a representative of another newspaper makes no difference in this case. Moreover if you believe the testimony of defendant's editor that he read the account published in The New York Times and other papers and believed that the facts stated therein have been given out by plaintiff for publication, it is for you to determine whether defendant's editor was justified in believing that such statements had been in fact given out by the plaintiff for publication. In other words you must decide whether he was justified under all the circumstances in believing that the plaintiff had stated to the reporter for The Times for purposes of publication the facts contained in The Times article. If you decide that he was justified in his belief, and that the article which forms the basis of this action is a reasonably fair, accurate account of the facts appearing in the article of The Times, then your verdict should be for the defendant. If on the other hand you are satisfied after a careful consideration of all the evidence that this plaintiff did not state the facts contained in this article to any reporter for any newspaper, and that the editor of the defendant newspaper was not justified in believing . . . that the plaintiff had given out for publication the statements contained in The Times article, then

your verdict should be for the plaintiff. [Campbell v. Sun Printing & Publishing Assn. Supreme Court of the State of New York, New York County, Trial Term Part XI, May 14, 1926]

In both cases, the juries found for the papers and sent Mrs. Campbell home without a cent.

The result was a magnificent victory for freedom of information because it gave reporters and editors wider latitude in publishing controversial news. But the cases could not be cited to judges in subsequent litigation because they were never published in the lawbooks. Mrs. Campbell did not appeal either the *Times* or the *Sun* decision, and, unless there is an appeal, the judge's instruction to the jury is not normally published.

Appellate Approval

Finally in January, 1956, the United States Court of Appeals for the Fourth Circuit supplied the authority needed for effective use of the defense. The decision came in two cases filed against the Baltimore *Sun* as the result of a story that Lawrence Westbrook, vice chairman of the Democratic National Committee, had negotiated a $9 million tungsten contract with the Federal Government for a Portuguese corporation.

Bert Andrews, head of the New York *Herald Tribune* Washington bureau, dug up the story. On checking with counsel, he was urged to ask Westbrook for comment. Andrews found Westbrook in a hotel in Dallas, where he was running House Speaker Sam Rayburn's campaign for reelection. Andrews told Westbrook what he had learned and asked for comment. Westbrook said that there was nothing improper about the contract and he did not want any publicity about it. Then, hoping that Andrews would drop the story if a better one came along, he said he thought Bert had called to ask how the campaign was going in Texas and predicted that the Democrats would win by a 60-to-40 margin. Andrews of course was not content with this reply, so he called Stephen A. Mitchell, the Democratic National Chairman, and told him about the article. Mitchell exploded. He phoned Westbrook, asked about the report and dismissed him then and there. With the cat out of the bag Westbrook decided he had better say something, so he called Andrews and gave him a long statement for publication. He also issued the statement to the wire services.

A year later, one day before the statute of limitations would have run, Westbrook brought libel actions against a number of newspapers, including the *Herald Tribune* and the Baltimore *Sun*. All the papers asserted that Westbrook, by commenting on the articles, had consented to their publication. The case against the *Sun*, which had used an Associated Press story based largely on the *Tribune's*, was the first to go before an appellate court. The *Sun* moved for summary judgment and the motion was granted, whereupon Westbrook took the case to the Circuit Court of Appeals. In affirming the lower court, the circuit court said:

> In view of the fact that Westbrook gave this statement to the press in an interview to be published, he is hardly in a position to complain of the publication with it of the charge to which it was an answer, even if the latter were otherwise objectionable. [Pulvermann v. A. S. Abell Co., 228 F. 2d 797]

Tennessee Case

Two students at Vanderbilt University put this defense into good use in a sensitive story in the student newspaper, *The Hustler*. The libelous matter had first appeared in the student humor magazine, *The Chase*, on May 17, 1954. In a layout poking fun at Mother's Day, *The Chase* had included four pictures with an over-all headline that said "Everyone Loves Mother." The upper left picture was a blank rectangle printed black, with the caption "Father Loves Mother" under it. The upper right picture was of a small child, with the caption "Daughter Loves Mother (And wants to be one too)." The lower left picture showed a boy in a T-shirt, his arm tatooed with a heart enclosing the word "Mother" and the caption "Sailor Boy Loves Mother." The lower right was a picture of an idiotically smiling face, partly covered by a hood, captioned "Midwife Loves Mother."

There was nothing else on the page, nothing to identify any person pictured there. But the cut of the child was actually a reproduction of a picture of Pamela Langford that her father, a Methodist minister, had delivered to the printer two years before for use on Christmas cards. Through a mistake this picture was used in the humor magazine's layout. When the issue of the magazine reached the Vanderbilt campus, someone recognized the picture and soon all but a few copies of the edition were seized and destroyed. In an act of self-chastisement, the Student Publications Board banned further publications of *The Chase*.

That seemed to end the matter, but when the fall term resumed there was talk that Langford was going to sue. Having learned to go to the source for a story, Ormond Plater, editor of *The Hustler*, and Joe Puryear, a reporter, called on the minister and asked for an interview. He granted the interview, confirmed the rumor that he was going to sue, let the two student journalists take some pictures and showed them some photos of his daughter, including one in a Vanderbilt T-shirt. He even told them they could select one photo to use with the story. But a friend of the minister who was present suggested that he check first with his lawyers. After doing so Langford told the students he would not release any picture and referred them to his lawyers for details of the suits.

But he was still willing to have a story published. Plater testified, "He told us that he wanted publicity in the matter, and to go and contact his lawyers for legal details." The minister did not contradict his lawyers on this point, for he said under cross-examination, "I wouldn't have minded having a fair statement of the facts presented to the public. I was not ashamed of what I was doing. I believed that I was doing the will of my Almighty God in fighting this and I didn't care if we had received publicity that would have presented it in its true light."

Acting on the minister's suggestion, Puryear went to see the lawyers and one of them promised to call when the suits were filed. On January 20, 1955, he phoned and said that the suits were being filed that afternoon. Puryear could get only a bulletin in the issue of *The Hustler* for the next day. But he and Plater then went to the court and read the papers filed in the suits. In legal language the suits charged that the Mother's Day pictures, through innuendo, implied that two-year-old Pamela Langford was interested in and amenable to acts of illicit sexual intercourse, that Mrs. Langford was sleeping in a darkened bedroom with a sailor and that Mr. Langford was having sexual relations in a darkened bedroom with someone unknown. Plater and Puryear then wrote an article that appeared in *The Hustler* under this headline:

$180,000.00 SUIT FILED BY LOCAL
MINISTER OVER CHASE PHOTO

CLAIMS ISSUE "LEWD, BAWD, VULGAR;"
"SPREAD SEX, FILTH, SLIME AND SMUT"

The article was an accurate summary of the six suits for libel and invasion of privacy. To illustrate the story, the offensive page from the Mother's Day issue of *The Chase* was reproduced and the objections to the pictures given. The minister, his wife and daughter then filed new suits—this time objecting to the handling of the report by *The Hustler*. The Circuit Court dismissed the cases and the Tennessee Court of Appeals upheld the decision. The appellate court pointed out that the article had been a fair report of a judicial proceeding, thus barring any damages. It also gave another reason:

> . . . we think this publication was absolutely privileged, as invited or consented to by plaintiffs. All the evidence shows that plaintiff Mr. Langford told these two students he wanted publicity, referred them to his lawyers for the legal details, the lawyers advised them when the suits were filed, and they made a fair and accurate statement of the pleadings, giving the alleged defamatory parts in plaintiffs' own words. [Langford v. Vanderbilt *et al.*, 44 Tenn. App. 694]

The Tennessee Supreme Court denied certiorari in *The Hustler* case. *The Chase* cases were never tried.

Beyond Consent

Sometimes the target of attack is so incensed that he not only consents, he also invites publication. A good example is a case that reached the Arkansas Supreme Court. On July 16, 1959, Governor Orval Faubus of Arkansas held a press conference at which he issued a release stating that an investigation had found irregularities in the operation of nursing homes in the state. He characterized the Trinity Nursing Home at Little Rock as "a sordid and shocking story of mismanagement and misdeeds" and announced that its operator, Mrs. Gladys Neal Brandon, had been dismissed as an assistant part-time attorney for the Welfare Department. The Arkansas *Democrat*, the evening paper, carried the story. Mrs. Brandon's attorney promptly called the morning paper, the *Gazette,* and invited a reporter and photographer to see the nursing home and judge it for themselves. The *Gazette* carried two page-1 stories on the charge under the headline "Faubus Says Probe Uncovers Scandal at Nursing Home."

One story, with a read-out headline saying "Shocking Conditions Are Alleged," told of the Governor's charges and mentioned that they had been denied. The other story, with a head saying "Trinity Denies Charges, Asks Probe by Jury," was based on the visit to the home and interview with Mrs. Brandon. It set out in full the details by Mrs. Brandon and her attorney of each charge and also quoted the Chief Sanitarian of the Little Rock Health Department that "to the best of my knowledge, we've had no unusual trouble up there." Praise of Mrs. Brandon's services to the Welfare Department was also mentioned.

In short, the *Gazette* gave Mrs. Brandon's side of the story in full. She even called the paper to express gratitude to the reporter, Patrick Owens, for his handling of the article.

Nevertheless, she sued. The following excerpts from the abstract of the case show the difficulty that a plaintiff like Mrs. Brandon faces once she is interrogated about her willingness to comment on the case:

> Q. Did you expect the *Gazette* to print your denial without telling the public who was reading the story what the Governor said?
> A. I didn't expect the story to be authorized, no sir.
> Q. Mrs. Brandon, did you want the *Gazette* to print your denial without putting in the story what the Governor accused you of?
> A. Yes. That is what I would like for them to have done.
> Q. You would have liked for them to have done that?
> A. Yes sir, because it is not so. I think when Mr. Owens went through, I think he knows it wasn't so.
> Q. Did you want the *Gazette* to write an article about you denying the Governor's charges without telling them what you were denying?
> A. I didn't want them to print a story period and I certainly didn't want my picture published.
> Q. You didn't want them to run the picture?
> A. That is right.
> Q. Did your attorney, Mr. Panich, invite them to go through the home?
> A. Mr. Panich invited them I believe. I don't know.

Q. Mr. Panich was your attorney on this thing?
A. That's right. Mr. Panich was my attorney and he would be here today if he was not flat on his back with a heart attack.
Q. And at that time he was authorized to speak for you?
A. Yes.
Q. If Mr. Panich invited them out there to speak for you, then that is what you wanted, wasn't it?
A. I wanted them to come out and look at the home and see it was not true.
Q. Then not print anything?
A. Mr. Carroll, I am not going into what I thought at the time because I was frantic and anyone in their right mind would have been half crazy if they had seen what I saw in the *Democrat* and I was goofy when Mr. Owens was out there. That is exactly the way I felt.

The photographs that the *Gazette* photographer took of Mrs. Brandon were not candid shots, taken when the subject was not looking. She obviously had posed for the cameraman. The picture that the *Gazette* ran with the article showed Mrs. Brandon in tears and was the one that would generate the greatest sympathy for her among readers.

When the case reached the Arkansas Supreme Court the outcome was never in doubt. The article was upheld, partly on the basis that Mrs. Brandon had consented to its publication (the court also noted that it was a fair report of an official proceeding). Regarding the consent, the court said:

It would appear from her testimony that Mrs. Brandon wanted the *Gazette* to print her side of the controversy without printing the charges that had been made, but we find it difficult to understand how one's denials to charges made can be published without also publishing the charges. [Brandon v. Gazette Publishing Co., 234 Ark. 332]

Consent is a good backstop for the newsman uncertain whether a particular story qualifies for any of the other legal defenses for publishing libel. Consider a situation like this: A civil-rights organization accuses the head of a squad of detectives of brutally beating a Negro boy. Since the courts in all states have not precisely defined who is a public officer under the New York Times rule, the reporter is uncertain whether that defense protects him if he reports the charge. If, however, he succeeds in getting the detective to comment on the charge, he has invoked the defense of consent. The reporter has not only substantially reduced the risk of damages, he has also written a more complete story. Similar problems sometimes arise in regard to the defense of reporting an official proceeding. A member of a state investigating committee may hold a news conference and name three pacifists he insists are Communists. The reporter cannot be sure that the courts will hold the news conference to be an official proceeding. But he checks with the three pacifists, gets their denials of Communist membership and writes the story. It is now a balanced story and reasonably safe from damages.

Absolute safety cannot be assured because the courts have not determined with exactitude what is and what is not assent to the publication of defamatory matter. Undoubtedly all the circumstances surrounding it must be taken into consideration. But in many cases the defense cannot arise unless the reporter takes the initiative.

The particular approach of the reporter often affects the outcome. The device used by *The New York Times* reporter on the Campbell story and Bert Andrews on the Westbrook incident can be effective. Both reporters informed the person that charges had been made public against him and said that in fairness he was being given an opportunity to answer at the same time. Of course, if the individual says he has no comment, that is not consent. The article should nevertheless include the fact that he replied, "No comment," when asked about the charges. If the target of the attack cannot be reached, the article should say that attempts to do so were unsuccessful. If the reporter cannot find the subject of the story but does reach his attorney, agent, public-relations man or even his wife, their remarks should be carried. If they are authorized to speak for the individual—and the defense can prove authorization—such statements would amount to consent. In most cases proof will be lacking, but the statements will still be of great value in a trial. The jury will be impressed by the newsman's sense of fair play. This absence of malice can hold damages down (as we shall see in Chapter 16).

Chapter 15

REPLY—THE SELF-DEFENSE

THE RIGHT OF SELF-DEFENSE RUNS ALL THROUGH THE LAW. IF YOU are attacked on the street, you have the right to defend yourself. You also have the right to protect your wife, your children or anyone close to you. In fighting back, the law says you are not restricted to merely blocking the blows of the attacker. You can take the offensive and use sufficient force to discourage him. But you cannot go too far. If a young punk jostles your wife on the subway, you have no right to pull out your derringer and blast away.

In the law of defamation a similar situation exists. The victim of an attack in the press has the right to hit back. A newspaper, magazine or broadcasting station has the right to carry his reply and can also rush to his defense and strike aggressively at the attacker. It can expose the attacker's infirmities and peculiarities and even libel him provided it is not actuated by malice and does not go too far.

The case that has been cited over and over again in support of this defense involved James Gordon Bennett of the New York *Herald* and John Fowler, American Consul in Chefoo, China. In 1908 Bennett brought a young man by the name of Li Sum-ling, the editor of the *Chinese Mail*, to the United States from China to further trade and educational ties between the two countries. The *Herald* made much of the Chinese visitor, setting up an interview between him and the Secretary of State, Elihu Root, carrying stories about his travels and statements and giving him much publicity.

In Boston, Li met Fowler, who was home on sick leave, at a hotel. Fowler was almost blind and very deaf, so most of the discussion had to be conducted by written statements. For some reason Fowler took a violent dislike to Li. Eventually Fowler insulted him, told him he was sorry he had called and left, stopping by the hotel manager's office to warn him to watch out for that Chinese fellow. Then Fowler went to the Boston *Journal,* the Hearst paper there at that time, and denounced Li as an impostor and fake. The *Journal,* which was squabbling with Bennett, was delighted with the news and ran a long article, quoting Fowler at length. The article created a public stir and exasperated Bennett, who hurried to Li's defense. The *Herald* branded Fowler a liar, commented extensively on his physical disabilities and intimated rather pointedly that he was crazy.

Mr. Fowler was sick, but not so sick that he could not find a lawyer and sue. Finding itself unable to prove the truth of its charge that Fowler was mentally ill, the *Herald* resorted to the privilege of self-defense. It said in effect that when Fowler attacked Li, the *Herald* had a right to go to his defense because it had been sponsoring him. Even if some of the statements about Fowler had not been true, the *Herald* argued, it had a right to publish them if it believed them to be true and was not motivated by malice. The trial judge disagreed, insisting that "the Chinaman had nothing to do" with the case. Its defense rejected, the *Herald* was assessed $16,000 in damages. But it appealed and the Appellate Division of the New York Supreme Court reversed the verdict and said that "the Chinaman" did have much to do with the case. Noting that the *Herald* had taken an active interest in promoting Li in this country, the court said:

> When, therefore, he was denounced by the plaintiff publicly as an impostor, the defendant's natural course, not only in defense of the man for whom it had thus stood sponsor, but also in defense of itself, was to defend the Chinaman from unjust attacks and false charges, even if such defense called forth a revelation or explanation of the infirmities or peculiarities of the plaintiff. The defendant had a qualified privilege so to do.

The qualification was that the *Herald* had the right to publish untrue, libelous statements about Fowler provided it believed them to be true, was not motivated by malice and did not go too far in its reply. In such cases the question of whether it exceeded its privilege, the court said, should be decided by a jury (Fowler v. New York Herald, 184 App. Div.(N.Y.)608).

Since then, court decisions have made it clear that the press has the right to transmit libelous remarks not only when it is a supporter of the person replying to an attack but also when it is in a neutral position of merely covering the news.

The United States Court of Appeals for the District of Columbia approved the defense of reply in 1948. In September, 1944, two young naval officers appeared one evening at the Statler Hotel in Washington to attend a dance. In another part of the hotel, a Teamster Union meeting was scheduled to hear an address by President Roosevelt. One of the naval officers, Lieutenant Randolph Dickins, Jr., and members of the Teamsters got into an argument in the corridor. Dickins said that he was slugged, and the Teamsters said that the lieutenant was drunk. A week later Dickins issued a statement to the press, and, it being wartime, the release received wide publicity. A month later Dan Tobin, the Teamster president, published the union member's side in the *International Teamster*. Lieutenant Dickins sued the union for libel.

Elisha Hanson, general counsel for the American Newspaper Publishers Association, who was trying the case for the Teamsters, induced the judge to charge the jury that the union had a conditional privilege to reply to the earlier attacks. The jurors brought in a verdict for the Teamsters, and when questioned by reporters, they all agreed that their verdict had hinged on the right of the union to reply. Dickins appealed but the Court of Appeals turned him down, explaining:

> When the author of a libel writes under the compulsion of a legal or moral duty, or for the protection of his own rights or interest, that which he writes is a privileged communication, unless the writer be actuated by malice. The appellant testified that, before the publication of which he here complains, he himself released to the press his own charges that members of the union assaulted him and his companion. His act in so doing cast upon the union the moral duty and consequently conferred upon it the legal right to publish a reply which, even if it were false, was privileged unless the plaintiff proved the defendant knew it to be false or otherwise proved actual malice in the publication. [Dickins v. International Brotherhood of Teamsters, 171 F. 2d 21]

When does a reply exceed the provocation? The rule is that the response must bear some relation to the original comment. The

Roy Campanella case is a good example. Roy was a catcher for the Dodgers when they played in Brooklyn. He hurt his hand in a game and was operated on twice, the second time by Dr. Samuel Shenkman. In due time Shenkman sent out a bill for $9,500, and when it was not paid he decided to go to court to collect. At the time he started his suit he put public pressure on Campanella and the Dodgers. His attorney called a press conference and issued a statement that included the following sentences:

> I sent the $9,500 bill to Mr. Campanella and it was promptly returned with the suggestion that the Brooklyn Dodgers Baseball Club was responsible for the bill. Then I sent it to the club and they immediately sent it back, informing me that Campanella alone was responsible for payment. Between Campanella and the club, I have been paid nothing.

The lawyer thought he should add something, so he said:

> After it was over, Campy expressed his deep gratitude and told Dr. Shenkman to send the bill to the Brooklyn Ball Club. He sent the bill there and then the Dodger front office said it wasn't their baby. They disclaimed any responsibility for it. And though Roy was grateful at first, he has apparently forgotten his obligation.

This was simply too much for Walter O'Malley, the talkative president of the Dodgers. When he saw the stories in the evening newspapers, he fired off his own press release for the morning papers. In it he said:

> I am shocked by the self-serving story appearing in evening papers in support of Dr. Shenkman's exorbitant claim of $9,500 for what will probably prove to be an unnecessary second operation on Roy Campanella's hand. The medical profession appreciates that the original operation was successfully performed by a recognized specialist, Dr. Herbert Fett. Dr. Shenkman telephone me in February and was most anxious to settle his claim, and admitted that he had not fixed a price or advised Roy that he contemplated such a charge. It appears that he thought he was operating on Roy's bankroll. I told him his charge was unconscionable and suggested he sue. He offered to arbitrate before a committee of doctors. I told him I preferred a jury of people who pay doctor's bills not send them. It took Dr. Shenkman a long time to get up courage to sue.

That did it. Dr. Shenkman sued O'Malley for slander. In discussing O'Malley's right to the defense of reply the court made two observations. The first was that a defamatory reply can be made only in response to a defamatory attack. "The occasion of a nondefamatory attack should not excuse false diatribe in reply," the court said. The second point the court made was that the reply must be related to the charge. In this regard the court noted that motives were pertinent, since they involved the reason for the original charge.

The court concluded that O'Malley was entitled to plead the defense. He had insisted he had been defamed at the Shenkman lawyer's news conference. His accusations that the operation might have been unnecessary and that the doctor thought he was operating on Campanella's bankroll were certainly relevant to the question of whether the $9,500 bill should have been paid.

As for whether O'Malley's response was excessive, the court said that a jury would have to make the determination on the basis of the evidence (Shenkman v. O'Malley, 2 A.D. 2d(N.Y.)567). Despite his victory in the early rounds of the case, O'Malley settled out of court on the third day of the trial, reportedly giving Shenkman $15,000, enough to cover his bill for the operation and most, if not all, of his costs of the libel suit.

Exceeding Provocation

Although the reply can question motives, it cannot go to the extreme that Westbrook Pegler did in hitting back at Quentin Reynolds. In a review of a book about Heywood Broun, the newspaperman, Reynolds had observed that Pegler had called Broun a liar and that Broun had brooded over this charge. Although he had been suffering from only a cold at the time, he could not sleep or relax and finally died. Pegler contended that this was a charge of moral homicide and that he was answering the accusation when he wrote his column of November 29, 1949:

> According to the New York *Herald Tribune*'s prejudicial custom of making political propaganda in its book reviews, a new biography of the late Heywood Broun was assigned for review to Broun's devotee, Quentin Reynolds.
>
> Broun was a fellow-traveler for many years, but he was also a voluptuary and, in the intellectual sense, a sneak. Thus he never joined the Communist Party and, in his last days, having, as some

contemporary said, "worshipped at all shrines," he embraced Catholicism and was funeralized with eclat by Monsignor Fulton J. Sheen at St. Patrick's Cathedral.

Like Broun, Reynolds was sloppy, and ran to fat but the fact was not to be established until we got the war which he had been howling for, that his protuberant belly was filled with something else than guts. Reynolds was a sycophant, a coat-holder for Broun and imitated his morals, and his equally frowsy physical and sartorial corpus.

In this review of the Broun biography, Reynolds wrote, in effect, that I was responsible for Broun's death, although he died of pneumonia, because about that time I wrote that Broun had lied about some matter in one of his columns.

I do not recall that particular accusation, but I will not trouble Reynolds for a bill of particulars. Broun was a notorious liar. For an example, which he never had quite the effrontery to deny, he lied when he wrote that J. B. Matthews, the chief investigator of the old Dies Committee, seriously testified that Shirley Temple was a dangerously subversive instrument of the communists.

The proposition that Broun was so cut up that he lost his will to live and to do for Connie, his wife and the only truly honest and devoted friend he had, just because I called him a liar, argues ill for Broun's courage.

Reynolds does his memory no honor here because Broun made his living at controversy. I would want better authority for the aspersion that, although he loved to dish it, Broun couldn't take it.

Broun was a dirty fighter. He had an ingratiating way which gave people to believe that his cruel ambition to run the lives of other newspaper workers and bend their necks or break them through the communist terror of his Newspaper Guild was but the philanthropic doing of a man who truly loved his fellow men.

Heywood shunned the company of his equals such as Alexander Woollcott and Robert Benchley because he couldn't fool them. They were onto him. So he cultivated a personal cult of four-flushers like Reynolds and sorry mediocrities or less who could be deceived by his pretense of heroic goodness.

There were at least as many self-respecting newspaper workers who knew he was running the Guild as a communist agency and simply would not dedicate their lives, their living, their human dignity and the welfare of their wives and children to his ulterior ambition.

He was in many communist fronts, and, once, by a lapse of judgment, he wrote that he never could be cajoled, coerced or persuaded to say a word against the Soviet Government because, to him it was the greatest effort ever made for human betterment.

Reynolds' medicine grew too strong even for *Collier's* which, I am told, incidentally, has "seen the light" and faced about. He is no longer an "editor" of *Collier's*. However, a fellow of his politics can do fairly well in Hollywood as I have been told he does.

Reynolds gives some false impressions. So I offer some corrective data.

Broun was a nudist during one phase of his soiled existence in his leafy retreat away from it all at Stamford, but he and his friends of both sexes practised their nudism in seclusion at his "lake," a mucky wallow, hidden from the road.

And Broun complained to me that Reynolds and his girl friend of the moment were nuding along the public road. Heywood said that, after all, the Yankee neighbors might not understand. If they saw Reynolds and his wench strolling along together, absolutely raw, they would call the State police and give him and his place a bad name.

There was no color line and a conspicuous Negro communist of the present day, by Broun's own word to me, seduced a susceptible young white girl at Heywood Broun's.

Connie Broun, Heywood's widow, for whom Reynolds now expresses noble sentiments, reflecting credit on himself, related that, as Reynolds was riding to Heywood's grave with her, he proposed marriage. But she said that some time later, after he had made an artificial reputation as a brave war correspondent in the London blitz, he snubbed her publicly and barely knew her. That would be credible.

Reynolds did fall in love with himself as a "celebrity" and, by forceful, opportune promotion, became one of the great individual profiteers of the war. Connie, by the way, soon after she married Heywood, cleaned out the whole parasitic, licentious lot, ran them down the road and turned Broun respectable.

Reynolds was largely an absentee war correspondent. He covered the ghastly Dieppe raid from a battleship and, when the invasion of Normandy was made, relieving the pressure on his Russian friends, he was safe in the United States cleaning up.

He cleaned up in the movies, in vaudeville, on the radio and on the lecture circuit. He cleaned up $2,000 of the ill-gotten loot of the Garsson brothers who, with Congressman Andy May, later were convicted of fraud in war contracts.

When I went to Boston to make a bad speech for $1,350, which was given to John B. Powell, the martyr editor, who was dying slowly as a consequence of his tortures at the hands of the Japanese,

Reynolds made a worse one, on the same program, for $2,000 for Quentin Reynolds.

Reynolds was an "interventionist." He loathed "isolationists." But though he was a giant and a bachelor, he let several million kids about 18 years old do the fighting. The old army regulars and their wives speak of his kind as the "let's you and him fight" school of heroes.

In the 1944 campaign, Roosevelt did his damnedest to beat Clare Boothe for Congress in Connecticut. The whole first team went up—Roosevelt, Wallace and many of the non-combatant warriors of the radio, stage and screen, including Reynolds.

Clare licked the whole varsity, single handed.

When she came to Reynolds, she peeled him of his mangy hide and nailed it to the barn door with the yellow streak glaring for the world to see.

This was strange conduct in a war correspondent, six feet two, weighing 250 and in the prime of life and health, Clare said, attacking a woman on the home front who had actually seen more fighting than he, and closer up, while high-school boys were pushing back the Nazi in the war that he had been asking for for the last ten years.

The judge held that the first part of the column bore some resemblance to a reply as it stated that Broun was a "notorious liar," a "dirty fighter" and "made his living at controversy." And the few shafts at Reynolds were acceptable. But Pegler's "corrective data" were held to have no conceivable relevancy to the review of the book. Reynolds was awarded $1 in compensatory damages and $175,000 in punitive damages from Pegler, the New York *Journal-American* and the Hearst corporation (Reynolds v. Pegler, 223 F. 2d 429).

Public Issues

The defense of reply is particularly useful to journalists because the essence of so much news is conflict. Take a not-unusual situation: In the 1950s the citizens of Fort Madison, Iowa, became embroiled in a controversy over the construction of a new dock and harbor on the Mississippi River. The leader of the opposition was Edmund A. Haas, a businessman. He communicated with the city council; he circulated handbills; he inserted paid advertisements in the local paper, the *Evening Democrat*. On November 3,

1955, just before an election, Haas issued a long attack on the proponents of the dock. He called on the voters to keep in mind what four council members, "Bean, Kiehne, Mosley and Johnston have done and what they stand for, and if you do, I do not believe your conscience will let you vote for them, you will vote against them and thank God that we have some good honest men who are opposing them." There were some references to "little dictators." Two weeks later Councilwoman Mary Esther Mosley responded in a letter to the *Evening Democrat*. It included these words:

> But let us not forget the workings of a man who could slander honest honorable citizens.
> This man shouted "dictator" so loudly at others that it was overlooked that he was employing dictator methods. Is it not the method of the dictator to grasp an untruth and shout it so long and so loud that the people become convinced that he might be right? And what happens to the person who is using dictator methods when he runs up against the law? . . . he just shouts longer and louder of "the rights of the people" and ignores the law. . . .
> I detest the methods this man has used to try to force people to think his way and no other. I think he has been cruel, abusive and unthruthful in his attacks on me. I think he has harmed innocent people . . . which is not to be condoned in this great free country of ours.

Haas sued the *Evening Democrat* for libel, citing the letter to the editor and other articles in the paper. He won a $75,000 verdict in a trial. The judge, however, reduced the over-all award by $48,000. When the case reached the Iowa Supreme Court, the justices threw out five of the seven counts on which damages had been awarded as not libelous. On the sixth, the letter from Mrs. Mosley, the court said:

> The limitations of space will not permit quotation here of the many attacks made by the plaintiff upon members of the city council or the proposed dock construction project. It will suffice to say that he was active and aggressive; and it is fair to comment that he took the lead in belligerency in his strictures on those who opposed him. If the whole controversy developed into a free-swinging affair in which there was considerable give and take, the plaintiff must bear his full share of responsibility. He was at no time a shrinking violet; he gave at least as much as he took.

. . . It is difficult to think that plaintiff expected his assaults on these people to be borne in silence. They had the right to ma'·e a fair reply; Mrs. Mosley did so, and we think she did not go beyond the bounds of fair defense and retort.

On the seventh count, the court decided that the *Evening Democrat* had gone too far in an editorial that said "there is no honorable reason for opposing a local boat harbor." It upheld a lower court order for a new trial on this count. (Haas v. Evening Democrat, 252 Iowa 517). Haas eventually received $3,413 in a settlement. The dock was not built.

In almost any dispute not much imagination is required to find something that prompted the libelous attack. Nor must the newsman find the target of the attack himself to invoke the defense. The right of reply also extends to those standing in place of the attacked person—his lawyer, a company's public-relations department, the president or counsel of an organization or even a wife or brother or sister. Anyone who could legitimately be called a spokesman can be quoted.

Using Third Party

An Oregon case shows that a reporter can lean on a third party in a pinch. The case resulted from the murder on November 21, 1933, of W. Frank Akin in his apartment in Portland. Akin was a public accountant and had been employed as a special investigator by the Governor to check into the fiscal affairs of the city's port. Two days later the Portland *Oregonian* carried this article:

Traces of "another woman" in the W. Frank Akin murder mystery were revealed yesterday in a startling story unfolded to state police by Mark M. Israel, jeweler and loan broker, of 2034 Northeast Twenty-first Avenue.

The lengthy statement made by Israel to Sergeant S. C. Linville at state police offices provided authorities with the first tangible motive for the slaying of Akin who was found shot to death in his living quarters at the Arbor Court Apartments, 1329 Southwest Fourteenth Avenue, about 9 A.M. Monday morning.

Israel, who said Akin had checked his books and made out his income tax reports for about four years, told Linville that the murdered man had told him on a number of occasions that a woman, with whom he had an affair, had repeatedly threatened his life.

AKIN AFRAID OF WOMAN

"I talked with Akin lots of times," Israel said, "and he told me about his woman and added that the only reason he kept seeing her was that he was afraid she would kill him. He said she had threatened to do so a number of times and on several occasions went so far as to point a gun at him."

Continuing his sensational narrative, Israel said that Akin had informed him that about five years ago he (Akin) had taken the woman on an automobile trip through the Grand Canyon. On their return to Portland, Akin's alleged paramour told him she would prefer a Mann Act charge against him if he ever deserted her, Israel said.

STORY HEARD OFTEN

"He confided in me often when he used the balcony of my store, the Century Loan & Jewelry Company at Third and Washington Streets, for an office. After this affair had lasted some time, Akin told me that he had confessed his infidelity to his wife and offered to give her a divorce. Mrs. Akin, I was told forgave her husband, but told him that he could leave with the other woman any time he desired."

NAME NEVER HEARD

"I know he went around armed," the jeweler related, "because I gave him shells for the weapon several times."

In all of these asserted conversations, Akin never once mentioned the name of the woman, always referring to her as "my girl" or "her."

Mrs. Akin previously had emphatically denied that any woman had entered her husband's life since their wedding and added that their married life had been exceptionally happy. Mrs. Bertha Goul, the dead man's sister, who was present at the time Mrs. Akin made the above assertions, amplified the statements by saying the couple had always been considered ideal mates and seldom if ever had any disagreements.

When the editor of the Portland News read the *Oregonian's* article, he assigned a reporter to check Mrs. Akin and get her side of the story. The reporter telephoned Mrs. Akin, but the widow was so upset that she was unable to talk more than a few minutes. Her sister-in-law, Mrs. Goul, picked up the phone and communicated the rest of the reply. Then the reporter wrote an article that included the following words:

The scandalous tale related to police by Mark Israel, pawnshop dealer, about a "jealous woman" in the life of W. Frank Akin, slain port investigator, was branded absolutely false Thursday by the widow of the murdered man.

"It is silly, in the first place," she said, "to suppose Frank might have confided in Israel on any private matter. He had no regard for Israel's integrity and frequently said so after being engaged to audit the books of that firm.

"He told me he knew Israel was stealing from his own father-in-law and he said he had no use for that kind of a man. Israel hated him after that, and he hated Israel. Can you imagine the police believing that those two would have confided in each other? That Frank would have confided secrets of his private life to him?

"It is ridiculous on the face of it, and the police are using it for a smoke screen in this whole thing. I suppose they will attempt to find all kinds of things to hurt him."

Israel's suit for libel was rejected by the Oregon Supreme Court. There was no question but that Mrs. Akin's charges had libeled Israel; she had accused him of stealing and cast doubts on his integrity. But the court said that the charges were privileged under the right of reply.

It would avail Mrs. Akin but little to simply deny the alleged defamatory matter in the article published by respondent, but if she could show an unworthy motive for the publication of such an article, it would then destroy the effect of the article itself. And this would be true whether the whole article was communicated by Mrs. Akin or part of it by Mrs. Goul, the sister of Akin. The sister would have a right to defend the good name of her dead brother. [Israel v. Portland News Publishing Co., 152 Ore. 225]

This privilege can often be invoked when the original attack is made during an official proceeding. A South Carolina case made that clear in 1927 when it held:

The plaintiff's claim, if allowed, would permit a member of the legislature, in a session open to the world, with reporter in sight, to make the most hurtful statements about a private citizen, knowing that they would be published to the world, and deny to the injured citizen the right to deny the truth of the charges anywhere. . . . We have been cited to no law, and know of none, to sustain such a proposition. [Duncan v. Record, 127 S.E. 606]

Official Proceedings

The reporter will find the right of reply valuable when he checks for the other side, of the story in governmental investigations and libelous remarks made at other official proceedings. If a witness at a legislative hearing asserts that Glockenspiel Red Neck is a member of the Ku Klux Klan, his testimony is protected by the privilege of reporting an official proceeding. If he calls Red Neck and asks him for comment, and gets an answer that libels the witness, such as, "He's a liar; he's been trying to blackmail me for months," this is not protected by the privilege of reporting a proceeding, but it is by the privilege of carrying a reply. The reporter should remember, though, that if the original charge is not libelous, there is no privilege in a libelous reply.

While most participants in political campaigns are probably covered by the New York Times rule, the privilege of reply can always be invoked as a second defense. If there is some question of whether a particular individual is a public figure within the meaning of *The New York Times* case, the newsman can often go ahead and carry the libelous material anyway because of the right of reply. A pre-*New York Times* case in Florida shows how effective this can be. In the 1954 gubernatorial campaign the Florida Political Survey and Poll reported that one of the candidates, Brailey Odham, appeared "to be slipping badly." Odham fired back at a rally in which he said that "the gamblers are making big talk and the phoney pollsters are bluffing, but you, the people, have the final say in this tremendously important decision of nominating your governor." He also named Joe Abram, author of the Florida Political Survey and Poll, as "one of the phoney pollsters."

Abram sued Odham and the Jacksonville *Times-Union,* which carried the reply. The Florida Supreme Court affirmed a lower court's dismissal of the case against the *Times-Union,* holding that it had a right to carry political news of wide interest, but noting in particular that Odham enjoyed the privilege of replying to the poll's report that he had been slipping. Because Odham also issued a handbill charging that Abram would rig a poll for a fee, the court sent that case back to the lower courts for a trial on the question of malice (Abram v. Odham, 6 Fla. Supp. 102). With the best hope for significant damages lost, the case was later dropped.

Racial controversies are also events that involve charges and countercharges and thus lead to the use of the defense of reply. One of the leaders in the fight against racial integration in Louisiana was Mrs. Bernard J. Gaillot, Jr., of New Orleans. As the result of her role in advocating disobedience against the Roman Catholic Archbishop's order for the integration of parochial schools she was excommunicated. She delivered lectures, appeared on television, gave newspaper interviews, wrote several pamphlets and waged a general crusade against the Church's racial teachings.

On September 2, 1962, the day before schools reopened, the Rev. John J. Sauvageau held benediction services for about forty parishoners in Our Lady of Guadalupe Church in New Orleans. He had worried about a report he had heard of a movement to boycott the integrated Catholic schools so he mentioned it in his sermon. No transcript of the sermon was made, but Father Sauvageau recalled it in these words:

> I was trying to direct my people into sending their children into school; in other words, in obeying our leader instead of the other side. I felt morally obligated to do so, and I also felt like it would be a good idea at the time to be precise enough. Now I said, whom are we going to follow. Are we going to follow our spiritual leader, who is the Archbishop, who is very capable and has proved it many, many a year, or are we going to follow Mrs. Gaillot who, according to what I hear, has been in an institution.

Mrs. Gaillot and her husband sued for slander, asking $100,000 in damages. There was a question as to whether the priest had said "institution" or "mental institution," but the Louisiana Court of Appeals said it did not make any difference because there was no doubt that Father Sauvageau intended to warn his congregation that Mrs. Gaillot might not be mentally responsible and should be ignored. Father Sauvageau acknowledged that he had been misinformed and had no evidence that Mrs. Gaillot had ever been in a mental institution. Nevertheless the court rejected the suit. It said:

> Defendant and his Church had a mutual interest in the preservation of respect for, and obedience to, the ecclesiastical edicts of their governing authority; with the qualified privilege to refute and negate the efforts of anyone publicly challenging its orders and teachings,

short of expressly or impliedly charging personal immorality or criminality. [Gaillot v. Sauvageau, 154 So. 2d 515]

That is the right of reply stated in other words.

This defense also protects against damages for articles and broadcasts of proxy battles in corporations, of labor disputes, of fights for the control of clubs and associations, of squabbles in churches, of arguments over social changes and foreign policy.

Chapter 16

MALICE AND DAMAGES

When the jury returned its verdict in Quentin Reynolds' libel suit against Westbrook Pegler, it announced an award of $1 in compensatory damages. For a fraction of a moment Pegler seemed to have scored a tremendous victory. One dollar's worth was all that the jury thought Reynolds had been damaged. But then the jury announced it had awarded $175,000 in punitive damages. That was how much the jury thought Pegler should be punished for his malicious column. The Pegler case should convince any newsman of the importance of malice in libel suits. The ability to recognize libel and to take advantage of the legal defenses for publishing it is not enough. The newsman must clear the hurdle known as actual malice before he can escape damages. This is not the same thing as legal malice, which simply means that the defendant is responsible for the offense, as in the case of a man whose pet tiger escapes and claws an innocent passer-by. Actual malice is definite behavior on the part of the newsman, either of omission or commission, that deprives the libeled individual of a fair shake.

The danger in actual malice is that if it is proved, the newsman loses most of the defenses the law provides for publishing libelous articles. He is pictured as a thief, armed with an acid pen, who seeks to steal the good name of upright citizens. Exposed as a villain, the journalist is punished at his weakest point—his pocketbook. In his heart the newsman may think he is right, but the law permits increased damages if actual malice is proved.

In early medieval days the man guilty of defamation could predict with a high degree of certainty what his penalty would be—his tongue would be cut out. After this punishment was abandoned, precise figures were set for specific words of slander.

The *lex salica* decrees provided: "If one call a man 'wolf' or 'hare' and cannot prove the truth of the charge, one must pay 3 shillings, while if one calls a woman 'harlot' and cannot prove it one must pay her 45 shillings."

In our more sophisticated society the amount of the damages depends on the worth of the individual, the extent of the harm and the presence of actual malice. There are three classes of damages recognized by the law when there is no complete defense.

Special Damages

Special damages are specific items of pecuniary loss caused by published statements which are false, whether libelous or not. If the statement is not libelous, the person referred to must prove special damages in order to collect. In such cases recovery is limited to the precise amount of pecuniary loss which has been proved. If the statement is ruled libelous, the person referred to is not required to prove special damages at all. Until recently he did not even have to prove any damages if there was no defense because the law, prior to the Gertz case (discussed on page 190), presumed there had been damage.

Special damages are never presumed. They must always be proved as facts, and the burden of proof rests on the plaintiff. He must establish the amount of loss that he has suffered in precise items of dollars and cents, and he must show that these specific items of loss were caused by the offensive publication and not by something else. So strict are the rules relating to proof that recovery of special damages is rare. That is why nonlibelous false publications should generate little worry unless maliciously made. Of course good newspaper, broadcasting and magazine people will try to avert minor as well as major errors. Their professional pride demands strict adherence to facts and scrupulous fairness to the individual. But the newsman ought to know, for his guidance in organizing and writing his story, whether he is dealing with libelous or nonlibelous material.

Malice has no bearing on the amount of special damages. They cannot be reduced or mitigated by anything the newsman has done, because they represent the plaintiff's actual loss from the false publication. Proof that the publisher's intentions were good, such as the fact that a correction was made, does no good in court. The only way to defeat special damages is to establish a complete defense.

Compensatory Damages

Compensatory or general damages are designed to offset the injury of the victim. If the article is not libelous, no compensatory damages can be recovered. Until recently, if the article was libelous and there was no defense, some damage was conclusively presumed. The plaintiff, where there was no defense, was entitled to at least a nominal recovery. The nominal recovery was six cents in the nineteenth and the early part of the twentieth century, but inflation has increased this nominal sum to one dollar. The doctrine of presumed compensatory damages received a death blow at the hands of the Supreme Court in 1974 in the Gertz case previously discussed. The court held:

> For the reasons stated below, we hold that the States may not permit recovery of presumed or punitive damages, at least when liability is not based on a showing of knowledge of falsity or reckless disregard for the truth.
>
> The common law of defamation is an oddity of tort law, for it allows recovery of purportedly compensatory damages without evidence of actual loss. Under the traditional rules pertaining to actions for libel, the existence of injury is presumed from the fact of publication. Juries may award substantial sums of compensation for supposed damage to reputation without any proof that such harm actually occurred. The largely uncontrolled discretion of juries to award damages where there is no loss unnecessarily compounds the potential of any system of liability for defamatory falsehood to inhibit the vigorous exercise of First Amendment freedoms. Additionally, the doctrine of presumed damages invites juries to punish unpopular opinion rather than to compensate individuals for injury sustained by the publication of a false fact. More to the point, the States have no substantial interest in securing for plaintiffs such as this petitioner gratuitous awards of money damages far in excess of any actual injury.
>
> We would not, of course, invalidate state law simply because we doubt its wisdom, but here we are attempting to reconcile state law with a competing interest grounded in the constitutional command

of the First Amendment. It is therefore appropriate to require that state remedies for defamatory falsehood reach no farther than is necessary to protect the legitimate interest involved. It is necessary to restrict defamation plaintiffs who do not prove knowledge of falsity or reckless disregard for the truth to compensation for actual injury. [Gertz v. Robert Welch, Inc., 418 U.S. 323, 349]

In theory, compensatory damages are supposed to be precisely commensurate in dollars and cents with the injury suffered, but since harm to reputation and the extent of pain and suffering are not susceptible to exact measurement in dollars and cents, a jury's verdict is bound to be more or less arbitrary and speculative. Emotions and prejudices—even how well the jurors slept the night before or whether they had a good breakfast—are sometimes controlling.

Prior to 1974, if the writer lacked a complete defense, the jury could award damages on three elements:

1. Injury to personal reputation
2. Mental and physical pain and suffering
3. General injury to business or occupation

All three apply to individuals. If the plaintiff is a corporation, the only element that can be taken into consideration is the harm done to its business. It has no personal reputation and cannot feel sorry for itself.

Since compensatory damages, prior to the Gertz decision, were presumed when the publication was libelous, the plaintiff was not bound to prove damages of any sort. He could sit back and say in effect: "You published this horrible thing about me and I will rest on my rights." He was aided by the legal presumption of damage, but he was not required to sit back and relax—and in most cases he did not. Ordinarily plaintiffs will give testimony concerning their injuries, real and imaginary. They will tell how their marital bliss was disrupted, their social standing—always surprisingly high—lowered and their business or professional reputation uniformly reduced from the top to the bottom. Frequently women plaintiffs will testify to intense mental and physical pain and suffering, of being unable to sleep, of suffering headaches and being forced to consult doctors. The purpose of this testimony, of course, is to demonstrate to the jury the status of the plaintiff as bearing on the amount of damage that was probably caused and to create a prejudice in favor of the plaintiff and against the defendant.

The only way to prevent a recovery of compensatory damages when the article is libelous is to prove facts constituting a complete defense. As a practical matter that means, in almost every case, proof of truth, of the privilege of reporting an official proceeding, of the privilege of publishing libel under the New York Times rule or of fair comment. Since compensatory damages are supposed to measure the plaintiff's actual loss, they are not affected by the publisher's good faith or by any other similar extenuating circumstance. Nevertheless, malice, or lack of it, inevitably has some effect on juries since their decision involves not only how much the plaintiff will receive but also how much the defendant will pay. Naturally, if a jury feels the newspaper, magazine or broadcasting station acted decently in the circumstances the damages will be less.

A good example of a jury's difficulty in separating its decision from the behavior of the defendants is shown by a Rhode Island case. John F. McBurney, a Pawtucket lawyer, represented a woman at a hearing in probate court on April 10, 1957. At the hearing the judge expressed doubt that McBurney had properly followed his duties as an officer of the court. He also made comments critical of McBurney's client. The Pawtucket *Times* carried stories on the hearing, playing up the judge's criticism of McBurney but not mentioning his comments about the client.

McBurney sued the *Times* for libel. At the trial he tried to prove three things: that he had been libeled; that the article had distorted the event, thus removing the paper's privilege of reporting a judicial hearing; that the paper was guilty of actual malice. In proof of the third point McBurney was allowed to testify about a phone conversation he had had with a Pawtucket *Times* reporter right after the hearing. He quoted the reporter as having said to him, "Boy, are you in hot water. We got you on this one." In his charge to the jury, the judge emphasized that the reporter did not decide what went into the paper and that the only malice that could be considered was any that existed on the part of executives at the *Times*. The three in charge, the general manager, managing editor and city editor, had testified that they bore no ill will toward McBurney.

The jury returned a verdict of $50,000 for McBurney. In reviewing it, the judge found that the jury had concluded that the articles had been defamatory and had not been a fair, impartial report of a judicial hearing. But he reduced the award to $25,000 and said that McBurney had not proved that the articles were motivated by malice. The *Times* appealed, contending, among other things, that testimony about the phone conversation with the reporter should not have been admitted and that the jury had been confused on the malice issue. The Rhode Island Supreme Court upheld the admission of the reporter's "hot water" testimony and the reduced verdict (McBurney v. Times Publishing Co., 93 R.I. 331).

Behavior in the courtroom is also important. A perfect example of how not to act was Westbrook Pegler's behavior during his trial in the Reynolds case. His evasive answers, arrogance, contradictions and outbursts against counsel for the defense antagonized virtually all present in the courtroom.

Under the present law, compensatory damages must be proved, but as the Supreme Court said, they are not limited to out-of-pocket loss. Plaintiff may recover if he can prove:

1. Impairment to reputation and standing in the community
2. Personal humiliation
3. Mental anguish and suffering

Although the Supreme Court did not say so, he can attempt to prove general injury to business and occupation.

Instead of relying on a presumption, the plaintiff must now produce a witness who will testify that after a publication the witness shunned the plaintiff by crossing the street when he saw the plaintiff coming. In a recent case, a plaintiff suing *New York* magazine testified in an examination before trial that after the publication his wife shunned and avoided him, but he had to admit on further examination that she had shunned and avoided him for several years prior to the publication.

Punitive Damages

Punitive damages are also known as exemplary damages, vindictive damages or "smart money." As the terms indicate, these damages are intended as punishment for the person who published them, as a warning to him not to offend again and as a deterrent to others who might have similar ideas. Punitive damages have nothing at all to do with special damages and compensatory damages, but are loaded on in addition to the first two if there is actual malice.

Punitive damages cannot be awarded unless the publication is libelous and unless actual malice is proved. Actual malice is never presumed. It must be proved as a fact, and the burden of proving it always rests on the plaintiff. If the evidence of both sides on the issue of malice is precisely equal, it is the duty of the jury to find that there is no actual malice. By requiring the plaintiff to prove actual malice the law helps the newsman who follows good journalistic practices stay clear of punitive damages. As will be seen, good professional habits are almost always a certain bar to recovery of heavy punitive damages.

The doctrine of punitive damages has been severely criticized and has been rejected by courts in a number of states. Some have abolished the entire doctrine or have substantially modified it through statutes. Generally these states permit punitive damages only on proof that the publisher refused upon demand to print a retraction as explained on page 289.

The Supreme Court in the Gertz case also reduced the effect of punitive damages by holding that a plaintiff could not get such damages unless he could show *The New York Times* type of malice—a known falsehood or reckless disregard. It said:

> We also find no justification for allowing awards of punitive damages against publishers and broadcasters held liable under state-defined standards of liability for defamation. In most jurisdictions jury discretion over the amounts awarded is limited only by the gentle rule that they not be excessive. Consequently, juries assess punitive damages in wholly unpredictable amounts bearing no necessary relation to the actual harm caused. And they remain free to use their discretion selectively to punish expressions of unpopular views. Like the doctrine of presumed damages, jury discretion to award punitive damages unnecessarily exacerbates the danger of media self-censorship, but, unlike the former rule, punitive damages are wholly irrelevant to the state interest that justifies a negligence standard for private defamation actions. They are not compensation for injury. Instead, they are private fines levied by civil juries to

punish reprehensible conduct and to deter its future occurrence. In short, the private defamation plaintiff who establishes liability under a less demanding standard than that stated by *New York Times* may recover only such damages as are sufficient to compensate him for actual injury. [Gertz v. Robert Welch, Inc., 418 U.S. 323, 350]

The result was that Gertz, who had been awarded $50,000, had to re-try the case.

Effect of Malice on Defenses

Since the presence or absence of malice has a direct bearing on damages, it is vital that the newsman know how it affects the legal defense he is relying on for publishing libelous material.

Theoretically, actual malice destroys the defense of truth in criminal prosecutions everywhere, although in some states, like Pennsylvania, court decisions have made it plain that truth alone is sufficient when evidence of malice is not strong. Malice also destroys the defense of truth in civil actions in a handful of states. These are states where the law requires a defendant to show that the matter was published with good motives or justifiable ends before truth can be invoked as a defense. They include Delaware, Florida, Illinois, Massachusetts, Maine, Nebraska, New Hampshire, Pennsylvania, Rhode Island, West Virginia, and Wyoming. Even in those states truth alone prevails unless there is overwhelming proof of malice. In most other states actual malice has no effect on the defense of truth. If the defense can show that the substance or gist of the libelous statement was true, it will win its case no matter how evil or malicious the publisher is.

That is what the law says. It is worthwhile to remember, however, that in trying a libel case, the attorneys and the litigants are dealing with practical considerations and practical problems. A newspaper in proving the defense of truth has to rely largely on the testimony of witnesses who are not in the employ of or under the control of the publisher, and all witnesses are subject to the common frailties of mankind. On occasion they are less positive than they should be. On occasion they utter indiscreet remarks. On occasion they forget. On occasion they collapse completely on cross-examination. On occasion they are liars.

Usually, the plaintiff has witnesses of his own who will give testimony that the article was false and testimony that contradicts what the defendant's witnesses say or are prepared to say. Thus, issues of fact usually arise, issues of veracity to be determined by the jury. The jury will more readily believe the defendant's witnesses on the issue of truth if there is no indication of malice on the part of the publisher. The jury will tend to believe the plaintiff's witnesses if there is evidence of actual malice on the part of the publisher.

Actual malice destroys the privilege of reporting an official proceeding, except in New York, California, Georgia, Michigan, Oklahoma, Texas and Wisconsin, where the defense is absolute. Since many suits are brought on articles reporting arrests and other police news, the newsman must make sure that he does not lose his privilege of reporting through actual malice.

The privilege of self-defense or reply is also lost if actual malice is proved. An individual has the right to hit back at his attacker, but if his intentions are proved to be malicious, the defense is lost everywhere.

Actual malice destroys fair comment and criticism in all states. All the other elements of this defense may be present, but if actual malice is proved the defense fails. The theory is that public policy justifies adverse comment on matters of public interest and concern, but not when it is dishonestly made with an evil intent.

The privilege of transmitting libelous statements about public men is also destroyed by actual malice. Insofar as this rule is concerned, the Supreme Court has defined actual malice in a very strict sense that is discussed later in this chapter.

The question of malice arises in almost every libel trial that goes to the jury for a determination. In view of the fact that malice carries the possibility of such drastic effects on news media, the reporter and editor usually assume that it means personal malevolence and that it is a simple thing to define. Unfortunately this is not so. Actual malice can be more than an evil heart. But the courts have hemmed and hawed over just what it means and what constitutes proof of it with the result that malice is a mass of confusion.

There are two types of actual malice. One is the definition set up by the Supreme Court in issuing its 1964 New York Times rule. The other constitutes the varying definitions reached by the state courts over centuries of libel suits.

Malice and the New York Times Rule

The New York Times decision established a test for malice in cases involving public officials that is beneficial for the newsman. The Supreme Court defined actual malice in issuing a libelous statement in the *Times* case as "knowledge that it was false or with reckless disregard of whether it was false or not." Moreover, the court said, malice must be proved by evidence of "convincing clarity."

What does this mean? In *The New York Times* case there was sufficient evidence to sustain a finding that someone employed by the newspaper knew the statements in the advertisement were false, or at least that it had negligently disregarded the truth. Any employee in the advertising acceptability department on the second floor of the *Times* had only to take the elevator to the newsroom morgue on the third floor and check the clips to discover that the ad contained factual misstatements. But, the court said, this failure to check the files was, at most, negligence, not recklessness. Thus, "recklessness" must mean something beyond the mere failure to observe standard care.

In its Garrison decision, extending the Times rule to criminal libel cases, the Supreme Court threw a little more light on the definition of malice. The Louisiana Supreme Court had held that malice had been proved, because the evidence was sufficient to support a finding of ill-will, enmity or a wanton desire to injure. The trial court had rested its conviction on finding that the defendant, District Attorney Garrison, had no "reasonable belief" that all eight district judges of the criminal court were subject to racketeer influences, as he had implied. The Supreme Court, in reversing the decision, held that "only those false statements made with a high degree of awareness of their probable falsity" could sustain a finding or recklessness. It specifically rejected absence of "reasonable belief," "ordinary care" or "mere negligence" as proof of reckless disregard of truth. (Garrison v. State of Louisiana 379 U.S. 64).

Thus, the desire to inflict harm on a public official is not sufficient to prove malice. Nor is the failure to observe the normal careful procedures in checking facts. The nation's highest court has clearly stated that only two situations fall outside the protection of the privilege of libeling a public official. One is the use of an outright known falsehood to inflict harm, and the other is the publishing of a false statement despite serious doubts about the truth by the defamer. The latter is the only method of establishing recklessness.

In 1967 the Supreme Court offered further clues regarding how far a newsman could go without recklessly disregarding truth. In reversing a judgment obtained by General Walker the Supreme Court held that the Associated Press had not been reckless. Walker point out (1) the article failed to state, as a United Press International dispatch had stated, that Walker had begged the students to cease their violence; (2) none of the hundreds of pictures taken had shown Walker leading a charge against the Federal marshal as the AP dispatch indicated and neither the UPI nor the other news media had reported that Walker had done so; (3) the AP cub reporter's dispatch had not been checked with other Associated Press reports at the scene, or with Walker, or with the Federal marshals, or with the state highway patrolmen; (4) in his first telephone call, on which the article was based, the AP reporter said Walker led the charge after delivering a speech, while in his second telephone call he said the charge came before the speech.

In 1968 the Supreme Court made it plain that to constitute recklessness "there must be sufficient evidence to permit the conclusion that the defendant in fact entertained serious doubts as to the truth of his publication." The case concerned a $5,000 judgment awarded Deputy Sheriff Herman A. Thompson of East Baton Rouge Parish, Louisiana, in a suit against Phil A. St. Amant for a television broadcast. In the broadcast St. Amant had read an affidavit in which a Teamster union member stated "money had passed hands" from a Teamster official to Thompson.

Although St. Amant (1) had no personal knowledge of Thompson's activity; (2) had relied solely on the affidavit; (3) and had not checked the charge with union officials, the Supreme Court ruled that there was no reckless disregard of truth and reversed the judgment. The court noted that St. Amant's source had sworn to his answer first in writing and then in the presence of newsmen. In addition, the court emphasized Thompson's failure to impeach the source's reputation for truth. But the Supreme Court did point out that a defendant could not obtain immunity merely by testifying that he had published in the belief that the matter was true. The court said:

> Professions of good faith will be unlikely to prove persuasive, for example, where a story is fabricated by the defendant, is the product of his imagination, or is based wholly on an unverified anonymous telephone call. Nor will they be likely to prevail when the publisher's allegations are so inherently improbable that only a reckless man would have put them in circulation. Likewise, recklessness may be found where there are obvious reasons to doubt the veracity of the informant or the accuracy of his reports. [St. Amant v. Thompson 390 U.S. 727]

The Butts case, decided in 1967, was the first in which the Supreme Court held that there had been reckless disregard of truth sufficient to establish malice. The article on Butts, an exposé, was published in the *Saturday Evening Post,* March 23, 1963. It alleged that Athletic Director Butts had given Georgia's football secrets to Paul Bryant, coach of Alabama, before their 1962 game. Alabama, which entered the game a 14–17-point favorite, won 35–0. The article was based on information supplied by George P. Burnett, an Atlanta insurance salesman, who said he had accidentally been connected into a long-distance telephone call between Butts and Bryant on September 13, 1962 and had taken notes on the conversation.

Burnett did nothing about his notes throughout the 1962 football season. On January 4, 1963, unable to restrain himself any longer, he told a close friend, who relayed the information to Georgia's head coach, Johnny Griffith. The coach asked to talk with Burnett, and on January 24, 1963, the two met in the Atlanta Biltmore Hotel. After listening to Burnett and reading the notes, Griffith is reported to have said to Burnett, "I didn't believe you until just this minute . . . but here's something in your notes you couldn't possibly have dreamed up . . . this thing about our pass patterns. I took this over from Wally Butts when I became coach, and I gave it a different name. Nobody uses the old name for this pattern but one man. Wally Butts."

Griffith did not move for about an hour after Burnett left the hotel room. Then he called a University of Georgia official. The university immediately began an investigation. At the request of officials Burnett signed an affidavit and took a lie-detector test.

On February 19, Roger Kahn, the *Post* sports editor, heard about the scandal. He assigned Frank Graham, an experienced sports-writer, to go to Atlanta to see if there really was a story, to get all available facts, an affidavit from Burnett and, if possible, a copy of his notes. Kahn cautioned Graham to be careful. In Atlanta, Graham met three times with Burnett and had him sign an affi-davit. Burnett's attorney promised to send a copy of the notes to Graham but never did.

While Graham was in Atlanta, university officials confronted Butts with Burnett's notes. After reading them briefly, Butts is re-ported to have said, "No doubt the guy heard what he said he heard. I don't blame him for placing the interpretation that he did on this conversation. If I had been in his place, I probably would have thought the same thing, but he is mistaken. It's just conversa-tion, ordinary football talk among coaches, and that you know I would never give old Bryant anything to help him and hurt Georgia. . . . If I did give any information to hurt Georgia it was not intentional." Butts was asked to take a lie-detector test but he refused. The next day Butts resigned as athletic director, citing the press of outside business interests.

When Graham finished his article, he turned it over to Davis Thomas, the managing editor. Thomas attached great significance to the fact that Burnett had executed an affidavit. However, when the contents of such documents is disputed they cannot be offered to prove the truth of a charge. They can only be used to demon-strate the good faith of the publication that relied on them. The article was also cleared by Clay Blair, Jr., then editor in chief of Curtis Publishing Company, as in line with his policy of "sophisti-cated muckraking," or as he defined it, a refined attack on corruption.

Both Butts and Bryant sued for libel. The Butts case was the only one that went to trial. Banking on Burnett's testimony, the *Post* sought to prove that the article was true.

What was especially damaging to the *Post* was the number of witnesses who cast doubt on Burnett's testimony. A former busi-ness associate of Burnett said that the notes were not the same ones that Burnett had shown him shortly after the phone conversation. Griffith, the Georgia coach, was a witness for the *Post*. He said that the notes identified two basic offensive formations of his team, but he also agreed that "a good number of Burnett's notes were incorrect and didn't even apply to anything Georgia had." An Alabama player said that one of the Georgia formations had caught his team by surprise. And Butts's attorneys argued with telling effect that the *Post* realized that Burnett could not be believed because they knew before running the article that he had been convicted of writing two bad checks totaling $75.

Moreover, a number of witnesses denied quotations attributed to them in the article. Mickey Babb, Georgia's leading pass receiver, was quoted in the article as saying that Alabama players knew Georgia's "eighty-eight pop" play and when this key play would be used. Babb testified that there was no "eighty-eight pop" play and Coach Griffith denied having said "I never had a chance."

As evidence of failure to check thoroughly—a key to malice—Butts's attorneys showed that no *Post* representative had examined Burnett's notes before the article was published, nor was a film of the actual game ever viewed

The article did show that the *Post* had checked with a great number of persons associated with the Georgia team, but their denials of specific quotations made it look as if evidence against Butts had been manufactured. Neither Butts nor Bryant was contacted by the *Post* or quoted in the story—a failure difficult to defend either journalistically or in court, although periodicals often deliberately avoid checking with targets of their attacks on the basis that flat denials can be predicted. To top off the proof of malice, evidence was introduced showing that the *Post* had rejected an emotional plea by long-distance telephone from one of Butts's daughters to withhold the article from publication and that the magazine had turned down a request for a retraction after it had run.

The jury awarded Butts $60,000 in compensatory damages and $3 million in punitive damages. The judge cut the punitive damages to $400,000. By the time the judgment was paid in 1967, interest had brought the total up to about $572,000.

Referring to the "slipshod and sketchy investigatory techniques" used by the *Post*, Chief Justice Warren noted, in casting the key vote in the 5-to-4 decision sustaining the verdict, that the *Post* had embarked on a policy of "sophisticated muckraking." He said:

Suffice it to say that little investigative effort was expended initially, and no additional inquiries were made even after the editors were notified by respondent and his daughter that the account to be published was absolutely untrue. Instead, the *Saturday Evening Post* proceeded on its reckless course with full knowledge of the harm that would likely result from publication of the article. This knowledge was signaled by the statements at the conclusion of the article that "Wally Butts will never help any football team again" and "careers will be ruined, that is sure."

. . . Freedom of the press under the First Amendment does not include absolute license to destroy lives or careers. [Curtis Publishing Co. v. Butts and Associated Press v. Walker 388 U.S. 130]

Another opinion in the case, joined in by a minority of four justices, throws some additional light on the extra care required of exposé articles. The opinion, written by Justice John M. Harlan, drew a sharp distinction between "hot news" like in the Walker riots case and articles based on investigations, such as the *Post's* "The Story of a College Football Fix." The Associated Press dispatch about Walker required immediate dissemination, Justice Harlan said, and nothing in the article seemed unreasonable to anyone familiar with the general's previous statements on the controversy. On the other hand, Justice Harlan went on, the *Post* had sufficient time, or at least should have taken it, for a more thorough investigation, but "elementary precautions were nevertheless ignored." The Harlan opinion is not controlling, since a majority of justices did not support it. However, it does offer sound advice.

Coach Bryant settled his suit involving the "fix" article, as well as a previous suit, out of court for $300,000. Since all this was considered to be compensatory damages, it was asserted to be tax free. Punitive damages are taxable.

Since responsible newsmen rarely tell deliberate lies—at least in print or on the air—they may possibly be lulled into a false sense of security by *The New York Times* doctrine and fall into sloppy habits which could lead to trouble. The defendant in *The New York Times* case was a newspaper that had received an advertisement from an outside source. It depended on the names signed at the bottom of the advertisement and the reputation of the advertising agency. It ran the advertisement without endorsement, somewhat similar to a bus that will pick up a passenger without regard to his ethical beliefs. In this respect newspapers—and broadcasting stations to a lesser extent—are open to all without censorship or endorsement. In the Garrison and St. Amant cases, unlike the *Times* case, the defendants were the originators of the material on which suit was brought. Unlike the press, they were not on the sidelines. The same test was applied.

But where a newspaper is in a position similar to the *Saturday Evening Post's* in the Butts case, and is in effect editorializing, it is possible in the future that a different standard of malice may be applied.

A case tried in Pennsylvania the year after *The New York Times* decision provides still another clue concerning malice. The case indicates that the newsman should make sure that he does not write one fact at one time and a totally contradictory libelous fact later. Despite the court's finding in the *Times* case, the editor should check the clips.

The article was a column written by Will Smith, editor of *The Evening Leader* of Lehighton, Pennsylvania, and published November 18, 1961. It said that Councilman George Reich had made a "fast buck" by selling property to the school district for "something like $17,500." It also said that Reich's "bosom pal" was Dr. Homer B. Fegley, "who just happens to be on the union school district board and chairman of the $2 million high school planning committee."

Reich and Fegley sued for libel, asserting that the column meant that they had conspired to jam through the school board a deal that gave Reich an excessive profit at the expense of the taxpayers. They also stated that the column was false in that the Perry Walp Estate, not Reich, had owned the land, and that the sale price was $10,500, not $17,500. When the jury awarded Fegley $4,000 and Reich nothing, the judge held that the verdicts were inconsistent and ordered a new trial. On appeal, the Pennsylvania Superior Court ruled that the cases were covered by the New York Times rule (Fegley v. Mortimer, 204 Pa. Super. 54).

The ruling meant that at the second trial the plaintiffs had to prove that Editor Smith either knew he was lying or recklessly disregarded the truth when he wrote the libelous column. Testimony indicated that Smith had gotten into an argument with Reich at a wedding reception a week before writing the column and had called him a thief and a robber. The argument moved out to the street where Reich knocked Smith down. Reich said that Smith went away vowing, "I'll write you up in my paper." Smith admitted that he might have said that. While this personal animosity would be good evidence in another kind of libel suit, it is of little value in negating the New York Times rule for defense. Personal ill will does not prove either lying or reckless disregard of truth.

To meet the stiffer test of malice, Laurence H. Eldredge, one of the attorneys for the plaintiffs, brought out that twice before penning the libelous column, Smith had written items with the correct facts on the school board's purchase of the land. In his defense, Smith said he had heard rumors on the street that Reich had made a fast buck on the sale and that at the wedding reception Reich had told him he had done so, suggesting the $17,500 figure. Reich denied this statement. The jury awarded each plaintiff $1 in compensatory damages and $2,500 in punitive damages. Answering specific questions submitted by the judge, the jury held that Smith had not lied about Fegley and Reich but had recklessly disregarded the truth.

There are two situations where the newsman should be especially careful even when banking on the definition of malice set by the Supreme Court. The first is when the target of the attack denounces the libel before its publication. He should certainly be given his full say in the original publication, to avoid any finding of "reckless disregard" of the truth. The second situation requiring special care is when a retraction is demanded. The Supreme Court declined to find the *Times* guilty of malice because it refused to retract for Commissioner Sullivan although it later did for Governor Patterson. It pointed out that the *Times* had a reasonable doubt that the advertisement referred to Sullivan, since it had not named him, and that the refusal to retract was not final. Nevertheless, it left open the possibility that a refusal to retract under other circumstances might prove actual malice. It is therefore suggested that replies to demands for retractions be worded in amicable terms, ask questions about what is specifically in error and not shut the door finally. If errors have been made, a correction—not a retraction—should be run, as discussed in full on page 286.

Malice and Other Defenses

Regardless of how the courts finally apply the standard of malice in cases involving public officials and public figures, the rule is bound to be more liberal than it is for other kinds of libel. The jury almost always decides whether malice is present, so the temper of the times and the effectiveness of the lawyers for each side, as well as the facts in the case, play a vital part in the outcome. Generally, actual malice in libel suits other than the cases involving the New York Times rule or, as the courts put it, common-law malice, can be divided into three kinds: personal ill will; gross carelessness or negligence that indicates a wanton disregard of the plaintiff's rights; and extreme falsity and atrocious character of the article.

Personal Ill Will

The classic case of personal ill will was discussed on page 108. It covered a fist fight between the late Mayor James Curley of Boston and Frederick W. Enwright, the publisher of the Boston *Telegraph*. Personal enmity need not reach the fist-swinging stage to show actual malice. In Minnesota a pamphleteer called the plaintiff a "son of a bitch" two or three years before the libelous attack. That, plus other evidence of ill feeling, was found sufficient to establish the existence of actual malice (Hammersten v. Reiling, 262 Minn. 200).

Fist fights, personal grudges and feuds are one way of showing personal ill will. In the old days journalists went around picking fights with people they did not like. Today they are better behaved and more responsible, so such evidence of ill will is rare.

One way to recognize personal ill will is to look for the aim behind the libel. If it is to oppose a person's ideas, there can be no quarrel, for he who offers himself and his ideas for public acceptance must be willing to submit himself to the test of opposing forces. The newsman devoted to informing the public must accept the fact that his reports will often injure the standing of some of his sources, often some of those he likes best. Reporters who covered Senator Barry Goldwater during the 1964 Presidential campaign liked him immensely, but this did not stop them from writing libelous stories about him. The test of ill will is whether the purpose goes beyond an attack on a person's ideas to an attack on the person himself in an attempt to harm and perhaps demolish him. Quentin Reynolds, for example, introduced evidence that Westbrook Pegler had written various organizations asking them to withdraw invitations to Reynolds to speak before them. That was direct evidence of ill will of a rare kind.

Another example is the blacklisting campaign conducted by Aware, Inc., in the 1950s against various personalities in the broadcasting industry. Here the intent was not just to combat ideas but to pursue the person and perhaps destroy him. Aware described its purpose as combating Communism in the entertainment and communication industries. It served as a consultant to sponsors and other institutions in radio and television, screening performers with respect to their political backgrounds. John Henry Faulk, who appeared daily on Station WCBS in New York, campaigned against Aware. Faulk, who was also an officer of the American Federation of Television and Radio Artists, charged that Aware used racketeering methods to intimidate and terrorize broadcasting networks, sponsors, producers and advertising agencies to pay for blacklists of performers accused of subversive connections. Aware struck back, sending out to every possible source of Faulk's employment a special bulletin and other material accusing him of being a Communist or pro-Communist and of exploiting his office and profession for the propagation of Communist doctrine. Faulk lost his job. He then sued Aware, Vincent W. Hartnett, one of its founders and its director, who wrote the special bulletin, and Laurence A. Johnson, the owner of a chain of grocery stores, who helped finance the campaign. Aware's ill will was easily proved and this deprived it of its defenses of reply and fair comment. On July 16, 1962, the jury awarded Faulk $3.5 million in damages, the largest libel verdict up to that time. Of that amount $1,000,000 was in compensatory damages against all three defendants and $2.5 million was in punitive damages, divided equally between Aware and Hartnett. There were no punitive damages against Johnson because he died the day before the verdict and an estate cannot be assessed such damages. Aware and Hartnett appealed. Johnson's estate did not enter an appeal. The Appellate Division of the New York Supreme Court reduced the judgment, cutting the compensatory award to $400,000 and the punitive damages to $50,000 against Aware and $100,000 against Hartnett, who was considered by the court "by far the more guilty of the two." In its decision, which was upheld by the state's highest court, the Appellate Division said this about malice:

> The proof in support of the plaintiff's case was overwhelming. He conclusively established that the defendants planned to destroy his professional career through the use of the libelous publications directed to the places where they would do him the most harm. He proved that they succeeded in doing so. The proof established that the libelous statements were not made recklessly but rather that they were made deliberately. The acts of the defendants were proven to be as malicious as they were vicious. The defendants were not content merely with publishing the libelous statements complained of knowing that injury to the plaintiff must follow such publication. They pursued the plaintiff with the libel making sure that its poison would be injected directly into the wellsprings of his professional and economic existence. They did so with deadly effect. He was professionally destroyed, his engagements were canceled and he could not gain employment in his field despite every effort on his part. [Faulk v. Aware, Inc., 19 A.D. 2d (N.Y.) 464]

Another way to prove actual ill will is to demonstrate repetition of the libelous matter. The plaintiff can offer evidence that there were previous libels of the same nature made by the same defendant. The theory is that the repetition of published statements of a similar character shows a continuing state of mind on the part of the publisher or a continuing purpose or intent to injure the person referred to. The most blatant form of repetition of a libel is the calculated falsehood. It is sufficient proof of ill will in any court and can result in heavy damage.

In 1948 the National Farm Labor Union, which later changed its name to the National Agricultural Union, began a campaign to unionize workers employed on the DiGiorgio Fruit Corporation's 19,000 acres at the southern end of the San Joaquin Valley in California. As part of the drive it made a film titled *Poverty in the Valley of Plenty*. It depicted workers on DiGiorgio farms living under conditions worse than those portrayed in *The Grapes of Wrath*. Tools and equipment were said to get better treatment than people. Nine or ten workers were shown living in one-room shacks, where they had to cook, eat and sleep and which lacked sanitary facilities. Twenty-five or thirty families had only a cold-water shower next to a cow pen for bathing. The narrator of the film said that workers were required to put in twelve hours of labor for eleven hours pay and had no medical facilities. DiGiorgio was also accused of joining other corporate farmers in hiring "headhunters" to smuggle Mexicans across the border in violation of the law.

The film stirred a great deal of interest and ultimately was shown to a Congressional investigating subcommittee, which decided that it had better look into the matter. In February, 1950, the subcommittee issued a report concluding that the charges in the film were false. The shacks were not on the DiGiorgio farms but on nearby land. The housing furnished workers had modern kitchens, toilets and bathing facilities. A doctor held office hours daily and a nurse was on full-time duty. DiGiorgio, which had filed a libel suit against the union, agreed in May, 1950, to settle the case out of court. Part of the agreement was the union's pledge to destroy all copies of the film it had and to try to induce third parties who possessed copies to destroy theirs.

In 1959, the Executive Council of the American Federation of Labor and Congress of Industrial Organizations decided to make another attempt to organize farm workers. To help in the campaign it resurrected the film and showed it almost daily in April and May at various places in northern California, primarily to audiences of agricultural workers, although the general public could attend.

Naturally DiGiorgio sued. The court found that although labor disputes are the subject of fair comment and criticism, the defendants had lost their privilege because they had uttered an outright lie. Proof that the defendants knew they were lying was unshakable because of the previous libel suit and agreement to destroy the film. Nevertheless, the defendants insisted that the conditions depicted in the film were true, a contention that the appellate court found "so utterly devoid of merit that it is difficult to understand how appellants can urge it seriously." It noted that the chief organizer of the union knew the history of the film and that it was not supposed to be shown. Moreover, none of those who showed it had ever investigated conditions at DiGiorgio. The defendants did win one point on appeal. Compensatory damages were reduced from $100,000 to $10,000 on the basis that most of those who had seen the film were only farm workers, not DiGiorgio customers. But punitive damages of $50,000 were allowed to stand (DiGiorgio Fruit Corp. v. AFL-CIO, 30 Cal. Rptr. 350).

The stricture against repetition does not mean that a libelous statement can be transmitted only once and then dropped. If there are continuing developments in a story, the libel can be repeated with impunity as long as the writer is careful to continue to invoke his defenses.

In a New Jersey case cited on page 132 two policemen sued the Passaic *Daily News* because it had carried a city manager's remark that they had not been promoted because they had been "insubordinate" and "should have been fired." The *News* invoked the defense of reporting an official proceeding. To defeat that defense the policemen tried to show actual malice on the part of the paper by citing nine articles that had quoted the libelous remarks. The New Jersey Supreme Court said that these were not needless repetitions of the libel, but provided necessary background information each time a development occurred in the situation (Swede v. Passaic Daily News, 30 N.J. 320).

Still another way to show ill will is testimony that the publisher refused to publish a correction. This testimony is rarely true and is an invitation to perjury. A plaintiff will testify that on the day of the publication of the article on which he is suing he telephoned the newspaper and said that the article was incorrect and demanded a correction. He will testify that he does not know to whom he talked. This leaves the publisher with the necessity of proving a negative, which is always difficult. Years may have elapsed between the date of the publication and the trial, and the defendant rarely knows until the trial approaches that such evidence will be offered. Or the plaintiff will testify that he sent a letter to the publisher demanding a correction. Several years ago an army officer who had started libel actions against all the New York newspapers contended that he had sent a letter to each of the papers demanding a correction. Not one of them was received.

Related to a refusal to publish a correction is a rejection of an appeal made before publication that the article or broadcast be withheld. Often these appeals are made too late to prevent the libel from getting out, but they are nonetheless effective and quite difficult to counteract. (Suggestions for handling corrections and demands for withholding items are discussed in full on page 285).

Finally, another method of proving ill will is by showing that the defendant tried but failed to prove the truth of the libel at the trial. This is harsh, but the law permits it. What the rule means is that the law lets a jury base a finding of ill will on the act of the defendant's trying to defend himself. But it is not an unmitigated evil. It gives the defendant a rebuttal right that few have in any kind of litigation. If the plaintiff contends that the unsupported allegations of truth in a newsman's answer constitutes ill will, the newsman has the right to call to the stand the attorney who drafted the answer. The attorney can then testify at length about the information that led him to believe that the defense of truth existed. The rule thus permits the defense to get into evidence all the reports that were available at the time—page after page of rumor, gossip and other matters that could not possibly be introduced in evidence in any other manner.

Gross Carelessness or Negligence

Common-law malice, however, is not confined to spite, vengeance, prejudice or calculated falsehood. It can be presumed from a wanton disregard of another's rights as the result of gross carelessness or negligence. The clue here is not how steadily the writer's heart beats but how carefully his mind functions.

Again, the law seems harsh, and it is. In many libel suits, perhaps most of them, there is evidence of some negligence. Infallibility is not a human trait, and while some sources may not believe it, writers, editors and commentators are human. In order to have a finding of actual malice, ordinary negligence is not enough. Gross negligence is required. The trouble is that the court will usually allow the plaintiff to introduce evidence of any negligence and leave it to the jury to decide whether it was gross. The jurors hear the evidence, and it is understandable if they get the impression that there is some basis for finding gross negligence. Most of them have never had to write a story against a deadline or to try to scribble down quotes with three people talking at once. Besides, the jury naturally assumes that since the court has permitted the testimony of slight negligence to get into the record, the evidence will also sustain a finding of gross negligence.

Unfortunately there are reporters who invent quotations and

facts to produce more readable stories. Those who fabricate their material may win pats on the back from fellow reporters, but they also lose libel suits.

On August 11, 1961, the Dallas bureau of United Press International sent out the following dispatch:

LITENBRITE

Dallas, Tex., Aug. 11 (UPI)—Bruce Mohs of Madison, Wis., is the kind of a guy who figures any port in a pinch. And he was . . . pinched.

He flew his plane to Dallas yesterday and by the time he got here he was low on fuel. His plane has pontoons and no wheels, so he landed smack in the middle of White Rock Lake, a residential area and park inside the city limits.

"Hey, get that thing out of here," a park patrolman yelled.

"Sorry," Mohs replied. "No gas left."

The patrolman crawled inside the plane and turned on the ignition. There was a quarter of a tank left. "You have plenty of gas to get to Lake Dallas [about 15 miles away]," he said.

Mohs disagreed and about this time L. M. Cook, Park Superintendent, arrived and ordered Mohs arrested and handcuffed. He took him to his office and began thumbing through a thick book of city ordinances to find one that fit.

He did and had Mohs charged with flying under 2,000 feet over Dallas and landing on a publicly owned lake. "I guess I could have looked a little longer," Mohs admitted. "I saw plenty of airports, but no water for a pontoon plane and I just set it down on the first thing that looked bigger than a puddle."

One of the few points in the story that was accurate was that Mohs did land his plane on the lake. He was not arrested, nor was he handcuffed. The park patrolman denied yelling, "Hey, get that thing out of here," or asserting that he had said that Mohs had replied that he was out of gas. The patrolman did not crawl inside the plane to check on the fuel. Mohs was not charged with low flying.

UPI had a rough time in court when Mohs sued. For one thing, it had carried a previous story on Mohs's landing. The first dispatch contained no statements of his being arrested, handcuffed or caught lying about being low on gas. The UPI man who wrote the libelous story testified that he had received his material from a string correspondent who had been reliable in the past. But evi-

dence was also introduced to show that someone at the UPI office
had called the police department and learned that Mohs had not
been charged with any offense. Even though this fact should have
flashed a caution light, no attempt was made to check with the
police substation for the park, the park patrolman, the park superintendent or anyone else to verify the libelous material. Nor did the
writer call the man who had written the first dispatch to try to
reconcile the conflict in facts.

UPI argued that it had sent out a complete retraction and that
therefore no evidence of malice had been offered. The court disagreed and, citing the failure to check sources, concluded that
either the writer or the string correspondent had "made up most of
the story, quotes and all, for the purpose of having an amusing
story published in the newspapers, without any regard for its effect
on Mohs." Fabrication, the court said, "was a willful and wanton
act sufficient to support a finding of malice." Mohs was awarded
$2,500 in compensatory damages and $5,000 in punitive damages
(United Press International v. Mohs, 381 S.W. 2d 104).

The usual proof of negligence is not fabrication, however, but
mere failure to make the routine checks that every reporter learned,
or should have learned, in his first few months on the job. The
newspaper morgue should be checked for background information
that throws light on the new development. Names and addresses
should be checked against the telephone directory, police logs,
Who's Who and other sources. A single source should not be accepted as final if there are other places to check. Most important of
all, as has been emphasized and reemphasized in this book, every
effort should be made to communicate with the maligned person
to get his side of the story. If he cannot be reached, his attorney,
his public-relations man or even his wife or a friend should be contacted. And if all efforts fail, the attempt to reach him should be
written into the story. Failure to even try to reach the person
named in the article will in almost every possible set of circumstances be allowed to go to the jury on the issue of gross negligence. If a newspaper, magazine or broadcasting company has
made a mistake, there is nothing quite so telling as the point that
it could have prevented the mistake by communicating with the
person who was libeled.

On page 51 the story is told of the Long Island clergyman who
was depicted as striking back when assaulted by a driver. Mr. Han-

cock, the minister, had not struck back, and the trial court held
that the article was libelous because it portrayed a minister brawl-
ing in the street. Mr. Hancock wanted punitive damages. Compensatory damages were not enough to satisfy this Christian
clergyman for this mild affront. So he argued that the *Tribune* had
been guilty of malice because it had neglected to ask him whether
he had struck the chauffeur instead of turning the other cheek.
That was all the proof he had of negligence. The *Tribune* said that
the facts had come from a Long Island correspondent who had
served it for twenty-one years without a complaint. Nevertheless,
the court allowed the jury to find gross negligence as a basis for
punitive damages, and an award of about $6,000 was made. In
what other field of human endeavor would it be regarded as gross
negligence for an employer to rely on an employe who had served
him for over twenty years without a single serious mistake?

The malice is compounded if the reporter not only fails to make
adequate checks but also disregards the information he does un-
cover. The publication falls under sharp suspicion if the material
selected for the article supports the publication's editorial position.
Here is a portion of an article from the September 18, 1958, edition of *Jet* magazine entitled "Rev. M. L. King's Court Fine Paid
by Police Commissioner," which the Alabama Supreme Court
found had shown malice:

> Actually, the minister had come to sit in on the courtroom hearing
> of bus boycott lieutenant Rev. Ralph D. Abernathy, who was press-
> ing charges against schoolteacher Edward Davis, 24.
> Earlier, Davis had attacked Rev. Abernathy with a hatchet and
> pistol after accusing him of an affair with his [Davis'] wife. Held on
> an attempted murder charge, he was the same Davis who resigned
> in June from a Greenville, Ala., grade school following charges of
> having sex relations with students. Montgomery Negroes speculated
> he was the pawn of persons seeking to embarrass Reverends Aber-
> nathy and King.

When *Jet* (which supported Dr. King and carried editorials by
him) refused to run a retraction, Davis sued for $150,000 in libel
damages. Davis asserted that students had brought copies of the
magazine to his class in Montgomery and had yelled, "Jet, Jet," at
him, that parents had demanded that he be dismissed and that he
had been shunned and ostracized by other Negroes. *Jet* replied
that the article was true. At the trial *Jet* showed how it had

checked on the facts. It displayed clips from the Baton Rouge (Louisiana) *Morning Advocate* and the Chicago *Sun-Times* and a press release which said that Davis had been "charged with" or "accused of" attacking Abernathy. *Jet,* however, had made an outright statement that Davis had attacked Abernathy with a hatchet and a pistol. On the witness stand a *Jet* editor said that he saw no distinction between a statement that someone had committed a crime and a statement that he had been "charged with" a crime. Davis was eventually acquitted of the charge.

Jet also showed that a reporter had called the superintendent of schools in Greenville. At the trial the superintendent, who had taken over the job after Davis had left Greenville, insisted that he had told the reporter that Davis' record was absolutely clean and he knew nothing that would indicate that the resignation was other than voluntary. The superintendent also said he knew of no facts "which in any way reflected on Davis' performance as a teacher." He did tell the reporter that shortly before Davis resigned, several Negroes had protested the hiring of a principal of a school and at that time one or more in the group had said that Davis ought to be fired because he was the father of children born to students. *Jet*'s next move would seemingly have been to check with the superintendent who was in charge at Greenville when Davis was there. It did not check with him, and when he was called to the witness stand he testified that he had heard the rumors, had investigated them and had found them to be groundless. Another logical person to check with would have been the superintendent of schools in Montgomery, where Davis had gone after leaving Greenville. If that superintendent had been contacted, the *Jet* reporter would have found out that he had investigated Davis prior to hiring him and had concluded that he had a good reputation both in Greenville and Montgomery. Finally, *Jet* should have checked with Davis himself about the charges made against him before, as the court noted, circulating them "on a national scale."

To back up its charges of Davis' having had sexual relations with students, a *Jet* executive testified that he had heard that Davis was the father of a child born to a particular girl. He could not name the source, and the girl told the court that another man was the father. Other unwed mothers testified, but the State Supreme Court commented that not one of them could give any facts to support the rumor about Davis. In rejecting *Jet*'s plea for a new trial, the trial court upheld the jury's verdict for Davis. On appeal the State Supreme Court cut damages from $67,500 to $45,000 (Johnson Publishing Co. v. Davis, 271 Ala. 474).

Extreme Character of the Language

Actual malice can also be shown if the article is false and the language is of a heinous, atrocious and extreme character. For a time some courts held that mere falsity was enough to prove malice, but this is no longer true. The libel must also be of an outrageous character. The best example is the Pegler column on Reynolds reproduced in full beginning on page 237.

Some courts, it is only fair to warn, have upheld a finding of actual malice from the wording of articles that do not seem particularly heinous or atrocious. In 1958 the West Virginia Supreme Court of Appeals thought the following editorial in the Charleston *Gazette* was so violent in character that it invalidated the defense of fair comment:

> Morality in government was a major issue of the 52nd Legislature, and it had the salutary effect of outlawing liquor accounts as political plums for officeholders.
>
> Now it's time the Legislature gives state insurance a long, searching study in view of the growing trend toward paying off political debts with fire insurance premiums.
>
> . . . .
>
> The Recipients of this lush piece of state business deny that they are parties to any wrong-doing. They argue, either out of stupidity or calloused disregard for their public trust, that their dealings with the state are right, proper and aboveboard.
>
> Perhaps, as they say, their dealings are outwardly legitimate. They get a premium as insurance agents, and the state gets insurance coverage from a reputable company. All would be well if the deal ended there, but by unfortunate circumstance it doesn't end in so innocent and blithe a manner.
>
> There is a third factor to consider that weighs heavily against these agents. They, as members of the Legislature, hold an allegiance to their constituents which precludes their doing business of any kind with the state while they are in office.
>
> . . . .
>
> If They Could Serve their own cause and that of the electorate

with equal fervor while holding state insurance contracts, all well and good. But they can't! Their past actions in the Legislature reveal them as peons of the politicians and lackeys of the administration.

We've watched them at work, and they follow the administration line with dutiful submission. They are the Governor's marionettes on the Senate and House floors and they jump when ordered to—like Kukla and Ollie of television fame.

It's easy to see that they've sold their votes—sold out their constituents—for a price. They're more dedicated to their own creature comforts than to the comforts and welfare of the folks back home.

The editorial then named the legislators who had sold fire insurance to the state. Two of them, J. Paul England and Paul Bower, sued the Charleston *Gazette.* England's $5,000 judgment and Bower's $8,000 judgment were upheld by the state's highest court. Today, under the New York Times rule, the case would be thrown out of court. Even under 1958 rules the decision is difficult to justify. But the West Virginia Supreme Court held that this editorial constituted "such a vehement and violent attack on the character of plaintiff as to make an abuse of the qualified privilege clearly apparent" (England v. Daily Gazette Co., 143 W. Va. 700).

Despite this aberrant ruling there is little to worry about in phrasing editorials if the writer is not motivated by an evil heart. There were other factors in the *Gazette* case that the court noted as bearing on the question of malice. One was the fact that the day after it was sued, the paper commented that it was "not backing down" from any statements it had made in the previous editorial—a repetition, in the court's view, of the libel. Another factor was the failure of the writer to check with the plaintiffs or any other member of the legislature.

Trends in Malice

In the third decade of the twentieth century (before the Supreme Court announced the New York Times rule) a more sophisticated approach to malice became noticeable. Not content with having two definitions of malice in libel—legal malice (to show responsibility) and actual malice (to show wrongdoing)—the law began to refine the latter in various ways, depending on the defense invoked. The multiplication of definitions began as a result of a question asked by legal scholars: Is the malice that will defeat the defense of fair comment and criticism the same malice that will defeat other qualified defenses and the same malice that will permit the plaintiff to obtain punitive damages?

The result was noted in 1938, when the American Law Institute issued volume 3 of the *Restatement of the Law of Torts,* an authority that carries great weight with the courts. In the section dealing with privileged criticism the word "malice" is dropped completely. The qualification on the defense is phrased this way: ". . . is not made solely for the purpose of causing harm to the other" (section 606, volume 3, *Restatement of the Law of Torts*). As even those not versed in law can see, this is quite different from personal ill will or gross negligence. The writer can hate the person whose performance he is criticizing with all the animosity his heart can muster, but if the comment is not made solely for the purpose of causing harm to him, there can be no finding of malice. The courts are now beginning to embrace the idea. The wider its acceptance, the more freedom the commentator will enjoy, for the newsman who cannot think of at least one reason, beyond harming his target, for publishing the criticism does not belong in the profession. Under this emerging definition the malice necessary to destroy the defense of fair comment has become a watered-down version of personal ill will, difficult for the plaintiff to prove.

In 1964, the Court of Appeals of the Second Circuit adopted the definition of the *Restatement of the Law of Torts* in a fair-comment case led by Dr. Linus Pauling against the New York *Daily News* (see page 182 for details) and held:

[6, 7] The privilege of "fair comment," the so-called "rolled up" plea, Gatley, Libel and Slander, 477-78 (1960 ed.), is defined in A.L.I. Restatement, Torts, § 606, as follows:

(1) Criticism of so much of another's activities as are matters of public concern is privileged if the criticism, although defamatory,
    (a) is upon,
        (i)   a true or privileged statement of fact, or
        (ii) upon facts otherwise known or available to the recipient as a member of the public, and
    (b) represents the actual opinion of the critic, and
    (c) is not made solely for the purpose of causing harm to the other.

Reports of Dr. Pauling's activities which the hearsay rule would render inadmissible to prove truth might be admissible for various purposes with respect to this defense. One would be to show that the comment was upon a "privileged statement of fact"; on this basis it was proper for the News to introduce reports of legislative and executive proceedings to show the "privileged facts" that formed a basis for its comment. If the News relied on such reports, these would also be admissible, again regardless of their truth, to show that the comment was "not made solely for the purpose of causing harm," in other words to negative "malice." [Pauling v. News Syndicate Company, Inc., 335 F.2d 659, 664-5]

The defense of reporting an official proceeding has passed through a similar experience. The reporter, acting in a sense as a historian, may despise some of the participants with a fierce hatred but still be able, because of professional ethics, to give an accurate and balanced account of the proceedings. He should not be placed in the position, simply because of personal dislike, of risking an adverse verdict from a jury in performing a task that he must do daily. In 1930 the New York Legislature embraced the idea by removing the qualification of malice from the privilege of reporting. Then the *Restatement of the Law of Torts* added its own remedy. It said that the privilege of reporting is lost if the publication was "made solely for the purpose of causing harm to the person defamed" (Section 611, Volume 3, *Restatement of the Law of Torts*). Again, the malice necessary to defeat the defense is a watered-down version of ill will. It is something done solely for the purpose of causing harm. In 1964 the Supreme Court issued its definition of actual malice. In *The New York Times* case the court defined it as a statement made with the knowledge of its falsity or with a reckless disregard of whether it is false or not. Courts, while describing this as actual malice, distinguish it from common-law actual malice.

Finally, in the Gertz case, the Supreme Court held that there could be no punitive damages unless *The New York Times* standard of malice is met.

The revision of the *Restatement of the Law of Torts* has recently been published (1977). This is not binding on courts but is frequently followed. With respect to fair comment, it has seized upon Justice Powell's statement in the Gertz case: "Under the First Amendment there is no such thing as a false idea." It has also revised the definition of defamatory expressions of opinion to read as follows: "A defamatory communication may consist of a statement in the form of an opinion, but a statement of this nature is actionable only if it implies the allegation of undisclosed defamatory facts as the basis for the opinion." This limits substantially any libel charge based on a statement of opinion.

A recent case provides a perfect example (Greenbelt Publishing Association, Inc. v. Bresler, 398 US 6). Bresler was a prominent local real-estate developer and builder and, during the period in question, was a member of the Maryland House of Delegates. Bresler entered into negotiations with the Greenbelt City Council to obtain certain zoning variances which would allow the construction of high-density housing on land owned by him. At the same time, the city was attempting to acquire another tract of land owned by Bresler for the construction of a new high school. The joint negotiations evoked substantial local controversy and several members of the community freely expressed their views. Some of the people at the public meetings characterized Bresler's negotiating position as blackmail, and the newspaper reported that they had charged him with blackmail. Bresler sued for libel and recovered $5,000 in compensatory damages and $12,500 in punitive damages. In reversing the Supreme Court said:

> No reader could have thought that either the speakers at the meetings or the newspaper articles reporting their words were charging Bresler with the commission of a criminal offense. On the contrary, even the most careless reader must have perceived that the word was no more than rhetorical hyperbole, a vigorous epithet used by those who considered Bresler's negotiating position extremely unreasonable. Indeed, the record is completely devoid of evidence that anyone in the city of Greenbelt or anywhere else thought Bresler had been charged with a crime. [Greenbelt Publishing Association, Inc. v. Bresler, 398 U.S. 6, 14]

If, on the other hand, no background material had been published, and a naked charge of blackmail had been made, this would have been libelous.

The new *Restatement* with respect to the privilege of reporting broadens the scope of privilege very substantially. *Restatement* § 611 now reads as follows:

The publication of defamatory matter concerning another in a report of an official action or proceeding or a meeting open to the public that deals with a matter of public concern is privileged if the report is accurate and complete or a fair abridgement of the occurrence reported.

While the privilege is referred to as a conditional (qualified) privilege, it is not qualified by reason of malice but only to the extent that the report is not substantially accurate and complete.

These definitions are just emerging and are still too indefinite to be understood completely. What is definite is that the newsman is enjoying more and more freedom and he should take advantage of it. In ticklish situations, however, he would be wise to err on the conservative side, keeping in mind that in many jurisdictions the courts will still define actual malice in the more strict sense explained earlier in this chapter.

Another trend is also apparent. The courts are putting the brakes on juries that go wild on punitive damages. In the Faulk case the $3.5-million award was reduced to $550,000. Damages against Representative Adam Clayton Powell, Jr., for calling a lady a "bag woman," meaning that she picked up graft for policemen, were cut from $211,500 to $46,500. In the Butts case the judgment was sliced from $3,060,000 to $460,000. The moral of all this is that the courts are acting to discourage gold diggers who take advantage of the libel laws to reap fortunes in windfalls and those who use the same laws as a club in an attempt to silence critics.

Chapter 17

DEFENSES AFTER PUBLICATION

Accord and Satisfaction

EVERY NEWSPAPER, MAGAZINE AND BROADCASTING STATION EVENTU-
ally communicates a libel it has no legal right to. The pressures of
time and competition combined with human frailties lead to errors.
When that occurs, what should be done? Happily, one complete
defense is still available even though all the copies of the publication have been distributed or the program has been broadcast.
The newsman can still pull out of trouble through a defense rarely
discussed in the lawbooks but a good one nevertheless. It is known
as accord and satisfaction and is based on the principle whereby
a tort is wiped out if the one who committed it and the victim
agree on a solution.

Several years ago there were two young actresses in New York
with the same last name. For our purposes let us call them Lulu
and Lili Lovely. One day Lulu became very depressed and decided to commit suicide. Because she was a real actress, she
wanted to go out dramatically. She could have just swallowed a
lot of sleeping pills—a bottle of them was right by her bed—
and lain down and died. Instead she went out in the back yard,
climbed a lonely pine and hanged herself from one of its whisper-
ing branches. When news of this untimely event reached the New
York *Herald Tribune,* an enterprising rewrite man went through
the clips and discovered that Lili Lovely, the other actress, had
recently played a minor part in an off-Broadway show. He jumped
to the conclusion that they were the same person. After writing the
facts about the suicide he added a line that the deceased had recently played a subordinate role in a play and he named the play.
The item was libelous, not because it made some readers think Lili

had died, since that happens to the good as well as to the evil, but because it said that she had committed suicide.

But it was not even the suicide report that Lili Lovely complained about when she telephoned the *Tribune* city desk in righteous anger. It was the description of her part in the off-Broadway play. "I did not play a subordinate role in that play," she exclaimed. "I had the lead." The man in charge of the city desk realized the potential of this conversation so he assured her that the *Herald Tribune* would be glad to publish a correction and place her in the lead role in this off-Broadway play. She was very apologetic and said she hated to bother him (she had not seen a lawyer yet) and said that if he would be good enough to publish a correction and put her in the lead of this show she would love the *Trib* forever. And then she added, "If you could give me a little boost my agent would also love you forever."

A correction was written and Lili was placed in the lead of the show, which had closed about a year before. At the end of the item a few sentences were added about her potential acting ability that did her more than justice. In fact, they somewhat compromised the integrity of the man who wrote the correction. He then called her and read the item, and she responded that she was delighted and reiterated her eternal devotion to the *Tribune*. What Lili had done was to agree to drop any cause of a libel action in return for the correction. In law the tort victim and the tort feasor had agreed on a solution and the tort was wiped out through accord and satisfaction.

Six months later Lili fell into the hands of an attorney who brought a libel action against the *Tribune*. The newspaper pleaded accord and satisfaction and the case was dropped before coming to trial. Now the only difficulty with an agreement like that with Lili would be to prove it. There would be no trouble at all if it were in writing; the accord would be in permanent form for all to see. But any request to a party to put the agreement in writing is bound to bring hesitations, reconsiderations and refusals. The editor should not take such a chance but should depend on an oral agreement, which is perfectly satisfactory as far as the law is concerned, but is harder to prove. In practically all cases of serious error the aggrieved party calls on the phone or in person with the complaint. To make it easier for the lawyer in case of a suit, the editor should instruct the reporter who hears the complaint to take extra pains in writing down his notes and to preserve them.

When the reporter is finished, the complainant should be switched to the editor so that he can offer his apology and in doing so ask in an offhand way if all is forgiven. This provides two witnesses to the agreement and sufficient details to impress a judge and jury.

In a case similar to Lili's, the court held that an oral offer of a correction made over the telephone on the very day of the objectionable publication, which was accepted by the aggrieved party, was sufficient to create an issue of fact regarding whether the requirements of the defense of accord and satisfaction had been met (Kasiuba v. New York Herald Tribune, Inc., 232 N.Y.S. 2d 258).

This defense is especially useful when the libel concerns personalities dependent on publicity to advance them professionally —entertainers, athletes, politicians, artists and writers, to name a few. They know that all information media hesitate to carry items about those who sue at the drop of a comma.

One word of caution about the defense of accord and satisfaction. Once litigation has started, the newsman should not attempt to reach a settlement except through his lawyer. Any attempt, even through an intermediary, to reach an amicable solution can be cited as proof of malice at the trial. Drew Pearson once was cross-examined by a plaintiff's lawyer seeking to prove that the columnist and radio commentator had sought through a third party to get the suit dropped. As the court pointed out, such evidence might have been construed as a lack of confidence on Pearson's part in his own good faith "and would have been some evidence of a consciousness of a weakness in his contention that he had made an adequate investigation and uttered the statement without malice." As it developed, Pearson was able to score a vital point for his side. He replied that he had not taken the initiative but that the third party had approached him and offered to act as intermediary. Later the intermediary told Pearson that the plaintiff was willing to drop the suit, but his lawyers objected because they were working on a contingent fee basis (Howser, v. Pearson, 95 F. Supp. 936).

Partial Defenses

There are times when a newsman for one reason or another cannot fall back on any complete defense. He has goofed somewhere or material fed to him has proved unreliable. In such cases what can the newsman do? If he has learned his libel law, he knows that he need not turn in his pencils. For in preparing his article or script he has automatically thought of partial defenses to help in time of need, and he knows that there are others still available. Partial defenses are those that will not bar the award of all damages but will tend to reduce them. The extent to which the damages will be reduced is ordinarily left to the jury.

Partial defenses can be of two kinds, those that tend to reduce compensatory damages and those that tend to reduce punitive damages. There can be no partial defense for special damages because these are specific losses proved in dollars and cents, and no evidence advanced by the defendant can change them. Compensatory damages, however, depend on the reputation of the individual. Anything the defendant can show to prove that the harm done was not as great as claimed can reduce such awards. The evidence need not have been known at the time the libel was transmitted, because the time element has no bearing on the plaintiff's reputation. Since punitive damages are predicated on actual malice, the only evidence that can be offered is that of good intentions and care—the opposite of ill will and gross negligence. Such evidence is limited for the most part to actions by the newsman, his editor and his employer at the time of publication. However, anything that shows good faith after the libel was transmitted, even after a suit is filed, is good evidence.

The law has not always permitted partial defenses in mitigation of compensatory damages. The thinking was—and still is in some states—that since the harm had already been done nothing the defendant could show could change matters and the judgment should be commensurate with the damage. But the courts and legislatures of some states eventually realized that actions of a newspaper, magazine or broadcasting station even after the libel was published could reduce the harm done. Moreover, evidence on the plaintiff's reputation often has a direct bearing on how much he really suffered. Partial defenses are now permitted in some states for both compensatory as well as punitive damages.

The value of this extended protection was shown in a case at the turn of the century, before partial defenses were allowed in mitigation of compensatory damages. The New York *Tribune* carried a story to the effect that a gardener employed on an estate had defrauded his employer by kiting checks. There was no arrest or criminal prosecution or any other kind of litigation involved at the time of publication, so truth was the only complete defense available. The *Tribune*, however, could not prove that the gardener had kited checks. Since there was no complete defense, the gardener was entitled to compensatory damages. The maddening fact was that raising checks was the only method of defrauding his employer that the gardener had overlooked. He had appropriated proceeds from the sale of flowers and garden produce; he had been an embezzler; he was a fugitive from justice. All of these facts would have proved that the gardener's reputation had been so tarnished before the article appeared that he had not been badly damaged. Since the law at that time did not allow these facts to be introduced in evidence, the gardener appeared before the jury as an upright citizen with an unblemished reputation. Fortunately this situation no longer exists everywhere.

As a practical matter the most important partial defenses are those that reduce punitive damages, since these can be heavy. The types of evidence available to rebut punitive damages fall into three categories: facts tending to show there was no ill will; facts showing there was no gross negligence; facts showing that the newsman believed that the matter was true and acted in good faith in transmitting it.

The writer, editor and commentator should keep alert to the possible ways to prove that ill will did not generate the libelous statement.

Friendly Items

One kind of evidence consists of articles, either prior or subsequent to the libelous publications, that are friendly in tone toward the plaintiff. These do not have to concern the same subject matter as the article objected to, but if they do, so much the better. They indicate that there has been no pattern of malevolence and that the plaintiff has not been the target of a continuous attack.

Corrections

The most important evidence of a lack of ill will that can be offered at a trial is a correction. A refusal to publish a requested correction is generally strong and dramatic evidence of actual malice. Any request should receive prompt and careful attention. There are only two situations in which a correction should not be published if the article is factually incorrect and there is no defense.

The first is when the article is a fair comment and the objectionable material is an opinion held by the newsman. Withdrawal of the opinion casts doubt on the honesty of the newspaper, magazine or broadcasting station that made it. If the aggrieved party is insistent on some further publication, he should be urged to write a letter to the editor expressing his opinion, and the newspaper or magazine should agree to publish it.

There is a corollary to this rule that applies when running a correction on false facts contained in an article of opinion or comment. The editor must guard against intensifying his comment so that he makes libelous an opinion that had been either non-libelous or borderline. An example shows how easily this can happen.

In the midst of a campaign against closed meetings of the city's library board, the *Daily Enterprise* of Bastrop, Louisiana, carried on January 21, 1954, an editorial that included this paragraph:

> Mr. Madison has no doubt made a good president of the Board. He was at the helm when the beautiful new building of which every resident of the Parish is proud was built. But he didn't do it by himself. Everyone had a hand in it. In fact, Mr. Madison received just as much as he gave. He was paid approximately $13,000 for the lot the library now occupies and it was while he was a member of the Board. . . .

The true facts were that Mr. Madison had been only one of the owners of the land and it had been sold to the town at a loss. Moreover, he had not voted when the Library Board decided to acquire the land.

After Mr. Madison had informed the *Enterprise* of these facts, it ran a correction in which it noted that he had not been the sole owner; but in doing so it wrote this fatal lead-in phrase: "The *Daily Enterprise* stated in one of its editorials that President James Madison of the Board got more out of the library than he had given. . . ." The editorial had said that Madison had received "just as much as he gave"; now it was "got more." As far as the Louisiana Supreme Court was concerned, that was a clinching proof that the *Enterprise* had meant to accuse Madison of using his unpaid position of honor and influence on the library board to gain a personal profit at the expense of the taxpayers. A $7,500 judgment for Madison was upheld (Madison v. Bolton, *et al.*, 234 La. 997).

The second situation where a correction is not indicated is a mistaken-identity case where the first publication does not clearly identify the aggrieved party. A correction may clearly identify him as the aggrieved party in the first article. If he wants an item published to the effect that John Ogle of Green Street is not the John Ogle who raped a ten-year-old child a week earlier, he should be willing to sign a general release from all damages and one should be insisted on.

In running a correction the editor should be generous. He should not bury it, but he need not give it exactly the same space or the same prominence as the original article, though it helps to display it in that way. Blind heads, such as "Editor's Note," should not be used. "A Correction" is better, but the kind that most impresses a jury is a standard news headline reflecting the story, such as "Priest Ate Fish, Not Meat at Banquet on Good Friday."

Such acknowledgment in large type calling attention to the previous story and detailing the error can go far in convincing a jury that the publication is striving to counterbalance the harm it inflicted.

An excellent device used by many good newspapers is to anchor all corrections in the same prominent position of the paper day after day, so readers come to look for them. A good lawyer can argue persuasively that more readers may have seen the corrections than saw the erroneous original article. The Boston *Globe* anchors corrections on page 3, which is an all-metropolitan news page. *The New York Times* runs corrections in its News Summary and Index on the first page of its second section.

In the article the word "correction," not "retraction," should be used. The editor is correcting a fact that was erroneous. The word "retraction" sounds as if the publication or station had taken an editorial position and is changing it. This should never be done.

A correction is more effective as a practical matter if made before a suit has been filed, but may also have a good effect if run afterward. In fact, the wise libel lawyer will, in almost every case, write the attorney for plaintiff along the following lines as soon as the summons and complaint are received:

> The receipt of the summons and complaint was the first intimation that the *Daily Bugle* had that anything published concerning your client was claimed to be libelous or erroneous.
>
> It is the uniform policy of the *Bugle* to correct any erroneous statement which may appear in its columns as soon as possible after the error has been discovered. This policy is applied whether or not the matter is libelous.
>
> This policy will, of course, be applied to your client if he so desires. Will you be good enough to point out what statement of fact in the article to which you object is claimed to be erroneous, and advise us whether your client wishes our client to publish a correction.

A correction is the last thing the plaintiff's attorney wants after the action has been started if the object is to win large damages, as is so often the case. Yet what can he do? He cannot refuse a correction, because that would look bad at the trial. Usually he has to write that the damage has been done and it is much too late. In effect, he is declining a correction. The newspaper's lawyer then prepares his answer and alleges as a partial defense that after the commencement of the action the defendant caused a letter to be written offering to make a correction, but that the plaintiff refused the offer. Both letters are attached as exhibits. The result is so embarrassing to the plaintiff's attorney that he moves to strike this defense as insufficient in law, but the skillful attorney invariably can convince the judge that it should be sustained.

Laurence H. Eldredge of Philadelphia, a libel lawyer who has often been on the side of plaintiffs, agrees in the value of corrections as a preventive of suits. He has written:

> Where an honest man has been seriously defamed by a newspaper article, an important function of a libel action is to obtain a public vindication of his good name by the verdict of a jury. However, if this vindication can be obtained promptly by a published retraction, adequately worded, the client will be better off than by getting even a large verdict two or three years later. This is certainly the case with a client who is more interested in his good name than he is in collecting damages ("Practical Problems in Preparation and Trial of Libel Cases," *Vanderbilt Law Review*, vol. 15, (1962) p. 1085).

Legislatures of various states have become so convinced that corrections in themselves are sufficient to restore the harm committed by libels that they have limited damages when a correction is requested and published. States with such statutes are Alabama, Arizona, California, Connecticut, Florida, Georgia, Idaho, Indiana, Iowa, Kentucky, Maine, Massachusetts, Michigan, Minnesota, Mississippi, Montana, Nebraska, New Jersey, North Carolina, North Dakota, Ohio, Oklahoma, Oregon, South Dakota, Tennessee, Texas, Utah, Virginia, West Virginia and Wisconsin.

An outright refusal to make a correction is dangerous anywhere, as a case involving Dr. L. G. Rice of Albuquerque, New Mexico, shows. On October 17, 1960, a thirteen-year-old girl, Cynthia Vigil, visited Dr. Rice, complaining about an infection of her foot. The infection required Cynthia to stay at home. Cynthia's mother did not want her to miss any classes so she asked the school to send a teacher to the house. In handling the request the school asked Dr. Rice for a report. Dr. Rice said later that he thought he was preparing a welfare form and listed the diagnosis of that illness as "pregnancy." Cynthia's mother was, to say the least, outraged and demanded that the school destroy the report. When it refused, she called Dr. Rice and asked him to correct or retract the report. She referred to the report as a letter. He checked his files and told Mrs. Vigil that he had found no letter, in fact, nothing except an indication that he had treated Cynthia for athlete's foot. He said that if Mrs. Vigil brought the letter in he would do what he could to correct any error he might have made. The school, however, would not give up the report, which was kept under lock and key in the principal's desk. Dr. Rice said he told Mrs. Vigil he believed the report was a mistake. Mrs. Vigil tried several times to talk to the doctor again but could not get past his nurse. Finally, in protest, Mrs. Vigil refused to pay the doctor's bill and, the court found, Dr. Rice turned it over to a collection agency. Again Mrs. Vigil called the nurse, telling her that the bill would be paid as soon as the school was informed that Cynthia was not pregnant. The next day she phoned and asked the nurse why the school had not been called. Annoyed, the nurse said that the school had not been called and there was no intention to call it. The Vigils then sued Dr. Rice for malpractice and libel. The jury returned a verdict in favor of the doctor on the malpractice count and in favor of the Vigils on the libel count. It awarded

Cynthia $2,000 compensatory damages and $5,000 punitive damages. In upholding the award the New Mexico Supreme Court said:

> We hold that evidence to show the defendant's refusal to retract is permissible to show malice. We have reviewed the record and find that the evidence is substantial to support and warrant a finding by the jury that actual malice was present, and we shall not reverse that finding. [Vigil v. Rice, 74 N.M. 693]

The same principle holds for news items. An actual correction is better than an offer to correct that is refused, but the offer alone will help. If the plaintiff is a substantial citizen and not a gold digger, as so many plaintiffs are, he may be satisfied with a correction and that may end the litigation.

A dilemma that a newspaper occasionally faces arises when an advertisement already published is shown to contain a libel that the publisher believes is indefensible. If he fails to publish a retraction he is open to a libel suit and assessment of possibly heavy damages, since he is responsible for everything in the paper. If he corrects it he may run into trouble with the advertiser. Usually the best course is to run a correction but in such a manner as not to cast any libelous aspersions on the advertiser. *Newsday,* the Long Island, New York, newspaper, faced such a situation as the result of an advertisement for Warehouse Willy, a discount house that sometimes obtained stock from insolvent concerns. The advertisement said that Warehouse Willy had purchased the stock of Northport Hardware through the Bankruptcy Court. The hardware store protested and established that this was not true. Since it is libelous to charge bankruptcy, *Newsday* wanted to correct the error and mitigate the damages claimed by Northport. It ran this item:

> In the Jan. 8 issue of *Newsday* an advertisement by Warehouse Willy stated that he had purchased the entire stock of Northport Hardware through the Bankruptcy Court. Northport Hardware Co., Inc. of Northport has not sold its stock to anyone, has never been in bankruptcy and is a long established going concern. Warehouse Willy mistakenly inserted the name of Northport Hardware in the advertising copy submitted to *Newsday.*

Both Northport Hardware and Warehouse Willy sued *Newsday* for libel. *Newsday* realized that Northport's cause of action could not be dismissed and settled out of court for a nominal sum.

Warehouse Willy protested the correction, asserting that the correction charged it with false advertising. But the court held that the correction had merely said that Warehouse Willy had made a single mistake in inserting the wrong name in the advertisement and that therefore it was not libelous (Warehouse Willy v. Newsday, 10 A. D. 2d(N.Y.)49).

Requests for corrections can usually be checked and granted if justified by the investigation. More troublesome in many ways are the requests before publication that the article be withheld. There is usually little time to investigate any further. In the case of magazines and newspapers, the type may already be locked in the page and the presses rolling. Perhaps the article has been widely promoted. In the case of broadcasting, the program has probably been listed in newspapers and television guides and promoted for some time. The temptation is to say that nothing can be done and let the requests go at that. But such action can have a deadly effect at libel trials.

In the Wally Butts case, the jury was told that one of his daughters had telephoned the *Saturday Evening Post* long distance and pleaded that the article be withheld. Who knows how many dollars in damages such heart-rending testimony adds up to?

Such appeals should not be dismissed out of hand. In every case the newspaper or magazine should go over the material again to make sure it is on safe ground. Often production schedules will not permit the postponement or cancellation of the article, but if a serious error is discovered, it can sometimes be corrected or blacked out. The pressmen can stop the presses long enough to hammer out key words in the libelous story. Readers may be puzzled or irritated by the blank spots in the paper, but the action may prevent heavy damages by showing that the publication desired to do what was right.

Judge and jury will also be impressed if the defendant can say that as soon as the objectionable matter was discovered the presses were stopped and every effort was made to retrieve papers that had left the plant. Such action is evidence that the article was indeed libelous, but jurors and judges have seen enough movies to know that the editor who yells "stop the presses" is on the side of the good guys. This procedure can save money, as the Brush-Moore Newspapers found out. Their Salisbury (Maryland) *Times* carried an article on November 14, 1956, reporting on an audit of county offices. It erroneously said that the audit had found that the sheriff's records were "incomplete" when it should have said "complete." The effect of the error was to charge the sheriff with noncompliance with the law. The press had scarcely started when the error was spotted. The press was stopped and the article corrected. The circulation manager sent an aide to try to retrieve the 250 copies of the paper with the error in it that had already been delivered, and he succeeded in finding most of them. A correction was also run the following day. Despite all these efforts the sheriff sued, and the court held that he had been libeled because the keeping of incomplete records by a sheriff is a crime. The court also ruled that the libel had been published because a few of the copies containing it had not been retrieved. The jury awarded the sheriff $12,000. When the case reached the Maryland Court of Appeals, the newspaper did much better. The court agreed that the sheriff had been defamed and that the libel had been published, but it said that the newspaper's action in stopping the press and trying to retrieve the copies containing the error tended to mitigate damages. It ordered a new trial (Brush-Moore Newspapers v. Pollitt, 220 Md. 132). The case was never retried but was settled out of court for approximately $7,500. The *Times* might have made out better in a new trial, but it did not want to take a chance of facing an antagonistic jury. The sheriff was popular in the community and the paper had been feuding with him over his refusal to show the jail log to the press.

Similar to a correction is an article revealing that the plaintiff has been acquitted. This device is available only if the plaintiff is suing on an article involving his arrest, indictment or confession or an event of similar import. If there was an error or an unfair report and the publication or broadcasting station followed up the case and carried an item concerning his acquittal, it may amount to a complete defense. Even if it does not, the item concerning his acquittal can be pleaded as a partial defense to show no ill will.

Special Statutes

In some states special statutes regarding subsequent publications have the effect of limiting the plaintiff's right to punitive damages.

The other partial defenses against punitive damages are designed to rebut gross negligence charges and show good faith. There are eight of these partial defenses.

Prior Articles

The first consists of prior articles in other publications making the same charges. This partial defense is frequently used. Morning papers cite articles in the evening papers of the preceding day; evening papers introduce articles published in the morning papers of the same date.

The New York *Daily News* used this defense in the libel suit brought by Dr. Linus Pauling. The *News* introduced publications made prior to its editorial calling Soviet Premier Khrushchev Pauling's "friend in the Kremlin." These prior publications were of two kinds: from other news media and from legislative investigating committees. As matters turned out, the *News* did not need this defense because it won the case outright (Pauling v. News Syndicate Co., 335 F. 2d 659).

Wire Service Copy

The second partial defense in this category is proof that the statements were received from reputable news-gathering agencies, such as the Associated Press and United Press International, or, on occasion, from some foreign news agency. As mentioned earlier, this defense does not protect completely against damages except in Florida, but it never does any harm and is regularly used in libel suits.

Of course the newsman does not want to involve anyone else in a libel suit, so his lawyer waits, if possible, until the statute of limitations has run with respect to the wire-service dispatch before disclosing to the plaintiff's lawyer that he is relying on such sources. Sometimes such a delay is not possible. If the plaintiff waits until just before the statute of limitation runs, there is no problem, but if he files right after the article appeared, the only thing the lawyer can do is plead reliance on a news-gathering agency in terms so vague that the source is not identified. If the plaintiff's lawyer is alert, he will force a definite answer.

Reasonable Cause

A third kind of partial defense is proof that the general conduct of the plaintiff was such as to give the newsman reasonable and probable cause to believe that the article was true. Such a defense is not very frequently available, particularly in large cities where the plaintiff may not be widely known. When it is available, it is extremely valuable because of its impact on the jury in fixing damages.

Not long after completing his studies at the Graduate School of Journalism of Columbia University, a young editor was sued by Mayor Frank Frankel of Long Beach, New York. The editor told his lawyer that a lawbook by Francis L. Wellman titled *The Art of Cross-Examination* contained a transcript of Frankel's testimony in a previous case. It was cited in the book as a classic example of how to show on cross-examination that a witness was a colossal liar. The lawyer pleaded, as a partial defense in the libel suit, that Mayor Frankel had been so indifferent to his reputation prior to the publication that he had achieved an unintentional immortality as a fine example of a liar. The chapter of the book was reproduced as an exhibit. Mayor Frankel quickly dropped his suit.

Rumors

Another partial defense consists of proof that there were rumors or common report to the same effect as the libelous publication. This defense is frequently used, because people are such gossipers that rumors of almost very hue are floating around all the time. This defense was worth $20,000 to the Baltimore *Afro-American* in one case. The newspaper had carried the following article:

> Oxford, Pa.—Mary J. MacRae, who died from gas poisoning, was buried Friday from Lincoln University where her father, James B. MacRae, is dean of students.
>
> Miss MacRae, 19, was found on Wednesday in New York City where she was residing for the summer. She was believed to have been despondent over her mediocre marks at Barnard College.
>
> It was rumored on the Lincoln campus that her mother, Mrs. Mary MacRae, was extremely displeased over her daughter's scholastic standing. Her father rated her as an "acceptable student."

Mary Jane, it was also whispered, had been told not to come home unless she improved her grades. Mrs. MacRae was so grief stricken that she did not go to the cemetery.

It has not been determined, however, whether Miss MacRae's death was suicide or accidental. A report from authorities is expected within a week or two, according to Lee R. Reynolds, Philadelphia undertaker, who was in charge.

Mrs. MacRae contended that the article depicted her as a cruel mother who had slammed the door of her home in her daughter's face and driven her to suicide. The jury awarded her $30,000 in compensatory damages and $20,000 in punitive damages, an unusual verdict because punitive damages are usually higher. The judge knocked out the punitive award on the basis that there had been no evidence of malice. The reporter, he noted, had testified that she had obtained all the defamatory information from "hearsay on the campus of Lincoln University where there was some rumor to support the story" (MacRae v. Afro-American Co., 172 F. Supp. 184).

Provocation

A fifth partial defense is proof that the publication was provoked by the plaintiff. Such evidence can be very useful; indeed, as noted in an earlier chapter, it can amount to the complete defense of reply. Failing that, it is good as a partial defense because it shows that the conduct of the plaintiff inspired, at least in part, the matter of which he complains. Of course there can be no actual malice on the part of the defendant.

In a series of thirty-four articles the Spanish language New York newspaper *El Imparcial* accused a rival, *El Diario*, of a multitude of crimes and unfitness to engage in journalism. *El Diario* struck back with three articles and an editorial. The court held that *El Diario* was not entitled to the defense of reply, but could plead provocation as a partial defense (Valdivieso v. El Diario Publishing Co., Inc., 18 A.D. 2d (N.Y.) 1072).

A slander case provides a clear example of how this defense can reduce an award. In April, 1959, Dr. Henry F. Kramer performed an operation at the Cary Memorial Hospital in Caribou, Maine. Mrs. C. Bernadette Farrell, a nurse, did not like the post-operative treatment given the patient and complained to hospital authorities. The result was a feud that led to the nurse's dismissal. Mrs. Farrell would not give up, though, and lodged complaints against Dr. Kramer with the Aroostook County Medical Association. This group cleared him, and there the matter rested for almost a year, until a new administrator at the hospital rehired Mrs. Farrell on the condition that she not discuss its affairs with outsiders. Dr. Kramer did not know that Mrs. Farrell had been rehired until he one day made a routine call to the hospital. Although the hour was very late he called the hospital administrator and said, "I wanted to ask you if you would stoop so low as to hire that creep, that malignant son of a bitch, back to work for you in the hospital." The doctor went on to say that he intended to make an issue of the rehiring. The hospital board discussed the case but decided to retain Mrs. Farrell. A year and a half later, in the spring of 1961, Mrs. Farrell, while checking the minutes of the hospital board, discovered what the doctor had said about her on the phone. She sued for slander and the doctor filed a countersuit. The jury awarded Mrs. Farrell $17,500 in damages, but did not say how much of it was compensatory and how much punitive. Reducing the judgment to $5,000, the Supreme Judicial Court of Maine said:

> The plaintiff began the feud which subsequently raged between the parties by launching an attack upon the defendant's professional competence. Implicit in her criticism was the thinly veiled suggestion that her judgment as to proper methods of post-operative treatment of a patient was better than his. Any professional nurse knows, or should know, that criticism of this sort will almost certainly induce irritation, annoyance and even anger on the part of any medical practitioner against whom it is directed. This attack was followed in due course by a direct complaint which forced the defendant to defend himself before a grievance committee of the medical association. This complaint must be deemed groundless. The decision of a competent board dismissing the charge is not under review and may not be challenged in the instant case. We are therefore presented with yet another instance of conduct on the part of the plaintiff well calculated to arouse the anger and hostility of the defendant. Human frailties, emotions and passions being what they are, it should not surprise anyone that the defendant deemed himself tormented and persecuted by the plaintiff and thereupon abandoned that caution

and restraint which is required by society. Although the slander is not thereby excused, such provocation will substantially diminish both the public interest in the punishment of the defendant and the plaintiff's right to have severe punishment inflicted [Farrell v. Kramer, 159 Me. 387]

Westbrook Pegler's right to reply was denied as a complete defense, because of the viciousness of his attack on Quentin Reynolds, but the court did allow the introduction of evidence of provocation as a partial defense. Although the $175,001 verdict indicated that this defense did him little good, it might have had some effect, because some of the jurors wanted to award Reynolds a much higher sum. The case is discussed at length beginning on page 237.

Because this defense is so useful, newspapers, magazines and broadcasting stations should retain in their files copies of every attack made against them. They might be worth lots of money some day in court.

Heat of Campaign

The sixth partial defense is proof that the publication was made in the heat of a political campaign. As far as the candidates are concerned, there is almost no danger now because of the complete defense offered under the New York Times rule. But evidence showing that the libel was published as charges and counter-chaiges were flying may still be valuable to show good faith and an absence of malice. It may also be needed in suits filed by those involved in campaigns who are not covered by the New York Times rule.

Mistaken Target

The seventh partial defense is a proof that the publication, although referring on its face to the plaintiff, was intended to refer to another person of the same or similar name concerning whom it was absolutely true. In the discussion on page 18 about

mistaken-identity cases it was said that the test is not at whom
the publication aimed but who was hit. There can be no complete defense in case of such a mistake, but there can be evidence
that motives were good, and this should reduce damages.

Care

The eighth partial defense consists of proof of all the defendant
did by way of investigation before publishing the article on
which the suit was brought. Included should be statements made
to reporters, documents in the hands of the newspaper, magazine
or broadcasting station, information in back files, interviews with
the plaintiff or with persons representing him, such as his lawyer
or relatives, letters from correspondents and the like. Interviews
with the plaintiff before publication are of the highest importance.
To emphasize again what has been stressed a half-dozen times,
any attempt to get the plaintiff's side of the story is the best
evidence that can go to the jury. When the plaintiff's side of the
controversy has been obtained and given adequate space, damages
in any substantial amount are rarely awarded.

The partial defenses affecting compensatory damages are more
limited in number. In practice, however, juries do not draw a
fine line of distinction between the mitigation of compensatory
and punitive damages. They weigh all the evidence at the same
time, and it is asking the impossible to demand that the distinction be made. The result is that in those jurisdictions where the
law bars proof aimed at reducing compensatory damages, some
of the same effect can be accomplished by evidence mitigating
punitive awards.

There are three general types of partial defenses affecting
compensatory damages:

Proof of Bad Reputation

Evidence that the plaintiff's general reputation was bad is
relevant because it has a direct bearing on how much the plaintiff
had to lose. If a boss of the Mafia sues, the defense has a right to

offer evidence of his generally unsavory reputation so that he does not collect as much in damages as, say, an outstanding citizen such as the Stated Clerk of the Presbyterian Church.

Favorable Items

In most states corrections are acceptable as evidence bearing on compensatory damages. The reason is that a correction helps restore the plaintiff's reputation in the eyes of the public. The same is true of articles published after the libel that cast a favorable light on the plaintiff. The importance of a correction in this regard was brought home in a case touched on on page 59. Fulton Lewis, Jr., the radio commentator, was sued by Mrs. Pearl A. Wanamaker, the Superintendent of Public Instruction in the State of Washington, for a broadcast on January 6, 1956. In criticizing a White House Education Conference, Lewis took issue with Mrs. Wanamaker's handling of the case of a Washington teacher who had invoked the Fifth Amendment's protection against self-incrimination when questioned about Communist activities. Lewis also said that Mrs. Wanamaker had a brother who had been in the Department of State but who had fled behind the Iron Curtain, renouncing his American citizenship for Communism. The broadcast was on a Friday. On the following Monday, the day of his next regular broadcast, Lewis admitted that he had made a "horrifying mistake." He said that the man who had fled behind the Iron Curtain was not Mrs. Wanamaker's brother but the brother of another person mentioned in the same broadcast. Lewis apologized for the mistake.

Mrs. Wanamaker sued in various jurisdictions throughout the country. The two parties decided that damages for the entire country would be decided in the District of Columbia case. The jury returned a verdict of $145,000 against Lewis, the Mutual Broadcasting System and Washington, D. C., Station WWDC. Mrs. Wanamaker had asked for $25,000 for the broadcast over WWDC. The jury thought that that was not enough and awarded her $45,000. The rest of the award, $100,000, was for the broadcast throughout the nation. All this was in the form of compensatory damages, although Mrs. Wanamaker's own witnesses testified that she had not been hurt by the broadcast. As for punitive damages, the jury concluded that Lewis had not demonstrated actual malice, and granted none. In view of its liberality with compensatory damages it is obvious that the move that saved Lewis and the other defendants from an even stiffer verdict on punitive damages was his swift and liberal correction. Even without any punitive award the judge was shocked by the size of the damages and ordered a new trial (Wanamaker v. Lewis, 173 F. Supp. 126). Eventually, the case was settled out of court on undisclosed terms.

Previous Recovery

Some states permit partial defenses under special laws. In New York, Section 76 of the state's Civil Rights Law includes the following provision:

> At the trial of any civil action for libel, the defendant may prove, for consideration by the jury in fixing the amount of the verdict, that the plaintiff has already recovered damages, or has received, or agreed to receive, compensation in respect of a libel or libels of a similar purport or effect as the libel for which such action has been brought.

This is a dangerous statute for defense lawyers to play with and has rarely been used in recent years. The mere fact that the plaintiff has recovered against another publication is likely to put improper ideas in the minds of the jurors. In theory this law is helpful, since it is aimed at reducing multiple suits, but in practice it should be shunned unless the article in question is laudatory in comparison with the one on which recovery has already been made.

Proof of a partial defense will not prevent the award of damages, but it will reduce them. Such defenses are highly important. The greatest of care will not always prevent libel suits from being brought or always furnish the defendant with complete protection. There is often uncertainty when a case goes to a jury, no matter how industrious, talented and knowledgeable the lawyer may be. These secondary defenses can play a great part in winning cases that otherwise might be lost.

Chapter 18

HOW TO APPLY THE RULES

Spotting Trouble

WITH THE PRINCIPLES OF LIBEL SO COMPLEX THAT EVEN THE COURTS get mixed up, how can the newsman, who is always pressed for time, reach sensible decisions—decisions that will permit him to communicate the maximum amount of information without needlessly harming the innocent or exposing himself to large libel damages? The trick is to develop a routine for spotting trouble and avoiding it without ruining the story.

Almost everyone from the copyboy up recognizes the perils presented by takeouts on racketeering, the Ku Klux Klan or a business fraud. But even the experienced reporter will sometimes overlook the danger in humdrum police news.

The habit that should become second nature to every writer and editor is to be always on the alert for libelous passages. Recognition of libel is the first consideration and the one on which all else depends. For if there are no libels present, but merely unpleasant words, the writer has maximum freedom to handle the material. Almost no danger of damages exists, even if the article should turn out to be factually wrong.

This rule gives the newsman the opportunity to write more effective news stories. On September 3, 1953, the Milwaukee *Journal* printed a story about the court appearance of a picket who had carried a sign doubting the hiring practices of "some Jews." The story began: "The customary sign in the hands of Dan Smith will be no more. That, however, is only on Smith's promise, obtained Thursday on the urging of the court."

In his libel suit Smith said the phrase "only on Smith's promise" implied that he was untrustworthy. The court, however, held that the statement was not libelous (Smith v. Journal Co., 271 Wis.

384). Thus the fact that the objectionable passage was not defamatory freed the *Journal* writer from the sometimes tight constrictions of reporting an official proceeding.

Editorial writers also can spread their wings wide if they select nonlibelous wording. A good example was printed in the *Dairymen's League News* of June 5, 1956. It contained these paragraphs:

> The Rev. John W. Dorney, New Jersey's apostle of the Get-Rich-Quick dogma, again moved into Central New York during the past week; this time following a promotional drumming of newspaper advertisements, radio entreaties, and handbill haranguing.
>
> Mr. Dorney, who accomplished the transition from Longshoremen's Union organizer to ecclesiastical cohort of the Teamsters Union by way of a Balesville, N.J., pulpit, was accompanied by high-salaried Homer Martin of Detroit, one-time organizer of the United Auto Workers and recent leader of the ill-fated Detroit milk strike. . . .
>
> The Rev. Dorney stuck to his gospel of $6 a hundredweight for all milk, but, as usual, carefully skirted how such a blend could be accomplished without pricing milk away from the consumer.

Mr. Dorney sued for $1,500,000 on the contention that the editorial depicted him as an "ecclesiastical faker." But the court held that there was no such imputation. Thus the use of such theological expressions as "dogma," "apostle" and "gospel" were permissible (Dorney v. Dairymen's League Co-op Assn., 149 F. Supp. 615).

If the article is libelous a different situation prevails. Then the next step is to determine if it identifies anyone. If it does not, there is no danger of damages. If it does identify the target of the libelous assertion, the article should be examined to see if there is a complete legal defense for publishing it. If one is found, there is only one more check to be made: to make sure that the target of the attack has been given his say. Besides being good journalism, it serves the purpose of proving good faith and a lack of malice.

When There Is No Complete Defense

What if a complete legal defense is lacking? Then the editor has only four choices:

1. He can hold the story until a complete defense is available.

2. He can modify the libelous passage so that it is nonlibelous, but still retain the identification of the target.

3. He can retain the libelous passage but remove the identification of the target.

4. He can take a chance and publish the article—libel, identification and all.

The choice will vary with the circumstances. Since the ideal story would say the most with maximum protection against damages, the preferred procedure would be to hold the story until a complete defense becomes available—until privileged documents are filed with an official agency, for example. Often the pressures of competition will not permit delay. The *Time* magazine reporter who has turned in a long memorandum on fraud in an oil company knows that a *Newsweek* staffer has gotten wind of chicanery. If *Time* holds up the article, *Newsweek* might break the scandal alone. A way must be found to run the article immediately. Sometimes, too, there is no indication that a complete defense will be available in the forseeable future. If *Time* does not tell the world about the sordid condition in the oil company, the scandal might be covered up. The magazine has a responsibility to publish what it thinks is the truth. As a practical matter, articles cannot often be delayed, and even when they can, there is a limit on how long they can be held up.

By far the most common and the safest procedure is to modify the libelous passage or fuzz the identification of the target. Either way something of the story will be lost, but the risk of damages is nearly eliminated. The choice will naturally depend on the circumstances of the story. If the name is vital, the libelous passage should be toned down; if the libelous charge is more important, identification will have to give way.

In the mid-1960s a financial news reporter for *The New York Times* heard about a revolt against the president of a large corporation by the heads of many of his departments. They drew up a petition charging the president with fraud, deceit, mismanagement, failure to reverse a downward trend in the company's affairs and a host of other bad practices. The petition had been circulated only among the top brass of the corporation. The *Times* had no way to prove the truth of the charges. They had not been filed with any government regulatory agency, so there was no privilege of reporting. The corporation's president had made no charges against his staff, so the privilege of reply could not be relied on. He could not be reached for comment, so the defense of consent could not be invoked. The defense of fair comment was in doubt, because the *Times* was not sure that the facts in the charges were correct. The story demanded to be told because the corporation was well known throughout the country, with thousands of stockholders. Under such circumstances the choice became obvious. The name of the president of the corporation would have to be used, but the charges modified to make them nonlibelous. The charges of fraud and deceit were deleted because the first was a crime and the second threw doubt on the executive's morality. The lead on the article reported that a score of staff members of the corporation had charged the president with mismanagement and demanded his resignation. Something was lost in editing out the libel. But the public did learn of the revolt against the corporate head, who was named and whose picture was used, and the sting of the charges was there—the accusation of mismanagement. Was not that libelous, too? No, because a single failure on the part of an executive does not imply that he is incompetent.

When the crux of the news lies not so much in the names of the individual but in the evil practice, then the technique of clouding the identification should be employed. An exposé of police graft might concern patrolmen the reader never heard off. The details of how the bookies and numbers-game racketeers were being protected by the police, how many policemen were involved, descriptions of payoffs and the amounts involved are the news. If the article fails to list the names of the cops, it loses part of its impact, but the main thrust is still there. The identification of the culprits is uncertain, but a story that should be told has been told. This, of course, is where identification of a class, as discussed on page 22, is vital.

Sometimes only one individual is the target of the attack. A young woman called *The New York Times* with a story of horrendous conditions at the House of Detention for Women, where she had been taken after her arrest while picketing as a pacifist. She told of filth, homosexuality and depravity. She said that a doctor had been brutal in giving her an internal examination and had asked a number of crude questions about virginity of college girls. She described the doctor in some detail. The problem with this story was that there was an uncertainty about whether a doctor in a municipal institution is covered by the New York Times rule as a public officer. To be certain of a legal defense, another had to be found. A quote from the doctor giving his side might have provided the defense of consent, but he could not be reached. Since the deadline was near, the problem was solved by removing the description of the doctor. Again the reader was deprived of a bit of the story, but in reducing the chances of damages the main element of the woman's charge remained—that shocking conditions existed at the House of Detention for Women. It is significant to note that charges led to an official investigation and promises of reform.

The newsman should remember that clouding of identification does not mean that no names can be mentioned. On October 17, 1958, United Press International sent a dispatch from its Atlanta bureau that wound up in litigation. According to the complaint, the dispatch read as follows; although the Associated Press material apparently was inserted in the story by an unnamed newspaper:

ATLANTA, Oct. 17 (UPI)—Five persons were indicted today in connection with the dynamiting of the Jewish Temple here.

The grand jury handed down indictments against the quintet that could possibly send them to the electric chair on charges of dynamiting of the house of worship on famed Peachtree Street last Sunday.

An Atlanta detective working on the case disclosed meanwhile that the identity is known of a so-called "fat cat" financier of such terrorist activity as the temple bombing.

Most investigators believe the bombing was part of an interstate, or possibly international, conspiracy.

Detective Capt. R. E. Little, Jr., said he "definitely" knows the identity of a person referred to in a confiscated letter as the "fat cat" financier who, the writer said, "is putting his $$$ where his mouth is, God bless him." The Arlington, Va., *Sun* said he is a resident of Baltimore.

Police released the text of a letter that spoke of the "fat cat" financier.

The Associated Press said an Arlington printer (George Lincoln Rockwell) who turns out anti-Jewish literature acknowledged today he wrote a letter which has figured in the bombing of a Jewish Temple in Atlanta.

Rockwell said the letter was written last July to Wallace H. Allen in Atlanta.

FBI agents interviewed Rockwell but the FBI declined to disclose the outcome.

It was learned in Washington that the FBI Thursday questioned Rockwell and Harold Noel Arrowsmith, Jr., described as a member of a wealthy Baltimore family.

Authorities today sought a mystery figure thought to be the mastermind of dynamitings in the South.

Further evidence of the "fat cat's" role was reported by police in a letter containing this line: "The big blast is all set for either next Sunday or Saturday . . . we will know tomorrow and will keep you informed."

Arrowsmith, whose case against the Providence *Journal* is discussed on page 119, contended that this dispatch identified him as the " 'fat cat' financier" behind the bombings and asked $10,000 for each release of the item to UPI's 5,624 outlets, or a total of $56,-240,000—a record asking price. He did not get a penny (Arrowsmith v. United Press International, 205 F. Supp. 56, reversed on other grounds, 320 F. 2d 219). The case was decided on jurisdictional grounds, but legal observers have also interpreted the lower court's decision to mean that the article did not describe Arrowsmith as the " 'fat cat' financier." The question, however, is a close one. The dispatch would have been safer if it had separated Rockwell and Arrowsmith instead of linking them in the third paragraph from the end.

If a writer wants to name the target of the libelous attack but not link him directly with the bad conduct, he should be careful to keep the passages distinctly separate. For example, if a grand jury has been investigating reports that a contractor has conspired with public officials to rig bids on highway construction, the article could report that fact in the lead. It could give as many details as are available—the amount of the payoffs, how long the conspiracy has been going on, color material on how the money was turned over. It should not name the specific projects, since these would identify the contractor. If other contractors had tipped off the prosecutor, that fact should be noted. Later in the story the reporter could state that C. Ment Mixer had appeared before the grand jury. It is a good idea to give Mixer a call and ask him when his next date with the grand jury is. He should also be asked what questions the grand jury asked him. In this way Mixer can appear to be either the culprit or one of the protesting contractors.

Another rule the editor and writer should keep in mind is one explained on page 87, that reports of occurrences at public places do not libel those establishments. Racial outbreaks at a restaurant, fights among young thugs at a theater, sale of narcotics at a tavern—all can be reported and the place named if the writer is careful to avoid charging the proprietor with wrongdoing. The shafts must be aimed only at the patrons, unless, of course, a complete defense exists for reporting accusations against the proprietor, too.

Almost all the problems that arise can be handled by modifying the libelous charge or by avoiding positive identification. The courts vary in their interpretation of just what is libelous and what is not, and they differ in deciding when an individual is identified. For this reason it is folly for the newsman to bank with 100 per cent certainty on the protection provided by changing a word here or there. If he is in doubt, he should turn to Chapter 5, 6, 7 or 8 and consult the section dealing with the particular type of libel involved. He should use his own judgment based on the principles in deciding whether to choose a particular word or phrase. In every instance where a complete defense is available the writer should select the strongest phrase that most accurately reflects the nature of the charge. If that phrase is libelous, so much the better for the story. In sticky situations, where defenses are uncertain, he should consult the newspaper's attorney.

Not Fit to Print

The editor must also realize that some stories should not be printed. Time, Inc., paid out its largest sum for a libel suit as the result of a series of editorial decisions violating its cautiously aggressive policy of handling risky stories. The case, noted in Chapter 12, involved an article in *Sports Illustrated* on January 13, 1964, about Jack Dempsey's 1919 fight with Jess Willard for the world's heavyweight boxing championship. The article, presumably narrated by the late Doc Kearns, Dempsey's manager, suggested that Dempsey had won the fight with "loaded gloves." According to the article, Kearns put plaster of paris in a talcum container and, after bandaging Dempsey's hands, drenched them with water to keep them "cool" and sprinkled them generously with powder from the can. In a few moments, Kearns said, Dempsey's bandaged hands were as hard as rocks. Dempsey sprang from his corner and gave Willard a fearful beating.

As a check on the article, the editors viewed movies of the fight. To their alarm, the film clashed with the article at a significant point. Kearns had said that he had talked Willard's manager into letting the boxers put their gloves on in the dressing rooms because of the heat—the fight was held in July. In this way Kearns indicated, he was able to cover up his trick. But the film showed the fighters entering the ring without their gloves on. Obviously *Sports Illustrated* could not go back to Kearns and question him regarding this discrepancy. The magazine had only two choices: to kill the piece or to make it conform to the movies. The editors decided on the latter and rewrote several hundred words. Hindsight is always 20-20, but *Sports Illustrated* should have known better. Its editors realized that Kearns had been a notorious liar. Proof of an untruth on a vital element in his story should have made the entire article suspect.

Compounding the magazine's trouble was the headline on the cover, "Dempsey's Gloves Were Loaded"—an unqualified statement. Inside, the title emphasized Dempsey's innocence—"He Didn't Know the Gloves Were Loaded."

When Dempsey sued, Time, Inc., insisted that the article was not defamatory because it had pointed out Dempsey's innocence. The court disagreed. The judge also saw evidence of a "reckless disregard of truth" because the magazine admitted that Kearns had been a confessed "rogue and rascal" (Dempsey v. Time, Inc., 43 Misc. 2d (N.Y.)754). Faced with the strong possibility of a jury's finding actual malice, Time, Inc., settled out of court for an undisclosed sum said to be equivalent to the cost it would have incurred if it had junked the cover and printed a new one. It also printed a declaration in *Sports Illustrated* that it accepted Dempsey's denial that his gloves had been loaded.

Exceeding the Rules

There are times when the editor knows that if he is going to do his duty to his readers he will have to exceed the rules. He will possess facts that cast light on a situation of such transcending importance that he must publish them, even though there is no complete legal defense. He will not weaken the libelous phrases to safe nonlibel. He will boldly point the accusing finger at specific individuals.

Before an editor goes ahead with such a story he should weigh three factors to determine if the risk is legitimate. The first is the policy of the publication. A tabloid that stresses sensational news would go further in adding nonprivileged matters concerning divorces, sex cases and crime than a more conservative newspaper would. An editor crusading against certain union practices would consider it a more legitimate risk to use material outside the protection of the law than an editor only trying to mirror the events of the day.

The second factor that must be weighed is the source of the facts. If the source is someone prominent in public life, then the risk is small if the libelous statement is given out publicly or circulated privately to a large number of persons. In a suit against the Baltimore *Sun* (discussed in Chapter 14), Lawrence Westbrook, a Democratic National Committee official, complained, among other things, about a statement from Dwight D. Eisenhower, who was running for President at the time. Westbrook had been dismissed from his party post because of disclosures that he had taken a fee for helping negotiate a contract with the Government. The *Sun* included this paragraph in its story about Westbrook:

> Gen. Dwight D. Eisenhower, in a speech in New York City today referred to the case as the "sort of crookedness (that) goes on and on in Washington." Of Westbrook, he said, "they had to fire him because someone caught up with him."

Westbrook's suit contended that the *Sun* had no right to carry this libelous remark about him. The United States Court of Appeals for the Fourth Circuit disagreed, saying:

> . . . where a high official in the national organization of a political party is dismissed from his position in the party because he has been accused of dealing with the government and where a candidate for the presidency of the country comments on the matter in a public address, it is unthinkable that newspapers should not be allowed to give publicity to the matter without fear of being held to liability

therefor in a libel suit. [Pulvermann v. A. S. Abell Co., 228 F. 2d 797]

Proxy fights and other business disputes sometimes pose problems for the writer because the charges are libelous and no complete defense is available. Again, if the charges are circulated to a large number of people, either at a meeting or through literature, and signed by identifiable persons, they can be used with little danger.

On September 4, 1954, a stockholders' protective committee of Timm Aircraft sent out a four-page circular accusing Charles D. Rudolph, the company president, of deliberately falsifying Timm's 1952 annual report by listing $48,000 in accounts receivable as cash. It also charged him with using company funds without authorization to purchase an automobile for his personal use, voting for a dividend of 2¢ a share to avoid a proxy fight, even though in 70 per cent of the cases the cost of issuing the checks exceeded the amount of the dividend, and various other acts of incompetence, mismanagement and disloyalty to the company. Rudolph sued Milton S. Koblitz, treasurer of the stockholders' committee, and others. A jury awarded Rudolph $250,000, which the judge ruled excessive (Rudolph v. Gorman, 169 Cal. App. 2d 666). At a second trial the jury set the damages at $85,000, which, with about $8,000 in interest, was eventually paid.

The *Wall Street Journal* and several Los Angeles papers published stories based on the libelous circular but they were not sued. They took only a slim risk, because the circular had been sent to 2,800 Timm stockholders and the dispute was made public. The plaintiff's quarrel in such cases is not with the newspaper, unless it gives a biased account of the dispute, but with those who originated the charges. The newsman who reports the libel is not on absolutely safe ground, but if he does not take sides and gives a balanced presentation, including the reply of the target of the attack, the danger of a suit is small. It is much easier for the plaintiff to prove malice against the originator of the charge than against the newsman who offers both sides to the question.

In crime stories the situation is less certain. The reporter must be more cautious before going ahead with a nonprivileged libelous story. He knows that corridor talk, quotes from "the police" or "the authorities" or a "source close to the mayor" or even a lawyer willing to be quoted by name outside court are not privileged. He knows, too, that proving the truth of the charge is tremendously difficult. Nevertheless, he may decide to publish the story because the source, even if he cannot be quoted by name, has proved, over the years, to be honest and knowledgeable—not just one, but both. Perhaps the counsel for an investigating subcommittee has proved in previous instances that his information is sound. District attorneys sometimes show grand-jury minutes to trustworthy reporters. In jurisdictions where such minutes are not privileged the newsman should attribute the statements to high officials or some other anonymous source even though the source's name cannot be used. This practice will not provide a complete defense against a libel suit, but it reduces the provocation for litigation, and if a case should develop and eventually go to a jury it will make an impression on the jury as a partial defense that will tend to mitigate damages.

The editor should also consider how much of a partial defense he has in regard to the character of the person he is defaming. Often it is a legitimate risk to print something about a particular individual when it would not be to print the same thing about another. Few editors would have hesitated to use, even without a legal defense, charges against the late Frank Costello, the racketeer, while none except those on the lunatic fringe would have printed the same material regarding Cardinal Spellman. In other words, if a person's reputation has already been somewhat tarnished, it is safer to print articles overstepping the limits of the law than about someone whose reputation is above reproach.

Sometimes it is safe to assume that a prominent person will not bring suit, either because he wants publicity—any kind of publicity—or because he does not want to give added circulation to the charges. Much of the material in gossip columns and movie magazines is used on this basis. Publications pandering to sex and sensation have lists of prominent persons about whom almost anything can be written—even if there is no basis for the stories. Prostitute writers fabricate wild libelous stories out of their imaginations about entertainers and those who operate on the shady side of the law. If the individual is not on the list, stories are still fabricated, but care is taken to make sure they contain no libelous charges. If, for example, a film star is on the list, the writer could say that she has left her husband and taken a trip to Europe with an old boy friend. That is libelous, but no suit is expected. The publisher

thinks the star is too vulnerable because of damaging material he
has in his files about her—material that has nothing to do with the
charge. If she is not on the list, the story could say that she fought
off a would-be rapist. The story is still false, but it is safe because
it is not libelous to report an unsuccessful rape attempt.

But sometimes stars do sue for libel. No film star of the mid-
twentieth century has received more publicity than Elizabeth Taylor. She has been involved in romantic affairs with married men
and been the subject of gossip all over the world. Yet even she
sued. She and her husband at the time, Eddie Fisher, complained
about the August, 1960, and December, 1960, issues of *Movie T.V.
Secrets,* a magazine whose title indicates its editorial policy. The
front cover of the August edition consisted of a picture of Liz and
Eddie and Eddie's former wife, Debbie Reynolds, with a headline
screaming: "Debbie Attacks Liz!" The court agreed that the
magazine could be read to mean that Liz was so unladylike as to
engage in a public brawl with her husband's former wife. And the
story, the court said, pictured her and Eddie as being so unprinci-
pled and mercenary as to have met with Debbie to arrange a joint
television spectacular to capitalize on the publicity that resulted
from the love triangle. The December issue of the magazine also
carried a picture of Liz and Eddie on the front cover. This time
the headline said, "Steven Boyd Has Split Up Eddie and Liz!" The
table of contents listed the story as "Confidential Exclusive Steve
Boyd-Liz Taylor—Steve Boyd Splits Eddie and Liz! (A new lover
enters the scene)." The court said that the reader might understand the article to mean that Steve and Liz were intimate or
lovers even though the indications were that the approach was uni-
lateral (Fisher v. Country Wide Publications, Inc., 213 N.Y.S. 2d
897). Eddie and Liz did not press the suit after their divorce.

The poor are also safe targets for the unconscionable editor. If a
Puerto Rican dishwasher, a Negro drifter, a Mexican farmhand or
an American Indian laborer is picked up by the police, the graphic
details of the alleged crime can be printed and the accusing finger
pointed with little probability of a suit. Usually such people
do not sue either because they do not know their rights under the
law or because they are faced with the more pressing problem of
trying to stay out of jail. Those who would like to sue would also
find that because they are poor their reputations are worth less and
any damage verdict would be small. The result would probably

not be worth the time and expense of filing a suit. It is unfortunate but nevertheless true that the law of libel discriminates against the poor.

Geography

One of the old rules of thumb in newsrooms is that distance reduces the threat of libel, that extra care must be taken regarding local people, while anything goes for those far away. There is a thread of truth in this rule insofar as small papers are concerned. Chances are slim that a Nebraska police chief will ever read an item in the Oiltown, Pennsylvania, *Lubricator* that somehow twists the facts in a murder case and libels him. Even if he does hear about it, the chief would probably not want to spend the time and money needed to press a case in a strange town far away, where his legal opponent would be surrounded by friends. The police chief is more likely to sue the Nebraska paper that makes such a mistake because the suit can be instituted with ease and the chances of recovery are greater in the local community where he is damaged more by the libel.

The rule about distances also applies to large newspapers and national magazines, if the defamed person lives in a foreign country, especially if that country is remote or Communist. But a large publication should be wary if the target of the defamation lives anywhere in the United States. Plaintiffs prefer to file suit at the local courthouse because juries have a way of bringing in large verdicts for the local boy maligned by a wealthy out-of-town publication. Even if the publication has only a sparse circulation in the community, the law often permits such suits to be filed there.

In any event, the responsible newsman on any publication will exert the same care regardless of how far away the man in the news lives. He will not let his guard down nor will he attempt to take advantage of the differences in state libel laws to try to get away with more about a man who lives in, say, Illinois, where the laws favor the defense, than in, say, Virginia. If the newsman is banking on differences in state laws, the distinction is so fine that only a lawyer who has specialized in defamation cases could give him sound advice.

Chapter 19

IN THE EDITOR'S HAND

WHEN A REPORTER TURNS IN HIS ARTICLE, HIS RESPONSIBILITY ENDS. If he is skillful and careful, he has protected the paper from libel damages. But all the writing skill and care in the world can be overthrown if the editors bungle. A badly written headline, an improper picture or caption or unwise makeup can wreck the immunity from damages that the writer tried so hard to invoke. When the judge considers the case, he weighs the entire article—headline, illustrations and layout—in addition to the text. While most libel suits are based on the phrasing of the articles, there are a surprising number that cite these other elements. For that reason the editor should alert his deskmen to be libel-conscious regarding heads, pictures and makeup.

Headlines

Like the writer, the copy editor must decide first of all if the material on which he will base his head is libelous. If it is not, he has a lot more freedom composing it. Not that the copy editor can write an unattributed headline on every nonlibelous story. Attribution might be demanded by responsibility, uncertainty or other factors, but from the standpoint of libel alone, attribution is not necessary in the headline if the charges are nondefamatory. If a surgeon should forget to remove a sponge from the patient before closing the incision, the headline writer can, if he wishes, say:

RED-FACED SURGEON OPERATES AGAIN
TO RETRIEVE SPONGE LEFT IN PATIENT

Since even the best surgeons make mistakes, it is not libelous to say this one did, and the head can reflect that nonlibelous fact.

On February 12, 1952, the Pocatello (Idaho) *State Journal* carried this headline on a story of two county commissioners leaving a public hearing on a county budget in anger:

TAXES AND TEMPERS

ALLEN-GOUGH WALKOUT AROUSES
ANGRY TALK OF RECALL MOVE

The two commissioners contended that the word "walkout" was actionable because it indicated that they were omitting a public duty. The Supreme Court of Idaho rejected their plea, holding that a statement of a walkout from an official meeting, even if false, was not libelous (Gough *et al.* v. Tribune-Journal Co. *et al.*, 73 Idaho 173).

If a college professor should call for a Communist victory in Vietnam, the head writer could characterize him as a leftist, since it is not libelous to ascribe left-wing opinions to anyone. It would be libelous to call him a Communist or a pro-Communist, because the courts have said that such charges are defamatory (Grant v. Reader's Digest Assn., Inc., 151 F. 2d 733).

A headline over an account of an official proceeding should be a fair and true index of the report. Like the story, the headline should not impute unchastity to a woman or crime to any person. *Movie T.V. Secrets'* title on an article mentioned in the previous chapter obviously violated this rule:

STEVE BOYD SPLITS EDDIE AND LIZ!

(A NEW LOVER ENTERS THE SCENE)

So does the headline that beginning copy editors often write:

3 BANDITS ARRESTED

concerning a report that three men suspected of robbing a bank had been picked up. The only exception to this rule would be when the newspaper, magazine or broadcasting station is carrying on an exposé or crusade, rather than merely reporting a current event. Even then the headline should be a flat statement only when the publication holds what its attorney believes is conclusive proof of the charge. The difficulties a newspaper can get into when the headline goes beyond the story are demonstrated by a case involving the Las Vegas (Nevada) *Sun*. The fourth of a series of articles on adoptions carried the headline.

BABIES FOR SALE

FRANKLIN BLACK MARKET
TRADE OF CHILD TOLD

The article told how George E. Franklin, Jr., an attorney, had arranged at a fee of $100 for the adoption of the child of an unwed mother. The consent signed by the mother did not disclose the names of the adopting parents. At the end of the article was this tagline promoting the next article:

TOMORROW—BLACKMAIL BY FRANKLIN

The tagline referred to a letter that Franklin wrote the mother when she sought to revoke her consent to the adoption. The letter contained the statement: "I feel that I must acquaint you with the fact that I am aware of certain developments which can only burden you if you continue to pursue your present course." A jury awarded Franklin $40,000 in compensatory damages and $150,000 in punitive damages. The *Sun*, insisting that it had proved the truth of the charges, appealed to the Nevada Supreme Court. The judges agreed with the newspaper that Franklin had not proceeded according to law in arranging the adoption, but it said that it did not follow that he was engaged in the "black-market" sale of babies. The court explained:

> The vice of the procedure followed by Franklin does not lie in the fact that it constitutes a black-market sale but in the fact that such procedure, if permissible, would open the door to black-market sales.
> Under any reasonable construction of the term "black-market sale" contemplates a sale contrary to regulations with a profit calculated either to compensate for the risk of apprehension or to match the buyer demand which has created the market. In the case before us the fact that the consent was properly secured is not enough to constitute the transaction a black-market sale in the absence of proof of a sale price or profit or that the law was deliberately disregarded in consideration for the attorney's fee.
> The record would indicate that Farnklin's failure to follow the requirements of statute was through his innocent misconstruction of the statute in the light of an earlier decision of this court.

As for the "blackmail" tagline, the court refused to rule that the letter from Franklin proved the truth of the charge. It said that he might just have been warning that he had facts that would make it difficult for the mother to prevail if she continued to press for revocation of the adoption. The court did throw a bone to the *Sun*. It found that because of the extensive research the newspaper had engaged in, damages were too high (Las Vegas Sun v. Franklin, 74 Nev. 282). (This case was settled out of court on terms disclosed on page 368.)

This case is another example of the difficulty of proving the truth of libelous charges and why editors should be wary of making exceptions to the rule against outright accusations of guilt. If however, the considered judgment is to proceed with such an accusation, on the basis that it can be proved, then there is no reason why the headline should not reflect it. As noted on page 125, the *Saturday Evening Post* proved its charge against Felix Bocchicchio, Jersey Joe Walcott's manager. The article carried the title:

DIRTY WORK AT RINGSIDE

FOR THE FIRST TIME, ROCKY DISCLOSES THE STARTLING TRUTH ABOUT HIS TITLE FIGHT WITH JERSEY JOE WALCOTT

In almost all other cases the most that a headline over such stories may properly do is to state that a charge of unchastity or a charge of crime has been made or sustained in a judicial, legislative or other official proceeding. It is true that newspapers regularly write headlines over jury verdicts that say flatly

JONES GUILTY

and get away with it. Strictly speaking, until all appeals are exhausted, the most that a headline over such a story should say is

JONES CONVICTED

The risk in a flat "guilty" head is low when there has been a jury verdict, especially if the trial has been front-page news. The reader presumably followed the case through trial until it went to the jury. When he sees the headline, he immediately understands that it was the jury that found Jones guilty.

When a baseball commissioner, a civil service disciplinary board, a Congressional committee or some other investigating unit makes the judgment on a person's guilt, the risk of an unattributed headline is much greater than when a judge or jury is involved.

A newspaper once printed a story that a police commissioner had found a policeman guilty of taking a bribe and had ordered him dismissed. This was an official proceeding protected by privilege. But the headline went further than the story. The headline said

BRIBERY OF A POLICEMAN

The story had said only that a charge of bribery had been sustained in an official proceeding. After the article had been published, the policeman fought back in court so successfully that he was cleared and his accuser was convicted of perjury and was jailed. Then the policeman sued the newspaper and recovered damages. The court held that the headline was not a report of a proceeding, but a false statement of fact.

Anyone who has worked on a copydesk knows that there are limits to how many letters you can jam into a headline. That is the major reason why guilt is unattributed so often. But this suit could have easily been avoided if the headline had read

POLICEMAN DISMISSED

or, if style had permitted the use of slang:

COP BRIBERY FOUND

The courts recognize that headline writers face problems. The judge's main concern is that the headline indicates that the article is a report and that it does not take sides. Use of the handy word "faces" has been approved by the Supreme Court of New Jersey to indicate that there has been some sort of accusation leveled that could bring steps toward punitive action. The case, studied on page 129, concerned the McCarthy committee's hearings at Fort Monmouth, New Jersey. The article said that McCarthy "moved" to have a radar scientist cited for perjury. His move was a statement that he would at some undesignated time forward the scientist's testimony to a Federal grand jury for possible perjury indictments. The headlines in the Newark *Star-Ledger* said

EX-FORT AIDE FACES INDICTMENT FOR PERJURY
MCCARTHY GIVING DETAILS TO GRAND JURY

In upholding the *Ledger* the New Jersey Supreme Court said that the headlines were not an abuse of privilege because they were in accordance with the contemplated action announced by McCarthy (Coleman v. Newark Morning Ledger Co., 29 N.J. 357).

Another favorite copydesk trick to get the most out of a story is to go along with a police report that the arrest of a number of suspects has broken a ring or a racket or a gang. Aside from the question of whether the police should be believed, which is not up for discussion here, there is little danger in using this device. On January 24, 1957, the Wichita (Kansas) *Beacon* carried a story, discussed on page 151, on some arrests. A banner headline said

WICHITA JUDGE, ATTORNEY IMPLICATED IN LOCAL BURGLARY GANG, POLICE SAY

The Kansas Supreme Court held that this was a fair index of the contents of the article (Stice v. Beacon Newspaper Corp., 185 Kan. 61).

Often the headline will merely say

NARCOTICS RING SMASHED

without any attribution. This is borderline, because there is an implicit assumption that someone is guilty without mentioning the three arrested persons and therefore not definitely linking them to the ring. If such heads are used, some attribution should quickly be given in the first bank, if there is one, such as

POLICE SAY ARREST OF 3 BREAKS $5 MILLION HEROIN RACKET

Definitely to be avoided is the headline that assumes the guilt of those arrested and links them to the ring:

DOPE RING SMASHED AS 3 ARE ARRESTED

Much better is a head that is attributed:

POLICE LINK ARREST OF 3 TO DOPE RING

Articles rounding up a situation, magazine pieces dealing with a variety of incidents or TV documentaries covering a broad sweep can carry headlines or titles that definitely imply guilt. No individual should be named in such heads or titles. *True* magazine was on safe ground when it titled its exposé on pep pills

THE PILL THAT CAN KILL SPORTS

although (as detailed on page 24) it lost a libel suit on other grounds (Fawcett Publications v. Morris, 377 P. 2d 42). The *Saturday Evening Post* ran into no trouble in putting this title on an article that dealt with a number of products (Drug Research Corp. v. Curtis Publishing Co., 7 N.Y. 2d 435):

DON'T FALL FOR THE MAIL FRAUDS

The courts permit a light touch in headlines, just as they do in articles. In February, 1959, an Atlanta reporter turned in an article on a petition by Roy Crook, Jr., to change his name to Cook. The copy editor scribbled this head on it:

MAKE NAME "COOK"
A CROOK ASKS COURT

The Georgia Court of Appeals rejected Mr. Cook's libel suit, which averred that the headline had made him out as a "swindler, sharper or cheat." The court said it was a mere play on words that accurately described the story (Cook v. Atlanta Newspapers, Inc., 99 Ga. App. 7).

The Supreme Court of Delaware has also upheld a headline with a pun in it. The article concerned Family Court Judge Francis A. Reardon and was published in 1959, when Delaware was considering revival of the whipping post. At a hearing for several teenagers who had escaped from a state school, stolen a car and almost killed several children at play, Judge Reardon asked, "Would lashes help?" Although he commented to a reporter that "I am not in favor of the whipping post," his first remark generated much adverse reaction. A member of the Governor's Youth Services Commission severely criticized Judge Reardon. Over the story of this criticism the Wilmington *Morning News* put this headline:

YOUTH SERVICES BOARD
LASHES JUDGE REARDON

Judge Reardon sued for libel, pointing out that the head attributed the criticism to the entire board while only one member had uttered it, and he objected specifically to the "degrading implications" of the word "lashes." In dismissing his case the Delaware Supreme Court said:

We do not think that the language of the headline is libelous. The word "lashes" as it appears in the headline, of itself, conveys only the meaning that the Board sharply disagreed with the language used by plaintiff. Considering the article as a whole along with the background information offered by plaintiff, it amounts at most only to a play on words, the humor of which, very understandably, escaped plaintiff. Defendant's attempt at a pun was, to say the least, not in good taste. It was to plaintiff a "pistol let off at the ear; not a feather to tickle the intellect." We feel that the use of such word, particularly in the setting in which it was used in this case, was not only inaccurate but unfortunate. It tended greatly to accentuate the adverse criticism of plaintiff appearing in the article. Moreover, the headline was inaccurate for the criticism did not emanate from the Board as a body, but from only one of its members and the headline further accentuated the criticism.

But we do not think that the statement was libelous. There was no attack upon plaintiff, either personally or in his professional capacity. [Reardon v. News-Journal Co., 53 Del. 29]

The courts also recognize that headline writers cannot make transitions as smoothly as the writer can in the article. On December 17, 1958, the New Orleans *Times-Picayune* printed the following headline over a story about two unrelated developments in a grand jury:

ORLEANS GRAND JUROR DROPPED
BURGLARY RING PROBE APPARENTLY BEGUN

The grand juror who had been dropped sued, contending that the bank of the headline made it appear that he was suspected of belonging to the burglary ring. The court said that it did not (Bellis v. Times Picayune, 226 F. Supp. 552).

A misplaced headline can bring trouble and should, of course, be corrected immediately regardless of whether it is libelous or not. The basis most courts seem to use for judging whether a headline over the wrong story is actionable is how the average fair-minded reader would react. The headline

TWO MEN BOUND TO HIGHER COURT IN AUTO THEFT

over an unconnected story about an automobile accident in Georgia was ruled harmless by the Georgia Supreme Court. The court pointed out that the article clearly dealt with an incident entirely different from that referred to in the headline, and since there was no ambiguity there was no libel (Ledger-Enquirer Co. v. Brown and Grimes, 214 Ga. 422).

The New York courts have also held that if a reader can recognize the fact that the headline is misplaced, then there is no ground for damages. A newspaper in Plattsburgh inadvertently printed a headline saying

MAN ARRESTED FOR CARRYING MARIJUANA

over a story about a man's arrest on disorderly conduct charges. The court said that any fair-minded person would recognize that the headline had been misplaced (Trudeau v. Plattsburgh Publishing Co., 11 A.D. 2d (N.Y.) 852).

Pictures

Something happens to an otherwise staid individual when he sees his picture staring out at him from a newspaper, magazine or television screen. If the event reflects favorably on him, he beams in rapture and tries to appear modest when friends mention that they saw it. If it cast a slight doubt on his eligibility for sainthood, he becomes enraged and rushes to his lawyer with a demand that he sue. For pictures, either standing alone or illustrating an article, can fulfill all the qualifications for libel: they are proof of publication; they can identify; they can make the reader think worse of the person. Since publication is something that the news photographer and the picture editor strive for, this aspect of libel offers little room for flexibility. The other two, however, present many problems that everyone who deals with pictures—the cameraman, the picture editor, the caption writer and the makeup editor— ought to become familiar with.

Pictures often definitely identify individuals and scenes, including any stores or businesses portrayed. Even without captions viewers recognize faces and buildings. Ordinarily, if the caption and accompanying articles are nonlibelous, there is no danger and no special precautions need be taken. *Life* magazine carried an article titled "Some Idiots Afloat," about the lack of care of many persons using boats. Eight pictures illustrated the article. No one in the pictures was named, but Sanford R. Cowan, a publisher of electronic magazines and a Long Island yachtsman, asserted that he was the individual at the tiller of a small boat holding four other persons. The caption on the picture said

RUB-A-DUB DUB, TOO MANY IN A TUB

The court threw out Cowan's suit for $500,000, saying:

> Here the plaintiff is charged with a single act of carelessness in that on the occasion when the picture was taken he permitted too many people in a small boat. While the word "idiot" may have the meaning ascribed to it by the plaintiff, in the context in which it is used, it may only be considered as a charge of lack of care [Cowan v. Time, Inc., 41 Misc. 2d (N.Y.) 198]

Extrinsic facts, however, can make an otherwise harmless picture libelous. On January 12, 1947, the Augusta (Georgia) *Chronicle* carried a routine announcement on page 1 of the wedding scheduled for the following month of Miss Kathryn Ann Beckworth. Accompanying the item was a picture of an attractive young woman holding a baby in her lap and apparently talking with a man whose face was turned from the camera and thus difficult to recognize. The picture looked somewhat like Kathryn Ann, but it was of a different girl. When the *Chronicle* reached the little town of Wrens, where eighteen-year-old Kathryn Ann lived, her friends began to laugh, and she, instead of glowing with pride, became somewhat hysterical. Here she was, pictured to all the world as the mother of an illegitimate child. Kathryn Ann duly married her fiancé. She also sued for libel. The *Chronicle* argued that the picture was not defamatory because there is nothing immoral about a single girl's holding a child in her lap. It convinced two judges of the Georgia Court of Appeals, but four agreed with Kathryn Ann that the picture was susceptible to the interpretation that she had had an illicit love affair (Southeastern Newspapers, Inc., v. Walker, 76 Ga. App. 57). A jury awarded her $500, according to reports.

Most libels resulting from pictures are caused by misidentification or inadvertent use of the wrong cut. Captions should be pasted on the backs of pictures to be filed—either the photographer's original caption or, preferably, since cameramen are known to have made mistakes, the editor's caption as checked with the photographer. If the pictures are from a photo service, the original caption should be affixed to the back. Dates of the photos should also be indicated.

In cases where the writer, for one reason or another, does not want to identify the target of the libel precisley, the picture editor must make sure that he does not do so either. If the picture adds sufficient detail to point the accusing finger at one individual, there is danger in an indefensible libel. On April 25, 1957, the Darlington (South Carolina) *News and Press* printed an article that began:

> You can get on a good drunk for less than 35 cents if you don't mind risking your life or the taste of bay rum. And hundreds of Darlington County residents are doing it, buying an estimated $1,000 a week in the once-popular shaving lotion.
> There ought to be something done about the problem, Chief J. Peele Privette told the *News and Press* this week, observing that one "back lot" store in Darlington is reported to have sold $500 in bay rum in one week.
> At 35 cents a pint, that would pay for over 1400 binges. Even the most seasoned vagrant wouldn't need over a pint.

Accompanying the story was a picture showing the store of Harold Timmons. The caption read:

> Here is a Darlington "back lot" on a busy day. In one week, $550 for bay rum was spent here by Darlingtonians whose aim is to feel, not smell, good. Police Chief J. P. Privette says something should be done to control the problem. The once-popular shaving lotion, 50 per cent alcohol costs one-ninth as much as more orthodox whiskey.

Timmons said that the newspaper knew that his store was the only "back lot" business in town, but in any case the photograph clearly showed his establishment. The South Carolina Supreme Court ruled that he had a cause for action (Timmons v. News and Press 232 S.C. 639).

It must be said for the record, although it should be obvious, that a picture should never be used in a libelous situation if the identity of the individual in it is not known. A perfect example of how not to choose a picture was dealt with on page 221. The Vanderbilt University humor magazine used a photo of a two-year-old girl that it picked up from the printer's shop in a sophomorish attempt to be funny about Mother's Day. Readers immediately recognized it and the University had a libel suit on its hands.

In the case of the motion picture *The Inside of the White Slave Traffic* (mentioned on page 87), the court held that a scene showing a factory and building bearing the name "Merle" identified the plaintiff and made the viewer think he was allowing his establishment to be used as a recruiting site for unwilling prostitutes (Merle v. Sociological Research Film Corp., 166 App. Div. (N.Y.) 376).

If libel is present and a good legal defense exists, identification is no problem, so a picture can be used. Even old pictures, unrelated to the current news event are usable as long as the caption makes the time of their taking clear. On May 26, 1954, the Topeka *Daily Capital* printed a story that the Kansas Attorney General had reported that the "key man" in a $60,000 grain-theft ring had been caught. He was identified as Keith R. Beyl, and a one-column picture of him illustrated the article. The caption merely gave his name. In the photo, across his chest, was a card with the notation:

SHERIFFS OFFICE
GREEN RIVER WYO
A 637
2 10 54

Beyl's libel suit denied wrongdoing and charged, among other things, that the picture would make the reader think that he had been arrested and photographed after having been jailed for a felony. While he did not deny that the picture was of him, he said that it had been taken by a Wyoming sheriff after he had been arrested and fined $10 for overloading his truck. The Kansas Supreme Court ruled that the picture was protected by the privilege of reporting (Beyl v. Capper Publications, 180 Kan. 525). The Topeka *Capital* would have been on safer ground if its caption had explained the circumstances of the picture and not just given Beyl's name.

Blind Photos

Even if a legal defense exists for publishing a libel, the picture editor should make sure that every person in the illustration is mentioned in the accompanying article and his role adequately explained. If for reasons of space that part of the article is dropped, then the publication is running a grave risk of libel. The passage should be restored or the picture dropped.

On March 9, 1962, the Boston *Traveler* carried a front-page story about a Congressional committee's investigation of fraud in taking land for the Federal highway program in Massachusetts. The banner headline said:

SETTLEMENT UPPED $2,000
—$400 KICKBACK TOLD

Immediately below the headline were three photographs. One was of Joseph I. Mirkin, a state negotiator who had been convicted of taking a $400 kickback for increasing the price of a settlement by $2,000. The second was of Arthur D. Wilcox, president of the National Association of Real Estate Boards, who, the article noted, was due to testify before the committee. The third picture was of Mitchell Mabardi, a Boston attorney, who had testified before the committee the same day, regarding what he described as his refusal to take part in the frauds. Mabardi had been mentioned as a scheduled witness in an early edition, but his name was edited out when the article was updated. The story did refer to an unidentified lawyer who had solicited cases of persons whose property had been taken. The Supreme Judicial Court of Massachusetts ruled, in passing on Mabardi's suit, that the presence of Mabardi's picture could, under the circumstances, be capable of a defamatory meaning. It explained:

> The defendant argues that a more likely meaning was that Mr. Mabardi was to be, as was Wilcox, a witness before the Blatnik Committee. But the role of Wilcox in the proceedings was explained in the article. That of Mr. Mabardi was not. There was reference to an unnamed lawyer allegedly engaged in the solicitation of legal business. The inference could have been drawn by a large number of readers that the plaintiff was involved in the wrongdoing cited in the headline and discussed in the article. Such an inference was encouraged by the juxtaposition of the plaintiff's picture and that of Mirkin, the headline, and the story. It was not discouraged by any clarifying textual reference to the plaintiff. And while the inference may not be a necessarily rational one, we cannot say that a considerable segment of the community would not make it. We are not im-

pressed with the defendant's argument that the insertion of Mr. Mabardi's picture should have been interpreted as a mistake. Where this publication is susceptible of both defamatory and harmless meanings, a jury should have the opportunity to decide in what sense the public did understand it. [Mabardi v. Boston Herald-Traveler Corp., 347 Mass. 411]

Captions

A full caption, explaining the circumstances, would also be sufficient. The caption must be carefully written so as not to make sweeping charges that go beyond privilege. In its issue of November 3, 1956, the *Saturday Evening Post* began a series of four articles titled "Confessions of an 'S.O.B.,'" by Drew Pearson, the columnist. Illustrating the article was a page of eight photographs under the caption "Pearson Has Many Enemies." One of the pictures was captioned "One of the three Congressmen Pearson helped send to jail." Another ex-Congressman was identified as having been "convicted of war-fraud charges after Pearson exposed him." Included in the layout was a picture of General Harry H. Vaughan, who was military aid to President Harry S Truman from 1945 to 1953. The caption under his picture read: "Many Pearson charges against Harry Vaughan were later confirmed by testimony before Senate committee." The only reference to Vaughan in the first article was in connection with a person whom Pearson "helped send to jail after exposing him for influence peddling under the shadow of Gen. Harry Vaughan."

Vaughan sued, contending that the caption conveyed to the public the idea that he had committed malfeasance in office and that charges of such wrongdoing had been confirmed by testimony before a Congressional committee. The *Post* pointed out that later installments of the series discussed Vaughan in great detail and thus explained the caption, but a jury awarded the general $10,000 in compensatory damages. The United States Court of Appeals for the District of Columbia upheld the verdict. In doing so it noted that in the second installment Pearson had written that "some of the things I had written" about Vaughan had been confirmed by the Senate inquiry. The court commented, "Had the caption here been so worded, we would have an entirely different problem." It also pointed out the danger in a caption's dependence on a passage in a subsequent publication. It said that "readers of the *Post* who bought and read the November 3, 1956 issue were not bound to buy and read the *Post* for the remainder of the month possibly thus to ascertain for themselves the basis for the *Post's* caption" (Curtis Publishing Co. v. Vaughan, 278 F. 2d 23).

The importance of an adequate explanation in the caption of the role of the person in a picture is shown by a case based on a *Life* magazine layout. It was titled "The Great Spy Swap . . . An Album of Intrigue" and dealt with the exchange of the convicted Russian spy Rudolf Abel for the American U-2 spy-plane pilot Francis Gary Powers. The caption writer followed a theme in his punch lines. The first picture, of the room where Abel had hidden, carried the capitalized introductory words "Abel's Cover." Captions for subsequent pictures began "His View," "His Admirer," "His Neighbors," "His Barmaid," "His Superintendent," "His Contact Point" and "His Comeuppance." Frank Gambuzza, a radio dealer, the man pictured in the "His Admirer" photo, sued *Life*, asserting that the caption made readers think that he thought highly of the Russian spy. The full caption said:

> HIS ADMIRER. Frank Gambuzza, a radio dealer, who sold Abel some part for a wireless receiver, praised the Russian for his electronic know-how.

The court dismissed the suit, asserting that the caption did not portray Gambuzza as an admirer of Abel as a spy. It said:

> Such impression can only be gathered if the words "His Admirer" are segregated and disassociated from the balance of the legend. However, these words are adjacent to and amplified by the words which give it an entirely different meaning. One cannot read the one without seeing and reading the other. . . .
>
> Even if we were to assume these words to be a headline, they are printed so close to the remainder of the legend as to be, for all intents and purposes, a part of the legend and inseparable. The staccato and provocative nature of the introductory phrases of the legends under each of the photographs are such as to invite, or even to compel a reading of the remainder of the legend. Particularly is this so when the balance of the legends is so short. With respect to the legend complained of it is inconceivable that a reasonable person who looks at the photograph would read the two words "His Admirer" alone and form a conclusion as to their meaning without reading the three following lines of explanation.

... a reasonable reading of the entire legend does not permit of a conclusion that plaintiff is identified as an admirer of Rudolf Abel qua Rudolf Abel, the Russian spy. To the contrary, the photograph complained of—as do all the other photographs and legends—attempts to show the activities of Abel in his guise as an ordinary law-abiding citizen. It depicts how various of his neighbors were deceived as to his true identity and how they felt towards him before they knew him to be an agent of the Soviet Government. Each of the photographs referred to the persons photographed in their relation to Abel before he was exposed. The only inference to be drawn from this photograph and legend is that plaintiff admired Abel for his skill and know-how in electronics. Attributing such admiration to plaintiff falls short of constituting a libel against him. [Gambuzza v. Time, Inc., 18 A.D. 2d (N.Y.) 351]

Fair Comment

The picture editor must not become overly cautious. He must not forget that all the defenses available to the writer are also available to him, and one in particular gives him great latitude in choosing photos and writing captions. It is the defense of fair comment. This is especially valuable when the editor is striving for action pictures that illustrate an article. The photo provides the facts on which the caption writer can base libelous comments. The disputed caption in the *Life* magazine article on carelessness in handling boats was not libelous, but even if the court had ruled that it was defamatory the plaintiff would not have collected, because there was a legal justification for publishing it. The court said that the caption

RUB-A-DUB DUB, TOO MANY IN A TUB

and the title

SOME IDIOTS AFLOAT

were fair comment. The beauty of this defense for the picture editor is that he usually does not have to worry, as the writer must, about proving that his facts are true. The picture almost always provides the proof. In the *Life* article, the picture showed clearly that there were five persons in the small boat. As long as the matter is one that concerns the public generally—and boat safety does—the caption writer need not worry about libelous comments. The picture cannot be a simple mug shot; it must include some action, but these are the pictures that good editors are looking for anyway. Needless to say, the picture must show clearly what is happening. A club descending on a racial demonstrator's head is good proof, if caught in the camera. So would a pickpocket's hand in a shopper's coat. But a shot of a white segregationist standing over a fallen Negro would not be proof that the white man had knocked the Negro down, or that anyone had. And the cameraman who snapped a seedy-looking individual handing a pouch to a policeman would not have real proof of a graft payoff. If the caption writer must add facts to explain a picture, he must be wary of libelous comment. If the picture provides all the vital facts needed, the comment can be libelous as long as it is fair. Such a picture and caption can also stand alone. No explanatory passage in an accompanying article is necessary, as it is with other pictures. If there is a reference, it should be checked to make sure it does not conflict with the picture. Those in the picture need not be named, although in most cases the editor will try to provide the names as facts that the reader will usually be interested in.

The editor can, of course, turn to professional models, who will sign releases, to pose for needed illustrations. Detective magazines do this regularly. These pictures fool no one. Far better are shots that mask identification by not showing faces or, if a business is libeled, by not displaying a recognizable establishment.

Libel in Layout

The Vanderbilt humor magazine case (discussed at length on page 227) also showed that a picture although unaltered or un-cropped could be libelous because of the context in which it was carried. The Vanderbilt layout poked fun at a minister's family. That is always dangerous. As noted on page 62, the New York *American* published pictures of Stanislaus Zbyszko, a wrestler, and a gorilla to illustrate a story on the theory of evolution. Since the comparison imputed the qualities of a loathsome animal to a human, the picture was held to be libelous. Fofo Louka, a classical Greek actress, was found to have been libeled by a Boston burlesque house that displayed a picture of her, fully clothed, along with photos of some scantily dressed cuties. She was not a performer in "Minsky's Midsummer Follies," although with a name like Fofo she sounded like one. She was awarded $2,688.75 for the libelous display of her picture (Louka v. Park Entertainments, Inc., 294 Mass. 268). Fofo was an unusual plaintiff. Having cleared her name, she never demanded payment of the damages.

It is perfectly safe to use pictures showing good characters with the bad, as long as some device is used to separate them. The reader should know as soon as he has read the overline or caption who is accused, who is the victim and who is the innocent bystander. It should not be necessary to read down the accompanying article to figure out the picture.

On May 17, 1947, the New Orleans *Item* printed a picture of six men leaving the Federal Court Building in New Orleans. One perpendicular line marked off four of the men, and another perpendicular line ran between the other two. The overline read:

MILK WAR INDICTEES PHOTOGRAPHED
DESPITE THEIR THREATS

and the caption said:

> Some of the men indicted by the federal grand jury on conspiracy charges growing out of the recent milk strike and other figures in the case were photographed by the *Item's* Bill Sadlier as they left the federal building despite threats to smash his camera. They are part of a large group from the Florida Parishes who appeared before Commissioner Carter and posted bonds. This was the second federal indictment to follow the milk war which raged for ten days last March and early April.

No names were given. Sheriff Loyd H. Mulina of Washington Parish was one of those marked off from the four. He had not been charged, but had, as a friend, accompanied some of the men to the Federal Building to help them if he could. In his suit for $50,000 he asserted that the picture carried the implication that he had been indicted. The Louisiana Supreme Court dismissed his case, emphasizing that the caption explained that only "some" of the indictees "and other figures" were shown in the photograph (Mulina v. Item Co., 217 La. 842).

The Camera Lies

The Wisconsin Supreme Court noted the difficulty that a plaintiff who protests a picture faces, because in citing the alleged libel he must of necessity introduce evidence that proves the truth of the charge:

> That the picture portrays plaintiff behind prison bars is disclosed, not by the defendant publisher, but by plaintiff's own pleading, wherein it is alleged that it is "a picture and true likeness and photograph of this plaintiff behind prison bars." Thus it appears that there is nothing in the picture itself which *falsely* tends to bring plaintiff into public disgrace or ridicule. [Smith v. Journal Co., 271 Wis. 384]

All pictures, however, do not necessarily accurately reflect a situation. A telephoto lens can distort distances between objects. An umpire can be made to look ridiculously wrong in calling a runner out in a baseball game because the camera's position gives the impression that the ball arrived late. A truck can appear to be sideswiping an automobile through photographic tricks.

Sometimes the camera shows more than intended—or more than reality. Such was the case in an advertisement that was the basis for a suit against *Collier's* and the *American Magazine*. The ad, which appeared in October, 1934, was for Camel cigarettes. It contained two pictures and textual matter. The larger picture showed Crawford Burton, a well-known steeplechase rider, seated outside a paddock with a cigarette in one hand and a cap and whip in the other. It was captioned "Get a lift with a Camel." There was certainly no offense in that, or in the text, which quoted Burton as saying that Camels "restored" him after a crowded business day. No offense, that is, until read in relation to the second picture. That one showed the steeplechaser about to be weighed in. He was carrying his saddle in front of him with his right hand under the pommel and his left under the cantle. The line of the seat was about twelve inches below his waist. Over the seat at the middle a white strap fell loosely, in such a way that it seemed to be part of Burton's anatomy. The court noted that so regarded, the photograph became obscene while the caption's reference to being "restored" could, without undue violence, be made to reinforce the ribald interpretation. Judge Learned Hand's opinion in the resulting libel suit said:

We dismiss at once so much of the complaint as alleged that the advertisement might be read to say that the plaintiff was deformed, or that he had indecently exposed himself, or was making obscene jokes by means of the legends. Nobody could be fatuous enough to believe any of these things; everybody would at once see that it was the camera, and the camera alone, that had made the unfortunate mistake. If the advertisement is a libel, it is such in spite of the fact that it asserts nothing whatever about the plaintiff, even by the remotest implications. It does not profess to depict him as he is; it does not exaggerate any part of his person so as to suggest that he is deformed; it is patently an optical illusion, and carries its correction on its face as much as though it were a verbal utterance which expressly declared that it was false. It would be hard for words so guarded to carry any sting, but the same is not true of caricatures, and this is an example; for, notwithstanding all we have just said, it exposed the plaintiff to overwhelming ridicule. The contrast between the drawn and serious face and the accompanying fantastic and lewd deformity was so extravagant that, though utterly unfair, it in fact made of the plaintiff a preposterously ridiculous spectacle; and the obvious mistake only added to the amusement. Had such a picture been deliberately produced, surely every right-minded person would agree that he would have had a genuine grievance; and the effect is the same whether it is deliberate or not. Such a caricature affects a man's reputation, if by that is meant his position in the minds of others; the association so established may be beyond repair; he may become known indefinitely as the absurd victim of this unhappy mischance. Literally, therefore, the injury falls within the accepted rubric; it exposes the sufferer to "ridicule" and "contempt." [Burton v. Crowell Publishing Co., 82 F. 2d 154]

Burton, who had accepted $500 for the testimonial, sued for $75,000 in damages. At the trial he recalled that fellow members of the New York Stock Exchange had given him an unmerciful ribbing after the advertisement appeared. A jury awarded him $2,500. Later he settled suits against the R. J. Reynolds Tobacco Company, other publications and the advertising firm of William Esty and Company for $22,550.

Sometimes an obscene effect can be created if the publication is folded a certain way or if the page is held up to the light so that a picture on the other side shows through. The moral seems to be that every newsroom and advertising department ought to have one man with a dirty mind to spot obscenities. Someone on *The*

New York Times noted the obscenity in the Burton ad for Camels and had the offensive detail blacked out.

Cropping

Cropping of pictures can also lead to trouble if a distorted idea emerges. The Worcester (Massachusetts) *Post* lost a libel suit because it cropped out the husband from a picture of him, his wife and their chauffeur (Thayer v. Worcester Post, 284 Mass. 160).

Makeup

The die is not cast on a libelous publication until the news editor decides the display he will give it or the producer the format of the broadcast. These decisions can play an important part in libel suits.

The section on pictures explained how the juxtaposition of two photos comparing a wrestler with a gorilla was libelous. Defamation can also result from the relationship of headlines, pictures and articles. The *Daily Alaska Empire* ran into that trouble when it broke a story on September 25, 1952, about a special Chilkoot Ferry Fund set up by the Territorial Board of Road Commissioners, consisting of Ernest Gruening, Henry Roden and Frank A. Metcalf.

The trouble stemmed not so much from the exposé as the makeup. The United States Court of Appeals for the Ninth Circuit explained:

> . . . the headline, in black type an inch and a quarter high, and extending across the entire eight columns of the front page, read "Bare 'Special' Ferry Fund." Beneath that headline was another smaller headline in ⅝ inch high black type five columns wide reading "Reeve Raps Graft, Corruption." This latter heading dealt with a one column story at the extreme left of the page regarding a speech made by a political candidate named Robert Reeve, and so far as its text is concerned, it had nothing to do with the ferry fund or appellees. Immediately next to the one column story and directly under the heading "Reeve Raps Graft, Corruption" was a photograph of a check drawn on the "special" ferry fund. Beneath the photograph of

BARE 'SPECIAL' FERRY FUND

Reeve Raps Graft, Corruption

Gruening, Metcalf, Roden Divert 'Chilkoot' Cash To Private Bank Account

Hitting out at corruption in government at every level and charging that the present administration has ruthlessly neglected the Territory of Alaska, Robert C. "Bob" Reeve last night addressed a standing-room-only crowd in the gold room of the Baranof Hotel.

Reeve, who is Republican candidate for Delegate in Congress from Alaska, closed by calling for a sweeping Republican victory at the polls on October 14.

That date, he reminded his audience, is also the birthday of General Eisenhower. "As Alaska grows, so does our nation—and the best birthday gift you Alaskans can present Ike will be a Republican victory."

Reeve cited lack of control of the finances by the Territory, the halt in payments of salaries, the beer-making withdrawal of public lands, destruction and discouragement of private enterprise, and many other items as showing the complete failure of the Democratic administration during the 20 years it has been in power.

The other featured speaker in last night's rally was William Boardman, Ketchikan life insurance agent, who is candidate for the House.

Reeve Tells Bartlett to 'Blow Horn'

Bob Reeve, the scrapping Republican candidate for Delegate in Congress, today dared fellow Democratic E. L. Bartlett to come out, res off the bandwagon.

Reeve, who returned today to his home in Anchorage after a campaign swing through South east Alaska, accepted a challenge that he said had been made at a time and place. The debate will be in Wasilla, near Anchorage.

START TALKING, BOYS

(An Editorial)

Disclosed in today's Empire is a story almost too fantastic for belief, but the facts have been personally verified by both the territorial auditor and assistant attorney general.

... between the auditor ... and signed by Ralph E. Coughlin ... the "special account" is ... without the knowledge of the auditor, without a territorial officer warrant, and by a man who is not a territorial officer.

The laws of Alaska, well-known to Gruening, Roden and Metcalf, carefully spell out the method in which public money may be appropriated for any expenditure by departmental heads. It will be made by warrant and approved by the auditor.

This is no vague technicality hidden away; in small print. It is a matter of law known, and followed by the original record might be barred.

McCarran Act Won't Trouble U.S. Citizens

SEATTLE, Sept. 25. —Immigration Director John P. Boyd said today that aliens in Alaska who possibly will face any trouble in entering the states from Alaska under the new immigration law ... are labeled as "erroneous ... er, exploited in a record ... of the normal Alaska ... that a U.S. citizen will record might be bar...

Roden, Metcalf Say 'Nothing Crooked' Here

Territorial treasurer Henry Roden and highway engineer Frank Metcalf today said that as the board of road commissioners set up a "special fund" at the operation of the ferry ... the following explanation of how it was done:

In spring of 1961, when the owners of the M. V. Chilkoot decided to sell the ferry, there were no buyers available. There was a danger that it would cease operation, and Juneau, going out of business.

The board did not want to see the ferry go out of business, because it was a ...

Auditor Neil Moore and Assistant Attorney General John Dimond Halt Payments From Fund

By Jack D. Daum

To avoid paying territorial money into the general fund as provided by law, Governor Gruening, Treasurer Roden and Highway Engineer Frank Metcalf have set up a "special fund" at a Juneau bank, territorial auditor Neil Moore disclosed today.

Illegal Payments

The "special fund," which dates back to early last year, is in the B. M. Behrends bank under the name "Chilkoot Ferry—by Robert E. Coughlin," the name of the operator of the ferry which was purchased by the Territory in May, 1961, and there have been thousands of dollars of illegal ... and disbursements recorded ... of the fund to date, Moore charged.

After perusal of six months, Auditor Moore and assistant attorney general John Dimond ordered the account drawn against the account.

AUDITOR NEIL MOORE

The special account, established and maintained without knowledge of the auditor, to enable the highway department, Frank Metcalf, to keep the ferry Chilkoot out of the normal Alaska laws, of territorial finance, Moore ... Metcalf latches the most

the check was a two-column editorial entitled "Start Talking Boys" which dealt with the special ferry fund. To the right of the page and as a sub-headline to the main headline three lines deep and in type one-half inch high, was a statement "Gruening, Metcalf, Roden Divert 'Chilkoot' Cash to Private Bank Account."

. . . Plainly here there was plenty of room for a finding that the publication charged, and that it was well calculated to charge, embezzlement involving theft and conversion to appellees' own use. Defamation can be accomplished in a multitude of ways, and the manner in which the front page of defendant's newspaper was made up on the occasion here in question, could well be regarded by the jury as a deliberate defamation by indirection, insinuations and associations, even if a direct and categorical charge were lacking.

. . . The fact that the text of the article under the heading relating to graft and corruption refers to a wholly different matter is a circumstance which the jury had a right to consider, but it did not compel them to ignore the very possible purpose sought in weaving all these headlines together, especially in view of the substantial evidence of actual malice on the part of the publishers. The jury could conclude that the headline was placed where it was for its effect upon the reader in connection with the other headlines. It was immediately opposite the headline, in comparable type, reading "Gruening, Metcalf, Roden Divert 'Chilkoot' Cash to Private Bank Account." The two column wide editorial on this same page immediately below the reproduction of the check, is headed, "Start Talking, Boys." Not only is that heading of the editorial an apparent simulation of the way a detective would address a crook in a cops and robbers movie, but it has sarcastic comments upon other "deals" with which Gruening had been connected, and whose defense of a named former proceeding is referred to as one which "still rings stridently in the ears of all honest Alaskans."

The court upheld awards to each of the three plaintiffs of $1 in compensatory damages and $5,000 in punitive damages (Empire Printing Co. v. Roden, 247 F. 2d 8).

Pictures added to the trouble the New York *Daily News* faced in a suit discussed at length beginning on page 166. The plaintiff, Paul J. Kern, insisted that his picture, under a headline that said "Tag 5 Project Mgrs. as Red," carried the implication that he had been responsible for their hiring. The use of pictures of two Communists on the jump page with the caption, "Shared speaking chores with Kern," added to the *News* troubles during the trial. Kern kept reminding the jury of the juxtaposition of the picture and headline until the *News* attorney protested, "This is the fifteenth time he has mentioned 'over the picture of plaintiff.'" Kern replied, "This was published in two million copies." The jury sided with Kern (Kern v. News Syndicate Co., 20 A.D. 2d(N.Y.) 528).

Makeup that gives a libelous impression to readers certainly falls within a court's jurisdiction. But the courts sometimes go beyond and stick their noses in an area where they do not belong. The judges base decisions on such immaterial factors as where a story is played and how heavily it is played.

In a case referred to on page 38, the Boston *Record American* was found to have libeled a woman in a front-page banner and an inside story concerning the possibility of exhuming two bodies buried on Cape Cod. The United States Court of Appeals for the First Circuit said in its decision:

> It must not be overlooked in such cases that the very fact a matter is viewed as newsworthy, particularly when given special prominence, means that something of possible importance is being communicated. Taking the article as a whole we believe it would be only natural for even reasonable readers to assume that they were being furnished with something more than necrology, or trivia concerning the relict [sic] of a routinely posted cadaver, and that they could well conclude that the plaintiff was suspected of having engaged in highly sinister conduct. [Perry v. The Hearst Corporation, 334 F. 2d 800]

The same court in the Second Circuit has gone even further and ruled that it should judge the newsworthiness of the story as a factor in a libel suit. The case concerned the following article from *The New York Times* of October 4, 1958, under the headline "Dice Raid in Stamford Follows The Script of a Keystone Comedy":

> STAMFORD, Conn., Oct. 3—Scene One: A deserted corner in downtown Stamford. Time: Just before daylight.
> A truck bearing the name of George's Flower Shop, 525 Main Street, arrives. Six policemen carrying night sticks pile out into the autumn chill and advance warily on a group of ten men rolling dice in the gleam of a corner street light.
> It is apparent that the police have used the truck as a decoy—to avoid suspicion.

> Scene Two: The same. Time: Later.

The policemen surround the players. They order them into the rear of the truck.

"Get moving," says one of the patrolmen to a straggler. "Inside, you!"

The suspects begin climbing in and then, one by one, they discover the truck has a front entrance near the driver's seat.

"Come on, let's get out of here," says the first man in. There's a scramble for the exit.

Scene Three: Still the same. Time: Even later.

The patrolmen start after the escaping suspects in the darkness. Night sticks are swung right and left. Patrolman Thomas Maloney strikes out at a shadowy figure. It proves to be a fellow officer, Patrolman Lawrence Hogan, who slumps to the pavement with a badly bruised head.

The chase finally ends but with only four of the ten suspects in custody. After the prisoners are booked at headquarters it is discovered that four of the police night stricks are missing—presumably grabbed in the darkness by the suspects who got away.

A Keystone Kop comedy? No, it really happened that way in Stamford early this morning.

In upholding a jury award of $6,020 for Patrolman Hogan and $6,125 for Patrolman Maloney, who had contended the article was false, the Court of Appeals said:

> Certainly the evidence is sufficient to sustain a finding that The Times' sole purpose in publishing the article was to amuse its readers at the expense of the plaintiffs. That The New York Times, a newspaper of international pre-eminence, devoted to extensive reporting of important current events, should find the raid of an open-air crap game in Stamford to constitute news fit to print—and on the front page at that—is quite enough evidence by itself. It is irrefutable that the story was not as newsworthy as were its companion articles on the front page [concerning Pope Pius and Cardinal Spellman, President Eisenhower, Charles de Gaulle, Mayor Wagner, George Meany, nuclear talks and space research]; it was obviously there only for its entertainment value. Noting particularly the setting of the item, we find it difficult to be impressed by the belated suggestion that the purpose of publication was the benevolent one of commenting on the small town police ways with crapshooters or at least that the jury must so find. Moreover, it was already stale news, having appeared the day before in the

local Connecticut paper. [Hogan and Maloney v. New York Times Co., 313 F. 2d 354]

This is a dangerous concept—that the courts should judge the relative newsworthiness of an article, whether it should be used because it considers the item "stale" or whether it should be played on the first or an inside page. Such a doctrine infringes on the freedom of the press as guaranteed by the Constitution. The *Times* proved that it was not intimidated by the court by continuing to run light bits of Americana on the front page, including one that in many ways is remarkably parallel to the Stamford story. It appeared on March 5, 1965, in approximately the same position as the Stamford story, with the same style of headline, and began:

> PHILLIPSBURG, N.J., March 4—Two snooping Keystone State Cops were caught today in this frontier town and forced back across the Delaware in the latest round of the whiskey war between the Garden State and Pennsylvania.

A much sounder legal rule on the play of a story was propounded by the Georgia Court of Appeals. The article concerned a feature story about the way a lawyer drove his ancient car, a reckless driving charge leveled against him and his acquittal. In running the story on September 25, 1959, the city editor of the Savannah *Morning News* put it on a page devoted to important local news and used a picture of the lawyer with it. The lawyer sued for libel, asserting he had been ridiculed. At the trial it was brought out that the reporter who wrote the story had objected to the way it had been displayed. Specifically, he asserted that its position in the paper and use of the picture were in bad taste and "ballooned" the article. In reversing a $5,000 verdict, the Georgia Court of Appeals said:

> Whether the article be regarded as in good taste or in poor taste is irrelevant in determining whether it was libelous. Though written in the best of literary styles and given the most conservative of treatment on the inside pages of the paper without a picture, if it contained statements about the plaintiff that were false, material and defamatory, it was libelous. On the other hand, a news item written in the poorest of tastes, as for example, including lavish and undue praise of an individual, his skills and accomplishments, accompanied by his picture and given the most prominent space in the paper, may be wholly free of any libel.

Nor can the personal preferences, wishes or predilections of the reporter who wrote the story constitute any standard for determing whether it was libelous. Suppose the reporter had wanted the story given the feature treatment, accompanied by a picture and carried in a prominent place in the paper, but the city editor had determined that it should have no more than a routine treatment, published in the want ad section and without any picture, could it be said that the mere violation of the reporter's wishes rendered the story libelous? Something more must appear.

Further, when the matter of whether there was malice in the publication of the story is considered, the violation of the reporter's wishes may indicate some friction existing between the city editor and the reporter, but shows nothing of any malice on the part of the city editor or of the publisher against the plaintiff. Again, something more must appear.

We may observe that the matter of what is "good taste" or "poor taste" in a newspaper story is a very nebulous and elusive thing, just as is what is "good taste" or "poor taste" in women's styles and fashions. In the newspaper world there is a variety of publications, giving a variety of treatment to the stories carried as news, ranging from the tabloid to the sophisticated; and all are generally accepted by the reading public. Some readers like one type while others prefer another. So long as it is not libelous those who are in charge of the newspapers must be left to judge as to the kind of treatment a story is to receive, and whether reader interest may be stimulated by the carrying of a photograph concerning the subject matter. The mere fact that the treatment of a news item is, in the opinion of some, in "poor taste" does not make it libelous.

With that instruction as a background, the court said that the treatment of the news could be considered in deciding whether the newspaper showed malice by departing from its normal custom (Savannah News-Press v. Hartridge, 110 Ga. App. 203). The Georgia rule thus gives the press the freedom it requires to select and handle the news without letting it use that liberty as a weapon to vent malice on an individual. The Savannah *News-Press's* primary interest in the case was to uphold truth as an absolute defense. After winning that point, it settled the case out of court for $1,500.

A point emphasized throughout this book has been the value of getting the other side of the story. The news editor can add to proof of fairness by playing both sides of the story properly. On page

229, the Arkansas Supreme Court's ruling in the case of a nursing-home proprietor's suit was discussed as an example of approval of the defense of consent. The Arkansas *Gazette* invoked this defense not with just a mention of her denial in the main story detailing the charges against her, but also with a separate story giving her side of the question. A headline covering both stories was based on the charges:

> FAUBUS SAYS PROBE UNCOVERS
> SCANDAL AT NURSING HOME

The readout head on the main story,

> SHOCKING
> CONDITIONS
> ARE ALLEGED

was matched by the readout head on the sidebar:

> TRINITY DENIES
> CHARGES, ASKS
> PROBE BY JURY

Brandon v. Gazette Publishing Co., 234 Ark. 332). Such makeup gives the accused his day in court. What more can he ask?

Even if the article is an exposé or a crusading piece or a policy story of some sort, the editor would be wise to point out the other side's reply. A sidebar with a complete explanation is best. If there is not enough material, a box will call the reader's attention to it. A good makeup editor will, whenever he has a chance, back up the picture and copy desks on possible libel in captions and headlines, as discussed earlier in this chapter.

There is one charge that some plaintiffs make that seemingly falls within the makeup man's jurisdiction but which he does not have to worry about: the accusation that the paper showed malice by overpublication of the libel by including it in all editions, even those that go to areas with little or no interest in the article. The courts have held that a paper is not required to have special editions for each community it serves (Swede v. Passaic Daily News, 30 N.J. 320).

Chapter 20

RADIO AND TELEVISION

WHEN COMMERCIAL RADIO FIRST CAME INTO ITS OWN IN THE 1920S, the courts did not quite know how to apply the law of defamation to the new medium. Initially judges, following the logic of the division of defamation into spoken or written form, decided that radio broadcasts were slander, not libel. For broadcasting this was fine, because the law is much more lenient for slander than it is for libel. Some terms, like "son of a bitch," may be libelous but not slanderous. Moreover, damages for slander are smaller than for libel, removing much of the danger of large verdicts.

With the rapid growth of radio, the impact of broadcasting on an audience soon became apparent. A single broadcast could reach tens of millions of people, far more than the nation's largest-selling magazine. An individual could be damaged far more extensively by a radio program than he could be by an article in a magazine or a newspaper. Justice called for a new approach, and in 1932 the Nebraska Supreme Court acted.

Richard F. Wood had used the following words in a broadcast over KFAB in Lincoln in opposing the reelection of C. A. Sorensen as Attorney General:

> In his acceptance of the Attorney General's office he took an oath before God and man that he would uphold the law justly and honestly. His promises to man are for naught and his oath to God is sacrilege, for he is a nonbeliever, an irreligious libertine, a mad man and a fool.

The Nebraska Supreme Court said there was "little dispute" that the words constituted libel rather than slander (Sorensen v. Wood, 123 Neb. 348).

In 1947 the Court of Appeals of New York handed down a decision that has had great effect on the law. The case concerned a broadcast by Walter Winchell. In discussing a World War II pacifist organization known as Peace Now, Winchell had said:

> This outfit yaps about loving peace. Its leader is George W. Hartmann. . . . It blames America for killing children in Europe and Asia. But they do not discuss the children murdered by the Sneakinees and the Nazis.
>
> Peace lovers my eye! They never talked about peace when Hitler was winning. Instead of a dove [their] symbol [ought] to be a jackass—or a skunk.

The New York court decided that since the remarks had been read from a script they consituted libel, not slander. The court did not decide whether extemporaneous statements over the air were libel or slander. A concurring decision suggested that all broadcast defamation was libelous because of the wide audience reached (Hartmann v. Winchell, 296 N.Y. 296).

Many jurisdictions follow the rule of terming defamation read from a script libel and ad-lib defamation slander. But the tendency has been, more and more, to consider all defamatory broadcasts as libel. The safest approach for the newsman in the electronic media is to act on the basis that the stiffer rules apply. If he does, then the principles laid down in this book for printed defamation will be good guides to follow. Since the goal of these principles is to permit the transmission of the maximum amount of public information, the newsman with a sense of responsibility will find he has a wide area of freedom on TV and radio.

While the principles of libel are the same in broadcasting as they are in printed media, the problems are sometimes different. One reason is that only a limited number of stations can occupy the available airwaves. As a result, the Federal Government has set up standards that stations must meet to obtain or renew the licenses necessary to operate.

Other problems arise from the fact that libels are transmitted in a different way by broadcasts than by newspapers, magazines and books. The use of sound or sound combined with pictures creates hazards unknown to those who deal only with the printed word.

Was It Published?

A broadcasting station's control over the actual publication of a libel is much less certain than even the fastest-moving newspaper. A radio or TV crew often picks up a news source at the scene and broadcasts his statement live. If he should blurt out a libelous remark, it is transmitted instantaneously to the audience. The moderator on a panel show can usually see perilous situations developing and steer the discussion to safer areas, but he can never be certain of preventing a trigger-tempered guest from libeling someone.

On March 6, 1960, Congressman Adam Clayton Powell, Jr., was being interviewed over WNTA-TV in New York about a campaign he was waging against organized gambling and police corruption. At one point he described Mrs. Esther James, of Harlem, as a "bag woman," or collector of graft, for the police department. Mrs. James sued Powell, NTA Television Broadcasting Corporation, which owned WNTA-TV, and the Associated Food Stores Corporation, sponsor of the program, for defamation. The station and the sponsor settled for $1,500. At Powell's trial the jury awarded Mrs. James $11,500 in compensatory damages and $200,000 in punitive damages. On appeal the total judgment was reduced to $46,500 (James v. Powell, 20 A.D. 2d (N.Y.) 689).

Commercial messages on television can run into the same trouble. On October 14, 1962, Frank Valenta noticed that a car was parked on his business property in Los Angeles. Although the car belonged to one of his customers, Valenta jumped to the conclusion that someone from one of the used-car lots next door had parked it there. Angry, Valenta called E. L. White, who owned the used car lots, to demand that the car be removed at once. Told that White was delivering a live television commercial, Valenta slammed down the receiver and stormed over to the car lot. With the TV cameras still whirring, he rushed past an attendant toward White, gesturing menacingly. He said something that no one heard very clearly but a viewer understood to be "you son of a bitch." This viewer said she thought that Valenta had been a customer angered over treatment he had received. Valenta insisted that it was White who had said, "son of a bitch," and had done so in ordering him off the property. White sued Valenta for slander and was awarded $5,000 in compensatory damages and $2,500 in punitive damages (White v. Valenta, 44 Cal. Rptr. 241). Mr. Valenta paid; Mr. White went out of business.

An obvious way to limit these dangers is to prerecord the shows. Almost all on-the-scene reports and panel discussions are taped. The benefits are apparent. The producer has better control over the show, because he can edit out the poor sections, keeping only the best. The writer has a chance to weave meaningful comments around the spot. And the show can be cut or expanded to fit the precise amount of time of the broadcast. Entertainment shows are usually recorded before a studio audience. Any defamation committed at such taping sessions undoubtedly meets the legal definition of being published. But as a practical matter the deletion of offending statements before airing will eliminate most damages.

When WNBC in New York changed its format to emphasize interviews with listeners who telephoned in, the station decided that the best way of limiting the danger of obscenity and defamation was to record the conversations but delay their broadcast for seven seconds. In this way spontaneity was not lost and some control was maintained.

The television program "That Was The Week That Was" posed special problems. The program was broadcast live. It was satire keyed to the news, and many of the skits bordered on the libelous. Much of it was written on deadline from ideas that popped up at the last minute. But a lawyer worked right with the staff, clearing everything before the skits went on the air. In the two years of the program only one defamation suit, and that a minor one, was filed on the basis of objectionable skits.

Did It Identify?

The possibility exists that sound alone may be found to identify an individual. The United States Court of Appeals for the First Circuit noted the possibility in a case brought by Bert Lahr, the comedian. Lahr had sued the makers of the cleaning fluid Lestoil for a television commercial featuring a duck with a voice that he said was a poor imitation of his distinctive vocal delivery. The suits charged invasion of privacy, defamation and unfair competition. The court did not pass on the question of whether the voice did make viewers think that they were hearing Lahr, but it noted that "it has never been held in defamation that a plaintiff must be identified by name" (Lahr v. Adell Chemical Co., 300 F. 2d 256). The comedian won an undisclosed sum in an out-of-court settlement.

On television, identification can be made by pictures alone, just as in newspapers or magazines. Usually, however, the basis is a combination of words and pictures. On April 11, 1950, Arthur Godfrey gave his audience some advice about buying ukeleles. He showed three brands. The first, he said, cost about $11 and was a good instrument. The second, Godfrey explained, cost about half the price of the first and was suitable for beginners. The third cost $2.99, Godfrey said, and then went on to express the opinion that while its sale as a ukelele might not violate the law, those who sold it ought to be jailed. The manufacturer of the $2.99 ukelele sued for defamation, and the defense did not even raise the question of identification (Tex Smith, The Harmonica Man, Inc., *et al.* v. Godfrey *et al.*, 198 Misc. (N.Y.) 1006). Tex Smith won an undisclosed sum in a settlement.

Jokes can lead to trouble. On Jack Paar's *Tonight Show* on December 26, 1957, Louis Nye held up a package and said, "Snooze, the new aid for sleep. Snooze is full of all kinds of habit-forming drugs. Nothing short of a hospital cure will make you stop taking Snooze. You'll feel like a run-down hound dog and lose weight."

Unknown to Nye, a product was being sold under the brand name "Snooze." The manufacturers, Harwood Pharmacal Company, Inc., were not sleeping. They sued, noting that a competitive product was advertised on the same program on other evenings but not on the night in question. The cause of action was upheld by the court (Harwood Pharmacal v. NBC *et al.*, 9 N.Y. 2d 460). As the case was headed for trial it was settled for $3,500. The National Broadcasting Company was fortunate. Writers and producers should check to make sure they are not identifying a product or person in scripts that depend on ridicule for their effect.

Many of the suits in broadcasting are filed by people who insist that they have been identified in dramatic productions. Sometimes names are identical, sometimes names and occupations coincide. Even some of the circumstances of the drama may jibe with the complainant's past. These cases are more annoying than costly, and broadcasters follow the sound practice of not letting the complaints inhibit them. The selection of fictitious names on the basis of the suggestions on page 30 is a good defense in case the complaints reach court.

When shows are based on history or other actual events, the broadcasters face a much more difficult situation. A number of cases indicate the extent of the problem.

The American Broadcasting Company dramatized on the program *The Untouchables* on January 5 and January 12, 1961, a two-part story titled "The Big Train." The episodes dealt with an attempted escape by the gangster Al Capone while being transferred from the Atlanta Federal Penitentiary to Alcatraz in 1934. An officer of the United States Bureau of Prisons was depicted accepting $1,000 from Capone to help in the escape. The officer slipped the date and time of the prison train's departure to Capone in a library book, and Capone passed the information to his gangster friends on the outside who were devising the escape plan. The officer went along on the train as a guard and gave Capone the key that the prisoner used to unlock his leg irons.

The dramatization showed only one guard in the railroad car, but in reality there had been two. One of them, E. L. Simpson, was living in retirement in Georgia. He sued for defamation, asserting that *The Untouchables* had been billed as an authentic portrayal of actual events. As proof that the show had tried to convince viewers that it was historically accurate, the suit noted that the date of Capone's transfer to Alcatraz, his prison number, the name of the Attorney General and scenes from the Federal Penitentiary at Atlanta were factual. But, the suit went on, those parts of the drama that showed the bribery of the guard and his aid in the escape attempt were false.

The court held that since Simpson was one of only two guards who had been in the real Capone car, he had a good case, and his claim was upheld. If he had just been one of the sixteen guards who had been on the entire prison train—and not one of the two assigned to the Capone car—the court indicated that he would have had no case (ABC v. Simpson, 106 Ga. App. 230). Simpson received an out-of-court settlement.

Two other cases also indicate that identification is the key in fictionalized accounts of actual events. If libel is present, the television producer ought to make sure that he can prove the events to be true or that he has some other legal right to put on the show. When defenses are weak, the producer must make the same decision as the newspaper or magazine editor: he will have to fuzz the identification or soften the libelous passages.

Metro-Goldwyn-Mayer did neither in the motion picture *Rasputin, the Mad Monk*, as noted on page 44. As a result, the court held that the Princess had been identified and that she had been defamed in scenes showing that she was either raped or seduced. The book and the film *Anatomy of a Murder* indicate that the fine line between safety and peril can be drawn. The novel and motion picture constituted a study through fiction of an actual murder trial, yet libel and invasion-of-privacy counts against the publisher of the book and distributor of the film were dismissed.

The novel was written by Robert Traver, the pen name of John D. Voelker, defense counsel at the murder trial. The suit was brought by Hazel Wheeler and Terry Ann Chenoweth. Hazel Wheeler noted that she was the widow and Terry Ann the daughter of Maurice K. Chenoweth, who was shot and killed by Lieutenant Coleman Peterson for the "rape" of Peterson's wife. Peterson was tried for murder at Marquette, Michigan, in 1952 and acquitted on the defense of insanity. In the novel and the film Janice Quill is the divorced wife and Bernadine Quill the daughter of Barney Quill, who is shot and killed by a Lieutenant Manion for the "rape" of Manion's wife. Manion is acquitted on the ground of insanity. Scenes for the picture were filmed at the tavern where the slaying took place and in the courtroom where the actual trial was held.

Admittedly, the court said, Barney Quill represented Chenoweth. But it held that no one who knew Hazel Wheeler could reasonably identify her as Janice Quill, "that dame with the dyed red hair and livid scar on her right cheek who had sworn at him in everything but Arabian. . . . Who'd ever forget such a noisy, foul-mouthed harridan?" Hazel Wheeler stated that she had scratched her face and had used a henna rinse during the time of the trial. Even so, the court insisted, those who knew she was Chenoweth's widow and Terry Ann's mother could not reasonably identify her with Janice Quill because Hazel Wheeler denied having any of the "unsavory characteristics" of the fictional character.

As for Terry Ann, the court pointed out that she was nine at the time of the actual trial, while in the book and the film Quill's daughter was sixteen. This age differential and the inconspicuous role of Quill's daughter in the fictionalized versions convinced the court that Terry Ann had no cause of action (Wheeler v. Dell Publishing Co., 300 F. 2d 372).

Some publishers try to head off trouble with a note in the book that "all characters in this book are fictional and any resemblance to persons living or dead is purely coincidental." Movie makers do the same. Such a note may have just the opposite effect, inducing the public to look for the identification of an actual person. Nevertheless, notes may be useful in convincing juries that no identification was intended.

In the Rasputin film, M-G-M went to the other extreme. After listing the eight principal characters, it said that "a few of the characters are still alive; the rest met death by violence." M-G-M was attempting to sell the film as a true story, although when it went to court it defended it as fiction. In such cases the safer course would be to run an explanatory note saying that the story is based on actual events but some of the characters and situations are fictional.

Did It Harm?

The writer whose material goes out over the air should judge the possible harmful effects of his broadcasts on the basis of the principles discussed in Chapters 5–8. In applying these principles the writer should not forget the distinctive nature of his medium. In television, particularly, he must always be conscious of the fact that words and pictures go together and that the timing of one with the other is crucial.

On March 30, 1954, Harry Luttbeg, secretary and manager of a Better Business Bureau, narrated a program over KGGM in Albuquerque, New Mexico. He displayed an advertisement of the Day and Night Television Service Company that had run in the local newspaper and commented on it. The ad said:

Television Service

$2.50   Call

Why Pay More?

Our skilled electronic technicians will now repair and adjust your television set

for only $2.50 plus parts. Open 7 days a
week from 9:30 'til 9:30

Day and Night
Television Service
2413 Fourth St. NW Phone 2-2737

The comment included these phrases:

. . . certain of the T. V. servicemen are misleading and cheating
the public. . . . They did not bring in any tools except a screwdriver
in one of their pockets. . . . This is what has been referred to in the
trade as the ransom. Ransom, the ransom racket. The technique of
taking up the stuff after first assuring the set owner that the
charges would only be nominal, and then holding the set for ransom
much as the way you would kidnap an individual and hold that
individual for ransom.

The New Mexico Supreme Court noted: "Standing alone, neither the advertisement nor the words used by Luttbeg could be
construed as libel. But the two combined impute fraud and dishonesty to the company and its operators (Young v. New Mexico
Broadcasting Co., 60 N.M. 475).

With proper care the two elements could have been kept separate and the gist of the message still communicated to the audience. A jury returned a $1,000 verdict against Luttbeg and $2,250
against the Association of Radio and Television Services, which
aided in the broadcast. The judge reduced the total award to
$1,000. The station escaped without any damages. Other factors in
the case tended to keep the verdict down.

The use of video tape resulted in an unusual defamation suit in
California. C. Robert Bupp was a staff announcer for television
station KXTV in Sacramento under the professional name of Bob
Stone. As part of his duties he made video-tape recordings of commercials and announcements on a fee basis. On September 26,
1960, Bupp went out on strike with other members of the American Federation of Television and Radio Artists. The station stayed
on the air and continued to use Bupp's video tapes without payment of fees. Bupp said that he had been defamed, because his
continued appearance on TV would make the audience think that
he was a strikebreaker. The court disagreed (Bupp v. Great Western Broadcasting Corp., 20 Cal. Rptr. 106).

Is There a Defense?

The defenses discussed in Chapter 10–15 are as good for broadcasters as they are for newspapers, magazines and books, Again, however, the distinctive nature of broadcasting leads to advantages and disadvantages.

Pictures are always impressive evidence of truth, and the station or network that wants to expose gambling or narcotics traffic or other forms of crime would be on safe ground if it had a lot of film showing the racketeers in operation. A jury would not only be entertained by the show, it might also be swayed to believe it had seen the truth.

Television and radio enjoy the same privilege of reporting official proceedings as do newspapers and magazines. But there is intense pressure on producers of news programs to exceed the rules. The problem arises from the fact that the best programs star the central characters of the news, not the announcer or reporter. Some of TV's best moments have been presentations of official proceedings such as those held by the Senate rackets committee. But television cameras are not usually permitted at official proceedings. TV reporters are allowed to attend and then report their accounts over the air. Much better film is obtained if the participants are interviewed as they leave the proceeding. These interviews are not privileged, and stations that use them should be extremely careful to avoid broadcasting indefensible libel.

The trouble can be compounded if the authorities are eager to star in a television show. On January 17, 1961, Constable B. P. Justice of Mills River Township, Henderson County, North Carolina, called the Skyway Broadcasting Company, which operates television station WLOS in Asheville and said he was about to make an arrest in a sensational rape and robbery case. Justice waited until a Skyway crew arrived at the Henderson City Hall, then, accompanied by several officers, he went out and seized Edward D. Greer. As Greer was taken into city hall the TV cameras took pictures of him handcuffed and surrounded by the police. The television crews followed Greer inside and took more pictures. The woman who had been robbed and raped was then brought into the room and asked in the presence of the TV crews if Greer was the man who had attacked her. When she did not identify Greer as the attacker, Justice took her into another room and talked to her. Ten minutes later he returned and said that the woman had identified Greer as the man who had attacked her. That night Skyway broadcast an item on its eleven o'clock news program that Greer had been arrested on a charge of rape and robbery and had been identified by the victim. The next day the station showed pictures of Greer in handcuffs and announced that he had been positively identified but refused to admit his guilt. At a hearing a few days later the victim looked at Greer and others in the courtroom and said that she did not see the man who had raped and robbed her. Charges against Greer were promptly dismissed, and he sued Skyway and Justice for defamation. The North Carolina Supreme Court held that Greer had stated a case of conspiracy between the constable and the station to commit libel (Greer v. Skyway Broadcasting Co., 256 N.C. 382). Skyway was fortunate; Greer settled out of court for a mere $500.

Much has been said in this book about how much safety is provided against libel suits by getting the other side of the story. This basic news-gathering procedure can also serve broadcasting companies well. An example of how expensive negligence in reporting both sides of the story can be is shown by a libel verdict won by Austin Purcell, who was in the car-repair business in Philadelphia. Purcell had been arrested in February, 1955, with four others. At a hearing in magistrate's court at which only prosecution witnesses testified, all five were convicted of violating the city ordinance regulating car-towing. Purcell's lawyer announced in the presence of Paul Taylor of the news staff of radio station KYW that an appeal would be filed. On March 4, an appeal was filed and in September his summary conviction was stricken from the record. Purcell was indicted by the April grand jury, but the charges were dropped early the next year. Thus Purcell was wholly exonerated of all charges filed against him.

Meanwhile, however, on March 20, while Purcell's appeal from his summary conviction was pending, KYW broadcast an exposé of the tow-car racket. The principal performer on the show was Paul Taylor, the man who had covered the magistrate's hearing. In the broadcast Taylor spoke in the first person. He recalled how he had been disturbed by a complaint about a "gouging" by a tow-truck driver. Taylor told how he had gone to District Attorney Richardson Dilworth and interviewed him. The show switched to the taped interview, with the District Attorney warning of "the very tough mugs who run this towing-car racket" and of how motorists were being "gypped." Taylor also narrated his conversation with two detectives. One detective mentioned that "many people" had been bilked by the "so-called G. & M."—a shop where Purcell had once worked as foreman. A detective also spoke of victims of the towing racket who did not want to prosecute because "they were fearful of reprisals."

Then Taylor broadcast anonymous voices of a number of men and a woman. They related how they had been "bilked" by the towing racketeers. A detective once again spoke out from the tape recorder, noting that many persons had told him they had been "roped." Another announcer broke in to tell the public of Paul Taylor's excellent investigation and of the good work of the District Attorney's office. Then he announced, "Now the pot was ready to boil."

At this point Taylor described the hearing in magistrate's court, saying, "I was at that hearing held in magistrate's court on February 24, 1955. The witnesses you heard earlier on this program and others were called to give their testimony."

Commenting on this point of the show, the Pennsylvania Supreme Court said:

> The impression was here conveyed that the statements made by the anonymous voices into Taylor's tape recorder were exactly the same statements made at the magistrate's hearing, which they were not. Taylor summed up the whole matter by relating that Purcell had been fined $500 and that he was held in $1,000 bail for action by the grand jury on "other counts."
>
> He did not stop here. He went on to say that "There are, unfortunately, dishonest persons in any line of endeavor," and, that "the sentencing of a few racketeers is not enough." He then inserted into the broadcast an utterance he had gotten from the District Attorney and thus projected the illusion that the District Attorney was directly commenting on the Purcell conviction. The words of the District Attorney were: "In any lucrative racket you will always find some thugs getting into." He deplored that motorists who are in accidents are "very frequently quite terrified of the kind of mugs who sign them up" and that his office will see to it that justice is done to the "gentlemen who gypped them."
>
> Thus, through this manipulation of the audio tape and the employment of anonymous voices, the public was made to believe that

Purcell was a "mug," a "thug," a "racketeer," one who "gypped" others and one who "terrified" his victims who were afraid of "reprisals."

Taylor, who knew the realities, did not acquaint the public with the fact that Purcell announced, after the magistrate's action, that he would file an appeal and that the appeal was indeed officially filed long before the broadcast. Taylor said nothing to even suggest, which he of course had to know, that the Magistrate's proceeding was only a preliminary hearing and that, therefore, Purcell's side of the story was not heard. All the derogatory phrases and attacks on character employed in the broadcast were funneled by Taylor into a blunderbuss which was fired pointblank at Purcell, although the accusatory voices had not accused Purcell of illegally towing away cars.

No one at KYW ever called Purcell to get his side of the story. A jury awarded Purcell $60,000. Of that, $10,000 was compensatory damages and $50,000 punitive damages. In upholding the verdict, the state Supreme Court reduced the punitive damages to $30,000 (Purcell v. Westinghouse Broadcasting Co., 411 Pa. 167).

As far as public figures are concerned, the New York Times rule extends to programs originated by stations much of the same protection against damages that they have enjoyed since 1949 in broadcasts by political candidates themselves. In that year the Supreme Court considered a broadcast that A. C. Townley, a candidate for the United States Senate in North Dakota, made in 1956 over WDAY, a television and radio station in Fargo, North Dakota.

In his speech Townley accused his opponents and the Farmers Educational and Cooperative Union of America of conspiring to "establish a Communist Farmers Union Soviet right here in North Dakota." The Farmers Union sued Townley and WDAY for defamation.

WDAY pointed out that the Federal Communications Act required broadcasting stations to let all candidates for an office use their facilities if they permitted one to do so. At the same time, the law prohibited censorship of the broadcasts. Therefore, it argued, the station was immune from liability for defamatory statements made by speakers. The Supreme Court of North Dakota agreed that under such circumstances libel laws did not apply.

The Farmers Union then appealed to the United States Supreme Court. In a momentous five-to-four decision the high court held that broadcasting stations were immune from liability for libelous material broadcast by political candidates. The majority opinion explained:

> The decision a broadcasting station would have to make in censoring libelous discussion by a candidate is far from easy. Whether a statement is defamatory is rarely clear. Whether such a statement is actionably libelous is an even more complex question, involving as it does, consideration of various legal defenses such as "truth" and the privilege of fair comment. Such issues have always troubled courts. Yet, under petitioner's view of the statute they would have to be resolved by an individual licensee during the stress of a political campaign, often, necessarily, without adequate consideration or basis for decision. Quite possibly, if a station were held responsible for the broadcast of libelous material, all remarks even faintly objectionable would be excluded out of an excess of caution. Moreover, if any censorship were permissible, a station so inclined could intentionally inhibit a candidate's legitimate presentation under the guise of lawful censorship of libelous matter. Because of the time limitation inherent in a political campaign, erroneous decisions by a station could not be corrected by the courts promptly enough to permit the candidate to bring improperly excluded matter before the public. It follows from all this that allowing censorship, even of the attenuated type advocated here, would almost inevitably force a candidate to avoid controversial issues during political debates over radio and television, and hence restrict the coverage of consideration relevant to intelligent political decision. We cannot believe, and we certainly are unwilling to assume, that Congress intended any such result. [Farmers Educational and Cooperative Union v. WDAY 360 U.S. 525]

Broadcasting stations should pay more attention to the troubles that reliance on wire services can get them into. Radio and TV stations are notoriously deficient in original reporting. Some operate with only press-service radio wires. Others make a few checks here and there, skimming the cream off the obvious news. Dependence on reliable sources, such as press associations, is, as noted on page 293, a partial defense in a libel suit, but it will not completely eliminate the danger. Broadcasting stations should make the effort to check with local people mentioned in press dispatches to make certain that their side of the story is carried. An attorney for a plaintiff would not have to be overly clever to convince a jury that a wealthy TV station neglected the rules, not just of good journalism but also of decency, in failing to check both sides of a question.

The advice on corrections given on page 285 is equally applicable to broadcasting stations. If a station makes a mistake it should be willing to correct the error. Stations should also set up systems of checking on telephoned complaints of libel instead of dismissing them out of hand. During the trial of KYW, discussed earlier in this chapter, the wife of the plaintiff testified that she had called the program director the day of the broadcast, after she had read an advertisement for it, and had pleaded, "Would you please hold off broadcasting this program until the charges against my husband are either proved or disproven? . . . An appeal has been filed, and I think you should at least wait until this man has an opportunity to prove his innocence." The court noted that the jury must have regarded the refusal to cancel or postpone the broadcast as a mark of malice. An adept producer would usually not have to go so far as to throw out the entire show—but only to observe Federal Communications Commission regulations requiring broadcasting stations to give men in the news a square deal. There is no better practice for avoiding costly libel verdicts.

Chapter 21

DETECTIVE WORK

In television shows newspapermen are often pictured as investigators who crack cases that puzzle the cops. Such goings-on are so rare in the profession that the shows bring only snorts of disgust from reporters and editors. They know better. They know that the real detective work in the communications business goes on in the libel suits. Big papers and magazines hire their own gumshoes who dig up dirt that can be valuable in building up partial defenses at the trial. Some metropolitan papers are known to have full-time investigators. One such individual was listed as a reporter, although all his reports went to the front office. Other publications use law firms with trained private investigators whenever a suit is filed.

These investigators check into the background of the plaintiff, unearthing everything they can of his past. If he has made mistakes—and who hasn't?—they go into the dossier. Every aspect of his personal life, his schooling, his military service, his business affairs, his relationships with people is checked. If there has been an extramarital affair, a request while in military service to return to stateside duty from overseas, a secret business deal, a questionable ethical practice—almost any misstep from the straight and narrow path—he had better think again about the libel suit.

Sometimes the investigators can find enough evidence to prove the truth of the libelous charge. A perfect example was the experience of the *Independent* of Wilkes Barre, Pennsylvania. In 1951 it had accepted advertisements from both sides in an election campaign in nearby Nanticoke. One of the ads, labeled "Rags to Riches," noted that Nanticoke Mayor Anthony B. Dreier had acquired a $15,000 home and a new automobile after his election to the $100-a-month job and commented, "Not bad, Mr. Mayor."

Mayor Dreier protested that the ads pictured him as corrupt. He hired a lawyer to file a $100,000 libel suit against the *Independent*.

Believing that they needed a bigger gun to fight the battle, Mayor Dreier and his attorney went to Philadelphia and asked Laurence H. Eldredge, one of the country's leading libel lawyers, to try the case. Eldredge pointed out that the *Independent* had pleaded truth as its defense and said, "Mayor, have you any skeletons in your closet? If you have, I don't want to handle this case." Dreier assured Eldredge that he was an honest man and kept insisting on his innocence, even to the point of refusing a substantial cash settlement offered by the *Independent*.

Forced to fight the case, the *Independent* retained Richardson Dilworth, the Philadelphia District Attorney, who subsequently was elected Mayor, as its lawyer and ex-FBI agents as investigators. The former FBI men did a remarkable job. A banker testified that Dreier's home had cost only $5,150, with a $4,900 mortgage outstanding. But on cross-examination Dilworth forced Dreier to admit that about $9,000 in improvements had been made to the house, some by city employes. On the second day of the trial Dilworth asked Dreier about the appointment of Ralph Farmer to the Nanticoke police force.

> Q. When he came down, you said to him, he was number three on the civil service list and he could go to work Monday morning provided he paid you $250 in cash?
> A. No. I didn't.

When Eldredge objected, Dilworth said, "If I can't produce the truth and I can't produce Mr. Farmer, not only should there be a large verdict, but I should be disbarred." Farmer soon testified that he had gone to Dreier's office in the city building, where the Mayor told him that "the job was a political job and the boys had asked him to get $250 from me."

> Q. Did he identify the boys?
> A. No, he didn't. I told him I couldn't afford that much money as I was on relief at the present time. Then he told me maybe I could arrange it for $200 and I told him that was still too much money. I couldn't afford it, I was living on relief. Then later in the afternoon I saw him again. He asked me if I could pay $50 down and I could have the job and pay him later on.

Farmer said he had borrowed $50 from his landlord, had given it to Dreier and had been appointed to the police force the following day. Eldredge took much of the sting from Farmer's testimony by noting in cross-examination that a political campaign was under way and implied that perhaps the request had been for a political contribution. The next witness broke the case wide open. The ex-FBI men had traced Dreier's former secretary, Helene Stock, to Washington, where she was working for the Department of the Interior. Miss Stock told the court how Dreier had asked that she lie to a Federal grand jury investigating rackets if she were asked about his relationship with a pinball-machine operator. Then she related that Dreier had at first instructed her to keep a docket listing information on traffic tickets and fines paid. After two or three months, she said, Dreier told her to tear out the pages. From then on, she said, she was told to pick up from the police each day a box containing the traffic tickets and money. At the end of the month she totaled these and reported the amount to Dreier.

> Q. Can you tell us whether or not he turned in as much money as the receipts showed?
> A. Not always.
> Q. After the sheets were torn out, what was the regular practice as to how much he turned in as against the amount of the receipts that were shown?
> A. It all depended on the amount of money collected for traffic violations.
> Q. Can you give us a typical example?
> A. If $150 was collected for traffic violations he would report $97.
> Q. Now, who would tell you to report $97?
> A. The Mayor.

After a conference in the judge's chambers, Eldredge, obviously shaken, rose and asked for permission to dismiss the case with prejudice—meaning the suit could not be reinstated. The judge granted the motion and told Eldredge that his action "is a great credit to you and is evidence of the high reputation you bear among members of your profession." Mayor Dreier was later tried and convicted of criminal charges.

Tarnished Characters

The Dreier case is unusual in that the investigators found sufficient information to prove the truth of the charge. More often the investigators dig up material that shows that the plaintiff has a tarnished character. Evidence that would be barred at other trials is often permitted in libel cases. The reason is that this evidence is germane to the question of how good the reputation of the plaintiff was prior to the publication, and it goes to the issue of credibility. The jury receives this evidence at the same time that it is considering all the other aspects of the case. The law presumes that jurors can separate the evidence about the defendant's sources and about how much the plaintiff was damaged from the question of whether he was damaged at all. As a result, on the issue of good faith on the part of the publisher, hearsay, gossip and otherwise inadmissible evidence about the plaintiff are offered with devestating effect.

Investigators are highly confident of their ability to find prejudicial material against even the most upright citizen. This confidence was demonstrated by a remark made by a private eye employed by United Press after it had been sued by Gerard Hartzog, a Charleston, South Carolina, attorney, for reporting that he had been forcibly ejected from a Republican executive committee meeting in 1950. Three weeks after the suit was filed the investigator was heard to boast, "We will have Hartzog broke and in jail before the Republican National Convention." The case did not turn out that way. Hartzog was awarded $1,000 in compensatory damages and $4,000 in punitive damages. Later the verdict was overturned on the basis that the investigator's boast had been erroneously admitted as evidence of the news association's malice. The court pointed out that the investigator could not have had anything to do with the libelous dispatch because he had not been employed until after the suit was filed (Hartzog v. United Press Assns., 233 F. 2d 174). This United States Court of Appeals decision suggests that a publication or broadcasting station is not taking a chance on being found guilty of actual malice for hiring a private detective to check on a plaintiff. Hartzog eventually accepted a $3,250 settlement.

A Chicago libel trial illustrates how a large publication digs up personal material about a plaintiff and attempts to put it in the record. The case resulted from an item in the Chicago *Tribune* on March 30, 1952, concerning a vice raid on an apartment. The article (referred to on page 21) said that among those arrested was "Dolores Reising, 57, alias Eve Spiro and Eve John, who, police said, was known years ago as Accardo's woman friend." It also described her as the suspected keeper of the apartment. A second article gave the arrested woman's name as Dorothy Clark, but still listed Eve Spiro and Eve John as her aliases. Living in the same building on another floor was Eve Spiro John, and she sued for libel. Ultimately she lost her case, because the Illinois Supreme Court said that an alias meant a false name and that therefore the articles referred to someone besides Mrs. John. It also noted that under the innocent-construction rule followed in Illinois the article would have to be construed in the light most favorable to the defendant and that therefore the *Tribune* was not liable. But at the trial the *Tribune* lawyers could not assume such a favorable outcome. They had to be prepared to offer evidence that her reputation had not been greatly damaged. The *Tribune's* investigation of Mrs. John disclosed that she had been working for her doctor's degree in psychology and had written a thesis. A copy of the thesis was obtained at the University of Chicago library, and at the trial the *Tribune's* lawyer asked Mrs. John about it:

Q. This book dealt with sex in part and intersexuality, did it not?
A. Not as commonly construed at all.
Q. Well, did it deal—forgive me for asking these questions, but did it deal with attitudes toward sexual activities for example?
A. There was one rating scale which I used in determining the state of mental health of the subjects and that rating scale was used, yes. It related essentially to show how these people regarded loving others.
Q. Well, did it?
A. This is called sexuality in psychology, but it is not what the common man refers to, I think, by sexuality.

The appellate court explained what happened:

The defendant then offered the thesis in evidence, to which offer the plaintiff objected. The book was admitted in evidence. It appears in the record as a book of 155 typewritten pages. In it there is a discussion of hetero and homosexuality, and on at least one page of the book the discussion is quite frank and of a character which could be easily misunderstood by a person not familiar with the psychological connotations therein involved. The reason for offering the book apparently was not at the time it was offered, nor in this court, crystal clear to the defendant. In the trial court the defendant took the view that it tended to impeach the plaintiff, since the plaintiff had by implication indicated that she did not know that her landlady was keeping a house of prostitution.

The plaintiff objected to the introduction of the book on the ground that it was immaterial, irrelevant and prejudicial.

In this court the defendant contends that the document was relevant and impeaching evidence; that if plaintiff had been aware of her landlady's activities it would be a matter for the jury to consider in determining "reputation and damages;" that the fact that the plaintiff wrote this book would indicate that she had the kind of education and knowledge which would cause her to be aware of the house activities; and that it was not prejudicial because, as said in its brief: ". . . the obviously scientific discussion of sexual attitudes contained in the latter portion of the work is to be expected in light of today's widespread discussion and interest in the relationship between sex and human behavior."

The appeals court said that the thesis could not be considered as evidence tending to mitigate damages because it was prejudicial regarding Mrs. John. The *Tribune* stressed that the jury could have read the entire book and judged it, but the court said that "where a book of this character is involved, it does not require much time for a juror to pick out the salient passages and call the attention of the other jurors thereto." The extract of the case does show, however, how the *Tribune*'s law firm's staff of private investigators followed up depositions of the plaintiff's educational background. Once they knew she had written a dissertation, there was no problem finding it at the University of Chicago Library and making a copy of it. In this case the investigators, in various guises, also called on Mrs. John, her neighbors and employers to ascertain what they could about her background. (John v. Tribune Co., 28 Ill. App. 2d 300, 24 Ill. 2d 437).

Another example of investigation is the Johnson Publishing Company's effort to find information to support its article in *Jet* magazine that Edward Davis had had sexual relations with students while a teacher in Greenville, Alabama. (This case was cited on page 273 to illustrate another point.) If *Jet* had investigated Davis before publication as thoroughly as it did after he filed suit, it would not have found itself in such a fix. The following extract from the Alabama Supreme Court's decision reveals the extent to which it went:

The final effort made by the defendant to support the assertion relative to Davis's having sex relations with students was the testimony of Mary Frances Scott, a young woman who was living in Pensacola, Florida, at the time of the trial. She testified that she had sex relations with Davis while she was a student at the Greenville High School. She left school in November, 1956, approximately two months after Davis came to Greenville and almost three years before his resignation. The plaintiff introduced in evidence her own signed statement. In this statement she said that she had heard a rumor that Davis had something to do with some of the girls but she "didn't know anything about it." She further testified that one of the teachers at the Greenville School had told her that the publishing company would probably "pay any witness to tell the truth" about Davis. Mary Frances further testified that she told the teacher "she didn't want anything to do with that kind of money." She admited, however, in her testimony that she had contacted Ruth Howard and had told her that Johnson Publishing would arrange for her to go to college if she would make a statement against Davis. We note that Mary Frances Scott admitted that she had been offered money to testify in the instant case and in turn had invited Ruth Howard to testify against Davis for a payment of a college education and testify to a relationship with Davis, which he denied. Her testimony is totally unsupproted except by her contradictory statements. [Johnson Publishing Co. v. Davis, 271 Ala. 474]

Davis won that case, but how many libeled individuals would be willing to go through the ordeal of a trial, facing the possibility of such testimony?

In many jurisdictions the courts attempt to limit such material by permitting only evidence relating to the general character of the plaintiff or to acts specifically related to the one involved in the libelous publication. In the football libel case discussed in detail in Chapter 16, the *Saturday Evening Post* was permitted to introduce testimony by University of Georgia officials that Athletic Director Wally Butts' character was "bad" and that they would not believe what he said under oath. The officials were also allowed to testify that there was general dissatisfaction with Butts. But an attempt to show that a woman other than his wife had traveled with him to the Bahamas and on various other occasions had visited him in hotel and motel rooms and had been given a car by him was rejected. The *Post* argued that such evidence was admissible to refute Butts's testimony that he had never done anything to injure the university, to mitigate damages and "to prove that the plaintiff was a corrupt man." In denying admission of this evidence the court held that proof that the plaintiff had been guilty of offenses other than those imputed to him were not competent in mitigation of damages. The *Post's* information about Butts was obtained by private investigators. The magazine's law firm regularly makes use of them—as do attorneys serving other large news media. Time, Inc., keeps a firm of investigators busy checking for evidence it can use in libel suits.

While investigations are most likely to aid the defense, such tactics are a two-way street. The Reynolds-Pegler case is a prime example of the fact that the lawyers on both sides search out the past of their adversary for weak spots. An American priest in Moscow, the wife of the editor of *The New Yorker* and an admiral were among those testifying about stories they had heard about Reynolds. But Louis Nizer, Reynolds' lawyer, showed that he had looked into Pegler's life, too. Among other facts, he brought out that during World War I Pegler had worked as a hotel clerk in the Navy, instead of serving aboard a fighting ship. This point was effective in countering Pegler's contention that Reynolds had been a coward in World War II.

Use of Reporters

The newspaper's own reporters can be of value in investigations. In the nineteen-thirties a radio personality broadcast under the name of "The Mystery Chef." He told housewives how they could become the best cooks in the world. They did not have to take any cooking lessons; they did not have to read any books. All they had to do was settle down in a comfortable chair, light a cigarette, listen to him in the morning and use a lot of the baking powder he was advertising. Professional chefs who worked at night had a little spare time in the morning and they were listening, too. They soon became infuriated, and at a meeting of the American Culinary Federation, Inc., the president arose and bitterly denounced The Mystery Chef. Among other things, he said:

> There is one unknown man who admits to his radio audience that
> he is not a cook and not a chef, but yet gives out formulas that

are faulty and disgusting. He is cowardly, too. If he is really honest, why in hell doesn't he tell his name, hey?

A reporter for the New York *Herald Tribune* wrote a light story about it and then The Mystery Chef got angry. Under his real name, John MacPherson, he brought a libel action against the newspaper and a slander action against the president of the Culinary Federation. A number of defenses were available to the *Tribune*, including that of truth, which it could probably have proved, and of the right of reply, which was probably less troublesome. But the *Tribune*'s lawyer wanted to make sure that he was not overlooking any partial defenses either, so he ran a check on MacPherson's promotional material. In this material The Mystery Chef had boasted that he had been an extremely wealthy man in Scotland before he had left the Old World to teach cooking to the housewives of the New. In one of his brochures there was a picture of an imposing castle that MacPherson said was his boyhood home. Another photo showed MacPherson in kilts. A copy of the picture of the castle was sent to the *Tribune*'s London bureau with the question of what building it was. A British architect had no trouble identifying it as the Royal Naval Academy Building in Portsmouth. As for the kilts, a reporter found experts who asserted that every plaid in Scotland was represented in the costume. He also found a man who had rented the costume to MacPherson. The trial could have been a lot of fun, but MacPherson got an inkling of what was in the wind and, as the jury was about to be selected, decided to drop the case.

Reporters have also helped win cases in which truth had to be proved. Johanna Gadski was the wife of an officer in the Imperial German Army who was military attaché at the German Embassy in Washington prior to World War I. After the war Mrs. Gadski, who had been an opera singer, attempted a comeback, inspiring this comment from one of the *Tribune*'s music critics:

> Why give financial aid and comfort to the enemy of our country? At the home of one of the singers of an opera the sinking of the *Lusitania* was celebrated with quip and song amid the clinking of glasses.

Mrs. Gadski sued for libel. To sustain the defense of truth the *Tribune* had to show that a guest at Mrs. Gadski's home had sung a song commemorating the sinking of the *Lusitania* on May

7, 1915. Proof of the truth had to come from one of the persons who attended the party, which meant one of her friends. Complicating the difficulty was the fact that the song had been sung in German. The witness would have to be sufficiently bilingual to translate freely from German into English. Where could such a witness be found? The *Tribune* found her by resorting to the thinking that every good trial lawyer or investigatory reporter uses: when you need information about a woman, find a woman she has snubbed or shunned. She'll talk. At the trial a woman who had been Madame Gadski's guest at the party testified that she had heard the song sung and identified the singer.

The *Tribune's* lawyers also realized that its best hope of influencing the jury was to re-create the emotions that had swept the United States at the time of the sinking of the *Lusitania*. It had been nearly ten years since the helpless passenger ship had been torpedoed by a German U-boat. How could the outrage at the dastardly deed be revived? The *Tribune's* counsel decided that he would show that the *Lusitania* had been sunk. For the greatest dramatic impact the best witness would be a mother who had lost her child in the sinking. A reporter was assigned to find such a witness. Using the ship's manifest as a guide, he searched and searched. He could not find a mother who had lost a child, but he did come up with the next-best witness: a woman schoolteacher who had saved a child in the sinking. At the proper time the little schoolteacher was called to the witness stand. Was she on the *Lusitania* on its last trip? MacDonald De Witt, the *Tribune's* lawyer, asked. Yes, she was. Mrs. Gadski's attorney jumped to his feet, demanding to know the purpose of the testimony. Back came the answer: The article said that the *Lusitania* had been sunk and the *Tribune* was ready to prove every statement of fact in it.

"Well," said Mrs. Gadski's attorney, "I will concede that the *Lusitania* was sunk."

"We do not ask for a concession," DeWitt replied coldly. "We do not want a concession. We are here charged with a malicious libel. We are here to prove the truth of every statement of fact in our article as we have a right to."

The judge agreed to allow the testimony. The little schoolteacher then was led through the dramatic account of the sinking. She described the scene at the dinner table when the torpedo hit the ship. She told how she had struggled and finally had reached the deck. There she saw a baby, separated from its parents. She explained how she had lifted the child up and dropped it into the arms of someone in a lifeboat, thus saving the child's life. Did she remember how many people had lost their lives in the sinking of the *Lusitania?* She had been briefed, so she recalled the exact number—1,198. And how many were babies? "Thirty-five." "And there would have been thirty-six if you hadn't saved this one, would there not?" DeWitt asked.

"Yes."

The jury was out only fifteen minutes before bringing back a verdict for the *Tribune.*

The point need not be labored. A newspaper, magazine or broadcasting station should use the skill of its investigatory staff to help it in trials of libel cases. It should also look ahead, when gathering material for a sensitive story, to the possibility of litigation. In such situations it is wise to assign, somewhere along the line, a newsman who would make a good witness. In the eyes of the jury the defense witnesses are the defense. Of course, assignments cannot be made solely on this basis, but it is a factor to keep in mind. A clean-cut reporter, a soft-spoken desk man, a forthright editor can do much to give the publication the image of honesty and square dealing it needs to counteract the plaintiff's attempt to portray it as a sensation-seeking yellow rag recklessly ruining reputations just to sell papers.

Every newspaper should also maintain, under lock and key, a confidential file of material, especially adverse reports, on controversial persons who might be in the news. Every scrap of evidence should go into the folders. The editor will find the file valuable in making judgments on stories, and the lawyers will find the material useful as starting points in investigations if there are libel suits.

The newsman should not make any written notes about libel points that arise on a story, especially those expressing doubt about the advisability of carrying the item. Nor should such material be put in with the old clips or discussed in memos, cables or FYI's. The plaintiff can subpoena the defense files and offer, as damning evidence of malice, a memo that questioned the truth of the facts, the legal right to use the material or the possibility of harming the individual named in the article.

Detective work is only part of the effort that goes into the preparation of the defense in a libel suit. It is an indication of the care taken to make sure that nothing is overlooked. Few other legal cases are prepared with such concern for detail as the defense in a suit against a metropolitan newspaper, a magazine or broadcasting network. Smaller papers and broadcasting stations and the individuals who want to speak their minds benefit by the legal precedents set as the result of this careful work, as witnessed by *The New York Times* decision in the Sullivan Case. Fighting that case cost the *Times* a half-million dollars in legal fees.

Insurance

Libel insurance is good protection. It can be purchased from various companies. The policy should cover punitive damages, because they are the only real danger in libel litigation. The terms should permit the publisher or broadcasting station complete freedom in litigation. He should not be compelled to settle if the insurance company wants to. The upholding of an important principle may be worth the legal expenses even though an out-of-court settlement would save money. In addition, news media that settle without a fight soon become known in the legal profession as soft touches and are much more likely to be sued than those that refuse to make deals.

The Las Vegas *Sun* demonstrated to the Employers Reinsurance Company of Kansas City, one of the largest libel-insurance policy writers, why a newspaper should not give up. In a case mentioned on page 315, a jury awarded the plaintiff $190,000 because of references to his role in the "black-market sale" of babies. Employers Reinsurance, which had written the policy for the *Sun*, was willing to settle, rather than appeal, and negotiated an understanding with the plaintiff for $90,000 settlement. At this point H. M. Greenspun, the *Sun* publisher, called in a Washington, D.C., lawyer, Edward P. Morgan. Morgan told Employers Reinsurance that the *Sun*, a crusading newspaper, could not afford to get the reputation of making costly settlements. He suggested that the insurance company give the *Sun* the $90,000 in return for a complete release from its liability under the policy. Employers Reinsurance agreed. The *Sun* then battled the case to the Nevada

Supreme Court, where it was remanded to the lower courts for a new trial. As the new trial was about to start the plaintiff suggested a settlement amounting to about $7,000. The *Sun* accepted. This is probably the only case on record in which a newspaper made money on a libel case.

Chapter 22

CRIMINAL LIBEL

LIBEL IS SELDOM PROSECUTED BY THE STATE AS A CRIME. THE OUT-raged citizen who wants the district attorney to punish the libeler almost always is turned away. The DA does not want to be bothered, since a civil remedy exists for the wrongdoing. Most likely he will tell the complainant something like this: "Why don't you sue? If what you tell me about this fellow is true and I prosecute, I may be able to have him thrown in jail for a few months and fined a couple hundred bucks. But if you sue you have a good chance of collecting a big wad of dough. That'll not only hit him where it hurts, it'll also give you traveling money for a vacation in Acapulco, where you can forget about the lies he's been telling about you."

Before criminal libel was abolished in New York, the District Attorney for New York County would not touch a criminal libel case unless important personalities were involved and then only when the plaintiff succeeded in persuading a criminal court to hold the defendant for indictment. In the rare instances where this occurred, some assistant District Attorney was usually assigned, and he prosecuted with only mild enthusiasm. An example involved an action against Walter Winchell. One day in his column he coined the word "Arabastard"—a combination that did not get by an Arab, who was referred to by name. He got quite angry and decided that he would have Winchell thrown in jail. Revenge, not money, was his motive. So he swore out a complaint in the Magistrate's Court and got a summons, and Walter Winchell was required to put up a legal defense. After a long hearing the magistrate wrote an opinion that endeared him to Winchell's following, which in those days was large. The magistrate said he was not sure what "Arabastard" meant. But, he went on, assuming it meant "Arab bastard," what was so bad about that? Were not

Erasmus and Alexander Hamilton bastards? And do you not frequently greet an old college friend at a reunion by slapping him on the back and exclaiming, "How are you, you old bastard?" So the magistrate concluded that the term "bastard" was not a word of opprobrium but of endearment—a finding that few other courts would uphold.

A more recent example occurred in 1954 when the late Mike Quill, then head of the Transport Workers Union, made a statement for publication to the effect that a member of the New York Transit Authority had agreed to support his demands against it if the Congress of Industrial Organizations would support the Authority member as a candidate for Special-Sessions judge. The District Attorney prosecuted. Four years later Quill moved to dismiss the indictment, and the complainant stated that he did not request the grand jury or the District Attorney to indict nor did he consider that he had been libeled. After all, he said, it had been made in the heat of a labor dispute, without any malice and for the purpose of gaining advantage for his union in the negotiations. The court dismissed the indictment only because the District Attorney joined in the request and added:

> But criminal libel is a special kind of crime. Criminal prosecutions are infrequent. The theory, in simplest terms, is that when an individual is libeled, he has an adequate remedy in a civil suit for damages. The public suffers no injury. Vindication for the individual and adequate compensation for the injury done him may be obtained as well in the civil courts. Thus the rule has always been, that the remedy of criminal prosecution should only be sought where the wrong is of so flagrant a character as to make a criminal prosecution necessary on public grounds. [People v. Quill, 11 Misc. 2d (N.Y.) 512, 514]

Criminal Libel More Sweeping

There is no substantial difference between what constitutes a libel of a living person or of a corporation in a criminal prosecution and in a civil action. Any publication that would be defamatory for the tort of libel would also be defamatory for the crime of libel.

But the criminal law goes a little further. A publication defamatory of the deceased will support a prosecution under the criminal law, although it cannot be the basis for a civil suit for damages unless there is a state statute permitting such action. As a practical matter, defamation of the dead is virtually never prosecuted.

In some states libeling an entire class can lead to criminal charges. These states have special laws permitting prosecution for defamation of religions, races, nationalities and groups with or without identification of individuals—a possibility not overlooked in combating extremist groups.

Criminal libel is usually a misdemeanor, not a felony. In New York prior to repeal, the punishment prescribed by statute was not more than one year in prison or a fine of not more than $500 or both. In the case of a corporation, obviously only the fine can be imposed.

Slander, although a tort, is not usually a crime. The person who feels great resentment against someone can vent his spleen without risk of jail if he uses the spoken rather than the written word. He might, of course, be hit with a slander suit and suffer a money judgment.

Nuts and Kooks

Newsmen who work for a paper, magazine or broadcasting station will almost never face a criminal-libel prosecution. Even the writer who goes off the deep end and publishes a particularly heinous defamation without a complete defense is not likely to be prosecuted. But let that same newsman turn into a nut or kook or join a radical group of either the left or the right and the district attorney will take a closer look at him. Now the public peace is considered threatened because the actions of some extremist groups can lead to riots. In such cases the criminal-libel laws have been used.

On March 22, 1962, eight adherents of the American Nazi party drove to a Chicago theater that was showing the film *Sergeants Three*, starring Sammy Davis, Jr., the Negro entertainer who adopted the Jewish faith and who married May Britt, a Swedish girl. At the theater some of the Nazis, wearing storm-trooper-like uniforms, began to march up and down carrying signs with such inscriptions as "How to Be a Jew, Lesson No. 1 By Sammy the

Kosher-Coon." They also passed out leaflets emblazoned with large headlines:

NIGGERS!

YOU TOO CAN

BE A JEW!

It's Easy!   *It's Fun!*   *Insult the White Folks!*
Make More Money!   *Love the White Women!!!!*

Continuing for a number of hundred words, the leaflets offered a "correspondence course" so "you can become a Jew Nigger and be rich, famous and arrogant." Within a few minutes more than 200 people had gathered, and the police asked the Nazis to stop picketing. Soon a man appeared with a baseball bat, another with a metal pipe and a third with a sash weight and the crowd started to push forward. The police then arrested the Nazis, three of whom were later convicted of criminal defamation and disorderly conduct. Two received a year in jail and one 90 days (City of Chicago v. Lambert, 47 Ill. App. 2d 151).

The United States Supreme Court has thrown doubt on the use of criminal libel laws in such instances. Overturning the six-month jail sentence and $3,000 fine of a youth, who put out a mimeograph sheet libeling law enforcement officers and a newspaper official in a Kentucky coal strike, the court said in 1966 that care must be taken "lest, under the guise of regulating conduct that is reachable by the police power, freedom of speech or of the press suffer." (Ashton v. Kentucky 384 U.S. 195).

Foes of Public Officials

In addition to being used against extremists, the criminal-libel laws have also been invoked by district attorneys to clear fellow public officials. The case of Mayor Curley of Boston, discussed on page 108, was a criminal prosecution. In Oregon, a common scold was prosecuted for writing a letter to the City Manager of Baker in which he said:

> I would like to bring to your personal attention the action of Fred Still, Chief of Police, in coming to my home, waving a gun in a menacing manner, swearing, and threatening me; all in front

of children and my nice neighbors. . . . Also for your personal attention the fact that my home was entered by Baker police and searched; rather ransacked is more appropriate, and four (4) of my good suits and an $880.00 diamond ring are missing. I have witnesses for the two (2) times that I know my home was robbed by the Baker police. . . .

The trial judge expressed the conviction that the case suggested medical, rather than criminal, procedures and the Oregon Supreme Court agreed (State of Oregon v. Kerekes, 225 Ore. 352).

The Tennessee Supreme Court upheld the indictment of Erwin Police Chief Leonard T. Guinn for writing a letter to the Johnson City *Press-Chronicle* on July 6, 1960. Referring to an investigation by the Attorney General into complaints by citizens, Chief Guinn wrote:

I have nothing to hide. Let them investigate me to their heart's content, but let them do so in an open and honorable fashion and according to the concepts of American justice. I resent, and the people resent, their Hitler-like tactics.

The trial judge ruled that the letter was not libelous. The State Supreme Court said that the term "Hitler-like" might not be defamatory when applied to an ordinary citizen or to a lawyer, but it certainly was to a district attorney, who was presumed to be acting impartially in the interests of justice (State of Tennessee v. Guinn, 208 Tenn. 527). An agreement was eventually reached whereby Guinn pleaded guilty and paid a $50 fine and costs.

If the defamation is particularly vicious, the public officials prefer a criminal prosecution. For some defamed a state prosecution shows purity of motives—they cannot collect any damages and prosecution will be by a third party, the district attorney. Such a case involved Senator Thomas H. Kuchel of California, who, in 1964 and 1965, was the target of widespread gossip. The rumors, spread by right-wing extremists, were that the Senator had been arrested in Los Angeles in 1949 in an incident involving drunken driving and homosexuality. Lending substance to the rumors was an affidavit of a former Los Angeles police officer. Senator Kuchel asked the Los Angeles authorities to investigate. They found the charges against Kuchel to be baseless. Four men were indicted on charges of criminal defamation and, while the case was settled short of a trial, Senator Kuchel was cleared through a series of retractions and apologies.

In other criminal prosecutions, like the Curley-Enwright case, the motive is obviously vengeance. The Supreme Court's decision in *The New York Times* case and extension of the rule to criminal prosecutions in the Garrison case (as discussed in Chapter 12) fortunately prevent most of these prosecutions. The court's 1966 ruling in Ashton v. Kentucky also seems to bar such cases.

Truth as a Defense

As to the defense of truth, the New York Penal Law, before its repeal in 1966, provided: "The publication is justified when the matter charged as libelous is true and was published with good motives and for justiable ends."

Note that the defense of truth is qualified. In a civil action New York law holds that the defense of truth is absolute, regardless of actual malice on the part of the publisher and regardless of the publisher's motives and purposes. But in a criminal prosecution for libel, truth is a qualified defense. To satisfy the defense of truth the accused must show that the matter was published with good motives and justifiable ends. The reason for this is that the purpose of the criminal law is to prevent riots and other violence, not to decide the justice of an accusation.

In their appeal from conviction for defamation while picketing the Sammy Davis movie, the American Nazis insisted that there was nothing libelous about their signs and leaflets. They explained that "Kosher" meant "pure," and that "coon" was used in songs and literature without any offensive imputations. Besides, the Nazis said, the statements were true. But the Appellate Court of Illinois denied the defense of truth, noting that the state law permitted this defense in criminal defamation only when "communicated with good motives and for justifiable ends." Those conditions, the court said, did not exist.

Reports of Proceedings and Officials

The defense of reporting an official proceeding and the defense under the New York Times rule are the same for criminal cases as they are for civil. The Supreme Court set the same standard for judging the actual malice necessary to lose the latter defense in both kinds of cases—knowledge that the defamation was false or reckless disregard of whether it was false (Garrison v. State of Louisiana, 379 U.S. 64). The Kuchel case is an excellent example of actual malice through lying.

Fair Comment

In fair-comment cases, the malice that will defeat the defense in a criminal prosecution is equated with a dishonest expression of opinion.

Partial Defenses

No partial defenses exist in criminal-libel prosecutions. Neither are there degrees of guilt. The publisher is either guilty or not guilty. However, the same sort of facts that would constitute a partial defense in a civil action would receive favorable consideration by a court in determining the sentence.

In a trial of a civil action, a great deal is heard about the bad reputation of the plaintiff, if he or she happens to have a bad reputation. But in a criminal prosecution little or nothing is heard concerning the reputation of the complainant—good, bad or indifferent—except on the issue of credibility. Theoretically, in a criminal prosecution, since the issue is not damages, the reputation of the person who has been libled is immaterial. Since the purpose of the criminal law is to prevent breaches of the peace, a bad man or a man with a bad reputation is as likely to disturb the peace as a man with an unblemished reputation. This reason was pointed out by a court with these words:

> A criminal libel is prosecuted in the name of the people, not for the purpose of redressing an injury done to an individual, but is so prosecuted and punished as a crime, for the reason that it tends to provoke animosity and violence, and to disturb the public peace and repose, and certainly it will not be for a moment contended that the threatened danger to the public peace is not as great when the person libeled is a bad man as when he is a good man. In a civil action, brought by an individual to obtain satisfaction for an injury to his reputation caused by the publication of a libel, the bad reputation of the complainant becomes material as affecting the measure of damages, while in a criminal action brought in the name of the people the individual libeled, so far as personal redress and satisfaction are concerned, is not considered. [People v. Stokes, 30 Abbott's New Cases (N.Y.) 200, 24 N.Y. Supp 727]

Now this may be good law, but followed to its logical conclusion it is absurd. The court says in effect, that libel is a crime because it tends to disturb the peace and that a libel of a bad man is at least as likely to disturb the public peace as the libel of a good man, and, therefore, the character of the person libeled is immaterial. If the person libeled is bad, there is more likelihood of causing a little private war such as that between the Hatfields and the McCoys than there would be if the person libeled were a good man. On that theory it would be a worse crime to libel Tony (Ducks) Corallo than it would be to libel a Roman Catholic Cardinal, for Tony would surely call on his Mafia pals to disturb the peace, while the Cardinal would more likely offer up a prayer for the person who defamed him. Despite the theory, anyone with an overwhelming urge to become a defendant in a criminal libel prosecution would be well advised to pick on a man like Corallo rather than one like the cardinal.

Chapter 23

ONE LAST WORD

The picture that emerges from this study of libel is one that heartens and at the same time appalls the observer. He is heartened by the trend in the law toward more freedom to speak out on public affairs. He is appalled by the possible use of that freedom to wreck an innocent man's reputation.

There is no question that the danger of abuse exists. The New York Times rule arms the irresponsible, as well as the responsible, journalist with a weapon of awesome power. The privilege of reporting an official proceeding is constantly being expanded. Fair comment is becoming easier and easier to invoke. Malice is harder and harder to prove.

Undoubtedly some newsmen misuse their power. Untruths can lead to the ouster of dedicated and capable public officials. Misstatements of facts do result in the adoption of unwise policies. Good men are sometimes maligned and bad men do sometimes prevail. Without question the newsman who wants to destroy a man has a good chance of doing so and getting away with it. But the trend toward freedom must be considered in its historical context.

From its earliest beginnings the law of defamation has evolved by the balancing of conflicting interests—the interest of the individual in the protection of his reputation, the interest of the writer in communicating facts and ideas to his readers and the interest of the public in information. As our democratic society develops, the interest of the public in information weighs ever more heavily on the scales when the conflicting interests are balanced. There are times when the scales seem tipped against the individual.

The solution for this problem is not a tightening of the libel laws. As John Stuart Mill said in "On Liberty," "[to] argue sophistically, to suppress facts or arguments, to misstate the elements of the case, or misrepresent the opposite opinion . . . all this, even to the most aggravated degree, is so continually done in perfect good faith, by persons who are not considered, and in many other respects may not deserve to be considered, ignorant or incompetent, that it is rarely possible, on adequate grounds, conscientiously to stamp the misrepresentation morally culpable; and still less could law presume to interfere with this kind of controversial misconduct."

This argument—that whatever is added to the field of libel is taken from the field of debate—may be sound, but, in the end, only the newsman can make sure it prevails. Others, of course, enjoy the same freedom of expression, but it is the practicing journalist who exercises it most publicly. In the past some publishers, writers and editors have shown lack of care in getting the facts, unconcern about telling all sides of a controversy and blind disregard of the individual's rights. These failings make it difficult to defend the expanding freedom the press enjoys. It is up to the newsman to prove that he can measure up to the trust the law has placed in him.

Epilogue

PRIVACY

THE JOURNALIST IS NOT HOME FREE JUST BECAUSE HE HAS ERECTED defenses against libel. There is a growing trend in law that poses increasing dangers: the concept of privacy.

Privacy and libel, although sometimes confused, are separate, distinct torts, with different origins and developments. The only common denominator is that both involve the written word or visual reproduction. Whereas libel deals with injury done to a person's reputation, privacy is designed to protect an individual's right to live a private existence safe from public stares.

The right of privacy has been defined as the right to be let alone; the right of a person to be free from unwarranted publicity about his personal life; the right to live without unwarranted interference by the public regarding matters that the public has no need to know. One author referred to the right of privacy as a principle designed to fill the breach in social justice formerly occupied by the horsewhip. This description is unnecessarily dramatic, but it does indicate the origins of privacy.

The law of privacy does not predate the twentieth century. The English common law did not recognize a right of privacy; yet, paradoxically, such a right was recognized in other systems of jurisprudence, some predating common-law origins.

Privacy was recognized in the Greek law as *contumelia*, and in the Roman law as *iniuria*. The German law gave it recognition under *Personlichkeitsrecht*. In France, while there was no special tort, the right of privacy received wide protection under the doctrine *la droit de la personnalité*, and the Swiss Codes called it *Geheimsspare*.

Even though the English common law did not recognize a right of privacy as such, it did afford some protection against a private invasion if the litigant could point to some collateral property right or the violation of a confidential relationship. Thus, early in the nineteenth century, a British Court of Chancery restrained the publication of a private letter, and later a student's publication for profit of lectures delivered by a surgeon, on the ground that the writer and surgeon had property rights in the documents. Midway through the nineteenth century, a British court enjoined the reproduction of several etchings that Queen Victoria and her Prince Consort had made for their amusement on the ground that the etchings had been procured through the violation of a confidential relationship.

It was not until 1890, when yellow journalism, with its sensationalized human interest stories, obsession with gossip, sex and murder, and unrestrained emotional advertising, was dominating the American press, that the doctrine of privacy was given its philosophic underpinnings in the United States. The authors were Charles Warren and Louis Brandeis, who later became a great associate justice of the Supreme Court. They wrote a brilliant article in an early edition of the *Harvard Law Review*. Their thesis was that all the cases which they collected could be rationalized only through a privacy doctrine and they contended vigorously that public policy required a forthright recognition of a right of privacy. To buttress their argument, they criticized the press and, among other things, wrote:

> The press is overstepping in every direction the obvious bounds of propriety and decency. Gossip is no longer the resource of the idle and of the vicious but has become a trade which is pursued with industry as well as effrontery. To satisfy a prurient taste the details of sexual relations are spread broadcast in the columns of the daily papers. To occupy the indolent, column upon column is filled with idle gossip which can only be procured by intrusion upon the domestic circle. [4 *Harvard Law Review* 193]

The full impact of this article was not felt for over half a century, but no law-review article has had a greater cumulative effect on the law.

Twelve years after publication of the article, the New York Court of Appeals was called upon to decide whether the right of privacy should be recognized as a common-law right. A flour company had used a picture of a young girl, Abigail Roberson, with-

out her consent to advertise its flour. She was the "flower of the
flock" and the "best of the bunch." Her red cheeks were attributed
to eating food made from flour from the Franklin Mills. By a 4–3
vote, the Court of Appeals decided that there was no recognizable
common-law right of privacy but expressed sympathy for her
and suggested that the legislature act (Roberson v. Rochester
Folding Box Co., 171 N.Y. 538).

A storm of professional and popular disapproval greeted the
opinion. The press joined the chorus and *The New York Times*
criticized the court severely in an editorial. Indeed, the criticism
was so great that one member of the court took the unprecedented step of writing an article in the *Columbia Law Review*
justifying the opinion.

The New York legislature acted swiftly, and in its next session,
1903, passed what is now known as Sections 50 and 51 of the
Civil Rights Law. Section 50 makes it a misdemeanor in New
York to use a living person's name, picture or portrait "for advertising purposes or purposes of trade" without his or her written
consent. Section 51 gives the victim the right to sue.

Two years later, the Georgia Supreme Court was called upon
to review a similar case. The Georgia court unanimously decided
that there was a recognizable right of privacy under the common
law, and permitted recovery of damages for the unauthorized use
of the name of the litigant for advertising purposes (Pavesich v.
New England Life Ins. Co., 122 Ga. 190).

Utah and Virginia followed New York's lead and adopted statutes. Both of these statutes are similar to New York's and both
prohibit the use of a person's name, portrait or picture "for advertising purposes or purposes of trade." The Virginia statute limits
damages to persons who are residents of that state.

Privacy Extension

The right of privacy has now been judicially recognized as a
common-law right in 37 jurisdictions: Alabama, Arizona, Arkansas, California, Colorado, Connecticut, Delaware, District of
Columbia, Florida, Georgia, Hawaii, Idaho, Illinois, Indiana,
Iowa, Kansas, Kentucky, Louisiana, Maryland, Michigan, Mississippi, Missouri, Montana, Nevada, New Hampshire, New Jersey,

New Mexico, North Carolina, Ohio, Oklahoma, Oregon, Pennsylvania, South Carolina, South Dakota, Tennessee, Texas and West Virginia.

The right of privacy has been rejected in three states—Nebraska, Rhode Island and Wisconsin. The situation in Oklahoma requires a word of explanation. A Federal District Court in Connecticut held that there was a common-law right of privacy in Oklahoma although no Oklahoma state court had so decided. Then Oklahoma adopted a privacy statute similar to the New York law. So, presumably, Oklahoma litigants have it both ways, as a common-law right and a statutory right.

In four states, Alaska, Massachusetts, Minnesota and Washington, courts have referred to the right of privacy without directly passing upon it.

In only four states, all sparsely settled, has there been complete silence: Maine, North Dakota, Vermont and Wyoming.

Some states have special privacy statutes that deal with specific situations, such as police material. In Massachusetts, for example, it is against the law to give out or receive the arrest records of an individual, although police blotters are open to inspection by reporters. Thus it is illegal for the police or the district attorney in Massachusetts to do what their counterparts in other states do: release the previous record of a man picked up for murder.

There is a Federal statute prohibiting the registration of a portrait of a living person as a trademark without his written consent. Nor may the portrait of a deceased President of the United States be used during the lifetime of his widow.

The right of privacy has developed along remarkably similar lines in the states that recognize it as a common-law right and the states that recognize it as a right by statute. While the right is limited in the states that have statutes, cases in common-law jurisdictions are frequently cited in the statutory states, and vice versa.

The right of privacy has not been recognized in England, although a case a few years ago suggests that recognition may be in the offing. A newspaper photographer attended a wedding reception uninvited, and began taking pictures contrary to the wishes of the groom, who punched him in the nose. When the groom was sued for assault and battery, the court castigated the photographer.

To determine how far protection is to be extended, certain conflicting interests must be balanced, exactly as conflicting interests are balanced in the law of defamation. Thus the right of the author or writer to express himself has to be balanced against the right of an individual to be protected against undue and sensational publicity; there is also the right of the public to information and news, and even some entertainment at the expense of a public figure.

Personal Right

The right of privacy is a personal right and, in common-law states, in the absence of a statute granting legal standing to survivors, terminates with the death of the offended individual. Thus, the widow of Al Capone, the Chicago mobster of the 1920's and 1930's, learned to her dismay that there was no survivorship. She complained about a motion picture which she alleged appropriated Al's name, likeness and personality for commercial gain. She was ushered out of court empty-handed (Maritote and Capone v. Desilu Productions, Inc., 345 F.2d 418).

One of the grandchildren of Robert Schumann sued Loew's Theatre when it showed *The Song of Love,* a motion picture about the life of her grandfather, the German composer who died in 1856. She claimed a derivative right to protect the privacy of her grandfather, who was no longer in the court's jurisdiction. She too was sent home empty-handed (Schumann v. Loew's Inc., 135 N.Y.S. 2d 361). The New York Statute expressly uses the term "of any *living* person" so that non-survivorship is clear. The Virginia statute, however, endeavors to extend the right to the surviving spouse or next of kin, and the same thing is true of the Utah statute. Both laws raise problems that need not be discussed here, and no one who has traveled through Virginia and noticed the number of Thomas Jefferson Hotels and James Madison Motels can believe that the survivorship provision of the Virginia statute is taken seriously.

One hypersensitive person sought to enjoin the use of a photograph of his dog, but the court quite properly decided that neither he nor his dog had a right to privacy in the dog's picture.

Limits of the Doctrine

On September 16, 1934, the New York *Sunday Mirror* published an illustrated article about the Hindu rope trick. The title to the article was "I saw the famous rope trick—but it did not really happen." The article was illustrated with a picture of Sarat Lahiri. He had nothing to do with the rope trick, but he was a Hindu musician, and his picture did have a remote connection with the article. When the plaintiff sued, New York Supreme Court Justice Bernard L. Shientag outlined certain rules applicable to unauthorized newspaper publications of photographs (and of course the same rules apply to the unauthorized use of names) as follows:

1. Recovery may be had under the statute if the photograph is published in or as part of an advertisement, or for advertising purposes.
2. The statute is violated if the photograph is used in connection with an article of fiction in any part of the newspaper.
3. There may be no recovery under the statute for publication of a photograph in connection with an article of current news or immediate public interest.
4. Newspapers publish articles which are neither strictly news items nor strictly fictional in character. They are not the responses to an event of peculiarly immediate interest but, though based on fact, are used to satisfy an ever-present educational need. Such articles include, among others, travel stories, stories of distant places, tales of historic personages and events, the reproduction of items of past news, and surveys of social conditions. These are articles educational and informative in character. As a general rule, such cases are not within the purview of the statute. [Lahiri v. Daily Mirror, Inc., 162 Misc. (N.Y.) 776,782]

The court held that Lahiri fell within the last category and sent him home.

The 1937 Lahiri case has become a landmark, and the rules listed above have been repeatedly referred to in court opinions in subsequent litigation.

Advertising

The first Shientag rule relates to advertising. The contents of a newspaper or magazine can be roughly divided into two classifications: editorial matter and advertising matter. An advertisement is a solicitation of patronage for a particular service or product. It is designed to sell wares or ideas. It is physically segregated from other material in a publication and is obviously so segregated. It is usually paid for by someone not identified with the newspaper or magazine wherein it appears, although publishers sometimes promote their own product through advertisements in their own publications. All other matters in a newspaper or magazine, such as news, special features, editorials, letters to the editors, crossword puzzles, comics and cartoons, whether written by the staff or produced from other sources, constitute editorial copy.

The right of an individual to prevent the use of his name, picture or portrait in an advertisement is fairly clear. One should not be able to profit from the commercial use of another's name or picture and use the name or picture of an individual without his consent to sell whiskey or cosmetics. Courts have been fairly strict with respect to advertisements, but there are two exceptions.

The most notable exception is the incidental use of a name or picture in a segregated news dispatch or gossip commentary in connection with a paid advertisement but wholly unrelated to the advertised product or business.

In addition, some advertisers use their space to discuss public issues. The advertisement is of course signed, but the use of a person's name in the editorial copy within the advertisement is not a forbidden use.

A television case illustrates the correct way to keep advertising segregated. Arsene Gautier was a successful trainer of animals who had agreed to perform between the halves of a professional football game in Griffith Stadium in Washington, the home of the Redskins. Instead of dancing girls, he had some dancing dogs. He announced to the Redskins management before the game that while he was being paid well for his performance before the 35,000 people who would be in the park, he was not being paid to perform before the great unseen audience and did not wish to have his show telecast without additional compensation in a substantial amount. The management considered this a shakedown, and told him that the telecast of the intermission show would go on anyway. After pocketing the agreed sum, he brought a privacy action and alleged that his name and picture had been used without his consent to advertise Chesterfield cigarettes, which had sponsored the telecast of the game. The New York Court of Appeals held that since Gautier's name and picture were segregated from the commercial, there was no violation of the New York statute, and the mere fact that the telecast was sponsored did not constitute a violation. Gautier was no shrinking violet. He had exposed himself and his dogs to a vast audience, and privacy was the one thing he did not want or need in his occupation (Gautier v. Pro Football, Inc., 304 N.Y. 354).

The other exception is the use in an advertisement of editorial copy that by itself would not violate the right of privacy. A *New York* magazine case demonstrates the freedom to publish such material. In December, 1974, *New York* published a year-end edition concerning events at mid-century. Included in this review was an article by Betty Friedan, describing how 25 years earlier, prior to her emergence as a leader of the feminist movement, she had been a contented housewife. She produced a picture taken in 1949 of herself, her former husband, Carl Friedan, and their son Danny, which was used to illustrate the article. There was no privacy violation because it was used to illustrate editorial copy. *New York* magazine promoted its December, 1974, issue with telecasts on four major television stations. To illustrate the article, the picture of Betty, Carl and Danny was flashed on the screen. Carl Friedan took exception and brought suit, but since the advertising use of his picture was from editorial copy that was not objectionable, the court held that the advertisement shared the privilege of the article itself and that his right of privacy was subordinate to the public interest in the news (Friedan v. Friedan, 414 F. Supp. 77).

The Shirley Booth case goes one step further. The actress was vacationing in a prominent resort called Round Hill in Jamaica. A photographer for the travel magazine *Holiday*, while taking photographs of Round Hill and its guests, snapped Ms. Booth. While she never consented in writing to the publication of her picture, the use of it in editorial copy describing the attributes of Jamaica and Round Hill was a permitted use. These pictures were taken in January, 1958, and the photographs appeared in the magazine's February, 1959, issue. In June of 1959 the same photograph was used in a full-page advertisement that *Holiday* inserted in the *New Yorker* magazine and *Advertising Age*. The reproduction of her picture to illustrate the quality and contents of the periodical, even though it appeared in another medium, was not considered a violation of her right of privacy (Booth v. Curtis Publishing Co., 15 AD (N.Y.) 2d 343, aff'd. 11 N.Y. 2d 907). Aside from these two exceptions, the privacy of an individual is violated by the use of his or her picture in an advertisement without his or her consent.

Purposes of Trade

The other three situations outlined by Justice Shientag in the Lahiri case relate to the purposes of trade. There is, of course, no violation of the statute for the use of a picture in a news article. Courts have recognized the overriding social interest in the dissemination of news, and an almost absolute privilege has been extended to the use of names and pictures in connection with reporting of news events. This privilege includes names and pictures not only in newspapers, but also in newsreels, magazines and even comic books, and courts have not undertaken the dangerous task of passing value judgment on the content of news. The deliberations of the United Nations and the chit-chat of a society editor have received equal protection.

A classic case involved William James Sidis, a famous child prodigy in 1910. At the age of 11 he lectured to distinguished mathematicians on the subject of four-dimensional bodies. At the age of 16 he graduated from Harvard. After that, he sought to live his life as unobtrusively as possible. Years later, *New Yorker* magazine published a biographical sketch of him, along with a cartoon. It was a merciless dissection of the intimate details of his personal life, with elaborate accounts of his passion for privacy and the pitiable lengths to which he had gone to avoid public scrutiny. But he had been a public figure, and his life was of interest to the public. The Court of Appeals of the Second Circuit held that his privacy had not been invaded and said: "Everyone will agree that at some point the public interest in obtaining information becomes dominant over the individual's desire for privacy" (Sidis v. F-R Pub. Corporation, 113 F.2d 806, cert. denied 311 U.S. 711).

Duncan Murray was in the habit of attending the St. Patrick's Day parade in New York, clownishly dressed, with a green tie and high hat crowned with a garland of shamrocks. His picture was taken by a photographer seeking feature pictures of the parade, and was published two years later on the cover of *New York* magazine to illustrate its St. Patrick's Day issue. Murray sued for invasion of privacy, but was denied damages. The New York Court of Appeals said:

> The law is settled, however, that "A picture illustrating an article on a matter of public interest is not considered used for the purposes of trade or advertising within the prohibition of the statute . . . unless it has no real relationship to the article . . . or unless the article is an advertisement in disguise." [Murray v. New York Magazine Co., 27 N.Y. 2d 406, 408-9]

Fictionalization

The second and fourth categories of Justice Schientag's outline of rules may be treated together. The question here involves unauthorized use of a picture or name in an article of fiction, or the fictionalization, in part, of an educational article, such as one dealing with historical personages, past events or surveys of social conditions.

Here, the balancing of conflicting interests is paramount in reaching a definitive answer. If the person whose name or picture is used is a public figure, more leeway is allowed than for a private individual.

One of the earlier cases involved a newsreel. John R. Binns was the wireless operator aboard the S.S. *Republic*. On January 23, 1909, the *Republic* and the *Florida* collided at sea. Binns sent out the distress call "C.Q.D.," which was received by the steamship *Baltic*. The messages exchanged by the *Baltic* and the *Republic* resulted in the *Baltic*'s going to the rescue of the *Republic*'s pas-

sengers, who were picked up and transported to New York. Soon
after the event, the Vitagraph Company produced a series of pictures entitled: "C.Q.D. or Saved by Wireless; A True Story of the
Wreck of the Republic." The pictures, except for one of the *Baltic*
entering New York harbor, were made in the studio of Vitagraph
Company. Actors were employed, and one impersonated the
plaintiff. The series of pictures commenced with a sub-series entitled "John R. Binns, the Wireless Operator in his Cabin Aboard
the S.S. Republic." This sub-series was followed by others, the
last entitled "Jack Binns and his Good American Smile."

Either Binns did not like the pictures, or he felt that he should
have been compensated for them. Although the Court did not use
the word "fictionalization," that was the basis of its decision. It
emphasized that the pictures were imaginary and not real, and
that Binns was impersonated by a professional actor. He
recovered a judgment of $12,500 (Binns v. Vitagraph Company,
210 N.Y. 51).

The degree of fictionalization is important. Serge Koussevitzky
was an eminent conductor of a world-renowned symphony
orchestra and an outstanding international figure in the field of
music. When an unauthorized biography of him was published,
Koussevitzky sought an injunction, complaining that it contained
much objectionable, untruthful, fictitious and defamatory matter.
The court noted that the book dealt almost entirely with the
plaintiff's musical career and that very little was said about his
private life. There were some statements in the book that Koussevitzky might naturally find to be highly objectionable if he
were at all sensitive, but there was no revelation of intimate
details calculated to outrage public tolerance or anything repug-
nant to a sense of decency. Consequently, the court denied a preliminary injunction (Koussevitzky v. Allen Towne and Heath, 188
Misc. (N.Y.) 479, aff'd. 272 App. Div. (N.Y.) 759).

Robert Goelet, Jr. also failed to prevent the publication of an
unauthorized biographical article. He and his wife complained
that the primary purpose of an article in the January, 1956, issue
of the gossip magazine *Confidential* was to amuse and astonish
the public, not for legitimate news or the description of actual
events. The court decided that while the article was a lurid and
spicy delineation of the activities of the plaintiffs, it obviously
was not fictionalized nor was it a treatment of public figures dis-

tinct from the dissemination of news and information. The court refused to pass judgment on the reading taste of the American public and pointed out that the increased circulation of magazines such as *Confidential* was mute testimony that the public is interested in the kind of news these magazines carry (Goelet v. Confidential, Inc., 5 A.D. 2d (N.Y.) 226).

A case related to one discussed in Chapter 5 on libel illustrates the difficulty in drawing the line between fact and fiction. Felix Youssoupoff was one of the killers of Rasputin, the evil Russian priest who had a strange influence on the Czarina in the early part of the twentieth century. The Columbia Broadcasting System telecast a dramatic production titled "If I Should Die." A professional actor played the part of Youssoupoff and portrayed an actual occurrence in which Youssoupoff had admittedly participated. Youssoupoff charged invasion of privacy. The event was of historical import. The production was fictionalized and the dialogue, setting, expression and gestures of the actors were all the result of the imagination of the writers and producers of the presentation. Both parties moved for summary judgment and both motions were denied. The Appellate Division noted that it could not determine from the record whether the telecast was a legitimate portrayal of history in a slightly fictionalized form so as to deny the plaintiff recovery, or whether the converse was true, and it set the case down for trial (Youssoupoff v. Columbia Broadcasting System, Inc., 19 AD 2d (N.Y.) 865). The trial resulted in a defendant's verdict so the plaintiff recovered nothing.

When the victim is not well known, even slight fictionalization of a past event in a feature article may permit recovery.

During the Second World War, a young American aviator with the romantic name of Valentine Lawless was shot down over Austria. He left a holographic will—that is to say, a will without witnesses, entirely in his own handwriting. The will left his entire estate to his brother, in trust, to furnish each Saturday morning for eternity a perfect rose to the secret object of his affection, Mildred Fitzpatrick. She was described as pretty and popular and, according to her account, entirely ignorant of the deep affection that the decedent bore her. The will, of course, was void since it created an illegal trust, a trust for the benefit of a rose. The will contest that took place in Norfolk, Virginia, resulted in extensive news coverage. Mildred had yielded in the meantime to the entreaties of a more ardent and aggressive suitor, and, by the time of the will contest, had become Mrs. Harold Sutton. She said she was surprised and touched, but roses were not for her.

Five years later, the Hearst papers published a feature article on this incident in a Sunday issue. The article was not the least bit unsavory and could hardly be described as sensational. It compared the prospective donee, Mrs. Sutton, now the mother of one child and the expectant mother of another, with great heroines of romantic history: Juliet, Beatrice, Heloise, Roxanne and others. Why Mrs. Sutton objected to this article is one of life's minor mysteries. One would have supposed that she would have cherished it and preserved it for her delight when time had wrought its toll, or saved it for the edification of her grandchildren. Perhaps the hard decision to sue was forced on Mrs. Sutton by her husband. In any event, she sued and pointed out that the article contained an imaginary sketch of Mrs. Sutton (which, incidentally, did her more than justice) tenderly fondling a perfect rose. Now the fact was that Mrs. Sutton never had received a rose, so this amounted to a minor fictionalization of an otherwise substantially accurate report of an event that had occurred five years before. The New York Appellate Division of the First Department split 3–2 on the case. The majority held that this slight fictionalization created an issue of fact for a jury to determine whether publication was made solely for the "purposes of trade" (Sutton v. Hearst Corp., 277 App. Div. (N.Y.) 155).

The Suttons decided not to pursue the matter, and after the lapse of a year or two the case was dismissed for lack of prosecution.

The Suttons were scarcely known to the general public. In the case of public figures, the courts permit much more fictionalization. Warren Spahn was a famous professional baseball pitcher. Milton Shapiro wrote a book for adolescents entitled *The Warren Spahn Story*. The book was highly fictionalized. The author used the literary techniques of invented dialogue and imaginary incidents, and attributed imaginary thoughts and feelings to Spahn. This technique was employed with respect to Spahn's childhood, his relationship with his father, the courtship of his wife, important events during their marriage and his military experience. Mr. Shapiro gave him an unearned Bronze Star. Because of the degree of fiction, Spahn was awarded a judgment of $10,000. This was affirmed by the New York Court of Appeals, but the Supreme Court of the United States reversed and sent it back for reconsideration in view of the Time v. Hill case, which will be discussed shortly. When the Spahn case came back to the New York Court of Appeals for reconsideration, the court, in a split decision, decided to adhere to its original determination (Spahn v. Julian Messner, Inc., 21 N.Y.2d 124). Spahn's troubles did not end there, because the Supreme Court of the United States agreed to hear the case again. This was too much for Spahn. He hung up his glove and consented to dropping his complaint. (For more on the Spahn case, see Chapter 12.)

Constitutional Limitation

The foregoing shows that generous fictionalization may be permitted in describing the events in the lives of public figures. In 1967 the Supreme Court handed down a ruling that made it clear that even in the case of individuals like the Suttons, who were far from public figures, the writer is quite free to fictionalize if the subject is of wide interest.

In that year, the Supreme Court of the United States applied the New York Times rule to privacy cases. James Hill, his wife and five children involuntarily became the subjects of a front-page story after being held hostage for 19 hours in their suburban Philadelphia home by three escaped convicts in September, 1952. The family was released unharmed, and in an interview with reporters after the convicts left Hill stressed that the convicts had not molested the family. Shortly thereafter, Hill moved to Connecticut and discouraged all efforts to keep his family in the public spotlight.

In 1953 Joseph Hayes wrote a novel entitled *The Desperate Hours*. The story described the experience of a family of four held hostage by three escaped convicts. Unlike the Hills, the family in his story suffered violence at the hands of the convicts, but the Hill experience undoubtedly inspired the Hayes novel, which was made into a play. The play reviewed in an article appearing in *Life* in February, 1955, entitled "True Crime Inspires Tense Play," with a subtitle "The ordeal of a family trapped by convicts gives Broadway a new thiller 'The Desperate Hours.'" To illustrate the review, *Life* took some of the actors to the actual house in which the Hills were besieged. The text of the article read as follows:

> Three years ago Americans all over the country read about the desperate ordeal of the James Hill family, who were held prisoners in their home outside Philadelphia by three escaped convicts. Later they read about it in Joseph Hayes's novel, *The Desperate Hours*, inspired by the family's experience. Now they can see the story re-enacted in Hayes's Broadway play based on the book, and next year will see it in his movie, which has been filmed but is being held up until the play has a chance to pay off.
>
> The play, directed by Robert Montgomery and expertly acted, is a heart-stopping account of how a family rose to heroism in a crisis. *Life* photographed the play during its Philadelphia tryout, transported some of the actors to the actual house where the Hills were besieged. On the next page scenes from the play are re-enacted on the site of the crime.

On the ensuing two pages were a picture of the son being "roughed up" by one of the convicts (entitled "brutish convict"), a picture of the daughter biting the hand of a convict to make him drop his gun (entitled "daring daughter") and a picture of the father throwing his gun through the door after a "brave try" to save his family was foiled.

Hill sued for invasion of privacy and recovered a judgment in the New York Supreme Court of $50,000 compensatory and $25,000 punitive damages. On appeal, the New York Appellate Division ordered a new trial as to damages but sustained the jury verdict as to liability. On the new trial a jury was waived and the court awarded $30,000 in compensatory damages without punitive damages. The New York Court of Appeals affirmed and the defendants went to the United States Supreme Court. In the Supreme Court, Hill was represented by Richard Milhous Nixon, who would be elected President of the United States in 1968. The defendant was represented by Harold Medina, Jr.

In reversing the $30,000 verdict, the Supreme Court held that neither fictionalization nor factual error was sufficient unless actual malice of *New York Times* vintage—knowledge that the statements are false or reckless disregard of truth—was proved. It held:

We hold that the constitutional protections for speech and press preclude the application of the New York statute to redress false reports of matters of public interest in the absence of proof that the defendant published the report with knowledge of its falsity or in reckless disregard of the truth.

The guarantees for speech and press are not the preserve of political expression or comment upon public affairs, essential as those are to healthy government. One need only pick up any newspaper or magazine to comprehend the vast range of published matter which exposes persons to public view, both private citizens and public officials. Exposure of the self to others in varying degrees is a concomitant of life in a civilized community. The risk of this exposure is an essential incident of life in a society which places a primary value on freedom of speech and of press. "Freedom of discussion, if it would fulfill its historic function in this nation, must embrace all issues about which information is needed or appropriate to enable the members of society to cope with the exigencies of their period." Thornhill v. Alabama, 310 U.S. 88, 102. "No suggestion can be found in the Constitution that the freedom there guaranteed for speech and the press bears an inverse ratio to the timeliness and importance of the ideas seeking expression." Bridges v. California, 314 U.S. 252, 269. We have no doubt that the subject of the Life article, the opening of a new play linked to an actual incident, is a matter of public interest. "The line between the informing and the entertaining is too elusive for the protection of . . . [freedom of the press]." Winters v. New York, 333 U.S. 507, 510. Erroneous statement is no less inevitable in such a case than in the case of comment upon public affairs, and in both, if innocent or merely negligent, ". . . it must be protected if the freedoms of expression are to have the 'breathing space' that they 'need . . . to survive' " . . . [Time, Inc. v. Hill, 385 U.S. 374, 387-8]

Under this ruling, fictionalization is not enough to create liability except for very private matters. In order to recover in any article involving a matter of public interest, the victim must show that the fictionalization hurt him and was intended to hurt. By this standard, because she had been involved in an earlier public will contest and was not hurt by the article on the gift of roses, Mrs. Sutton could not possibly have recovered damages.

False Light

Professor Prosser, in the fourth edition of his book *Law of Torts,* classifies acts violating privacy into four categories: intrusion, appropriation, disclosure and false light.

Intrusion involves illegally entering someone's home, illegal searches and illegal wire tapping. Intrusion does not involve the written word or visual representation, and so does not affect the newspaper writer or publisher.

Appropriation roughly corresponds to advertising and the use of the victim's name and picture to promote someone's products or ideas. This has already been covered.

Disclosure involves writing about an individual and subjecting him to publicity of an objectionable kind, and this has been covered by the paragraphs on fiction or fictionalization. There are a few cases, however, in common-law states that involve no fictionalization at all but are condemned under this category. The classic one is the case of a motion picture which revived the history and disclosed the present identity of a reformed prostitute who, some years before, had been the defendant in a notorious murder trial (Melvin v. Reid, 112, Cal. App. 285, 297 P. 91). This case would probably not be followed in any of the states in which privacy is dependent upon statute.

The final category is placing the plaintiff in a false light in the public eye. The leading case in that category is a Supreme Court case decided in 1974. Margaret Cantrell's husband, Melvin, was killed in December, 1967, along with 43 other people when the Silver Bridge across the Ohio River at Point Pleasant, West Virginia, collapsed. Five months after Cantrell's death, the Cleveland *Plain Dealer* carried a follow-up feature article. The article stressed the family's abject poverty, the ill-fitting clothes worn by the children and the deterioration of their home. The writer used the Cantrell family to illustrate the impact of the bridge's collapse on the lives of the people in the surrounding area. There were a number of inaccuracies and false statements in the article. Mrs. Cantrell was not present at the time the reporter visited her home, but the article said: "Margaret Cantrell will talk neither about what happened or about how they were doing. She wears the same mask of non expression she wore at the funeral. She is a proud woman. She says that after it happened, the people in town offered to help them out with money, and she refused to take it." There were other misrepresentations, including details of the dirty and dilapidated conditions of the Cantrell home. The district judge charged the jury that liability could be imposed only if it concluded that the false statements in the Sunday magazine feature article about the Cantrells had been made with knowledge of their falsity or any reckless disregard of the truth. The jury brought in a verdict of $60,000 for Mrs. Cantrell. The Court of Appeals set aside the verdict, but the Supreme Court reversed and restored the verdict (Cantrell v. Forest City Publishing Co., 419 U.S. 245). The doctrine that there is a right of privacy infringement if a private individual is placed in a false light can be considered established in common-law states.

Defenses

Unlike libel, truth is not a defense in privacy cases. But truth may be valuable in demonstrating that the article is either not fictionalized or fictionalized only to a small degree.

Written consent is a complete defense under the New York statute and is a complete defense in common-law states. Oral consent is not a defense under the New York statute, but it has been held to be a partial defense. Oral consent is a defense in common-law jurisdictions, but consent voluntarily given without consideration can be withdrawn at any time. To be protected, payment should be made for consent so that it is a binding contract that may not be withdrawn. Courts have limited consent to the exact use originally contemplated. Mrs. Katherine Feeney consented to the use of the pictures taken for scientific purposes of her undergoing a Caesarean section. Her consent was held to be limited to that scientific use and did not cover the use of these pictures as a part of a publicly shown film, appealing to the general public (Feeney v. Young, 191 App. Div. (N.Y.) 501).

Damages

Damages have not been large in privacy cases. Binns obtained a verdict of $12,500; Cantrell a verdict of $60,000; Spahn recovered an initial verdict of $10,000, but ended up without anything. Hill's $30,000 judgment was reversed. A woman named Julie Myers complained that a nude photograph of her had been published without her consent. Although mental stress was obviously involved, the court limited her recovery to $1,500 (Myers v. U.S. Camera Pub. Corp., 9 Misc. 2d (N.Y.) 765). *Front-Page Detective* magazine published in its January, 1953, issue an article entitled "Gang-Boy." Three young men, all under the age of 21, brought suit because of the use of their pictures to illustrate the article. They were described as a gang, which was entirely fictitious. In addition to claiming invasion of privacy, they argued that the article libeled them. The jury brought in a verdict of $9,000—$3,000 for each of the three plaintiffs—which the court reduced to $5,100, or $1,700 apiece (Metzger v. Dell Pub. Co., 207 Misc. (N.Y.) 182).

Punitive damages are recoverable if the victim is able to make a strong showing of malice. In the Cantrell case, the District Court applied *The New York Times* standard for the purpose of establishing liability, and although liability was established, refused to permit a finding of punitive damages. The Supreme Court supported this finding, and said:

> In a false-light case, common-law malice—frequently expressed in terms of either personal ill will toward the plaintiff or reckless or wanton disregard of the plaintiff's rights—would focus on the defendant's attitude toward the plaintiff's privacy, not towards the truth or falsity of the material published. [Cantrell v. Forest City Publishing Co., 419 U.S. 245, 252]

Thus, in privacy cases, in order to obtain punitive damages a showing of personal ill will seems to be required.

Privacy is a new and growing tort, and while damages have not been large thus far, they may increase as time goes on and the law develops.

Additional Problems

New concern about privacy developed early in the seventh decade of the twentieth century. In part, this concern grew from the fear that those with access to computers storing personal material about millions of Americans might release this information for their own purposes. Added to the fear were revelations of controlled leaks by government officials of personal data, such as that contained in income tax returns and health records, as well as revelations designed to injure enemies of the administration or of individual officials. The police and prosecutors regularly gave out information about suspects so damaging that convictions were easy. Wire tapping by businesses and individuals, as well as by the government, became a developed practice.

The reaction has been the adoption of special laws and agency regulations designed to protect private records. Both the Internal Revenue Service and the Social Security Administration adopted such regulations, and state welfare agencies adopted a practice of not naming the relief recipients. Mental hospitals kept their records confidential. Notwithstanding such regulations, there is frequently legitimate news in personal data. The revival of gossip columnists has provided new outlets for such material, and each publication and broadcasting station obviously must follow its own standards in deciding what personal material is to be published or broadcast. Each editor must weigh the value of the personal material to the readers and the public, and this depends on whether the person in the news is sufficiently public to require his accountability to the public at large.

This guide can be followed:

1. The Providence *Journal* was justified in publishing the fact that President and Mrs. Nixon paid only $1,370.84 in Federal income taxes in 1970–71. He certainly was a public figure and his taxes were a matter of public interest.
2. Almost everything relating to President Nixon's private life, such as reports of his heavy drinking in the weeks before his resignation, his profanity, his weeping, his praying, can be justified on the ground that the public had a right to know about his physical and emotional condition. Perhaps disclosure of Mr. Nixon's inactive sex life was justified on

the same basis, although some editors would argue that even a President deserves privacy in such matters. Of course, if there was evidence that sexual conduct affected a President's decision making, there would be no question about privacy.

3. The Boston *Globe* was correct in publishing the fact that a worker on the city payroll was also drawing welfare benefits. The public had the right to know it was being defrauded.

4. The Knight newspapers were on firm ground in reporting the emotional difficulties of Senator Thomas Eagleton, who was the Democratic vice-presidential candidate for a short time in 1972. This disclosure bore on his fitness to serve, and led to his removal from the ticket.

5. It was proper for newspapers to carry the details of Supreme Court Justice William Douglas's incapacitation after his illness, despite court efforts to hide the facts.

6. The privacy of a public figure's family is difficult to judge. If a public official uses the family as a political asset, the family would be as open to disclosure as the official. Anything about their personal lives that conflicted with the image of a happy couple would be fair game. Some editors would argue that personal stability is so important to a public figure's performance in office that family affairs are the public's business. On this basis, it was proper to report that Senator Edward Kennedy's wife had mental problems and had entered a health clinic. Other editors would disagree, pointing out that Mrs. Kennedy seldom took part in her husband's campaigning or public affairs. The same difference arises regarding the private escapades of children of public figures. There is no conflict over the validity of publishing family events involving the police or other safety officers, such as Mrs. Kennedy's arrest for drunken driving or a student's participation in a demonstration.

7. The release of a subscriber's telephone calls, although forbidden by telephone company rules, is justified when, as in the Watergate investigation, they throw light on the conduct of a public figure.

8. It is also in the public interest to publish the details of a public figure's financial condition, including the amount of his

pension and the fact that he was rejected as a credit risk.

9. It is acceptable to publish the fact that a person is a homosexual, provided the information bears on a public issue such as support for gay rights. It would also be defensible to carry a news item saying that a murder victim had been frequenting gay bars, since the information might lead to the apprehension of criminals.

This list is obviously not complete. There are borderline instances which may require writers, editors and broadcasters to pause before disclosing facts in their possession. The policy of a particular newspaper or broadcasting station also has to be considered. In all close instances the right of the public to have valid information must be weighed against the right of the individual to preserve his privacy.

Index of Cases

Almost all cases discussed in this book can be found in any good law library. Here is a list of the citations needed to find them in various law reports:

Page

Abram v. Odham—6 Fla. Supp. 102; 89 So. 2d 334   *245*
American Broadcasting-Paramount Theaters, Inc. v. Simpson—106 Ga. App. 230; 126 S.E. 2d 873   *347*
Anthony v. Barss—346 Mass. 401; 193 N.E. 2d 329   *73*
Archibald v. Belleville News-Democrat—54 Ill. App. 2d 38; 203 N.E. 2d 281   *199*
Arrowsmith v. United Press International—205 F. Supp. 56, reversed on other grounds, 320 F. 2d 219   *306*
A. S. Abell Co. v. Kirby—227 Md. 267; 176 A. 2d 340   *211*
Ashton v. Kentucky—384 U.S. 195   *373*
Associated Press v. Walker—388 U.S. 130   *183, 258*
Atkins v. Friedman—49 A.D. 2d (N.Y.) 852   *187*
Barr v. Matteo—360 U.S. 564   *176*
Barton v. Barnett—226 F. Supp. 375   *66*
Battersby v. Collier—34 App. Div. (N.Y.) 347; 54 N.Y. Supp. 363   *76*
Beauharnais v. Pittsburgh Courier—243 F. 2d 705   *212*
Beckley Newspaper Corp. v. Hanks—389 U.S. 81   *181*
Bell v. Simmons—247 N.C. 488; 101 S.E. 2d 383   *74*
Bellis v. Times-Picayune—226 F. Supp. 552, aff'd, 341 F. 2d 300   *321*
Bennett v. Williamson—4 Sandf. (N.Y.) 60, Super. Ct. (N.Y.) 60   *41*
Beyl v. Capper Publications—180 Kan. 525; 305 P. 2d 817   *325*
Binns v. Vitagraph Company—210 N.Y. 51   *390*
Birmingham v. Daily Mirror—175 Misc. (N.Y.) 372; 23 N.Y.S. 2d 549   *58*
Bocchicchio v. Curtis Publishing Co.—203 F. Supp. 403   *125, 317*
Bock v. Plainfield Courier-News—45 N.J. Super. 302; 132 A. 2d 523   *166*
Bon Air Hotel, Inc. v. Time, Inc.—426 F. 2d 858   *186*
Booth v. Curtis Publishing Co.—15 A.D. (N.Y.) 2d 343, aff'd, 11 N.Y. 2d 907   *388*
Borg v. Boas—231 F. 2d 788   *142*
Bowen v. Independent Publishing Co.—230 S.C. 509; 96 S.E. 2d 564   *64*
Bradley v. Conners—169 Misc. (N.Y.) 442; 7 N.Y.S. 2d 294   *93*
Brandon v. Gazette Publishing Co.—234 Ark. 332; 352 S.W. 2d 92   *231, 341*
Briarcliff Lodge Hotel v. Citizen-Sentinel Publishers, Inc.—260 N.Y. 106; 183 N.E. 193   *146, 154*

Bridgewood v. Newspaper PM, Inc.—276 App. Div. (N.Y.) 858   *139*
Brown v. Du Frey—1 N.Y. 2d 190; 151 N.Y.S. 2d 649; 134 N.E.
   2d 469   *49*
Brush-Moore Newspapers, Inc. v. Pollitt—220 Md. 132; 151 A. 2d
   530   *292*
Bupp v. Great Western Broadcasting Corp.—201 Cal. App. 2d 580;
   20 Cal. Rptr. 106   *350*
Burton v. Crowell Publishing Co.—82 F. 2d 154   *333*
Campbell v. New York Evening Post—245 N.Y. 320; 157 N.E. 153   *136*
Campbell v. Sun Printing & Publishing Assn.—Unpublished charge
   to jury   *226*
Cantrell v. Forest City Publishing Co.—419 U.S. 245   *397, 398*
Cardiff v. Brooklyn Eagle, Inc.—190 Misc. (N.Y.) 730; 75 N.Y.S.
   2d 222   *51*
Carlisle v. Fawcett Publications, Inc.—201 Cal. App. 2d 733; 20 Cal.
   Rptr. 405   *48*
Cepeda v. Cowles Magazines and Broadcasting, Inc.—328 F. 2d 869,
   cert. denied, 379 U.S. 844; 392 F. 2d 417   *196*
Chapadeau v. Utica Observer-Dispatch, Inc.—38 N.Y. 2d 196, 199   *192*
Charles Parker Co. v. Silver City Crystal Co.—142 Conn. 605; 116
   A. 2d 440   *186*
Cherry v. Des Moines Leader—114 Iowa 298; 86 N.W. 323   *214*
City of Chicago v. Lambert—47 Ill. App. 2d 151; 197 N.E. 2d 448   *373*
City of Chicago v. Tribune Co.—307 Ill. 595; 139 N.E. 86   *98*
Cohalan v. N.Y. Tribune—172 Misc. (N.Y.) 20; 15 N.Y.S. 2d 58   *209*
Cohen v. New York Times Co.—153 App. Div. (N.Y.) 242; 138 N.Y.
   Supp. 206   *51*
Coleman v. MacLennan—78 Kan. 711; 98 P. 281   *174, 184*
Coleman v. Newark Morning Ledger Co.—29 N.J. 357; 149 A. 2d
   193   *130, 318*
Commonwealth v. Donaducy—176 Pa. Super. 27; 107 A. 2d 139;
   appeal dismissed, 349 U.S. 913   *17*
Cook v. Atlanta Newspapers, Inc.—99 Ga. App. 7; 107 S.E. 2d 260   *320*
Cook v. Patterson Drug Co.—185 Va. 516; 39 S.E. 2d 304   *64*
Cosgrove Studio and Camera Shop, Inc. v. Pane—408 Pa. 314; 182
   A. 2d 751   *83*
Costas v. Florence Printing Co.—237 S.C. 655; 118 S.E. 2d 696   *86*
Coursey v. Greater Niles Township Publishing Corp.—239 N.E. 2d
   837, 40 Ill. 2d 257   *181*
Cowan v. Time, Inc.—41 Misc. 2d (N.Y.) 198; 245 N.Y.S. 2d 723   *323*
Crellin v. Thomas—122 Utah 122; 247 P. 2d 264   *112*
Crosby v. Time, Inc.—254 F. 2d 927   *24*
Curtis Publishing Co. v. Butts—388 U.S. 130   *262, 280, 291, 363*
Curtis Publishing Co. v. Vaughan—278 F. 2d 23, cert. denied, 364
   U.S. 822   *328*
Daly v. Engineering & Mining Journal—94 App. Div. (N.Y.) 314;
   88 N.Y. Supp. 6   *72*
Danziger v. Hearst Corp.—304 N.Y. 244; 107 N.E. 2d 62   *139*
Davila v. Caller Times Publishing Co.—311 S.W. 2d 945   *116*
Dempsey v. Time, Inc.—43 Misc. 2d (N.Y.) 754; 252 N.Y.S. 2d 186,
   aff'd, 22 A.D. 2d 854, 254 N.Y.S. 2d 80   *308*

Den Norske Ameriekalinje Actiesselskabet v. Sun Printing & Publishing Assn.—226 N.Y., 1; 122 N.E. 463 — 84
De Seversky v. P. & S. Publishing, Inc.—36 N.Y.S. 2d 271 — 67
Dickins v. International Brotherhood of Teamsters—171 F. 2d 21 — 235
Di Giorgio Fruit Corp. v. A.F.L.-C.I.O.—215 Cal. App. 2d 560; 30 Cal. Rptr. 350 — 269
Dilling v. Illinois Publishing and Printing Co.—340 Ill. App. 303; 91 N.E. 2d 635 — 70
Dolcin Corp. v. Reader's Digest Assn.—7 A.D. 2d (N.Y.) 449; 183 N.Y.S. 2d 342 — 208
Dooley v. Press Publishing Co.—170 App. Div. (N.Y.) 492; 156 N.Y. Supp. 381, aff'd,224 N.Y. 640; 121 N.E. 865 — 40
Dorney v. Dairymen's League Co-op Assn.—149 F. Supp. 615 — 302
Droner v. Cowles Communications Inc. and World Journal Tribune, Inc.—34 A.D. 2d (N.Y.) 823 — 125
Drug Research Corp. v. Curtis Publishing Co.—7 N.Y. 2d 435; 199 N.Y.S. 2d 33; 166 N.E. 2d 319 — 89, 320
Dunaway v. Troutt—232 Ark. 615; 339 S.W. 2d 613 — 116
Duncan v. Record Publishing Co.—131 S.C. 485; 127 S.E. 606, aff'd, 145 S.C. 196, 143 S.E. 31 — 244
Edmonds v. Delta Democrat Publishing Co.—230 Miss. 583; 93 So. 2d 171 — 207
Emde v. San Joaquin County Central Labor Council—23 Cal. 2d 146; 143 P. 2d 20 — 206
Empire Printing Co. v. Roden—247 F. 2d 8 — 336
England v. Daily Gazette Co.—143 W. Va. 700; 104 S.E. 2d 306 — 276
Estill v. Hearst Publishing Co.—186 F. 2d 1017 — 60
Express Publishing Co. v. Gonzales—326 S.W. 2d 544; 350 S.W. 2d 589 — 164
Express Publishing Co. v. Orsborn—151 S.W. 574 — 18
Fairbanks Publishing Co. v. Francisco—390 P. 2d 784 — 161
Fairbanks Publishing Co. v. Pitka—376 P. 2d 190 — 110
Farley v. Evening Chronicle Publishing Co.—113 Mo. App. 216; 87 S.W. 565 — 95
Farmers Educational and Cooperative Union v. WDAY, Inc.—360 U.S. 525 — 355
Farrell v. Kramer—159 Me. 387; 193 A. 2d 560 — 297
Farrell v. New York Evening Post, Inc.—167 Misc. (N.Y.) 412; 3 N.Y.S. 2d 1018 — 147
Faulk v. Aware, Inc.—19 A.D. 2d (N.Y.) 464; 244 N.Y.S. 2d 259, aff'd, 14 N.Y. 2d 899; 252 N.Y.S. 2d 95; 200 N.E. 2d 778 — 267, 280
Fawcett Publications, Inc. v. Morris—377 P. 2d 42, cert. denied, 376 U.S. 513 — 24, 320
Feeney v. Young—191 App. Div. (N.Y.) 501 — 397
Fegley v. Morthimer—204 Pa. Super. 54; 202 A. 2d 125 — 263
Fisher v. Country Wide Publications, Inc.—29 Misc. 2d (N.Y.) 96; 213 N.Y.S. 2d 897 — 312
Fleckenstein v. Friedman—266 N.Y. 19; 193 N.E. 537 — 122
Fletcher v. Norfolk Newspapers—239 F. 2d 169 — 118
Foley v. Press Publishing Co.—226 App. Div. (N.Y.) 535; 235 N.Y. Supp. 340 — 217

Fowler v. Curtis Publishing Co.—78 F. Supp. 303, aff'd, 182 F. 2d
377   *23*
Fowler v. New York Herald Co.—184 App. Div. (N.Y.) 608; 172
N.Y. Supp. 423   *234*
Francois v. Capital City Press—166 So. 2d 84 (La.)   *149*
Franklin v. World Publishing Co.—183 Okla. 507; 83 P. 2d 401   *64*
Friday v. Official Detective Stories, Inc.—233 F. Supp. 1021   *149*
Friedan v. Friedan—414 F. Supp. 77   *387*
Gaillot v. Sauvageau—154 So. 2d 515 (La.)   *247*
Gambuzza v. Time, Inc.—18 A.D. 2d (N.Y.) 351; 239 N.Y.S. 2d
466   *329*
Gauitar v. Westinghouse—396 F. Supp. 1042   *187*
Garriga v. Richfield—174 Misc. (N.Y.) 315; 20 N.Y.S. 2d 544   *68*
Garrison v. State of Louisiana—379 U.S. 64   *175, 193, 257, 376*
Garrison v. Sun Printing & Publishing Assn.—74 Misc. (N.Y.) 622;
134 N.Y. Supp. 670   *61*
Gates v. New York Recorder Co.—155 N.Y. 228; 49 N.E. 769   *43*
Gautier v. Pro Football, Inc.—304 N.Y. 354   *387*
George v. Time, Inc.—259 App. Div. (N.Y.) 324; 19 N.Y.S. 2d 385   *154*
Gertz v. Robert Welch, Inc.—418 U.S. 323   *188, 191, 250, 255*
Gilberg v. Goffi—21 A.D. 2d (N.Y.) 517; 251 N.Y.S. 2d 823, aff'd,
15 N.Y. 2d 1023; 260 N.Y.S. 2d 29; 207 N.E. 2d 620   *184*
Gilligan v. King—29 A.D. 2d (N.Y.) 935   *181*
Giraud v. Beach—3 E.D. Smith (N.Y.) 337   *91*
Goelet v. Confidential, Inc.—5 A.D. 2d (N.Y.) 226   *391*
Gough v. Tribune-Journal Co.—73 Idaho 173; 249 P. 2d 192   *315*
Grant v. Reader's Digest Assn.—151 F. 2d 733, cert. denied 326
U.S. 797   *4, 68, 315*
Greenbelt Publishing Association v. Bresler—398 U.S. 6   *187, 279*
Greer v. Skyway Broadcasting Co.—256 N.C. 382; 124 S.E. 2d 98   *352*
Gregoire v. G. P. Putnam's Sons—298 N.Y. 119; 81 N.E. 2d 45   *103*
Gross v. Cantor—270 N.Y. 93; 200 N.E. 592   *25*
Haas v. Evening Democrat Co.—252 Iowa 517; 107 N..W 2d 444   *242*
Hamilton v. Eno—81 N.Y. 116   *214*
Hammersten v. Reiling—262 Minn. 200; 115 N.W. 2d 259   *265*
Hancock v. New York Tribune, Inc.—198 App. Div. (N.Y.) 917   *52*
Hanson Co., W.T. v. Collier—51 Misc. (N.Y.) 496; 101 N.Y. Supp.
690   *89*
Hartmann v. Winchell—296 N.Y. 296; 73 N.E. 2d 30   *343*
Hartzog v. United Press Assns.—202 F. 2d 81; 233 F. 2d 174   *360*
Harwood Pharmacal Co. v. N.B.C.— 197 N.Y.S. 2d 413, aff'd, 9
N.Y. 2d 460; 214 N.Y.S. 2d 725; 174 N.E. 2d 602   *346*
Hearst Consolidated Publications, Inc. v. American Newspaper
Guild—294 F. 2d 239   *82*
Henry v. Collins—380 U.S. 356   *180*
Hoeck v. Tiedebohl—74 N.M. 146; 391 P. 2d 651   *30*
Hogan v. New York Times Co.—313 F. 2d 354   *339*
Hope v. Hearst Consolidated Publications, Inc.—294 F. 2d 681, cert.
denied, 368 U.S. 956   *17*
Hornby v. Hunter—385 S.W. 2d 473   *15, 156*

Hotchner v. Castillo-Pouche—404 F. Supp. 1041 · 187
Howser v. Pearson—95 F. Supp. 936 · 123, 283
Hudson v. Pioneer Service Co.—218 Ore. 561; 346 P. 2d 123 · 79
Hulton v. Jones—[1909] 2 K.B. 444 · 31
Irving v. Irving—121 App. Div. (N.Y.) 258; 105 N.Y. Supp. 609 · 45
Israel v. Portland News Publishing Co.—152 Ore. 225; 53 P. 2d
529 · 244
James v. Gannett & Co., Inc.—40 N.Y. 2d 415 · 187
James v. Powell—20 A.D. 2d (N.Y.) 689, aff'd, 14 N.Y. 2d 881; 252
N.Y.S. 2d 87; 200 N.E. 2d 772 · 105, 280, 344
John v. Tribune Co.—28 Ill. App. 2d 300; 24 Ill. 2d 437; 181 N.E.
2d 105 · 21, 362
Johnson Publishing Co. v. Davis—271 Ala. 474; 124 So. 2d 441 · 275, 363
Josephs v. News Syndicate Co.—5 Misc. 2d (N.Y.) 184; 159 N.Y.S.
2d 537 · 160
Julian v. American Business Consultants—2 N.Y. 2d 1; 155 N.Y.S.
2d 1; 137 N.E. 2d 1 · 27, 223
Kapiloff v. Duna—27 Md. App. 514 · 181
Karrigan v. Valentine—184 Kan. 783; 339 P. 2d 52 · 28
Kasiuba v. New York Herald Tribune, Inc.—232 N.Y.S. 2d 258 · 283
Katapodis v. Brooklyn Spectator—287 N.Y. 17; 38 N.E. 2d 112 · 57
Kehoe v. New York Tribune, Inc.—229 App. Div. (N.Y.) 220; 241
N.Y. Supp. 676 · 20
Kellems v. California Congress of Industrial Organizations Council—
68 F. Supp. 277 · 222
Kenney v. Hatfield—35 Mich. 498; 88 N.W. 2d 535 · 55
Kern v. News Syndicate Co.—20 A.D. 2d (N.Y.) 528; 244 N.Y.S.
2d 665 · 169, 337
King v. Lake—Hardres 470; 145 Eng. Rep. 552 · 8
Kirkman v. Westchester Newspapers, Inc.—287 N.Y. 373; 39 N.E.
2d 919 · 93
Klaw v. New York Press Co.—137 App. Div. (N.Y.) 686; 122 N.Y.
Supp. 437 · 80
Kornblum v. Commercial Advertiser Assn.—164 N.Y. Supp. 186,
aff'd, 183 App. Div. (N.Y.) 615; 170 N.Y. Supp. 249 · 72
Koussevitzky v. Allen Towne and Heath—188 Misc. (N.Y.) 479,
aff'd, 272 App. Div. (N.Y.) 759 · 390
Lahiri v. Daily Mirror, Inc.—162 Misc. (N.Y.) 776, 782 · 385
Lahr v. Adell Chemical Co.—300 F. 2d 256 · 346
Langford v. Vanderbilt University—44 Tenn. App. 694; 318 S.W. 2d
568 · 229, 324
Las Vegas Sun v. Franklin—74 Nev. 282; 329 P. 2d 867 · 317, 368
Lawson v. New York Post Corp.—10 A.D. 2d (N.Y.) 832; 199
N.Y.S. 2d 154 · 67
Layne v. Tribune Co.—108 Fla. 177; 146 So. 234 · 117
Ledger-Enquirer Co. v. Brown—214 Ga. 422; 105 S.E. 2d 229 · 322
Lee v. Brooklyn Union Publishing Co.—209 N.Y. 245; 103 N.E. 155 · 141
Linn v. Local 114, United Plant Guard Workers—383 U.S. 53 · 97
Lonardo v. Quaranta—205 A. 2d 837 · 15
Louka v. Park Entertainments, Inc.—294 Mass. 268; 1 N.E. 2d 41 · 331

Lunn v. Littauer—187 App. Div. (N.Y.) 808; 175 N.Y. Supp. 657   *42*
Mabardi v. Boston Herald-Traveler Corp.—347 Mass. 411; 198 N.E.
  2d 304   *327*
MacRae v. Afro-American Co.—172 F. Supp. 184, aff'd, 274 F. 2d
  287   *295*
Madison v. Bolton—234 La. 997; 102 So. 2d 433   *287*
Maritote and Capone v. Desilu Productions, Inc.—345 F. 2d. 418   *384*
Marlin Fire Arms Co. v. Shields—171 N.Y. 384; 64 N.E. 163   *88*
Martin v. Press Publishing Co.—93 App. Div. (N.Y.) 531; 87 N.Y.
  Supp. 859   *57*
Mawe v. Piggott—[1869] 4 Ir. R.C.L. 54; 32 Digest 60   *33*
McAuliffe v. Local 3, International Brotherhood of Electrical
  Workers—29 N.Y.S. 2d 963   *70*
McBurney v. Times Publishing Co.—93 R.I. 331; 175 A. 2d 170   *253*
McCarthy v. Cincinnati Enquirer, Inc.—101 Ohio App. 297; 136
  N.E. 2d 393   *202*
McFadden v. Morning Journal Assn.—28 App. Div. (N.Y.) 508; 51
  N.Y. Supp. 275   *53*
Meeropol v. Nizer—381 F. Supp. 29   *188*
Melvin v. Reid—112 Cal. App. 285, 297 P. 91   *396*
Merle v. Sociological Research Film Corp.—166 App. Div. (N.Y.)
  376; 152 N.Y. Supp. 829   *87, 325*
Merren, H.O. & Co. v. A. H. Belo Corp.—228 F. Supp. 515, aff'd,
  346 F. 2d 568   *185*
Metzger v. Dell Pub. Co.—207 Misc. (N.Y.) 182   *398*
Mitchell v. Tribune Co.—343 Ill. App. 446; 99 N.E. 2d 397, cert.
  denied, 342 U.S. 919   *65*
Monitor Patriot Co. et al v. Roy—401 U.S. 265, 274-5, 277   *194*
Moore v. Francis—121 N.Y. 199; 23 N.E. 1127   *56*
Moore v. P. W. Publishing Co.—3 Ohio St. 2d 183; 209 N.E. 2d
  412, cert. denied, 86 Sup. Ct. 549   *65*
Moriarty v. Lippe—294 A. 2d 326, 162 Con. 371   *181*
Mosler v. Whelan—28 N.J. 397; 147 A. 2d 7   *70*
Mulina v. Item Co.—217 La. 842; 47 So. 2d 560   *331*
Murray v. New York Magazine Co.—27 N.Y. 2d 406, 408-9   *389*
Myers v. U.S. Camera Pub. Corp.—9 Misc. 2d (N.Y.) 765   *398*
Natchez Times Publishing Co. v. Dunigan—221 Miss. 320; 72 So.
  2d 681   *64*
National Dynamics Corp. v. Petersen Publishing Co.—185 F. Supp.
  573   *119*
National Variety Artists v. Mosconi—169 Misc. (N.Y.) 982; 9 N.Y.S.
  2nd 498   *93*
Neiman-Marcus v. Lait—13 F.R.D. 311   *26*
New York Bureau of Information v. The Ridgway-Thayer Co.—193
  N.Y. 666; 87 N.E. 1124   *84*
New York Society for the Suppression of Vice v. MacFadden Pub-
  lications—260 N.Y. 167; 183 N.E. 284   *91*
New York Times Co. v. Sullivan—376 U.S. 254   *99, 172*
Notarmuzzi v. Shevack—108 N.Y.S. 2d 172   *8*
November v. Time, Inc.—13 N.Y. 2d 175; 194 N.E. 2d 126   *78*

Nunnally v. Tribune Assn.—111 App. Div. (N.Y.) 485, aff'd, 186
  N.Y. 533; 78 N.E. 1108   17
Ogren v. Rockford Star Printing Co.—288 Ill. 405; 123 N.E. 587   68
Osmers v. Parade Publications, Inc.—234 F. Supp. 924   104
Owens v. Clark—154 Okla. 108; 6 P. 2d 755   25
Parker Co., Charles v. Silver City Crystal Co.—142 Conn. 605; 116
  A. 2d 440   186
Pauling v. News Syndicate Co.—335 F. 2d 659, cert. denied 379
  U.S. 968   176, 182, 293
Pavesich v. New England Life Ins. Co.—122 Ga. 190   382
Pearson v. Fairbanks Publishing Co.—413 P. 2d 711   183
People ex rel. Richardson v. Reid—Unreported N.Y.   42
People v. Quill—11 Misc. 2d (N.Y.) 512; 177 N.Y.S. 2d 380   371
People v. Stokes—30 Abb. N. Cas. (N.Y.) 200; 24 N.Y. Supp. 727   376
Perry v. Hearst Corp.—334 F. 2d 800   39, 337
Phillips v. Murchison—252 F. supp. 513   137
Phoenix Newspapers, Inc. v. Choisser—82 Ariz. 271; 312 P. 2d 150 163
Pittsburgh Courier Pub. Co. v. Lubore—200 F. 2d 355   155
Pitts v. Spokane Chronicle Co.—63 Wash. 2d 763; 388 P. 2d 976   43
Pogany v. Chambers—206 Misc. (N.Y.) 933; 134 N.Y.S. 2d 691,
  aff'd, 285 App. Div. (N.Y.) 866; 132 N.Y.S. 2d 828   59
Ponder v. Cobb—257 N.C. 281; 126 S.E. 2d 67   174
Porcella v. Time, Inc.—300 F. 2d 162   221
Post Publishing Co. v. Butler—137 F. 723   18
Powers v. Durgin-Snow Publishing Co.—154 Me. 108; 144 A. 2d
  294   54
Purcell v. Westinghouse Broadcasting Co.—411 Pa. 167; 191 A. 2d
  662   354, 356
Pulvermann v. A. S. Abell Co.—228 F. 2d 797   227, 310
Reardon v. News-Journal Co.—53 Del. 29; 164 A. 2d 263   321
Reporters' Assn. of America v. Sun Printing & Publishing Co.—186
  N.Y. 437; 79 N.E. 710   81
Reynolds v. Pegler—223 F. 2d 429, cert. denied, 350 U.S.
  846   240, 248 253, 266, 275, 297, 364
Richman v. New York Herald Tribune, Inc.—7 Misc. 2d (N.Y.)
  563; 166 N.Y.S. 2d 103   87
Richwine v. Pittsburgh Courier Publishing Co.—186 Pa. Super. 644;
  142 A. 2d 416   85
Robbins v. The Evening News Assn.—373 Mich. 589; 130 N.W. 2d
  404   70
Roberson v. Rochester Folding Box Co.—171 N.Y. 538   382
Roberts v. Breckon—31 App. Div. (N.Y.) 431; 52 N.Y. Supp. 638   9
Roberts v. Love—231 Ark. 886; 333 S.W. 2d 897   161
Rogers v. Courier Post Co.—2 N.J. 393; 66 A. 2d 869   138
Rosenblatt v. Baer—383 U.S. 75   178
Rosenbloom v. Metromedia, Inc.—403 U.S. 29   190
Rovira v. Boget—240 N.Y. 314; 148 N.E. 534   35
Rudolph v. E. W. Scripps Co.—83 Ohio L. Abs. 538; 169 N.E. 2d
  300   75
Rudolph v. Gorman—169 Cal. App. 2d 666; 338 P. 2d 218   310

Salvo v. Edens—237 Miss. 734; 116 So. 2d 220   47
Sanford v. Bennett—24 N.Y. 20   143
Savannah News-Press, Inc. v. Harley—100 Ga. App. 387; 111 S.E.
  2d 259   38
Savannah News-Press, Inc. v. Hartridge—110 Ga. App. 203; 138
  S.E. 2d 173   340
Schachter v. News Syndicate Co.—270 App. Div. (N.Y.) 378; 59
  N.Y.S. 2d 693   154
Scheinblum v. Long Island Daily Press Publishing Co.—37 Misc. 2d
  (N.Y.) 1015; 239 N.Y.S. 2d 435, aff'd, 18 A.D. 2d (N.Y.) 841;
  239 N.Y.S. 2d 533   19
Schneph v. New York Post Corp.—23 A.D. 2d (N.Y.) 822; aff'd,
  16 N.Y. 2d 1011   181
Schumann v. Loew's Inc.—135 N.Y.S. 2d 361   384
Schy v. Hearst Publishing Co.—205 F. 2d 750   95
Sciandra v. Lynett—409 Pa. 595; 187 A. 2d 586   158
Shenkman v. O'Malley—2 A.D. 2d (N.Y.) 567; 157 N.Y.S. 2d
  290   71, 237
Shepard v. Lamphier—84 Misc. (N.Y.) 498; 146 N.Y. Supp. 745   14
Sheridan v. Crisona—14 N.Y. 2d 108; 249 N.Y.S. 2d 161; 198 N.E.
  2d 359   105
Shubert v. Variety, Inc.—128 Misc. (N.Y.) 428; 219 N.Y. Supp.
  233, aff'd, 221 App. Div. (N.Y.) 856; 224 N.Y. Supp. 913   80
Sidis v. F-R Pub. Corporation—113 F. 2d 806, cert. denied 311
  U.S. 711   389
Smith v. Fielden—205 Tenn. 313; 326 S.W. 2d 476   75
Smith v. Journal Co.—271 Wis. 384; 73 N.W. 2d 429   301, 332
Smith v. Smith—73 Mich. 445; 41 N.W. 499   49
Snively v. Record Publishing Co.—185 Cal. 565; 198 P. 1   173
Sorenson v. Wood—123 Neb. 348; 243 N.W. 82   342
Southeastern Newspapers, Inc. v. Walker—76 Ga. App. 57; 44 S.E.
  2d 697   323
Spahn v. Julian Messner Inc.—43 Misc. 2d (N.Y.) 219; 250 N.Y.S.
  2d 529, aff'd, 23 A.D. 2d (N.Y.) 216; 260 N.Y.S. 2d 451; 21
  N.Y. 2d 124   186, 393
Spanel v. Pegler—160 F. 2d 619   69
Spriggs v. Cheyenne Newspapers—63 Wyo. 416; 182 P. 2d 801   107
State v. Kerekes—225 Ore. 352; 358 P. 2d 523   374
State v. Guinn—208 Tenn. 527; 347 S.W. 2d 44   374
Stevenson v. News Syndicate Co.—302 N.Y. 81; 96 N.E. 2d 187   159
Stice v. Beacon Newspaper Corp.—185 Kan. 61; 340 P. 2d 396 152, 319
Stillman v. Paramount Pictures Corp.—2 A.D. 2d (N.Y.) 18; 153
  N.Y.S. 2d 190, aff'd, 5 N.Y. 2d 994; 184 N.Y.S. 2d 856; 157 N.E.
  2d 728   86
Sutton v. Hearst Corp.—277 App. Div. (N.Y.) 155   392
Swartz v. World Publishing Co.—57 Wash. 2d 213; 356 P. 2d 97   153
Swede v. Passaic Daily News—30 N.J. 320; 153 A. 2d 36   133, 269, 341
Sweeney v. Patterson—128 F. 2d 457   118
Sydney v. MacFadden Newspaper Publishing Corp.—242 N.Y. 208;
  151 N.E. 209   29

Szalay v. New York American—254 App. Div. (N.Y.) 249; 4 N.Y.S.
  2d 620 ... 117
Tabart v. Tipper [1808] 1 Camp 350; 10 R.R. 698; 32 Digest 20 ... 196
Tex Smith, The Harmonica Man, Inc. v. Godfrey—198 Misc. (N.Y.)
  1006; 102 N.Y.S. 2d 251 ... 346
Thackrey v. Patterson—157 F. 2d 614 ... 49
Thayer v. Worcester Post Co.—284 Mass. 160; 187 N.E. 292 ... 334
Thompson v. G. P. Putnam's Sons—40 Misc. 2d (N.Y.) 608; 243
  N.Y.S. 2d 652 ... 76
Thompson v. Upton—218 Md. 433; 146 A. 2d 880 ... 74
Thuma v. Hearst Corporation—340 F. Supp. 867 ... 180
Time, Inc. v. Firestone—424 U.S. 448 ... 189
Time, Inc. v. Hill—385 U.S. 374, 387-8 ... 395
Time, Inc. v. Johnston—448 F. 2d 378 ... 187
Time, Inc. v. Pape—401 U.S. 279 ... 180
Timmons v. News and Press, Inc.— 232 S.C. 639; 103 S.E. 2d 277 ... 324
Tobin v. Alfred M. Best Co.—120 App. Div. (N.Y.) 387; 105 N.Y.
  Supp. 294 ... 92
Triggs v. Sun Printing & Publishing Assn.—179 N.Y. 144; 71 N.E.
  739 ... 263
Trudeau v. Plattsburgh Publishing Co.—11 A.D. 2d (N.Y.)
  202 N.Y.S. 2d 412 ... 322
Twiggar v. Ossining Printing and Publishing Co.—161 App. Div.
  (N.Y.) 718; 146 N.Y. Supp. 529, aff'd, 220 N.Y. 716; 116 N.E.
  1080 ... 76
Union Associated Press v. Heath—49 App. Div. (N.Y.) 247; 63 N.Y.
  Supp. 96 ... 83
United Press International, Inc. v. Mohs—381 S.W. 2d 104 ... 272
United States v. Associated Press—52 F. Supp. 362 ... 2
Valdivieso v. El Diario Publishing Co.—18 A.D. 2d (N.Y.) 1072;
  239 N.Y.S. 2d 640 ... 295
Valenti v. New York Herald Tribune, Inc.—N.Y.L.J., January 28,
  1959, p. 14 ... 151
Vandenburg v. Newsweek, Inc.—441 F. 2d 378 ... 187
Vigil v. Rice—74 N.M. 693; 397 P. 2d 719 ... 290
Vosbury v. Utica Daily Press Co.—183 App. Div. (N.Y.) 769; 171
  N.Y. Supp. 827 ... 72
Wanamaker v. Lewis—173 F. Supp. 126 ... 59, 300
Warehouse Willy, Inc. v. Newsday, Inc.—10 A.D. 2d (N.Y.) 49;
  196 N.Y.S. 2d 787 ... 291
Warren v. Pulitzer Publishing Co.—336 Mo. 184; 78 S.W. 2d 404 ... 145
Washington Post Co. v. Chaloner—250 U.S. 290 ... 41
Webster v. American Broadcasting Companies—N.Y.L.J., October 1,
  1976, p. 5 ... 187
Wheeler v. Dell Publishing Co.—300 F. 2d 372 ... 349
White v. Valenta—234 Cal. App. 2d 243; 44 Cal. Rptr. 241 ... 345
Wildstein v. New York Post Corp.—40 Misc. 2d (N.Y.) 586; 243
  N.Y.S. 2d 386 ... 45
Williams v. Holdredge—22 Barb. (N.Y.) 396 ... 57

Williams v. P. W. Publishing Co.—76 Ohio L. Abs. 404; 140 N.E.
  2d 809   *160*
Willis v. Eclipse Mfg. Co.—81 App. Div. (N.Y.) 591; 81 N.Y.
  Supp. 359   *80*
Witcher v. Jones—17 N.Y. Supp. 491, aff'd, 137 N.Y. 559; 33 N.E.
  743   *3*
Wolfson v. Syracuse Newspapers, Inc.—279 N.Y. 716; 18 N.E. 2d
  676   *103*
Woolworth v. Star Co.—97 App. Div. (N.Y.) 525; 90 N.Y. Supp.
  147   *58*
W. T. Hanson Co. v. Collier—51 Misc. (N.Y.) 496; 101 N.Y. Supp.
  690   *89*
Young v. New Mexico Broadcasting Co.—60 N.M. 475; 292 P. 2d
  776   *350*
Youssoupoff v. Columbia Broadcasting System, Inc.—19 A.D. 2d
  (N.Y.) 865   *391*
Youssoupoff v. Metro-Goldwyn-Mayer Pictures—50 Times L.R. 581;
  99 A.L.R. 864   *44, 348*
Zbyszko v. New York American, Inc.—228 App. Div. (N.Y.) 277;
  239 N.Y. Supp. 411   *62, 330*
Zepeda v. Zepeda—41 Ill. App. 2d 240; 190 N.E. 2d 849   *15*

Subject Index

Abandonment of spouse, 48
Aberration, sexual, 55
Abnormality, 53, 56
Abusive, 241
Accardo, Tony, 21, 361
Accord and satisfaction, defense of, 281
Accuracy not proof of truth, 112
Accusations, risk in, 72
Actor
  general rules for criticism of, 195, 198, 201, 212, 213, 311; atrocious performance of, 203; burlesque performance billing with, 331; Communist link with, 26, 222; corrections about, 281; enemy link with, 365; Jew-nigger description of, 373; ludicrously inadequate performance of, 212; marital misconduct of, 28, 311; misidentification of, 18; ridiculous performance of, 13; sexual conduct of, 29, 47, 198, 311; taking charm course, 29
Addresses, wrong, 20
Ad libs on radio and TV, 343, 344
Admirer
  of Soviet system, 69; of spy, 328
Adoption, illegal, 316
Adultery (see Marital misconduct; Sexual conduct)
Advertising (see also Commercials)
  correction of, 290; deceptive, 208; false, 290; fraudulent, 349; high-powered, 207; leeway in criticizing, 201; misleading, 209, 350; misrepresentation in, 118; need for checking, 82, 261; phoniest, 208; picture distortion in, 332; risk in, 83, 170, 201
Advertising Age, 388
Affidavits
  limit on use of, 155, 260, 374; value of, 118
Ages, use of in identification, 20, 348
Aliases, 21
Alien, 67
Alien to American way, 70
"All but one," use of in exposés, 25
Ambiguity, use of in exposés, 22
Ambulance chaser, 10
American Broadcasting Company, 187, 347
American Business Consultants, 27, 223
American citizen, failure to be, 67
American Magazine, 332
American Opinion, 188
American, un-, 69
Amusement park, right to report actions at, 85
Analyses, risk in, 196
Anatomy of a Murder (book and film), 348
Anglo-Saxon bias, 66
Animalism, 85
Animals, comparison of man to, 62, 330
Anti-Negro bias, 63

Anti-Semitism, 118, 119, 305
  leeway in expounding, 22, 373
Antitrust law violation, 81
Apalachin crime convention, 150, 157
Apology (*see* Corrections)
Arabastard, 370
Arbuckle, Fatty, 28
Architect (*see also* Business and professional men)
  dangerous structure designed by, 71
Arizona Republic, 162
Arkansas *Democrat*, 229
Arkansas *Gazette*, 113, 230, 341
Army officer (*see* Military officer)
Arrests (*see also* Crime)
  general rules for, 147; background of, 152; citizens', 147; civil rights, 149; determination of, 147; false report of, 271; illegal, 154; non-libelous wording for, 149; police blotter entries of, 148; political pickets, 150
Arrowsmith, Harold Noel, 106, 119, 305
Art criticism (*see also* Actor; Artist)
  general rules for, 195, 198, 201, 212, 218, 311; leeway in, 75, 76, 201, 212, 218; risk in personal comments in, 203
Art discoveries, right to doubt, 218
Artist (*see also* Actor)
  fallen down badly, 76; as public figure, 187
Artificial reputation, 239
Assault, 153, 273
Associated with woman, 45
Associated Press, 2, 107, 113, 116, 181, 227, 258, 293, 305
Athlete (*see* Sports figures)
Attorney (*see* Lawyer, Business, and Professional men)
Attorney general, right to report findings of, 146, 150
Augusta (Ga.) *Chronicle*, 323
Author, 187

Baby black market, 316
Baby's name, ridicule of, 203
Bachelor (*see also* Sexual conduct)
  accused of fathering child, 28
Back copies, care in showing, 104
Background information, leeway in publishing, 152
Bag woman, 344
Baltimore *Sun*, 210, 227, 309
Bank cashier, mentally ill, 55
Bankruptcy, 72, 79, 81, 97, 290
Bar associations, right to report proceedings of, 144
Baseball player (*see also* Sports figures)
  in dog house, 197; uncooperative, 197
Basketball coach, 187
Bastard, 8, 15, 370
Bastrop (La.) *Daily Enterprise*, 286
Baton Rouge *Morning Advocate*, 148
Battery rejuvenator, worthless, 118
Bay rum sales, 324
Beauty, doubt of, 46
Beer drinking on job, 74
Belleville (Ill.) *News-Democrat*, 198
Belly dancer, 187
Bias (*see* Negro; Racism; Racist)
Bigamy, 43
Birch, John, Society, 188
Birth announcements, risk in, 27
Blacklisting as indication of malice, 266
Blackmail, 316
Black market in babies, 316
Blackmun, Harry A., 191
Black Muslims, 65
Black Nationalists, 65
Bleached blonde bastard, 8
Blunders, 215
Boards of aldermen, right to report proceedings of, 127
Bomb throwers, 68
Bookie, leeway in libeling, 78, 304
Book reviews (*see also* Actor; Drama criticism)

general rules for, 195, 198, 201, 212; distortion in quoting, 75
Booth, Shirley, 387
Bootlegger, 193
Boston *Globe*, 287
Boston *Journal*, 234
Boston *Telegraph*, 108
Boston *Traveler*, 326
Boxer (*see also* Sports figures) fixing fight, 217; wearing loaded gloves, 186, 307
Boxing manager accused of dirty work, 123
Brandeis, Louis, 381
Brawl, 312
Brennan, Justice William J., Jr., 176, 191
Bribery, 113, 122, 173, 318
Brick throwing, 182
Broadcasts
general rules for, 342; ad libbing in, 9; commercials on, 345, 346; corrections of, 299; exposés in, 346, 347, 349, 351; fictitious names in, 346; films to prove truth of, 351; identification in, 345; imitations in, 345; libel, not slander, in, 8, 343; live, 9, 343, 344, 345; monitoring live, 9, 345; New York Times rule in, 354; official proceedings in, 351; police conspiracy in, 351; post-proceedings reports in, 351; prerecording of, 345, 350; leeway of privacy in, 386, 391; ridicule in, 345, 346; right to air political speeches in, 355; scripts for, 9; sponsor liability for, 344; wire-service use in, 355; withholding of programs of, 356
Broken man, 60
Brooklyn *Standard Union*, 140
Brother, link to, 59
Broun, Heywood, 212
Brutality, 98, 304
Bryant, Paul, 259
Bullyragging, 215

Burglary, 151, 160
Burlesque billing, 331
Business (*see also* Advertising; Business and professional men)
general rules for, 71; advertising claims for, 118, 208; antitrust violation of, 81; bankruptcy of, 72, 79, 81, 82, 290; bay rum sales by, 324; boycott of, 204; cheating by, 72, 80, 82, 83, 92, 350; closed to public, risk in libeling, 87; closing plants by, 82, 185; corporations, leeway in libeling, 80, 185; corporations, nonprofit, risk in libeling, 90; criminal link with, 84; debt, nonpayment of, 41, 79; discontinuance of products by, 82; dishonesty of, 72; embargo violation by, 84, 185, 221; factories, risk in identifying, 87; false advertising of, 290; financial difficulties of, 55, 72, 79; fraud by, 72, 79, 83, 88, 92, 134, 154, 163, 224, 303, 310, 352; gouging of, 80; harming innocent people by, 241; illegal, 78; insolvency of, 72, 79, 81; labor contract violation by, 204; labor law violation of, 96; labor relations unfairness of, 96, 267; leeway in criticizing, 76, 87, 184; losses by, 82; merges of, 81; mistreating employees by, 267; open to public, leeway in libeling, 85, 86, 87; partnerships, risks in libeling, 91; patrons, leeway in libeling, 85, 86, 87; personal violence by, 81; political campaign link with, 185; price cutting by, 80; products, worthlessness of, 87, 118, 208, 346; profiteering by, 42, 239; proxy fights of, 310; pure-food law, violations by, 80, 81, 146; rackets of, 23, 61, 304, 350, 352; ransom by, 350; rape by, 81; robbery by, 81; running out on oral agreement by, 42; sale of, 185; sharp practices of, 80; single

mistake by, 76; single loss by, 82; smuggling wetbacks by, 268; trading with enemy by, 185, 221; unfairness to employees of, 96, 204, 267; with public interest, leeway in libeling, 185, 187, 189

Business and professional men (*see also* Business)

general rules for, 71; abusive conduct of, 241; adoption black market of, 316; as architect of frame-up, 188; arrest of, 271; artificial reputation of, 239; bankruptcy of, 72, 79, 81; blackmail by, 279, 316; botching case by, 143; bribery by, 113; brutality of, 304; cheating competitors by, 83; cheating customers by, 72, 80, 82, 83, 92, 350; Communist link with, 58, 68, 166, 182, 188, 266, 315; cowardice of, 240; criminal link with, 17, 26, 58, 84, 113; cruelty of, 241; death in office of, 11; debt, nonpayment of by, 41, 79; designing dangerous structure by, 71; dictator methods of, 241; disclosing confidence by, 77; dishonesty of, 72, 365; drunkenness of, 75; elbowing others aside, 78; falsifying report by, 310; "fat cat" description of, 305; fighting by, 51; financial difficulties of, 72, 79; firing of, 109; forcing partner to retire by, 80; fraud by, 37, 72, 79, 83, 90, 92, 154, 248, 245, 310, 350, 351; grotesque conduct of, 77; harming innocent people by, 241; Hitler-like conduct of, 36; honor, lack of by, 244; illegal acts of, 78; illiteracy of, 75; inability of, 36; inability to support wife by, 58; incapacity of, 25, 78, 295; informing on criminals by, 33; insolvency of, 72, 79, 82; integrity, doubt of, 244; intelligence quotient of, 56; labor contract violation by, 204; labor law violation

by, 96; labor relations unfairness of, 96; leeway to criticize, 76, 78, 89, 181, 185; liquor used for medicine by, 34; losses by, 82; love of money by, 58; love of self by, 239; lunacy of, 204; lying of, 237, 241, 244, 294; marital misconduct of, 36, 145, 273; mental illness of, 54, 204; misappropriation of money by, 139; mismanagement by, 229, 304; misrepresentation by, 201; misuse of funds by, 310; NAACP link with, 66; nudism of, 239; peddling smut by, 189; pennilessness of, 57; phoney actions of, 245; price cutting by, 80; profiteering by, 42, 239; pure-food law violation by, 80, 146; quackery of, 10, 79; racket of, 350; ransom by, 350; reckless driving of, 339; refusal to make payments by, 41; risks in libeling, 71; running out on oral deal by, 42; scandal link with, 20; seizing profits by, 80; sexual conduct of, 25; sharp practices of, 80; sideline of, 75; single mistake of, 76, 82, 314; son-of-a-bitch description of, 344; statute-of-fraud invocation by, 42; suggestion for jailing of, 346; theft by, 244; treason by, 221; un-Americanism of in labor relations, 70; unconscionable fee of, 71, 236; unethical conduct of, 71, 72, 80, 107, 118, 188, 209, 236, 252; unfairness to employees by, 96

Butchers, cheating, 72

Butts, Wally, 181, 183, 256, 259, 280, 291, 363

Buxom brunette, identification of, 17

Cabinet officers, leeway in libeling, 176, 179, 180

Cabinet sub-officers, leeway in libeling, 179

"Cahoots, in," 161

Camden (N.J.) *Evening Courier* and *Morning Post,* 138
Cantor, Eddie, 25
Capone, Al, 384
Captions (*see also* Pictures)
  general rules for, 327; animal-human comparison in, 62; association with spy in, 328; cheating charge in, 72; criminal association in, 60; fair comment in, 329; incomplete, 327; misidentification in, 29, 323; misidentifying couple as married in, 30; need for reference in accompanying articles, 326; nonlibelous, 323; obscenity in, 332; racial, 63
Carelessness, 323
Car-repair company, fraud by, 352
Cartoons, 6, 108, 173
Cashier, mental illness of, 55
Cepeda, Orlando, 196
"Certain," value of term, 24
Charities, leeway in libeling, 90, 145, 201
Charleston (W.Va.) *Gazette,* 275
Charm course, taking, 29
Cheating, 72, 80, 82, 83, 88, 92, 350
Checking facts, value in, 261, 272, 273, 276, 298, 352, 356
Check kiting, 275
Chef, dishonest, 365
Cherry Sisters, 213
Chicago *Herald-American,* 60
Chicago *News,* 97
Chicago *Tribune,* 20, 97, 360
Child bride, 47
Children of public figure, 400
Children's court, right to report proceedings of, 139
"Chinks," leeway in using term, 67
Christian Science practitioner, suit by, 134, 164, 224
Church boards, right to report proceedings of, 145
Church, membership in, 3, 36
Churches, risk in libeling, 201

Churchwarden, marital misconduct of, 30
Cincinnati *Enquirer,* 201
Circulation
  back copies, 104; no complete defense in small, 15; not factor in malice, 341; risk in large, 337
Citizens Council, membership in, 65
City councilmen (*see also* Public officials)
  leeway in libeling, 180, 264
City councils, right to report proceedings of, 127, 132
City, right to libel, 97
City managers (*see also* Public officials)
  leeway in libeling, 180
Civic Clubs, right to report trials of, 145
Civic libel, definition of, 6, 371
Civil rights
  foes, leeway in libeling, 172, 180, 183, 246; leaders, leeway in libeling, 149, 172; protests, 142, 149, 183, 201; violations, right to report, 98, 172
Clay, Cassius, 217
Clay Center (Kan.) *Dispatch,* 27
Clergymen (*see also* Business and professional men)
  adultery of, 145; drunkenness of, 75; fighting by, 51, 272; fraud by, 134, 224; get-rich-quick dogma of, 302; informing on criminals by, 33; misappropriation of money by, 140; refusal to turn other cheek by, 51, 273; ridicule of, 51, 302; risk in libeling, 311, 377; union-supporter ridicule of, 302
Clergyman's daughter, ridicule of, 227
Clergyman's wife, ridicule of, 227
Clerks, government, risk in libeling, 181
Cleveland *Call & Post,* 160
Cleveland *Plain Dealer,* 396

Closed hearings, right to report proceedings of, 129, 130
Cocotte, 35
Coffins, making own, 53
Collier's, 89, 121, 332
Columnists
   defense for, 196; gossip, 16, 143; leeway in libeling, 183; risk in, 16, 118, 143, 177, 237; unpaid, 177
Commercials, 345, 346 (*see also* Advertising)
Communist (*see also* Socialist)
   agent, 68; in broadcasting, link with, 26, 266; clique, 167; dupe, 222; exposé of, 26; fellow traveler, 26, 68, 169, 222; fronter, 188; innocent, 26; left-wing, 27, 66, 315; link, 3, 26, 59, 283, 299, 328, 336, 354; pro-Communist, 4, 34, 68, 266, 315; sellout to, 98; sucker, 222; supporter, 26; sympathizer, 68; tool, 222; transmission belt, 26
Complaints, legal, right to publish, 135
Concord (N.H.) *Monitor*, 193
Condemned house, 75
Conductor, 390
Coney Island singer, 43
Confessions, forcing of, 98
Confidential files, value of, 367
Confidential (magazine), 390
Conflict of interest, 184, 226, 275
Congress (*see* Legislative bodies)
Consent, defense of, 224
Consumption, 56
Coon, 373 (*see also* Negro)
Cop (*see* Policemen)
Coroners, reliance on, 150
Corporation (*see also* Business)
   general rules for, 80; antitrust violation by, 81; credit, 81; leeway in libeling, 80, 185; management (*see* Business and professional men); nonprofit, risk in libeling, 90

Corpus Christi *Caller Times*, 116
Corrections
   general rules for, 282, 285, 287, 299; crime story, 292; form of, 282, 286; headlines for, 287; offer of, 282, 288; quick, 299; radio and TV, 299, 356; risk in refusing, 264, 269, 286, 289, 292; states limiting damages for, 289; value of, 271, 282, 299; when to refuse, 286
Corruption, 173, 214, 357
Court referee, denunciation of, 209
Courtroom behavior, importance of, 252
Courts-martial, right to report proceedings of, 146
Cowardly, 240, 365
Crazy, 234
Credit risk, 401
Creep, 296
Crime (*see also* Arrests)
   general rules for charging, 33, 41, 147; accusation of, 37, 284; anonymous sources for, 310; background of, 152; business in, 84; convention, 158; corrections for stories of, 292; delegate, 158; exposés of, 22, 26, 58, 147, 156, 303, 308; false report of, 271; guilty of, 37, 352; headlines for, 315, 316, 317, 318, 319, 320; hints of, 38, 148; links to, 17, 22, 26, 58, 84, 113, 148, 304, 347; meetings, 157; pictures, 325; right to print reports of, 147, 158, 173; suspicion of, 37, 148, 173
Criminal libel, general rules for, 6, 174, 370
Criminal libel
   fair comment of, 376; good motives of, 375; official proceedings of, 375; public officials and, 97, 174, 373; truth of, 107, 375
Criminals, leeway in libeling, 311
Critics, suit by, 75
Cropping of pictures, 334

Cross examination to prove truth, 119

Cruelty, 241, 295

Crusades (*see* Exposés)

Cub reporter, 182

Curley, James, 108, 265, 373

Customers, right to report actions of, 87, 307

Daily Alaska Empire, 334

Dairymen's League News, 302

Dallas *Morning News*, 184

Damages
general rules for, 248; compensatory, 250; exemplary, 253; general, 250; limits on, 191, 250; multiple, 300; in privacy cases, 398; punitive, 253, 280; special, 249; vindictive, 253

Dance-hall girl, 111

Darlington (S.C.) *News and Press*, 324

Dashing blonde, 43

Davis, Sammy, Jr., 372

Dead, libel of, 7, 281, 372; privacy of, 383, 384

Death, false report of, 50, 51, 281

Debt, nonpayment of, 41, 58, 79

Deceptive, 208

Defense
general rules for, 100; absolute, 100; accord and satisfaction, 281; after publication, 281; care, 298; complete, 101; consent, 224; corrections, 282, 285, 299; exceeding, 308; fair comment, 195; favorable items, 285, 299; heat of campaign, 297; mistaken target, 297; New York Times rule, 170; partial, 101, 283; previous recovery, 300; prior articles, 293; privilege of participant, 104; privilege of reporting, 126; proof of bad reputation, 298; provocation, 295; qualified, 101; reasonable cause, 294; reply, 233; rumors, 294; special statutes, 292; statute of limitations, 102; truth, 106; wire-service copy, 293

Delta (Miss.) *Democrat-Times*, 206

Demagogues, 69

Demotions, 146

Dempsey, Jack, 307

Den of iniquity, 87

Dentist (*see also* Business and professional men; Physicians)
negligence of, 76; unskillful work of, 76

Depositions, right to report, 137

Derangement, 54

Desertion of spouse, 49

Desertion from duty, 75

Designer, homosexual, 26

Designer, scenic, Communist link with, 59

Des Moines *Leader*, 213

Detectives (*see also* Policemen)
use in suits, 357

Diabolical plot, 180

Dictator methods, 241

Dilettante, 187

Dillinger, John, 60

Diphtheria, 56

Dirty fighter, 240

Dirty football player, 121

Disability compensation board, leeway in libeling, 180

Discrimination (*see* Negro; Racism; Racist)

Disease, 36, 56

Dishonesty, 37, 72, 365

Dishonorable conduct, 37, 242

Dishwasher, leeway in libeling, 312

Disloyalty, 67, 221

Disorderly conduct, 18, 109

Distortion of fact, 207

District attorney (*see also* Policemen; Public officials)
criminal link with, 60; Hitler-like tactics of, 36, 374; right to quote, 150; right to report proceedings of, 146, 150

Ditchdigger, illiterate, 75

Divorce, risk in reporting, 42, 154, 160, 189

Divorce court, right to report closed proceedings of, 139

Doctor (*see* Physician; Business and professional men)

Documentary (*see also* Exposés) headlines for, 317, 319; risk in, 347, 352

Dodge, Horace, 17

Doe, John, as fictitious name, 32

Dog, privacy of, 384

Dog house, in, 197

Dolcin Corporation, 208

Drama criticism (*see also* Actor) general rules for, 196, 200, 203, 211, 212, 213, 311; leeway to criticize performance, 200, 203, 212; risk in personal comments, 200

Dress designers, homosexual, 26

Drifter, leeway in libeling, 312

Drinking, 399

Drive-in, incidents at, 85

Driving, reckless, 339

"Dropped," right to use term, 321

Drugs harmful, 208, 346; possession of, 148; use of, 24; worthless, 88, 208, 346

Drunkenness of clergyman, 75; crowd, 85; driver, 75; mayor, 108; military officer, 235; newsman, 75; sharpshooter, 18; wife of public official, 400

Drunkenness, risk in reporting, 57

Dr. Williams' Pink Pills for Pale People, 89

Dubious characters, leeway in libeling, 311

Ecclesiastical faker, 302

Editorials general rules for, 196; exceeding limits of, 203, 221; facts for, 206, 209; limiting risks in, 302; non-libelous comment in, 198; scope of, 200, 203, 215, 302; strong language in, 275; test of fairness in, 211

Educator (*see also* Business and professional men; Public ofcials) Communist link with, 59, 299, 315; firing of, 109; leeway in libeling, 184; marital misconduct of, 28, 273, 362; risk in libeling, 180, 203; sexual conduct of, 273, 362

Either-or technique, 26, 215

Eldredge, Laurence H., 264, 288, 358

Embargo, violating, 185, 221

Enemy, aiding, 365

Entertainer (*see* Actor; Drama criticism)

Espionage, 58, 129, 178

Evolution, 62

Executive proceedings, right to report, 146

Ex-officials, leeway in libeling, 178

Ex-parte hearings, right to report, 165

Exposés general rules for, 22, 26, 58, 166, 196, 217, 221, 262, 303, 307; Communists, disclosure in, 26, 336; Congressional investigation, use in, 166; criminal libel in, 372; exceeding rules in, 308; headlines for, 315, 319; pictures for, 324; 325, 327, 328, 336; public opinion aid in, 221; risks in, 90, 303, 307, 336, 352, 372; test for fairness of, 341, 352

Extremism, 65, 70, 372

Extrinsic facts danger in, 29; definition of, 27; in pictures, 323

Eyewitness, 182

Fabrication, risk in, 271

"Faces," right to use word, 318

Faggots, 25

Fair comment
general rules for, 195; art-criticism reliance on, 201, 218; crowd-opinion reliance on, 217; drama-criticism reliance on, 212; exceeding limits of, 221; exposé reliance on, 217; facts for, 203, 206; fairness in, 211; labor-relations-criticism reliance on, 204; malice role in, 277; nonlibelous, 198; opinion requirement in, 203; product-criticism reliance on, 207; public interest requirement in, 200; risk in correcting, 286; sports-criticism reliance on, 196, 217

Fairbanks *Daily News-Miner*, 108, 183

Fairy colony, 26

Fakery, 217, 302

Fallen women, 43

Falsehood, relation to libel, 10

Falsehood, nonlibelous, 11, 30, 301

Falsifying, 310

Fanny Hill (book), 75

Far right, 70

Fascist, 106, 119 (*see also* Communist; Dictator methods; Gestapo-like; Hitler-like; Nazis)

Fast buck, 263

"Fat cat," 305

Faulk, John Henry, 266, 280

Federal Power Commission, right to libel, 146

Federal Trade Commission, right to libel, 146

Features
fair comment in, 195; play of, 339; ridicule in, 50, 144, 154, 165, 212, 220, 227, 337, 339

Fee, unconscionable, 236

Fellow traveler, 26, 68, 169, 222 (*see also* Communist)

Fifth Amendment, invoking of, 41

Fictionalized TV accounts, risk in, 347

Fictitious names

broadcasting use of 346; how to select, 31; mixing real with, 347; right to use, 31, 347; value of editors' note of, 349

Fighter, dirty, 240

"Fights," right to use term, 109

Film stars, leeway in libeling, 311

Financial embarrassment, 72, 79

Financier (*see* Business and professional men)

Firemen, leeway in libeling, 180

"Fired," right to use term, 109, 161

Firestone, Mary Alice, 189

Fisher, Eddie, 312

Fixed fights, 217

Fixing, 215, 259

Fluoridation foe, misrepresentation by, 201

Follow-up articles, risk in, 17

Fool, 342

Football fix, 181, 259, 363

Football player (*see also* Sports figures)
bullying of, 121; dirty playing of, 121; risk in libeling, 24; drug use by, 24

Foreigners, leeway in libeling, 67, 313

Foreign legislative bodies, right to report proceedings of, 128

Foundations, right to criticize, 90, 201

Fowler, Thomas W., 23

Fraud (*see also* Business and professional men)
government, 97, 173, 326, 327; labor union, 92; limiting risk by avoiding charge of, 303; mail, 320; suspicion of, 72; vote, 174

Friedan, Betty, 387

"Friend," use of term in relation to woman, 45

Friend in Kremlin, 181

Friendly, Judge Henry J., 175, 182

Friends, unsavory, 21, 26, 58

Frightening women, 55

Frigid woman, 48

Front-Page Detective, 398
Funeral, secondary role in, 14
FYI's, risk in, 367

Gamblers, risk in relying on, 114
Gambling, 166
Gang, 157, 319, 398
Gannett & Co., 187
Garbage man of fourth estate, 183
General (*see* Military officer)
Gestapo-like, 94
Get rich quick, 302
Ghoulish, 54
Godfrey, Arthur, 346
Goelet, Robert, Jr., 390
Good taste no test of malice, 339
Gossip, risk in, 16, 143, 294, 311
Gouging, 80
Government, right to libel, 97
Government agencies, right to report
    proceedings of, 146
Government officials (*see* Public of-
    ficials)
Graft, 139
Graft collector, 105, 280, 344
Grand jury, right to publish pro-
    ceedings of, 139, 306, 321
Grave, exhuming of, 39
Greater the truth, greater the libel,
    107
Grotesque conduct, 77
Group libel, value of, 22, 303
Groups, unincorporated, risk in libel-
    ing, 91
Guilt, assumption of, 145, 152, 317,
    318, 319, 320
Guilt by association, 22, 26, 58, 299
Gymnasium, right to report incidents
    at, 86
Gypped, 354

Half-truth, risk in, 110
Hand, Judge Learned, 2, 68
Handcuffed, 271
Hanging, right to report remarks at,
    142
Harming innocent people, 241

Hayes, Joseph, 393
Headlines
    general rules for, 314; attribution
    in, 315, 317, 318; corrections in,
    287; crime stories, 317; exposés,
    315, 317, 319; features, 156;
    going beyond story in, 308;
    implying guilt in, 145, 317, 318;
    misplaced, 321; nonlibel in, 314;
    official proceedings defense in,
    315, 318; puns in, 320
Hearst Corporation, 17, 180, 240,.
    392
Hints, risk in, 38, 72
Hitler-like, 36, 374
Holding hands, 48
Holiday (magazine), 387
Homosexuality, 25, 98, 194, 374,
    400 (*see also* Sexual conduct)
Honor, questioning of, 242, 244
Hoodlum, 157
Hope, Frederick H., 17
Hospitals (*see also* Nursing homes)
    mistreating of patients by, 86; right
    to criticize, 201; right to report
    wrongdoing at, 86; risk as source
    of information, 28
Hotel
    failure to pay bill by, 146, 154;
    poor service of, 186; right to re-
    port wrongdoing at, 87, 307
Hot water, in, 252
House of Representatives, 127 (*see
    also* Legislative bodies)
Hula-hoop girl, 198
Humor, risk in using, 227
Husband of public figure, 387
Hushing up witness, 215
Hustler, The (movie), 227

Idahonian, 141
Identification
    general rules for, 16; circum-
    stances for, 16; clouding of, 22,
    26, 303, 306; description for, 16,
    48; fictitious names for, 30, 346;
    group, 22; initials for, 16; mis-

taken, 18, 287, 297; need for, 12,
16; nickname for, 16; occupation
for, 17, 176; pen name for, 16;
picture use in, 322, 346; risk in
police reports of, 18; to only one
reader, 16; TV problems of, 346;
voice for, 345
Idiot, 54, 322, 329
Illegal proceedings, right to report,
140
Illicit love affair, 323 (*see also* Marital misconduct; Sexual conduct)
Illiteracy, 75
Ill will as test of malice, 265
Imbecile, 56
Immorality, 37
Imposter, 234
Incompetence, 25, 78, 210, 295
Indecent exposure, 199
Indictments, right to report, 139
Inefficiency, 174
Infamous, 210
Infantile paralysis, 56
Informer, 33
Informer, use of information from,
151
Initials for identification, 16
Innocent construction rule, 20
Innocent mistake, how to avoid, 20,
27, 28, 29
Insanity, 54, 56
Insolvency, 72, 79, 81
Institutionalized, 246
Insubordination, 132, 269
Insurance broker, fraudulent, 92
Insurance, libel, 368
Insurance policies, fake, 92
Integrationist, 66
Integrity, doubt of, 244
Interpretive articles, risk in, 196
Interstate Commerce Commission,
right to report proceedings of,
146
Interview, responsibility of source
for, 9
Interview, value of, 9, 224, 228
Investigators, value of, 357

I.Q., low, 56
Irreligious libertine, 342

Jackass, 343
Jacksonville (Fla.) *Times-Union*,
245
Jailing suggestion, 346
Janitors, risk in libeling, 176
Jet (magazine), 273, 362
Jews, leeway in libeling, 22, 372
Jew-nigger, 373
John Birch Society, 188
Johnson City (Tenn.) *Press-Chronicle*, 374
Jones, Artemus, 30
Judge (*see also* Public official)
criminal link with, 151, 153, 319;
excessive vacations by, 174; inefficiency of, 174; lashing of, 320;
laziness of, 174; leeway in libeling, 320; looting business by, 24;
malfeasance of, 24; mistake of,
141; misusing legal machinery by,
24; role in deciding libel of, 34
Judicial proceedings, 133 (*see also*
Official proceedings)
closed, 138; children's court, 139;
descriptions of court scenes, 165;
divorce court, 139; ex-parte, 165;
grand jury, 139, 306, 321; illegal,
140; one-sided testimony in, 165;
post-, 138; private, 144; start of,
136; unfair report of, 252; women's court, 139
Julian, Joe, 27, 222
Jury's role in deciding libel, 34

Kansas rule, 173
Keane, Doris, 29
Kearns, Doc, 307
Kellems, Vivian, 221
Keystone Cops, 337
KGGM Albuquerque, 349
Kickback, 326
Kikes, 67, 120
Kissing, 48
Kiting checks, 285

Knickerbocker, Cholly, 16
Kosher-coon, 373
Koussevitzky, Serge, 390
Kremlin, friend in, 182, 293
Kuchel, Thomas H., 374
Ku Klux Klan, 65, 183, 245, 301
    (*see also* Racism)
KXTV Sacramento, 350
KYW Philadelphia, 352, 356

Labor contract, violation of, 204
Labor leader, accused of
    agitation, 93; antibusiness views,
    93; Communist link, 68; conspir-
    ing with gamblers, 23; feathering
    nests, 92; gestapo action, 94;
    get-rich-quick dogma, 302; rack-
    eteering, 93; rule or ruin tactics,
    93; scabing, 95; strikebreaking,
    95; theft, 112; unfitness, 203;
    using force, 94
Labor-management disputes
    general rules for, 95, 96, 97, 144,
    145, 200; criminal libel and, 371;
    leeway in reporting, 97, 201, 204,
    267, 302
Labor unions
    general rules for, 90–97; belliger-
    ency of, 93; boards of, 145; com-
    pany, 93; libel by, 267; meetings
    of, 144; rackets of, 92; risk in li-
    beling, 93; use of force by, 95
Laborer, leeway in libeling, 75, 95,
    312
Laconia (N.H.) *Evening Citizen*,
    177
Lahr, Bert, 345
Lait, Jack, 25
Lashes, 320
Las Vegas *Sun*, 315, 368
Lawyer (*see also* Business and pro-
    fessional men)
    adoption black market by, 316;
    ambulance chasing by, 10, 127; as
    architect of frame-up, 188; black-
    mail by, 316; botching case by,
    143; Communism link of, 68, 166,

188; conflict of interest by, 183;
disbarrment of, 107, 118; criminal
link of, 17, 60; deliberately giving
erroneous advice by, 77; disclosing confidence by, 77; elbowing
others aside by, 77; Hitler-like
conduct of, 36, 374; hot-water status of, 252; improper conduct in
court of, 252; legal technicality
of, 161; leeway in libeling, 183;
lunacy of, 204; marital misconduct of, 17, 30, 36; as public
figure, 188; reckless driving of,
339; representation of rabble-
rouser by, 42; scandal link of, 20;
shyster conduct of, 79; single mistake of, 76; unethical conduct of,
209; value in quoting, 232, 242;
wretchedly poor ability of, 36
Laziness, 174
Left-winger, 66, 315
Left-wing group, 27
Legal action, start of, 136
Legal loophole, 185
Legal rights, invocation of, 41
Legal technicality, 161
Legal terms, synonyms for, 160
Legislative bodies (*see also* Official
    proceedings)
    general rules for, 127; closed
    hearings of, 131; committee pro-
    ceedings of, 127; illegal sessions
    of, 128; informal sessions of, 132;
    news conferences of, 129; official
    proceedings of, 127; open sessions
    of, 127
Legislators (*see also* Public officials)
    leeway in libeling, 180; selling
    votes by, 276
Lehighton (Pa.) *Evening Leader*,
    263
Leigh, Janet, 47
Leninist, 188
Leprosy, 56
Letters, private, 13
Letters to editor, risk in, 69, 87, 196,
    198, 214, 241, 373

Subject Index

Lewdness, 199
Lewis, Fulton, Jr., 59, 299
Lex salica decrees, 249
Libel and slander differentiated, 7
Libel
  civil, 6; criminal, 6, 174, 370;
  definition of, 12; falsity of, 10;
  first case of civil, 8; insurance,
  368; of dead, 7, 372; of govern-
  ment, 97; of thing, 87; oral, 9;
  per se, 35; pro quod, 35; repeti-
  tion of, 4, 103, 116, 225, 267,
  310; value of publishing, 2
Liberals, well-intentioned, 26
Libertine, irreligious, 342
Lie detector test, balking at, 210
Life (magazine), 217, 322, 328,
  329, 393
Liquor for medicinal purposes, 34
Loaded gloves, use of, 186, 307
Look (magazine), 125, 196
Los Angeles *Record*, 173
Lost records, 73
Love affair, illicit, 323
Love triangle, 312
Loving himself, 239
Lunacy, sheer, 204
Lying, 215, 237, 241, 244, 294, 310,
  342

Mad man, 342
Mafia, 17, 84
Magruder, Calvert, 14
Mail fraud, 88, 320
Makeup
  general rules for, 334; banner-
  headline use in, 334; fairness of,
  340, 341; feature story, 337, 339;
  good-taste test for, 339; malice
  proof in, 340; picture-story relationship in, 334, 335, 336; stale
  news play in, 338
Malfeasance in office, 24, 146, 327
Malice
  general rules for, 248; actual,
  248; legal, 248; trends in, 276

Malice, effect of on
  damages, 248; civil libel, 255;
  criminal libel, 255; fair comment,
  256, 277; New York Times rule,
  257, 264, 278; official proceedings
  reports, 256, 278; reply defense,
  256; truth as defense, 106, 255
Malice, risk of in
  blacklisting, 266; carelessness,
  270; desire to injure, 257, 266,
  278; extreme language, 265, 275;
  fabrication, 261, 267, 271; failure
  to check, 172, 261, 262, 272, 276;
  failure to prove truth, 270; failure
  to retract, 172; falsity, 257; fist
  fight, 108, 264, 265; ignoring
  facts, 264, 272, 273; intent to destroy, 266; labor disputes, 97;
  lying, 263, 267, 271; makeup,
  340; misquotation, 261; negligence, 270, 272, 285; personal ill
  will, 108, 264, 265, 277, 285;
  quoting rogue, 308; reckless disregard of truth, 258, 263, 308;
  refusal to withhold item, 261,
  269; rejection of correction, 264,
  269, 289; repetition of libel, 267,
  269
Mangy hide, 240
"Many," use of term in exposés, 24
Marciano, Rocky, 106, 123, 317
Marcus, Stanley, 25
Marijuana, carrying, 322
Marital misconduct (*see also* Sexual
  conduct)
  abandonment of spouse, 48; adultery, 28, 36, 145, 158, 273, 362;
  associated with man, 45, 334; bigamy, 43; delighted in female
  butterflies, 31;. desertion, 49; disagreements, 49; divorce, 36; double-dealing, 158; failure to fulfill
  obligation, 48; friend of man, 45;
  inability to support wife, 58; love
  of money, 58; lover, new, 312,
  315; public figures, 311; sexual
  relations with students, 273, 362;

triple-dealing, 158; traveling with Negro, 64; unfaithfulness, 61; unnatural relations, 160

Marlin Fire Arms Company, 87

Marriage, false report of, 28, 30

Mau Mau, 65

McCarthy, Joseph R., 128, 129, 318

Medical board, right to report proceedings of, 11

Medical societies, right to report proceedings of, 144

Medicine, worthless, 89

Mental hospital heads, risk in libeling, 176

Mental illness, general rules for, 54; abnormality, 55; crazy, 234; derangement, 54; emotional difficulties, 400; entering health clinic, 400; fool, 342; frightening women, 55; idiocy, 23, 54, 119, 322; insanity, 54, 56; institutionalization, 246; lunacy, 204; mad man, 342; moron, 56; nervous breakdown, 54, in occupation, 55; psychiatric treatment, 55; psychoanalytic treatment, 55; psychological upset, 54

Mergers of businesses, 81

Metro-Goldwyn-Mayer, 44, 348

Mexican, poor, leeway in libeling, 312

Military courts, right to report proceedings of, 146

Military manner entrance, 94

Military officer
courts-martial of, 146; desertion of, 75; drunkenness of, 235; fixing by, 215; former, 129, 181; homosexuality of, 98, 195; link with spy by, 129

Milk boards, right to libel, 146

Millinery designers, homosexual, 26

Milwaukee *Journal,* 301

Ministers (*see* Clergyman)

Minority groups, leeway in libeling, 22

Misconduct, 210

Misdeed, 229

Misfortune, general rules for, 54

Misleading, 208

Mismanagement, 229, 304

Misplaced headline, 321

Mistake, innocent, 27

Mistaken identity
risk in, 18, 28, 116, 361; risk in correcting, 287; value in correcting, 297

Misusing legal machinery, 24

Misusing office for personal gain, 263, 286, 357

Models, prostitute, 25

Models, use of professional, 330

Moll, link to, 58

Money, love of, 58

Moore, Mrs. Bertha B., 65

Mormon, 3, 36

Morning Journal Association, 53

Moron, 56

Morris, Dennit, 24

Mortimer, Lee, 25

"Most," value of using in exposés, 24

Mother's link to daughter's suicide, 294

Motion picture criticism (*see* Actor; Drama criticism)

Motives, doubting, 214, 237, 244

Motor Trend (magazine), 118

Movie T.V. Secrets (magazine), 312, 315

Muckracking, 260, 261

Mug, 354

Mulatto, 63

Municipal power companies, leeway in libeling, 180

Murderous, 38

Music criticism (*see* Actor; Art criticism; Drama criticism)

Mutual Broadcasting System, 299

NAACP, membership in, 66

Names, similar, 18

Narcotics
possession of, 148; ring, 319; sales, 307; use of, 24
National Broadcasting Company, 346
Nationalities, leeway in libeling, 63, 67, 373
National Labor Relations Board jurisdiction in libel cases, 96
Navy officer (*see* Military officer)
Nazis, American
link to, 120, 305; criminal libel by, 372
Negro
anti-Negro, 66; Black Muslim, 65; Black Nationalist, 65; calling a white man, 3, 36, 63; conservative, 65; coon, 373; cooperative, 65; extremist, 65; five percenters, 65; Jew-nigger, 373; leeway in libeling, 312; link to, 65; Mau Mau, 65; moderate, 65; mulatto, 63; nigger, 64, 373; nonaggressive, 65; Northern, 64; old-line, 65; prejudice against, 66; risk in libeling, 22; Southern, 63; Uncle Tom, 65
Neiman-Marcus Company, 25
Nervous breakdown, 54
Newark *Star-Ledger*, 129, 318
News conferences and releases, right to report, 9, 129, 146, 151, 174, 230, 236
Newsweek, 187
New Orleans *Item*, 331
New Orleans *Times-Picayune*, 321
Newsday, 290
Newsman, accused of
arousing fears, 201; artificial reputation, 239; bribery, 113; cowardice, 240; dirty fighting, 240; distortion, 73; drunkenness, 75; garbage-man status, 183; harmful acts, 201; ignoring facts, 73; incapacity, 25, 295; loving himself, 239; misrepresenting facts, 201;

NAACP link, 66; nudism, 239; profiteering, 239; sycophant, 238; yellow streak, 240; unfitness, 295
Newspaper, leeway in libeling, 201, 295, 373
New York *American*, 117
New York *Daily Mirror*, 58
New York *Daily News*, 120, 154, 158, 160, 166, 182, 293, 336
New Yorker (magazine), 388
New York *Evening Graphic*, 90
New York *Herald Tribune*, 16, 20, 30, 42, 51, 79, 82, 142, 151, 209, 226, 233, 281, 365
New York *Journal-American*, 151, 240
New York (magazine), 253, 387, 389
New York *Mirror*, 385
New York *Post*, 45, 66, 134, 147
New York *Recorder*, 43
New York *Sun*, 91, 203, 225
New York Times, The, 28, 50, 151, 164, 224, 287, 303, 304, 334, 337, 368, 382
New York Times rule, 170, 257
New York *Tribune*, 214, 284
New York *World*, 214
Nickname, risk in using, 16
Nigger, 64, 373 (*see also* Negro)
Nigger lover, 65
Night club, right to criticize, 87
Nixon, Richard, 394, 399
Nizer, Louis, 364
No comment, importance of, 232
Nonbeliever, 123
Noncitizen, 67
Nonlibel, right to publish, 11, 26, 27, 29, 30, 40, 198, 202, 301, 314
Norfolk Newspapers, 118
North American Newspaper Alliance, 193
Notable persons, misidentification of, 18
Notorious, 125

Nudism, 189, 239

Nurse called son of a bitch, 296

Nurses, risks in libeling, 176, 201, 296

Nursing homes (*see also* Hospitals; Public places)
shocking conditions at, 229, 341

Oakley, Annie, 18

Oath breaking, 342

Obituary, false, 50

Obituary list, omission from, 14

Obscene effect in distorted picture, 332

Obscenity cases, right to report proceedings of, 139, 189

Occupation
injury to, 71; role in identification, 16

Office worker, risk in libeling, 73

Official (*see* Public officials)

Official Detective Stories (magazine), 149

Official proceedings (*see also* Judicial proceedings; Legislative proceedings)
general rules for, 127, 141, 155, 156, 278; closed, 131, 138; exparte, 165; fair reports of, 156, 164, 279; illegal, 128; informal, 132; misinterpretation of, 164; open, 127; post-, 138, 146; true reports of, 156; unfairness in reporting, 352

O'Malley, Walter, 71, 236

Opening up town, 162

Opera singer's link to enemy, 365

Opinions as different from fact, 203

Opinions, misstatements of, 75

Oral business agreement, running out on, 42

Orgy, right to report, 85

Owens, O. O., 24

Paar, Jack, 346

Pacifists, leeway in libeling, 183, 201, 343

Panel shows, risk in, 344

Parade Magazine, 104

Parents, penniless, 57

Parks, right to report misconduct at, 85

Partnerships, risk in libeling, 91

Passaic (N.J.) *Daily News*, 132, 269, 341

Patriotism, 67, 221 (*see also* Communist; Fascist; Nazi; Pacifist; Spy; Subversion)

Patrolman (*see* Policeman)

Patrons of public places, right to report actions of, 87, 307

Pauling, Linus, 182, 293

Pawtucket (R.I.) *Times*, 252

Payroll padder, 147

Peace Corps worker, desertion by, 75

Pearson, Drew, 106, 118, 183, 193, 202 ,283, 327

Pegler, Westbrook, 68, 237, 248, 253, 266, 275, 297, 364

Pen name sufficient for identification, 16

Penniless, 57

Percentage girl, 110

Perjury, 110

Personal items, risk in, 53

Perversion, sexual, 160

Petitions, right to publish, 128

Phony, 208, 240

Photographs (*see* Pictures)

Physician (*see also* Business and professional men)
brutality of, 304; deaths in office of, 11; illegal practice by, 79; incapacity of, 76; leeway in libeling, 201; operating on bankroll by, 71, 236; performing unnecessary operation by, 71, 236; as public figure, 187; prescribing liquor, 34; quackery of, 10, 79; risks in libeling, 305; single mistake by, 76, 314; unconscionable fee of, 71, 236; unfitness of, 76

Picketing, 201, 301

Pig, 62

Pictures (*see also* Captions)

general rules for, 322; blind, 325; captions for, 30, 322, 327; comparing wrestler to gorilla, 62, 330; Communist link in, 328, 336; criminals in, 325; cropping of, 334; distorted, 332; erroneous, 29, 63, 323; 324; exposé use of, 324, 329, 336; humorous, 227, 324; layout of, 60, 62, 227, 328, 330; linking good characters with bad, 58, 331; misidentification, 323; motion, 44, 87, 325, 348; need for cross reference in stories, 326; obscenity in, 332; posed by models, 330; as privacy invasion, 381, 383, 385; proving defense of consent, 231; trick, 333

Pilot, arrest of, 271

Pink Pills for Pale People, Dr. Williams', 89

Pistol permit, request for, 151

Pittsburgh *Courier*, 85, 155, 211

Plague, 56

Plainfield (N.J.) *Courier-News*, 165

Planting false evidence, 210

Playing politics, 215

Plaintiff's character, how checked, 357

PM (newspaper), 139

Pocatello (Idaho) *State Journal*, 315

Police

blotter, 148; bookings, 148; bribery, 210, 318; charges, 149; investigations, 148; privacy of, 383, 384; questioning, 149; raids, 148; records, 149; role in misidentification, 18; trials of, 146

Policeman (*see also* Public officials)

Policeman, accused of

balking at lie detector test, 210; bribery, 173, 318; brutality, 98; criminal link, 347; diabolical plot, 180; drinking beer on job, 74; forcing confessions, 98; graft, 304; incompetence, 210; infamous conduct, 210; insubordination, 132, 269; keeping incomplete records, 292; Keystone Cop tactics, 337; making false charges, 210; menacing citizen, 373; misconduct, 210; murderous conduct, 38; padlocking college building, 171; planting false evidence, 210; racket, 74; refusing to obey orders, 210; ridiculous conduct, 74, 337, 339; ringing campus, 171; starving students, 171; swearing, 373; theft, 3, 155, 374; threats, 373; tin-horn cop tactics, 74; unjustified shooting, 38; waving gun menacingly, 373

Policemen

leeway in libel, 98, 172, 180, 290, 304; risk in libeling single, 99, 304

Political affiliations, right to report, 67

Political campaigns, right to report, 142, 162, 173, 174, 175, 183, 184, 200, 245, 309, 354

Political parties, right to report trials of, 145

Political polls, phoney, 245

Politicians (*see also* Public officials)

conflict of interest by, 226; correcting reports about, 283; criminal link with, 138

Polacks, 67

Poor, leeway in libeling, 178, 312

Poor white trash, 66

Portland (Oreg.) *News*, 243

Portland *Oregonian*, 242

Potter's field, 57

Poverty, 57

Powell, Adam Clayton, Jr., 105, 280, 344

Powell, Lewis F., Jr., 191

Praying, 399

Pregnancy, 29, 289

Prejudice (*see* Negro; Racism; Racist)

Presidential advisers, right to libel, 179

Presidential candidate, right to quote, 309

Press conferences (*see* News conferences)

Price cutting, 80

Priest (*see also* Clergyman)

Priest accused of
eating meat on Friday, 287; informing on criminals, 33

Prisoner, 37

Privacy
in advertising, 386; as appropriation, 396; of child prodigy, 388; of clowning spectator, 389; consent as defense, 397; defenses against, 397; as disclosure, 396; of dog, 384; of drinking, 399; as false light, 396; of family of public figure, 400; in fictionalizing, 389, 398; of financial troubles, 400; four classes of, 396; of gangs, 398; history of, 380; of husband, 387; as intrusion, 396; in names and pictures, 388; in New York Times rule, 393; of pension, 401; of praying, 399; of profanity, 399; rules on, 385; of sex life, 399, 400; of a spouse, 387, 400; status by states, 382; of tax payments, 399; of telephone calls, 400; of weeping, 399; of wife, 400

Private affairs, leeway in libeling, 191; risk in reporting, 173, 202

Private gatherings, risk in reporting, 143

Private organizations, right to report trials of, 145

Privilege of participant, 104

Privilege of reporting general rules of, 126
states in which malice limits, 126

Pro-Communist (*see* Communist)

Prodigy, child, 388

Products, libel of, 87, 118, 208, 320, 346

Profanity, 399

Professional man (*see* Business and professional men)

Professional societies, right to report actions of, 144

Professor
illiteracy of, 75; penniless, 57; ridiculing personal life of, 203

Profiteering, 42, 239

Prohibitionists, right to criticize, 207

Promise, only on, 301

Promotion, denial of, 132

Propaganda trick, 207

Pro-Red (*see* Communist)

Prosecutor (*see* District attorney; Lawyer; Policeman; Public officials)

Prostitution, 25, 35, 43, 110, 162, 325, 360; privacy of reformed prostitute, 397 (*see also* Marital misconduct; Sexual conduct)

Protection money, 139

Protests, right to report, 142, 148. 150

Protestant bias, 66

Providence *Journal*, 106, 119, 399

Provocation, defense of, 295

Proxy fights, right to report, 310

Psychiatric treatment, 55

Psychoanalytic treatment, 55, 400

Psychological upset, 55

Psychotic, 125

Publication
requirement of, 13; rule for determining date of, 103

Public figures, leeway in libeling, 181, 200, 257, 283, 311; leeway in reporting on private matters of, 399; risks in libeling, 188

Public institutions, right to libel, 97, 201

Public meetings, right to report, 142, 162, 217, 279, 309, 310

Public officials
definition of, 176–180; ex- , right

to libel, 178; leeway in libeling, 170, 172, 257, 311, 355; right to quote, 146, 150; risk of criminally libeling, 175, 373

Public officials accused of accepting stock, 214; anti-Semitism, 118; being fired, 161; blundering, 215; breaking promises, 342; bribery, 122, 173, 318; brutality, 98, 304; bullyragging, 215; Communist link, 354; conflict of interest, 275; corruption, 357; criminal link, 60, 347; diabolical plot, 180; diverting government cash, 334; drinking, 74, 399; financial troubles, 400; fixing, 215; fool, 342; gambling aid, 162; graft, 139, 304; Hitler-like tactics, 374; homosexuality, 98, 195, 374, 400; incompetence, 210; inefficiency, 174; insubordination, 132, 269; irreligious libertine, 342; keeping incomplete record, 292; kickbacks, 326; laziness, 174; looting business, 24; lying, 215; mad man, 342; making false charges, 210; making fast buck, 263; malfeasance, 24, 146, 327; marital misconduct, 311; menacing citizens, 373; mental illness, 234; misconduct, 210; mistake, 141; misusing legal machinery, 24; misusing office for personal gain, 262, 286, 357; murderous conduct, 38; oath breaking, 342; opening up town, 162; payroll padding, 147; padlocking college building, 171; planting false evidence, 210; private misconduct, 173, 192; profanity, 399; prostitution aid, 162; racket, 74, 98; refusing to obey orders, 210; ridiculous conduct, 337; rigging testimony, 215; ringing campus, 171; sabotage, 161; selling votes, 276; sexual conduct, 195; starving students, 171; stealing state secrets, 178; taking public funds, 357; theft, 3, 155, 374; unjustified shooting, 38; vote fraud, 174; walkout from meeting, 315; weeping, 399; whitewash, too much, 216

Public opinion, aid in exposés, 221

Public places (*see also* Hospitals; Restaurants)
right to report trouble at, 85, 307

Public relations campaign, right to criticize, 201

Public relations man, value in quoting, 232

Public nuisance, 198

Public utility commission, right to libel, 180

Publisher (*see also* Business and professional men; Newsman)

Publisher accused of distorting news, 73; ignoring facts, 73

Publisher's right to sue for libel, 72

Puerto Ricans, poor, leeway in libeling, 22, 312

Puns, risk in, 302, 320, 332

Pure-food law violations, 80, 146

Putnam's Sons, G. P., 76, 103

Quack, 10, 79

Quill, Mike, 371

Quotation marks, risk in using, 45

Quotations
fabrication of, 271; fair comment, use of, 196, 217; risk in relying on, 4, 45, 112, 258

Quasi-judicial agencies, leeway in libeling members of, 180

Quasi-judicial agencies, right to report actions of, 146

Race (*see also* Negro)
general rules for, 63; criminal libel of a, 372

Racial incidents, right to report, 246, 305, 330

Racial moderate, 65

Racism, leeway in expounding, 22, 65, 312, 372

Racist, 65, 183, 211, 245, 246, 305

Racket, 19, 22, 23, 61, 74, 93, 98, 304, 319, 350, 352

Racketeers in government, 98

Radio (*see also* Broadcasts)

Radio commentator accused of misrepresentation, 201; pro-Communism, 266

Radio script, liability for, 9, 343

Ransom, 350

Rape, 43, 348, 351

Rape, identification of victim of, 44, 348

Rasputin, 44, 348

Reader's Digest (magazine), 4, 207, 315

Real-estate developer, 187

Real-estate firm, as public figure, 187, 279; renting of condemned property by, 75

Reckless disregard for truth, 258, 264, 308

Reckless driving, 339

Recreation Magazine, 87

Red (*see also* Communist)

Red Channels (book), 26, 222

Refugee, 67

Refusing to obey orders, 210

Relationship with wrongdoer, 58, 299, 328, 331

Relatives, 58, 299

Religion
criminal libel of a, 372, 373; member of a, 3, 36; risk in libeling, 90

Repetition of libel, 4, 45, 105, 112, 116, 133, 225, 267, 310 (*see also* Wire-service dispatches)
from interview, 9; indication of malice, 113; warning of, 4, 113, 169

Reply, defense of, 233

Reply, limits to, 235

Reporters (*see also* Newsman; Publisher)

use of to check plaintiffs, 364

Reputations, bad, 298, 311, 357, 363, 376

Resort manager, criticism of, 177

Restaurants
incidents at, 87

Retractions (*see* Corrections)

Reviews (*see* Actor; Art criticism; Drama criticism)

Reynolds, Quentin, 237, 248, 266, 297, 364

Ridicule
general rule for, 50; picture distortion to, 332; right to, 212, 220, 339; risk in, 227, 339, 346

Rigging testimony, permitting, 215

Ring, 319

Riots, 181, 305

Rioters, taking command of, 181

Robbery, 351

Robbery, attempted, 153

Roe, Richard, as fictitious name, 32

Rowdyism, 85

Rumors, reliance on, 294

Rumors, risk in reporting, 274

Runaway wife, 61

Russians, sellout to, 98

Sabotage, 161

St. Louis *Post Dispatch*, 144

Salesgirls, prostitute, 25

Salesman, homosexual, 26

Salisbury (Md.) *Times*, 291

Saloon, incidents at, 87

San Antonio *Sunday Express and News*, 163

Satire (*see* Ridicule)

Saturday Evening Post, 22, 88, 106, 123, 181, 259, 291, 317, 327, 363

Savannah *Evening Press*, 37

Savannah *Morning News*, 330

Scab, 95

School boards, right to report proceedings of, 127, 146

School officials, right to libel, 146, 181

Subject Index

School teacher (*see* Educator)
Schumann, Robert, 384
Scientist (*see also* Business and professional men)
link to Kremlin, 182
Scranton *Times*, 157
Secret proceedings, right to publish, 131
Securities and Exchange Commission, right to report proceedings of, 166
Seduction, 44, 348
Segregation, 65
Seizing profits, 80
Self-defense, cleric's use of, 51
Self-incrimination, invoking protection against, 41
Selling votes, 276
Settlement of suits, risk in, 4, 283, 358
Senate proceedings, 127 (*see also* Legislative bodies)
Sexual conduct (*see also* Marital misconduct)
general rules for, 42; headlines about, 315; implications in pictures, 323, 332
Sexual conduct, report of
abnormality, 55; association, 45; bachelor's, 28; bigamy, 43; child bride, 47; clergyman's, 145; engaged girl's, 323; entertainer's, 28, 47, 198, 311; faggot, 26; fairy colony, 25; friendship, 45, 361; frightening women, 55; girl's, 198; homosexuality, 26, 98, 195, 374, 400; illicit affair, 323; kissing, 48; lewdness, 199; love triangle, 312; men's, 47; military men's 98, 195; model's, 25; perversion, 160; pregnancy, 29, 289; privacy of, 399; prostitution, 23, 35, 43, 110, 162, 397; public official's, 194, 374, 399; rape, 44, 348; runaway wife, 61; salesmen's, 26; seduction, 44, 348; student's, 289; teacher's, 273, 362;

433

unchastity, 35, 42–49; unnatural relations, 160; women's, 42
Sexual conduct, risk in reporting, 30, 42, 47, 145, 194, 273, 312
Sharp practices by business, 80
Sheriff (*see* Policeman; Public officials)
Shientag, Bernard L., 385
Shifty-eyed, 211
Shooting, 38, 40
Shyster, 79
Similarity of names, risk in, 18, 28
Singer, 390
Single mistake, right to report, 76, 82, 314
Single-publication rule, 102
Sinister, 211
Sinkhole, 87
Sister, link to, 58
Six-cent verdicts, 250
Skunk, 343
Slander, definition of, 7, 372
Smallpox, 36, 56
Smart money, definition of, 253
Smuggling, 268
Snake, comparing man to, 62
Socialist, 68
Society, risks in reports of, 16
Soldier (*see* Military officer)
"Some," use of term, 24, 331
Son of a bitch, 296, 342, 344
Sources, anonymous, 310
Spahn, Warren, 186, 392
Spanel, Abraham N., 68
Special editions, 341
Spectator, 389
Spies, children of, 188
Spokane *Chronicle*, 42
Spokesman, value in quoting, 232, 242
Sports fans, remarks of, 217
Sports figures
bullying of, 121; cheating by, 186, 307; carelessness of, 323, 329; comparing with gorilla, 62; corrections about, 283; criminal link with, 86; dirty playing of,

121; dirty work by, 123, 317; distorted picture of, 332; dog-house status of, 197; drug use by, 24; elbowing others aside, 78; fakery by, 217; fix by, 217, 259, 363; idiocy of, 322, 329; leeway in libeling, 186, 187; obscene picture of, 332; risk in libeling, 176, 186; uncooperative, 197

Sports Illustrated (magazine), 77, 186, 307

Sports scandal, 259

Spy, link to, 58, 129, 328

Starving students, 171

Statute of frauds, invocation of, 42

Statute of limitations for libel, 102

Statute of limitations, list of states by years, 102

Statute of limitations, right to report invocation of, 41

Stewart, Potter, 193

Stillman's Gym, 86

Stockholder meetings, risk in reporting, 144

Stockton Labor Journal, 204

Stock swindle, 166

Stopping presses, value of, 291

Stranger, leeway in libeling, 313

Strikebreaking, 95, 350

Strikes (see also Labor-management disputes)
  leeway in reporting, 201

Stripteaser, 198

Student, NAACP link to, 66

Subversion, 70 (see Communist; Fascist; Nazi; Spy)

Suicide, 125, 282
  driving to, 58, 294

Suspension from job, 161

Suspicion, risk in reporting, 37, 72, 294

Spy, 66 (see also Communist; Fascist; Nazi; Subversion)

Sycophant, 238

Syphilis, 57

Syracuse Journal, 103

Tape recording
  to check quotes, 123; to prove truth, 113

Taping radio and TV shows, 9

Taylor, Elizabeth, 312, 315

Taxicab driver, cheating by, 22

Tax payments, 399

Teachers (see Educator)

Teamster Union, 23, 204, 235

Telephone calls, 400

Television (see Broadcasting)

That Was The Week That Was, (TV program), 345

Theft, 155, 244, 351, 374

Theft of state secrets, 178

Thing, libel of, 87

Thompson, William Hale, 97

Thug, 354

Time (magazine), 23, 154, 180, 187, 189

Tin-horn cop, 74

Topeka Daily Capital, 325

Topeka State-Journal, 173

Town meetings, 127 (see also Legislative bodies)

Track coach, 187

Trading with enemy, 185, 221

Treason, 98, 173, 221

Trials (see Judicial proceedings)

True (magazine), 24, 319

Truth
  general rules for defense of, 106; accuracy not proof of, 112; cross examination to prove, 119; danger in trying to prove, 270; detectives' use to prove, 357; definition of, 108; documentary evidence to prove, 118; errors that defeat, 108; essentials of, 108; gamblers' testimony insufficient to prove, 113; half-truth, 110; how to prove, 118–125, 357; how to test for, 120; perjury proved by, 110; states permitting defense of, 107; "whore" proved by, 110; wire-service dispatches to prove, 116; witnesses that prove, 122

Tuberculosis, 56
Turn other cheek, refusal to, 51

Ultra old guard, 70
Un-American, 69
Un-American in labor relations, 70
Unchastity, 35, 42–49
Uncle Tom, 65
Unconscionable fee, 71, 236
Unemployment compensation board, right to libel, 180
Unfaithfulness of wife, 61
Unincorporated groups, 91
Unions (*see* Labor unions; Labor-management relations)
Union leaders (*see* Labor union leaders)
United Press, 107, 360
United Press International, 116, 271, 293, 305
University presidents, 176
Unnatural sexual relations, 160
Untouchables, The (TV program), 347
Untrustworthy, 301
Untruthful, 241
U. S. A. Confidential (book), 25
Utica (N.Y.) *Observer-Dispatch*, 192
Uvalde (Tex.) *Leader-News*, 15, 156

Vacations, excessive, 174
Vaseline, boxer's gloves smeared with, 106, 123
Vice, 174
  link to, 61
Vote fraud, 174
Votes, selling, 276

Wake, attendance at, 15
Walker, Maj. Gen. Edwin A., 181, 182, 258
Walkout, 315
Wall Street Journal, 310
Wanamaker, Mrs. Pearl A., 59, 299
War profiteering, 42, 239
Warren (Ark.) *Eagle Democrat*, 161

Warren, Charles, 381
Warren, Earl, 182
Washington *Post*, 40
Watchmen, risk in libeling, 178, 312
Water boards, right to report proceedings of, 146, 154
Waterworks superintendent, risk in libeling, 180
WDAY Fargo, N.D., 354
Weight-reducing pills, libel of, 88
Welch, Robert, 188, 191, 251
Weeping, 399
Westbrook (Maine) *American*, 53
Westchester Newspapers, 92
White slavery, 325
White supremacist, 65
Whitewash, too much, 216
Whore, 110 (*see also* Marital misconduct; Sexual conduct)
Wichita (Kan.) *Beacon*, 151, 319
Wife, runaway, 61
Wilkes-Barre (Pa.) *Independent*, 357
Williams', Dr., Pink Pills for Pale People, 89
Winchell, Walter, 343, 370
Wire service dispatches, cautions on, 116, 293, 313, 355
Wiretaps, illegal use of, 210
Withholding publication, request for, 261, 269, 291, 356
Witness (book), 59
Witnesses
  need for in defense, 122, 367;
  right to report conduct and emotions of, 165; unreliability of, 114, 252, 253, 261
WIP Philadelphia, 189
WKRC Cincinnati, 201
WLOS Asheville, N.C., 351
WMMW Meriden, Conn., 185
WNBC New York, 345
WNTA-TV New York, 344
Women engaging in contest for man, 52
Women of ill repute, danger in reliance on, 28

Women, risk in libeling, 28, 43, 139
Worcester (Mass.) *Post*, 334
Workers, leeway in libeling, 75, 95, 178, 312
Worker on make-work project, 58
Worker, ridicule of, 53
Working method for determining libel, 12, 301
World-Telegram, 209
World Telegram and The Sun, 151, 209
Worst performance, 212
Wrestler, compared with gorilla, 62, 330

Writer, incapacity of, 25; as public figure, 183, 187, 188
WWDC Washington, D.C., 299
Wyoming *Eagle*, 107

Yachtsman, careless, 323, 329
Yellow streak, 240
Yonkers (N.Y.) *Statesman and Daily Argus*, 154
Youssoupoff, Princess, 44, 348, 391

Zbyszko, Stanislaus, 62
Zenger, John Peter, 97